ALSO BY SARAH MENKEDICK

Homing Instincts
Wild River Blues

ORDINARY INSANITY

ORDINARY INSANITY

FEAR AND THE SILENT CRISIS OF
MOTHERHOOD IN AMERICA

Sarah Menkedick

 PANTHEON BOOKS | NEW YORK

All rights reserved. Published in the United States by Pantheon Books,
a division of Penguin Random House LLC, New York, and distributed
in Canada by Penguin Random House Canada Limited, Toronto.

Pantheon Books and colophon are registered trademarks
of Penguin Random House LLC.

Library of Congress Cataloging-in-Publication Data
Name: Menkedick, Sarah, author.
Title: Ordinary insanity: fear and the silent crisis of motherhood in America
/ Sarah Menkedick.
Description: First edition. New York: Pantheon Books, 2020. Includes index.
Identifiers: LCCN 2019036726 (print). LCCN 2019036727 (ebook).
ISBN 9781524747770 (hardcover). ISBN 9781524747787 (ebook).
Subjects: LCSH: Mothers—Psychology. Motherhood—Psychological aspects.
Postpartum psychiatric disorders.
Classification: LCC HQ759.M465 2020 (print) | LCC HQ759 (ebook) |
DDC 155.6/463—dc23
LC record available at lccn.loc.gov/2019036726
LC ebook record available at lccn.loc.gov/2019036727

www.pantheonbooks.com

Jacket photograph by Lobro78/iStock/Getty Images
Jacket design by Janet Hansen

Printed in the United States of America
First Edition
9 8 7 6 5 4 3 2 1

For Jorge

Contents

Introduction

Only one person warned me about what my life might look like after giving birth. Carlos—or Charly, as everybody called him—had the build and the face of an old tugboat. He wore little pageboy caps and often smoked a pipe. Charly, with his artiste's mustache curled up at the ends, was the type to quote Borges on the street at seven a.m. when you ran into him hungover. Years after my husband Jorge and I left Oaxaca, where we'd first met Charly, he married and had a daughter. When we returned for a visit a few months into my pregnancy, we bumped into him at a café. He offered congratulations, then he told us: "You'll go into some really dark places. Seriously. You'll have to confront the darkest parts of yourself." We nodded, and held that moment up as quintessentially Charly, a splash of artistic gravitas over huevos rancheros. Yet that was without a doubt the most humanizing and important insight anyone shared with me before my daughter's birth.

My fear had already begun by then, but like many women, I couldn't separate it out from the set of "normal," culturally and medically and socially solicited behaviors appropriate to new motherhood. I couldn't draw a line where my fear crossed over into the darker territory of illness. Pregnant women in the United States live in a universe of risk divorced from everyone else's reality; they operate on a dramatically reduced spectrum of human possibility, in which their behaviors, attitudes, and identities are carefully proscribed and charged with dangerous potential. Who wouldn't want to protect their unborn child from exhaust? From the smell of gasoline? From plasticizers in shampoo and bodywash and hand lotion? From pesticides? From the radiation of airplanes? From the toxins in cat poop? Was there ever any reason to say: *I'm not going to worry about this?* To answer the question *why risk it?* with *because I want to live a meaningful life?* When women become new mothers, they can talk about how tired they are, about the insane costs and waiting lists of day cares, about their partner's failure to cooperate in the ways they expected. What they do not talk about is their fear. They do not say, *Every time I pick up my baby I see her crushed skull on the tile.* They will not say, *I don't wear anything with buttons in case my baby grabs one and chokes.*

Fear—the debilitating and constant and I-know-it's-crazy-but-I-can't-stop kind of fear, fear that walls off the world and imprisons the self in a frantic scramble for control, fear that can never be satiated and that mimics care and love and intelligence so precisely it's impossible to recognize as an impostor—is the last major taboo of American motherhood. Fear has become the way American mothers police, educate, and define themselves. It is the ritual with which they commemorate their transition to motherhood. It is tightly baked into the historical strata beneath their everyday lives. It is built into their very brains. But they don't talk about it.

When I began researching this book, I thought anxiety was a growing and underdiagnosed problem affecting a sizeable percentage of American mothers, myself included. Yet as I began talking to others, I found that I was in the middle of an epidemic of fear. Some women are unable to function because of it, some grapple with it as a familiar daily pressure, and others experience it as a milder subterranean hum. But, cumulatively, fear is having a devastating, corrosive effect on maternal well-being in the United States today.

My life became a map showing the viral proliferation of disease, with red lines and dots expanding too far for me to trace. A conservative cousin in the suburbs of Cincinnati; a close friend in Seattle; a former colleague and now PhD student in California. On a plane, an older woman from West Virginia told me her daughter suffered from anxiety so extreme that she wouldn't let her child go to birthday parties at other kids' houses. "What is going on with your generation?" the woman asked me.

Online, in a closed Facebook group I'd been invited to join, I discovered that the wife of one of my daughter's preschool teachers was suffering from severe postpartum anxiety. Meanwhile, out in daily life in Pittsburgh, I would spot women from the support group I'd attended briefly: there was one in my daughter's toddler music class; one at Target; one at the big summer concert series for families, dancing with her daughter and eating ice cream. All of these women throughout the city and the United States go about their daily lives, nodding at one another in the grocery store, all the while dogged by hidden and secret and constant worry.

––––––

This book is the culmination of several years of research, interviews, thinking, and personal struggle. It is built around the stories of women to whom I am forever grateful for spending untold hours with me on the phone or in person, guiding me over and over through their experiences so that I could convey them as accurately and vividly as possible. Per their request, I have changed several of their names and the names of their children.

I spoke to neurobiologists about how the maternal brain changes throughout pregnancy and after birth, and here I argue that as a mother is building her infant she herself is also being remade and rewired, though very little attention has been paid to the science of her transformation. Interviewing psychologists, therapists, and academics, I discovered that the way "postpartum depression" (PPD) is defined and diagnosed is largely erroneous, and that the term itself does not begin to describe the struggles faced by the majority of new mothers: in particular, the fact that fear—not melancholia or apathy—will be their biggest tormentor, while simultaneously masquerading as good, smart, socially sanctioned parenting. I plunged into how risk during pregnancy and postpartum becomes a kind of manic obsession, and how the constant pursuit of zero risk to babies has created a toxic—and dangerous— culture for mothers. Researching the history of motherhood in the United States, I began to piece together the story of how motherhood shifted from a source of public, civic authority and power to a private identity and capitalist prize. I also discovered the role psychoanalysis has played in creating our modern obsession with the perfectly attuned, perfectly attached mother.

Delving into the work of female writers and historians, I learned the myriad ways male experts and leaders throughout history have attempted to co-opt and control women's reproductive power, from claiming that the fetus was actually fully formed in sperm to burning witches at the stake.

Interviewing black midwives, mental health providers, and mothers, I was shocked to discover not only the significant body of research demonstrating how systemic racism impacts the health outcomes of black mothers and babies, but also the largely lost history of black midwifery. The latter is an illustrative example of how the power of women has been usurped by a myopic, medicalized, and often counterproductive model of care obsessed with certain risks and ignorant of others. I was immensely humbled by how much I did not know about the history of black motherhood in the United States, including the scope of the forced sterilization of women of color, the damaging and persistent stereotypes assigned to black mothers, and the way feminism and women's movements have tended to neglect reproductive justice for all mothers in favor of reproductive choice for white women.

Finally, I explored how the lack of community and ritual in American life impacts mothers, and how a transition that may very well be the most consuming and transformative of a woman's life is largely unmarked and ignored by society, which focuses instead on the development of the perfect baby. I considered how central grief is to the experience of becoming a mother, and I found that women's stories—more than therapists, medicine, or other medical interventions—are central to healing mothers, and to remaking and reclaiming motherhood.

In the process of writing this book, I was consistently astounded by how little I knew about these psychological, neurobiological, historical, and cultural underpinnings of motherhood. Motherhood is relegated to the children's section of bookstores and considered a topic for how-tos and pastel homages to stereotype, with a handful of notable exceptions. As I got deeper into the research and my relationships with the women whose stories are told here, I recognized motherhood as a deeply frightening, potent source of power—a recognition that came five years into my experience of motherhood, largely because I'd been so conditioned to assume that motherhood was more of a dull hindrance or a cute aside than a world-shattering awakening. Becoming a mother is one of the few experiences in life that really remakes a woman, that dramatically unsettles her center of gravity, and there is opportunity here: to connect, collaborate, elucidate new visions, and change the status quo. Mother's stories are a missing piece in our culture, an ache we can't pinpoint, a void papered over with platitudes or warnings about danger and risk, a lack and ossified desire felt early in the experience of becoming a mother. Yet stories of motherhood are elemental as bone and teeth.

This is a book about women: their lives, loves, brains, history, struggle, triumph, pain, and healing. And yes, men can and damn well should read it, too. This is a book about building connections between women. It's about taking back motherhood by recognizing many of the historical, cultural, social, biological, and psychological machinations behind it, and the way in which its salient contemporary emotion is no longer love, but fear.

This past summer, I was at the pool with the mother of one of my daughter's preschool classmates watching our girls kick and splash, when out of nowhere she said to me, "I'm terrified of the pool. Actually, I'm terrified of everything." I wrote this book in response to the urgency and confusion of that suffering, to this sensation that all of us are clinging so hard to an untenable and unhealthy fantasy. We are in desperate need of new stories about motherhood, which claim ownership of its science, history, culture, and future.

Bell hooks writes, "False notions of love teach us that it is the place where we will feel no pain, where we will be in a state of constant bliss." We have labored for too long under these false notions. Through a detailed journey into the dark side of motherhood—into all that mothers do not say and might not acknowledge; into the veiled elements of this profoundly unsettling, transformative experience—this book aims to reshape the contemporary understanding of motherhood and create a path to a different kind of care, vision, and connection.

ORDINARY INSANITY

FOR ME, IT BEGAN WITH MOUSE POOP. *We lived in a nineteenth-century cabin, so mouse poop should not have been an anomaly. I'd brushed it aside before, but then one day anxiety lit it up. Like a virtuoso author of magical realism, anxiety infuses everyday objects with great power. Suddenly the mouse poop glowed with threat and I couldn't unsee it. I turned to the contemporary wizard of Google to learn my fate: was it innocuous, or could it kill my baby? It could kill my baby. There was a vanishingly small but devastating chance that mouse poop could transmit congenital CMV, one of the many conditions that barely arouse a cough in an adult woman but can destroy the brain of a fetus. The Google hive of experts warned against coming into contact with it.*

This is when I first felt that hot tingling of horror. It was like swallowing a spoonful of cayenne pepper and then feeling it shiver through the veins, pickle the stomach, sear the heart. I went on a cleaning frenzy that lasted for the next nine months. I stored bottles of Seventh Generation Disinfecting Multi-Surface Cleaner as if they were the sole line of defense between me and a looming invasion. I coated every surface in a layer of sticky, mint-reeking gunk.

Telling the story of my anxious episodes is a bit like an alcoholic recounting blackouts: they all follow the same pattern, becoming increasingly disturbing and severe, monotonous in their arc but gruesomely compelling in their details. Thinking always of my baby, I was afraid of the mouse droppings, glyphosate in Quaker Oats, the toxins given off by our new mattress, the microwave, fracking chemicals in the air, fracking chemicals in the water, preservatives in granola, synthetic fabrics. That's just a small selection. Meanwhile I ate peanut butter pie piled with whipped cream. I drove on sinuous country roads laced with ice. I cried a lot. I isolated myself from the world. I took risks, even big risks, but I did not see them as risks because I was fixated on toxins that I imagined would be poisonous to my baby's body. This is the nature of anxiety: it is not about actual threat, about reducing via rational measures a set of real risks, but about the personal horror show playing in an individual psyche, crafted by individual values and priorities. It is incredibly partial and irrational, almost comically so: iced tea might permanently damage your baby, *it says, though it utters nary a peep when you enter the crosswalk at a yellow light. It fits itself so tidily into the unique dimensions of a mental blind spot that its absurdity is undetectable.*

I figured throughout my pregnancy that after the birth, when the inscrutable womb would finally crack open and reveal—I hoped, I prayed—a healthy baby, my anxiety would go away. I imagined that the baby and I would travel, we'd eat at truck stops, we'd have no idea of the Air Quality Index on any given day.

Meanwhile, anxiety was rewiring my brain. Anxiety was remaking my relationship to the world so that by the time my baby was born it had become the dominant and singular fact of my life. My former, pre-pregnancy self was like a land from which I'd been exiled, whose customs and beliefs I couldn't imagine I'd ever unthinkingly accepted. Even if I wanted to go back, the bridge to that place had been washed away, and I was left staring at the torrent that had stranded me on the far side.

There was a brief reprieve in the newborn stage, when my daughter was breastfeeding and the day was a surreal sequence of tasks that I performed, disembodied by fatigue and awe, but then it ramped right back up. Established, fed, groomed, coddled, my anxiety had become very skilled at attaching itself to almost anything. Windowsills. Dog treats. Keys. The beaded eyes of stuffed animals. The horror struck my system, seared it, faded, again and again. It became normal. In between and around it, I was mostly happy.

It took nine months after the birth of my child for me to finally sense the anxiety as something more than typical worry, or even excessive typical worry. There came a tipping point. It would be the first of many: I would tip again and again, further and further down, until finally I hit bottom, and got help.

Jorge and I took the baby on a trip to San Francisco and stayed with friends in Berkeley. Clean, crunchy, organic Berkeley, where I thought, with palpable excitement and relief on the plane, we would be cocooned in the very best of American hippie liberal privilege. Our friends lived in a renovated house they'd bought for an astronomical sum. It was California impeccable: bright, airy, clean, contemporary with vintage touches. There was a new, separate bungalow out back in a garden of fruit trees. If I needed an Eden into which to escape, this was surely it. But my euphoria lasted less than twenty-four hours. I worried the deck, which had been varnished, had traces of lead on it. I bought a package of lead test strips at a nearby Home Depot and began testing, and on the back of their garage door, one came up red. I wouldn't do laundry in the garage. Wouldn't go inside it. Wouldn't touch the handle of its door. Wouldn't touch any bike or object that had been in it or near it. From the garage emanated invisible waves of contamination that rendered every surface suspect: the grass, the deck, even the floors inside the house, where I tried my best not to let the baby crawl. There was no point in time in that house when all the ligaments of my body were not drawn tight with tension over whether she would make one catastrophic move.

And yet my life was also normal, even lovely. We had Indian street food and microbrews for dinner. The baby started taking her first tentative steps amid soaring redwoods. We drove down Highway 101 and stopped at a wild windswept beach, stuck the baby's little feet in the cool sand; I asked to switch rooms twice at a hotel because each smelled like bleach; we ate Cheez-Its and drank beer above rugged cliffs while the baby slept in the Ergo on my chest. My illness was background or aberration, a mere quirk, even as every day felt like a held breath, my whole life felt like a held breath, like walking on the surface of a balloon that might pop at any second.

I first realized I needed help on that trip to California. Sometime after we returned, and before my daughter's first birthday, I made an appointment with one of the midwives at the practice in Columbus, Ohio, where I'd been seen throughout my pregnancy. She was not the one who'd delivered my baby, and I'd met her only once before. She was in her late fifties or early sixties, with a long gray braid. She'd delivered her thousandth baby that year, and a poster in the office featured her holding this lucky newborn, smiling. I decided she was my best bet. We chatted a bit about a medical question and then I offered, as if mentioning a curious weather pattern, that I'd been having some anxiety. She didn't lift her eyes from her computer screen. "Uh-huh," she said. I was half relieved and half terrified that she didn't show any concern at all. "Do you have any recommendations for maybe, um, seeing someone?" I ventured. Even asking felt like a blazing humiliation. "Sure," she said. "We can connect you with a social worker. Let me see here." She punched some keys on the keyboard, navigated around. I waited in silence. Then, I told her that my husband and I would be moving overseas that fall, but I'd like to try and talk with someone in the months before then. "Oh," she said, and immediately ceased her search. "If you're leaving Ohio, I can't help you. You should find someone, though. You know, anxious mothers make anxious children."

She gave me a curt smile and a handful of printouts with my height and weight, then left. I didn't talk about my anxiety with anyone else for another year and a half.

APRIL

1

The Mother's Brain

In a famous 1956 paper, psychoanalyst D. W. Winnicott describes a state of "normal illness" that overtakes mothers immediately postpartum and that is essential for proper mother-infant bonding. He calls it "primary maternal preoccupation" and explains that it "could be compared with a withdrawn state, or a dissociated state, or a fugue, or even with a disturbance at a deeper level such as a schizoid episode in which some aspect of the personality takes over temporarily." It is a condition of heightened sensitivity, in which the mother's ego is fused with the infant's so that she "can feel herself into her infant's place." At any other time in a woman's life, this would be considered a mental illness, and it is so all-consuming as she experiences it during this early period of motherhood that later she may have no memory of it, or, Winnicott speculated, repress it. It is an aberration from what one would typically consider the "normal" behavior of a functioning adult, and it is a vital one. Winnicott wrote, "I do not believe that it is possible to understand the functioning of the mother at the very beginning of the infant's life without seeing that she must be able to reach this state . . . and to recover from it." The crucial fact here is recovery: the woman descends into this illness, but then she has to emerge.

Many women now do not emerge. Some of these women have

biological, genetic, or epigenetic factors that don't properly enact, regulate, or shut down the neurobiological changes in the maternal brain. Some have personal histories that make them highly susceptible and vulnerable to such changes. But many, I believe, are also held in perpetual primary maternal preoccupation because there is little social or cultural impetus to climb out: the condition of American mothering has become a "schizoid episode," a state of illness, from which it is extremely difficult to extricate oneself.

No one wants mothers to need fixing. Mothers, after all, are the ones our lives depend on. Our sanity. Our future. Mothers are the ones we need abjectly at our weakest, most vulnerable moments—when, as children, we wake up screaming without knowing why.

Mothers are our foundation, yet they are not encouraged to step up, speak out, think for themselves, or shape society in the light of their understanding. Mothers are supposed to have it all figured out without ever being told, but they are also supposed to listen very carefully, like the best students in the class.

This cognitive dissonance lends itself to both the repression and the enthusiastic embrace of anxiety. Anxiety is a handy device with which to keep oneself in line with a grueling and ever-changing regimen of coded behavior: a thousand minuscule decisions, from the proper tone of voice to take with a screaming child to the proper daily serving of protein, each freighted with importance and societal judgment. Anxiety is thus necessary and normalized. But too much anxiety reveals weakness, and mothers who demonstrate this weakness are shamed. Mothers must try to somehow navigate their anxiety as if it were an ocean they were sailing at night. This has led to a situation in which not only has clinical anxiety, which necessitates diagnosis and professional treatment, become much more prevalent, but subclinical anxiety—which may not register on exams as notable, and which may not seem so urgent but still dominates a woman's life—has become the norm.

It is necessary and urgent to recognize postpartum anxiety, postpartum OCD, and other categories of perinatal mood disorders as diagnosable conditions with symptom profiles, and at the same time acknowledge that merely defining them as illnesses and highlighting their prevalence perpetuates an ongoing problem of dichotomizing motherhood into the pathological and the normal. The diagnostic and cognitive model that sees disease as a condition a person has or does not have prevents us from understanding the way a certain disease may infect everyone in a particular population to the point where the disease becomes a mindset. Anxiety has escaped its clinical definition and run wild, worming its way into nearly every mother's cells. Some may develop real, potent illness. Others may show enough symptoms to be hampered without recognizing anything out of the ordinary. And others may have just a few bouts here and there. It is critical to understand the normality of maternal anxiety and the ways it is sanctioned—in culture, in social life, in medicine—in order to truly grasp its pathologies, its insidious infection of the process of becoming a mother.

I first met April at a café in Lawrenceville, the so-called Brooklyn of Pittsburgh. Our meeting had been arranged by a local therapist who runs a support group for women with postpartum mood disorders. She thought it might be helpful for me to hear the story of another woman who'd experienced what I was experiencing. I was nervous. After years of silence, I was finally about to speak to someone like me.

I sat at a table for two by the window. When April came in, we recognized each other immediately. She had coppery blond hair and a soft green scarf and glasses, and on her chest was Oliver, six weeks old. He was her second. Her first, Ella, was two—the same age as my daughter when we met.

April was elegant, kind, together. Of course she was. So was I. There are so many women walking a very fine line between madness and an utterly standard American life that we can all be recognized as "normal"—this is in fact the normal milieu in which we live. I am reminded of this over and over, whenever I think *That sounds crazy, but she seems normal.* The truth is that she is normal and that is crazy: this is how many of us mother now.

April began telling me her story that day, and over the course of the next year she would recount the rest. Her fearless candor inspired me. Plainly, in the same way mothers acknowledge that babies don't sleep and toddlers are insane, she would say, *This, too, happens. It may be happening to you.* She was fierce and pragmatic, and every time I talked to her I felt tenderness and healing at all the cracked places, as if she made them glow.

April was born in South Philly to two hippies who'd met and fallen in love at Penn State. Her mom was a nineteen-year-old wild child; her father a tenderhearted romantic with an alcohol problem. Shortly after April's birth, her mother left her father and moved with April back to her hometown of Wexford, Pennsylvania. April grew up in the "split reality of South Philly life and Wexford white suburbia." She went to college at the University of Dayton, then left for the Peace Corps in West Africa. She was stationed out in the bush in Gambia, where she worked in health education. There was no electricity, no running water, no paved roads. She ate the same meal three times a day. For the first six months, it was the worst experience of her life, and then it became the best. She learned Mandinka, the local language. She built relationships. She adjusted to the pace of life. She was utterly immersed, and loved it there.

In Gambia, she met a young volunteer from Seattle named Alex. At a Peace Corps meeting in the capital, Banjul, they talked and danced all night. The village where April was placed was only two kilometers from him, and over the course of their final year in Gambia they fell in love.

They each returned home in 2006: she to Pittsburgh, he to Seattle. Two years later, Alex joined April, and they both started graduate programs at the University of Pittsburgh: hers a master's in international development, his a PhD in biology. In 2010, they married. They bought a house and decided they were ready to be parents together.

They had trouble getting pregnant. April's ob-gyns and doctors asked questions like, "Are you really trying?"

"What the fuck does that mean?" April wondered aloud. "Do you want me to stand on my head?" Alex had suffered from clinical depression and been on very high dosages of Wellbutrin and Effexor, which have commonly known sexual side effects. April asked her doctors if perhaps there could be something going on with him that might be preventing her from getting pregnant. "Oh no, no, no," she mocked, in an officious doctor tone. "They wouldn't even consider it." After two years of trying she finally forced someone to check his sperm count. They discovered an overactive vein that was, in April's charming, no-nonsense Pittsburgh cadence, "baking the sperm."

Alex had to have surgery to cauterize the vein, and then he had to wait ninety days in recovery before they could try again. Precisely one hundred days post-op, April was pregnant. She said this wryly, shaking her head. Two years of stress might have been avoided had someone acknowledged that a man played a crucial role in reproduction.

But, she was thrilled. She went on a cruise with her family. It was July, peak summer. Then, at ten weeks, she miscarried.

She woke up in the middle of the night with severe pain. Panicked, she hurried her dogs into the car and drove to her mother's house. Her mom took her straight to Magee, the women's hospital better known as Pittsburgh's "baby factory." There, they informed her that she was having a miscarriage. As she was lying on the table being examined, she heard the doctor say, "Nurse, here's the tissue." Prone, scared, the awareness of what was happening now dawning on her, she thought with a surge of fury: *That's not the tissue, that's my fucking baby.*

Ultimately, they found that her baby had a random chromosomal abnormality. The doctors told her it was not genetic, not a problem in the long term, and that she could start trying again in a couple of months. They also told her that her baby was a girl: a fact she had not wanted to know.

When she and Alex started trying again a few months later, she got pregnant right away. But this time was different. She had a very easy pregnancy. There was no sickness. April's mother was five miles away, her husband was supportive, she had a good job in the marketing department of an engineering firm. Everything, she wanted to say, was great—except that it wasn't.

A good partner, good family, okay financial situation, good food, healthy pregnancy, *yet*—many women live moment by moment in the vicissitudes of that *yet*. Everything is fine on paper, just as it should be. We should be having the happiest times of our lives. Yet we squint, visor our hands to our foreheads to try to make out the path, and all we see is shadow.

In the time a woman spends going through pregnancy and giving birth, her brain changes. Its pathways, structures, connections, and relationships change. The feeling that she can never return to her old life, her old self, is rooted in neurobiology. She has been made into a mother like a factory is made into lofts, a church into a concert hall, a barn into a house. The beams or bricks may be the same, but the interior energy is distinct, reprogrammed: new shafts of light, walls, nooks, conduits of movement.

What women enact in pregnancy and early motherhood is no less than the development of the mammalian brain. To caress, feed, worry, soothe, startle, hush, sing, is to relive the emergence of humanity. Whereas reptiles can lay an egg and slither right along, leaving their progeny to hatch and fend for themselves, mammals give birth to live, dependent young, whose survival demands nurturance. As mammals diverged from reptiles millions of years ago, they had to evolve a complex suite of maternal behaviors to keep their helpless young alive. Some scientists argue that the development of maternal behavior—heightened sensitivities, empathy, attention, skill—actually spurred the mammalian brain to evolve. In other words, because the puzzle of keeping a terrifyingly dependent creature alive had to be worked out, human beings could move on to developing agriculture and smartphones. As Kelly Lambert and Craig Kinsley, researchers at the University of Virginia, put it in a 2006 piece for *Scientific American,* "The hand—or paw—that rocks the cradle indeed rules the world."

And yet, in spite of the fact that we can attribute our development and dominance as a species in part to the neurobiology of maternal behavior, very little has been studied about it. In a theme echoed throughout much of the history of humanity, uniquely female contributions—pregnancy, birth, lactation—have historically been taken for granted, diminished, or ignored. Only recently have scientists turned their attention to the maternal brain. What they have found is that during the peripartum period—defined as the time span from pregnancy through lactation—the mother's brain is remade in dramatic ways.

Hormones initiate this process. The hormonal surge in estrogens in the first trimester alone is akin to taking four hundred birth control pills a day. Many women throw up from the effects and struggle with fatigue. They may weep or feel a startling blankness. This upswelling of hormones is not only vertiginous; it also lasts an incredibly long time. I sensed my hormones like a rising wave, bearing me to its searing crest and then plunging me down in childbirth, leaving in its wake a different person.

The best-known and -studied of these hormones, oxytocin, is present in the brains of both genders at all times, but its expression fluctuates depending on both how much is released and how many receptors for it exist in given brain areas at a given time. Oxytocin is well known as the "love hormone," released when mothers nurse or kiss or cuddle their babies, and during and after labor. In the peripartum period, oxytocin receptors pop up like spring shoots all over the brain. The arrival of the infant activates these signals by releasing a flood of oxytocin, which surges through the mother's body via a tug of the nipple, the smell of that sweet hay-and-milk body, the press of skin to skin. As Craig Kinsley and Elizabeth Amory Meyer put it in *Scientific American*, "The infant creates a rich environment that stimulates the mother, pushing her brain into a higher gear."

This involves risk. That higher gear both heightens attention and ups its stakes. The brain is rewiring itself. Every time a person thinks or behaves in a new way, the brain makes new connections, and each time the thought or behavior is repeated, those connections are strengthened. "Neurons that fire together wire together," as the saying goes in neuroscience. There are myriad opportunities here for protective behaviors to be overzealously reinforced, for complex circuits to be incorrectly triggered or excessively sensitive, and for lasting, powerful, potentially flawed associations to be formed.

Hormones prime and prep the maternal brain for the epic work of care. Hormones can raze and rewire us, and in pregnancy this happens on an unprecedented scale. Like a football coach in a Hollywood movie about the underdog team that wins the Super Bowl, the hormones arrive and begin whipping neurons into a frenzy. They are particularly influential in a region called the medial preoptic area, or MPOA, which can be imagined as a sort of staging area and ground zero for maternal behavior. There are receptors in the MPOA for all of the maternal steroid and peptide hormones, including the all-stars progesterone, estrogen, prolactin, and oxytocin. Neurons that "ascend" and "descend" from the MPOA to other regions of the brain are associated with basic caring behaviors like nursing, grooming, and carrying, and—as these neurons activate the limbic and dopamine systems—with a mother's motivation, memory, mood, and response to her infant.

Studies on rats—whose mammalian behaviors and brains are similar to those of humans—have shown how pregnancy hormones "rev up" MPOA neurons, increasing the length and number of their dendrites, or signal-receiving branches that extend from the cell body. The more dendrites, the more sensitive the neuron, and the more primed it is to receive signals and respond quickly to stimuli: in this case, the suckling or the cry or the smile of an infant. Lambert and Kinsley liken the nerve cells, beefed up with dendrites by the maternal hormones, to "thoroughbreds straining at the starting gate, awaiting their release for the race." These neurons are eager to set a mother leaping from bed at the sound of a hiccup. They convert a woman who may not have known how to pick up a mewling newborn into one who rocks and bounces a floppy seven-pound body in infinitely subtle ways. This neuronal effect can also be stimulated in virgin rats by priming them with progesterone and estradiol; their MPOA neurons will also grow more and longer dendrites, sensitizing and preparing them for maternal behavior. Rats whose MPOA has been damaged, meanwhile, will fail to exhibit certain crucial aspects of maternal behavior, such as building nests and retrieving pups who stray.

Hormones also ramp up the number of astrocytes in the brain. These star-shaped cells feed nutrients and oxygen to neurons and hold them in place. Pregnant and lactating rats have far more astrocytes and far more complex ones than virgin rats. The proliferation of these cells suggests that the maternal brain is taking on a task of significant magnitude, requiring reinforcement. As the hormone-primed neurons ready themselves for the marathon of infant care, they need the astrocytes to hand out the equivalent of Gatorade and PowerGel Shots and keep them on course.

Parallel changes can be theorized in women on the basis of numerous studies, which show that after an initial decrease in memory, attention, and word recall in late pregnancy and early lactation—otherwise known as "pregnancy brain"—mothers' verbal, semantic, and working memory undergo measurable improvements postpartum. This could be explained by a similar priming, ramping up, and remodeling of neurons in the hippocampus, strengthening that area with benefits not only to maternal behavior but also to other cognitive domains, particularly memory.

The maternal brain is not only remodeled by hormones juicing up neurons; it actually grows. Researchers have shown that in women, brain regions that govern maternal behavior—including the striatum, amygdala, substantia nigra, and hypothalamus (which includes the MPOA)—undergo structural growth over the first three months postpartum, as do other areas of the brain involved in empathy, processing sensory information, and regulating emotion.

The brain *grows.* Pregnant women often joke *I am making a human!* when their husbands ask them to do the dishes; in her Netflix special *Baby Cobra,* Ali Wong looks deadpan at her husband and shouts, "I'm busy making an eyeball, okay?" But she is not simply growing a human. She is also, herself, growing, or perhaps more accurately being grown.

It hurts to grow a muscle. It hurts to grow up. It hurts to grow new skin over a raw cut. The process of breaking and healing is painful and illuminating: what is formed is measurably different from what began, but also defined by the traces of its becoming. Yet we don't tend to understand becoming a mother in terms of this growth, but rather in terms of instinct, which kicks in or doesn't, like a car engine starting up. We don't see it as a process; mothers become mothers in an instant, or they don't. Yet to become a mother is to develop, in dramatic fits and starts and over time, a second, altered consciousness, a new brain layered over and woven into the old.

The growing maternal brain reorients itself to the world. Its systems work differently. This is particularly relevant in the case of the amygdala, an almond-shaped region that helps produce and process emotional reactions and memories. The amygdala controls both positive emotions and the rewards we get from them, and negative emotions and the impulses we have to avoid them. Ultimately, the amygdala organizes our emotional reactions to the landscape before us, legislating what resonates with us and in what way: whether we will weep at the sight of a limping dog, or rejoice at a whiff of pine. During the peripartum period, the amygdala not only grows, it also exhibits different responses to stimuli. Functional magnetic resonance imaging (fMRI) studies have shown that when parents and non-parents are asked to listen to recordings of laughing and crying babies, the amygdala of non-parents lights up more with the laughing, whereas the amygdala of parents lights up more with crying. This suggests that, at least for a significant stretch after birth, parents are primed to be more alert to an infant's distress than to his or her contentment. The fear is more salient than joy.

In pregnant rats, research has shown increased dendrites in the medial nucleus of the amygdala, which plays an important role in the olfactory system—prompting new rat mothers to seek out smells they previously might have found repulsive—and which controls defensiveness and avoidance behavior. Craig Kinsley has drawn a correlation here with new mothers, arguing that bulked-up amygdala neurons make mothers highly cautious and sensitive to the slightest hint of danger. A mother reads a news story about a baby who stopped breathing at day care and her amygdala generates an intense fear response, which commands her to check her own baby's breathing, after which she feels relieved, until a few minutes later she must once again place her hand before the miniature cave of the mouth and wait, heart pounding, for a warm gust. The amygdala codes all of this into memory.

The function of the amygdala seems to flip during pregnancy. In virgin rats, activation of the medial nucleus leads to fewer maternal behaviors—*hear a crying baby and run for the bar!*—whereas in mothers, activation of the medial nucleus leads to increased attentiveness to an infant, even to the point of obsessive preoccupation. The few fMRI studies conducted on the brains of women with postpartum depression found that contrary to major depression outside of pregnancy, in which the amygdala is more active than normal, in postpartum depression the amygdala actually has reduced function, which might explain why severely depressed mothers tend to be less responsive to their infants. The amygdala's activity and sense of emotional salience are meant to change and heighten in this period, sculpting the mother into a fine-tuned receptor for infant signals, an alarm that wails at the slightest blip.

Meanwhile, as the amygdala of new mothers is on high alert for distress, it is simultaneously flooding the body with tenderness at positive stimuli. The amygdala is laden with oxytocin and dopamine receptors and, in communication with other brain regions in the peripartum context, it receives the message to nurture from oxytocin, initiates the nurturing, and then rewards the nurturing with a hit of dopamine, in a loop known as a reward circuit. *Ping,* goes a woman's brain each time her baby gurgles or coos or coughs, and that ping is rewarded with the soft touch of the baby's skin and a surge of loving connection, which is how women like me go from being clueless vagabond artists to hyper-responsive caregivers in the course of a day.

Over time, the amygdala strengthens the mother's responses into sensory, emotional memories. I remember the first time my baby produced a real smile. It was five in the morning at a friend's house in Massachusetts. My friend didn't yet have children and, like most normal non-parents, was sleeping in the pre-dawn. I was desperate to keep my baby quiet for fear of waking my friend and her partner. In this desperation, I was making silly faces and flailing in a full-body effort to distract my daughter from the urge to wail. It worked. She smiled, a ridiculous little crinkle in her soft round face. I devoted hundreds of hours over the next year to soliciting that smile, and still have a video on my desktop, which I watch on a regular basis, of me feigning a stubbed toe and Elena bursting into a four-month-old toothless guffaw.

Meanwhile, each time I saw a reference to lead paint in the media, I seized up with fear. Dr. James Swain, a child psychiatrist at Stony Brook University Medical School, has hypothesized that an increase in circuits associated with arousal, anxiety, and obsessiveness in the amygdala is normal and temporary for most parents, but warned that if the circuits become permanently sensitized, they can lead to mental illness. For me, as for many mothers, maternal behavior became inextricably bound up with hypersensitivity to danger, with excessive wariness. A close friend of mine, who suffered from debilitating perinatal anxiety for which she ultimately went on Zoloft, put it this way: "My love manifested as fear."

April's baby girl, Ella, was born on July 24, 2014, after forty-eight hours of labor. The baby weighed nine pounds and came out face up. It was not an easy birth. But when Ella finally emerged April felt peaceful and blissful. It was 11:59 p.m., and the nurses had turned the lights low so that the room was dark. April's girl was beautiful and big and healthy. She latched on to the breast right away. April felt amazing.

But Ella, like most newborns, was not a sleeper, and April, like most new mothers, became more and more sleep-deprived. At around eight weeks, she began to notice something was off. She was so wound up she could not sleep even in the precious opportunities she had. Family would come to help take care of Ella, and she would grow paranoid they were going to drop or smother the baby. She lay in bed with rapid-fire thoughts of destruction playing over and over in her head. *The baby falling. Her head shattered on the floor.* In some ways, having help heightened her stress.

Her breaking point came one day when her mom was over. April was a mess, crying. Her mom said, "Please, go lie down, you have to get some rest, I have this." April obeyed and went to the bedroom only to lie there awake, alert as a hunted animal. *I have to sleep, I have to get some rest.* She heard the microwave start. Her brain pinged. *What if your mother is putting your baby in the microwave?* She knew this notion was utterly illogical—*I have a master's in International Development! I speak an African tonal language fluently! This is crazy!*—and yet she heard the microwave kick up and she saw a clear image of her baby in there. She leapt out of bed and raced into the kitchen and screamed, "What are you doing?"

Her mother told her she needed help: "You've got to call somebody." April knew this, too. She was not in denial; she simply had no idea how to stop or fight the thoughts, and no functional sense of when the danger was imminent and when it was an insane invention of her brain. Even if she sensed the unreality of her thoughts, she was powerless before them. She dug through the sheaf of papers she'd received from Magee after her delivery, and found a help line. She told the woman who answered, "Look, I really think I'm having some sort of postpartum condition here." *Ah, the baby blues,* the woman offered, but April clarified that she was not depressed. Her husband had been seriously, clinically depressed and she knew what depression looked like. Instead, she emphasized, "I'm constantly worried. Something isn't right."

The woman on the other end of the line was soothing. She said April was a new mom, and of course new moms worried about their babies! She echoed the refrain of nearly everyone in April's life: *This is fine, it's natural, you're a good mom.* For this woman, as for so many people, it was just an issue of calming April down, taming a fire that had gotten perhaps a little out of control but that was ultimately protective and warming and meant no danger, posed no real threat. Finally, desperate, April laid out the specifics of her thoughts. The woman referred her to a crisis line.

When she called, a young man picked up. He had no idea what to do. He had no idea what *postpartum* meant, or why there would be any particular set of issues around this. "If I was raped, if I was suicidal, he would have known where to put me," April said. But she wasn't depressed, and nothing terrible had happened to her. She'd just had a healthy, happy, beautiful baby. Finally, he offered one insight that did help: "I don't know what you're experiencing, but I can tell you're afraid," he said, "and the people who are really at risk of hurting others are the people who aren't afraid of those thoughts you're having, because they don't seem strange to them." April clung to this information. It was the only mental health resource she was able to obtain for seven months.

At six weeks, April went in for the one checkup mothers receive in their whole first year after birth. She was screened for postpartum depression. Unlike many mothers, who are understandably frightened about putting their complicated feelings before medical professionals, April was brutally honest; she circled all the bubbles that applied to her, even the embarrassing or potentially shameful ones. "I was like, 'I cry all the fucking time and I'm losing my mind.'" The doctors, unfazed, tried to placate her. "It's really hard," they said. "You have to get some sleep!" No one ever followed up, referred her, or told her that perhaps her situation was not normal. So her worry became the new normal, along with diapers and nursing and the standard newborn rigmarole.

April could not listen to or watch the news. She could not read the newspaper. A negative image or story would stick in her brain for days. There was a mother in Pittsburgh who had murdered her four-year-old daughter, then lied about it, initiating a massive search for the dead girl. Her face floated every night in April's mind while the story looped over and over.

Meanwhile, April went back to work. While she was there, she was better: the thoughts didn't have a target, and she could calm down. Occasionally one would pop up—*What if the day-care lady lets her fall?*—but for the most part, she felt safe. Yet the moment she came home, she was trapped in "a mental prison of what if, what if, what if." The thoughts were rapid-fire, devastating: a plastic bag over Ella's head, Ella stabbed by a knife. April hid all the bags and all the knives in the basement. Alex brought home a pocketknife, and she panicked, shouting at him to put it away.

April had no idea at the time that these thoughts were called *intrusive,* that they were both ruthless and useless. She had no way of separating them out from thoughts that might be sanctioned as informed, proactive, and healthy. How is a mother to know when her worry is no longer a measure of good parenting, and at what point? Plastic bags are covered in suffocation warnings. On Web forums, mothers issue stark proclamations of doom about women who dare to use baby soaps that contain one non-organic ingredient. Car seats, blind cords, treadmills, pillows: all, warn the doctors and the experts and the Internet, can kill.

The thoughts shoved themselves relentlessly to the forefront of her mind, even as part of her wondered if she was losing it. The mother in her, activated by the impulses in her brain and body, answered: *But your child could die.* What mother can respond to this with calm detachment? What mother stands up to the ob-gyn who leans over her and tells her that if she doesn't get the C-section, her baby might die? To the doctor who tells her that if she sleeps with her baby, her baby might die? To the friend or colleague or relative who tells her that if she uses this stroller, that pacifier, this toy, her baby might die? What mother can take the risk?

2

Postpartum Mood Disorders

Love is a factor of attention, and while the brain's goal is not necessarily to increase anxiety in mothers, it is certainly to direct and sharpen and sensitize attention. There is a very fine line between this careful attention and anxiety, and between protective, loving maternal behavior and obsessiveness. It is easy to cross without noticing, and once on the wrong side, it can be extremely difficult to cross back.

Alison Fleming, a professor of neurobiology at the University of Toronto at Mississauga, told me, "With depression it's pretty clear that it rarely seems beneficial . . . whereas anxiety gives you both types of outcomes, depending on the extent of it and the degree of social support and a variety of other factors. It feels less chronic and it's on again, off again." Fleming described studies of pregnant women that showed anxiety rising in pregnancy until it was quite high, then dropping after birth, then increasing again, which perfectly captured my experience and which apparently makes me common among mammals. This curve, she explained, "implies that a certain level of anxiety is important, and it might make you less avoidant, and it also might make you more attentive to the offspring because you're alert." Yet being too anxious could tip a mother into depression, or the excessive care that creates anxious offspring. It is a careful calibration, not a clear yes or no; it could be influenced by specific alleles in specific genes, by epigenetics, by personal history, or by social context, but no one knows yet because the research is not there. In the maternal context, Fleming explained, "Anxiety has multiple functions, some beneficial and some not."

A 2013 study by researcher Oliver Bosch, again on rats, found that highly anxious mothers exhibited more maternal behavior. Bosch worked in a lab that had bred two varieties of rats for research purposes: those with high anxiety-related behavior, or HAB, and those with low anxiety-related behavior, or LAB. The former were meticulously cultivated over eight generations to produce maximum anxiety. Bosch happened to notice that these rats were excessive in their mothering. They were constantly sitting on the pups, crouching over the pups, arching over them in the nursing posture, whereas the LAB rats did this only as often as necessary. The HAB rats had more of the neuropeptide vasopressin in their brains. When researchers blocked the receptors for vasopressin, the highly anxious rats demonstrated less maternal behavior. Meanwhile, when Bosch gave the low anxiety rats more vasopressin, they became more maternal. In the way of all good and dutiful scientists, Bosch would not draw a direct link between anxiety and maternal behavior. "When I compare the high and low anxious rats," he told me, "I see the high anxious rats are still the better mothers. If this is similar in humans I can't tell."

Vasopressin is very closely related to oxytocin, the aforementioned "love hormone." Vasopressin and oxytocin are almost identical save for two amino acids. Dr. James Leckman, a professor of child psychiatry, psychology, and pediatrics at Yale, knew that vasopressin was elevated in individuals with obsessive-compulsive disorder (OCD), and later discovered by sampling cerebrospinal fluid that men who had severe OCD in puberty also had very high levels of oxytocin. I asked Leckman whether he thought there might be a relationship between vasopressin, oxytocin, maternal behavior, and anxiety. If having higher levels of these neuropeptides increased mothers' sensitivity to babies, might it also make them anxious or encourage OCD-like behavior? Leckman described this as "not an unfair hypothesis." He told me, "If you look at the behaviors that are associated with higher levels of oxytocin in the mothers, it's the sensitive, responsive parenting where you see this very close attention to every detail of how the child is responding."

It seemed possible that significant amounts of these neuropeptides could lead to more maternal behavior, which could lead to higher amounts of neuropeptides, and so on and on in a narrowing circle that could come to be characterized as OCD. Dr. Joe Lonstein, one of the premier researchers on maternal anxiety in rats, explained to me that almost all peptides show "inverted U-shaped" relationships with outcomes of interest: both too little of the peptide and too much can lead to negative impacts.

Dr. Leckman's research has also demonstrated that OCD symptoms—strongly associated with anxiety—are the norm, not an aberration, in the postpartum period. Leckman found in a 1999 study that 95 percent of mothers and 80 percent of fathers experienced OCD-like intrusive thoughts in the weeks following birth, and that most of these thoughts were not the stereotypically absurd ones culturally associated with OCD but rather average concerns about cleanliness, safety, and health. What distinguished the parents who actually developed clinical OCD from the parents who simply experienced the thoughts was the level of behavior: how much time they spent checking, organizing, cleaning, avoiding, and ritualizing in response to their thoughts. If they had to check and recheck the door multiple times before leaving, for example, or clean the same surface repeatedly, the standard worry tipped over into debilitating illness.

Leckman revealed that mothers spent an average of fourteen hours a day exclusively focused on their infants in the immediate postpartum period. This was the norm. More than 80 percent of mothers worried about their baby's development, potential illness, and harm, and many "reported the persistence of graphic images in which they failed as parents." These images propelled them to compulsively babyproof their environment in an effort to get the baby's space "just right." Seventy-five percent of parents, meanwhile, felt driven to constantly check on their infant, and 83 percent of mothers reported that they would be "severely" or "moderately" distraught if prevented from doing so.

Leckman points out that from an evolutionary perspective, it makes sense that patterns of obsessive behavior devoted to protecting and nurturing offspring would be selected for and passed on. Only in the past century has infant mortality in the United States fallen dramatically, from 100 deaths per 1,000 births in 1900 to 6 deaths per 1,000 births in 2014. For most of human history, a majority of infants and children did not survive to adulthood. As Eula Biss notes in her book *On Immunity*, many older U.S. cemeteries do not have graves for babies: their deaths were too frequent. "Little wonder then," Leckman writes, "that a specific state of heightened sensitivity on the part of new parents would be evolutionarily conserved." Leckman makes the case for considering OCD less a malfunction or a disease than a dysregulation of healthy, evolutionarily promoted behavior. His interest in OCD in the postpartum period stems from seeing how his wife changed after the birth of their first child, how obsessed she became. Much of his research has painted a picture of OCD not as deviant or exceptional behavior but as an intensified, out-of-control version of innate tendencies. In pregnancy and early motherhood, when these innate tendencies are even stronger and are powerfully reinforced, OCD briefly becomes the norm. The question is why a significant number of women discover they cannot turn it off; why it grows until it becomes not just a period of preoccupation but a lifetime.

All of these transformations in the brain and body of a mother—the structural growth, the hundredfold increase in hormones and thousandfold increase in steroids, the flourishing of receptors, the activated or altered neural pathways—must be in place in order for healthy, "normal" mothering to occur. Any dysfunction, from early childhood adversity, previous post-traumatic stress disorder (PTSD) or mental illness, trauma, genetic predisposition, and/or biological irregularity could knock the system awry. Considering the fact that 1 in 4 girls will be sexually abused before she turns eighteen, that 1 in 6 women has been the victim in her lifetime of an attempted or completed rape, that 1 in 4 women will have an abortion by age forty-five, that 1 in 5 women has had a miscarriage, and that 1 in 3 women suffers from an anxiety disorder, the normative view of the transition to motherhood as inherently blissful, if a little ragged around the edges with sleep deprivation, seems absurd. According to Samantha Meltzer-Brody, one of the top researchers on postpartum depression, it is shocking that given the built-in risks, there are women who actually make it through pregnancy and the postpartum period with few or no mood symptoms.

If the neurobiology of the maternal brain is plastic—and this seems difficult to dispute, backed by a growing literature of solid evidence—then its plasticity must also be influenced to some degree by our culture and our environment. "The brain," writes Bessel van der Kolk in *The Body Keeps the Score,* "is a cultural organ."

Dr. Pilyoung Kim, a psychologist and professor at the University of Denver, told me, "Brain plasticity matters, because it sensitively responds to environment." In mice, if the environment consistently indicates to new mothers that their babies are not safe, the mice grow distracted or abandon their babies. It remains to be seen whether certain changes in the maternal brain are now being exacerbated by the environment in which we live, of persistent unreal threat and little real danger.

Primatologist Sarah Hrdy, whose book *Mother Nature: Maternal Instincts and How They Shape the Human Species* debunks many common myths and presumptions about motherhood, points out that throughout history the choices available to most women have been very limited, and few have been able to control their reproduction. But many contemporary women in the United States have an unprecedented array of options. "Today," Hrdy writes, "mothers in developed countries, and with them fathers and children, enter uncharted terrain. Without anyone raising their hands to volunteer, we have become guinea pigs in a vast social experiment." The abundance of choice—from breastfeeding to formula, day care to nannies to stay-at-home motherhood, all the way down to store-bought packets versus homemade purees and X gadget for social-emotional development over Y trinket for fine motor skills—both allows us to ignore the real changes at work in our bodies and minds and hijacks those changes, attaching life-or-death importance to organic applesauce. Hrdy warned, "Motherhood has become a minefield . . . without so much as a map to guide us."

Why are so many women now falling prey to debilitating anxiety? Neurobiologists have only just begun to tease out the "normal" functioning of the maternal brain, the standard repertoire of changes that might be expected in the average pregnancy, much less work out what factors—cultural, social, interpersonal, genetic, biological—might impact these changes and how.

One major problem is the fact that most scientific research has been done and is still done by men. "Research is me-search," goes the cliché: men tend to investigate male issues and problems. Over and over again in my reading of the scientific literature on postpartum anxiety, I came across laments about the shocking lack of research. Dr. Joe Lonstein and Dr. Jodi Pawluski, who have collaborated in studying maternal anxiety in rats, told me there has been far more research done on animals than on women, and there are only a few more than a dozen labs in the entire world focusing on postpartum anxiety in either humans or rodents. There is more research on fathers' postpartum depression than on anxiety in mothers.

Dr. Lonstein's overview of potential neurobiological sources of anxiety in the maternal brain notes that a literature search of Medline-indexed, non-review articles on humans from the past thirty-eight years for "anxiety" with either "postpartum" or "lactation" reveals five hundred articles, where "anxiety" and "men" yields more than forty-one thousand. A 2014 study on mindfulness as a treatment for postpartum anxiety stated, "Despite a great need for effective, non-pharmacological interventions, research specifically addressing treatment of anxiety disorders during pregnancy is seriously lacking, with no published studies of psychotherapeutic treatments for anxiety in pregnancy to date."

Meanwhile, a 2006 literature review on postpartum mood disorders found only four studies on the prevalence of OCD and four on postpartum anxiety. A 2016 literature review focusing on anxiety and broadening the criteria to include a set of search terms related to agoraphobia and other phobias, panic disorder, stress disorder, social anxiety, and PTSD—but, crucially, not depression—found a total of fifty-eight studies in the entire history of the three largest scientific research databases. This in spite of the fact that every researcher I have spoken with has emphasized that the peripartum period is a time in which women, and particularly women with preexisting risk factors, find themselves uniquely vulnerable to fear, sadness, grief, and turmoil.

As Dr. Kelly Lambert, a professor of psychology at Randolph-Macon College, put it: "There are so many opportunities for little things to not go right. For stress to not be reined in or held at bay." She characterizes reproduction as a time of immense volatility, when women are in a "chaotic storm" of hormones and the entire brain is being asked to come on board in various ways to tackle the complexity of creating and raising a human. "There's a lot of room for error," she warned, and "nature tries to protect against that, but it's just not good enough." Even more important, stress during this time actually changes the brain. As Dr. Kim explained to me, stress in the peripartum period can significantly influence parenting over the long term, even when the mother is no longer stressed.

There is a danger in describing mothers, and women in general, as "vulnerable." The female body is regulated because of its presumed vulnerability. Vulnerability can justify the excessive medicalization of childbirth; the patronizing and infantilizing treatment of mothers; the marginalization of women's voices and stories as emotional and hysterical. And yet understanding pregnancy and birth as simply "natural," as transitions in which a woman somehow becomes a mother in the way a storybook caterpillar becomes a butterfly—achieving her consummate female trajectory—ignores the immense tumult of this period and the fact that mothers, just like their infants, are complicated beings who need scientific, personal, cultural, and social care.

Many mothers don't want to appear vulnerable, both out of fear of being diminished, infantilized, or threatened with unwanted interventions, and because they know they are almost solely in charge of keeping a new human being alive. Who the hell has time for vulnerability? It is a profound testament to the strength and resilience of women that so many of them suffer from debilitating fear, sadness, and confusion and yet they soldier on working, taking care of their families, getting the myriad everyday chores done. The fact that they're asked to do so, to carry and bear alone not only the child but the chemical and biological shifts, the solitude, the loss, the grief, the complex questions of their own transformation, reveals a society that values mothers only as passive, docile, keeping their motherhood safely tucked in the sentimental cultural space reserved for it. The idea is not to study the mother, to listen to her, to recognize her in her fullness, to explore her becoming, but to keep her contained: prevent her from causing harm, encourage her to follow the rules. Anxiety is an excellent weapon for containing women; it needs only to be gently stoked in the context of pregnancy and women will weaponize it against themselves.

April was terrified to bathe Ella. She was certain she'd drop her, drown her. She masked her terror with justifications for why Alex needed to do bath time. "That's your time with her," she'd tell him. "You need to bond with her." This worked, but like all the fixes for anxiety, it offered a brutally short reprieve. After bath time came nursing, and April grew paranoid that as she nursed Ella on the bed she'd somehow roll over on the baby, crush her, break her neck. April started pinning her own arms behind her back while she nursed, restraining herself. When Ella finished, April, terrified of contact, would whisk her up in a rush and lay her as quickly as possible in her crib.

At first, the crib felt safe, but Ella was still in the same room with her. April began to worry that she would wake up, sleepwalk, and injure Ella in her sleep. She wanted to keep the crib in her room, because that was the recommended procedure, and April, like so many American mothers, didn't want to deviate from the myriad recommended procedures. What if her baby died because the crib was in another room? What if the baby was forever traumatized by the separation?

But what if she woke up in the middle of the night and sleep-walked and killed Ella because she was in the same room? April became obsessed with the latter possibility, despite the fact that she had never once in her life sleepwalked. It grew difficult, then impossible, for her to sleep in the room with the baby without Alex present. If he wasn't going to bed, she wasn't either, even if she was stone-cold exhausted.

One night, when she had a bit of a cough, she decided to sleep on the couch so as not to wake the baby. There, she realized she felt much better at a safe remove. She started to sleep on the couch every night. This offered a precious window of relief.

But soon enough, April began to wonder, *What if I get up off the couch and go up the steps to their room in the middle of the night?* She began putting on ankle weights. Nothing about this scenario seemed improbable to her: rather, it became increasingly urgent and crucial to enact. Every night, Alex strapped ankle weights on her.

"God bless him, because he was trying to be supportive and he was probably just like, *What is going on with my life?*" April laughed. The distance between then and now is palpable in that laugh, which has a bitter undertone of incredulity. She'd been swallowed by the beast, and her dark new reality was so convincing and so powerful that even her mellow husband, with a PhD in biology and an informed understanding of mental illness, was roped into its assumptions without question.

April not only felt awful, she felt awful about feeling awful. She would have an intrusive thought, go on a bender of intrusive thoughts, and then tear herself up for letting herself have the intrusive thoughts or follow them in the first place. April would dwell in guilt and blame, assuring herself that this new protection—the sleeping in another room, the ankle weights, the knives in the basement—was finally going to make it okay. Then another intrusive thought would worm into her mind and throb with imminent doom, and the cycle would kick up again.

Meanwhile, she was supposed to be happy. She was supposed to be awash with wonder and joy (while also dutiful to her child's breathing patterns and the nature of food additives and the potential safety hazards of dogs/appliances/shopping carts/the outdoors/houses/playgrounds). She felt none of the positive emotions, only their shadow sides. Thus, she concluded, she was a bad mom. She was failing. She'd lost a baby and it had totally, utterly wrecked her. All she had wanted was this, and she had it, and she could hardly live with it.

Soon, the ankle weights were not enough. She worried that she might still awaken and, in spite of them, find her way to the bedroom and damage the baby. The safer plan was surely to tether herself to her husband in bed, making it impossible for her to somehow slip away. So every night she'd tie herself to Alex. To all this, friends, family, acquaintances responded: "It's normal for new mothers to worry!"

It is normal for mothers to worry. It is normal for mothers in the United States to worry excessively. It is normal for mothers in this country to worry themselves sick, to worry as a second career, to worry as a demonstration of love and education and care, to worry to the point where they blunt and mute their own and their children's lives in the name of safety. When, then, does worry become not normal? Ankle weights? Tethering in bed? Hiding bags, hiding knives?

"In my mind," April said, "it's shades of gray." Some behaviors are clearly on the not-normal end of the spectrum. But many others, from concern about a dropped baby to fear of drowning, are common and encouraged. One high school friend of mine on Facebook shared a website that consisted of thousands of recorded live videos from neighborhood pools in which lifeguards had jumped in just in time to rescue drowning children. It was recommended to watch them all to recognize signs of drowning, which doesn't look like the stereotypical drama we often imagine. Is it abnormal to spend an entire afternoon, a day, days, watching video footage of children in pools to spot the exact instant when one starts to sink?

One differentiator for April between the normal and the not is a person's individual level of panic: "Are your palms sweating? Are you incapable of sleeping?" But ultimately, for most women—even those who experience such intense physical symptoms that their bodies seem alight with adrenaline—the terrain between sick and well, between protective and destructive fear, is shadowy.

———————

There is no established definition of postpartum anxiety, and no category for it in the *Diagnostic and Statistical Manual of Mental Disorders* (DSM), the standard reference work for classifying recognized psychiatric disorders. In the clinical imagination and the majority of medical literature, postpartum anxiety either does not exist or is merely a symptom of postpartum depression. Several years ago, when I first began checking, a Google search for "postpartum anxiety" yielded articles from *American Baby* magazine, the *Huffington Post, Today's Parent,* and *Scary Mommy,* but not a single official medical resource. Google intervened to suggest that perhaps I meant postpartum depression, offering, "People also ask: How long does postpartum depression last for? Can postpartum depression make you angry?"

I began tracking Google searches over time. Up popped an article from *Vogue. New York Magazine's* "The Cut." Gwyneth Paltrow's *Goop. Parents* wormed its way to the top with an article entitled "Postpartum Anxiety: The Other Baby Blues We Need to Talk

About." Not a single major medical website or institution—the reliable old places I might have gone to look up symptoms for, say, the flu, or stomach trouble—had a listing for postpartum anxiety. The American Pregnancy Association, the Anxiety and Depression Association of America, the American Psychological Association, the National Institute of Mental Health: each only offered a definition of postpartum depression.

From the perspective of a mother trying to figure out why she is afraid all the time, the only diagnosis available appears to be postpartum depression. Some of the leading hospitals in the country, including the Massachusetts General Hospital Center for Women's Mental Health, have no category for postpartum anxiety on their websites covering postpartum psychiatric disorders, and they reference anxiety only or primarily as a symptom of depression. While the MGH Center has recently added more information about studies on perinatal onset of OCD and anxiety, their bolded category headings are limited to postpartum psychosis, postpartum depression, and the postpartum blues. The webpage of the MGH Center actually describes the "baby blues" in this way: "Rather than feelings of sadness, women with the blues more commonly report mood lability, tearfulness, anxiety or irritability." The cognitive dissonance in this sentence is casual and stunning: the blues, which by definition should involve the *blue* feeling of sadness, actually stem from fear. Still, they remain "the blues," even though the center declares that "generalized anxiety is common" and "significant anxiety symptoms may occur."

I turned to Google because this is where most mothers—alone with their babies, their thoughts running tortuous loops around them—are likely to turn at three o'clock in the morning, desperate for answers. This is where, for better or worse, most medical odysseys begin in the mid-twenty-first century. The majority of the women I talked to started here, and if they were lucky, they found either a magazine article or one of the two major advocacy organizations for postpartum mood disorders: Postpartum Progress or Postpartum Support International. These two offer the only substantial definitions of postpartum anxiety as a distinct condition with its own symptom profile. They define it as debilitating, constant worry and dread, accompanied by disrupted sleep and eating, irritability and restlessness, and sometimes physical symptoms like nausea and sweating. Postpartum OCD is defined as a cycle of obsessive or intrusive thoughts, which are distressing to the thinker, and which the thinker understands are "crazy" but cannot ignore, followed by the use of compulsions—such as organizing, cleaning, or avoiding—that aim to reduce the anxiety produced by the thoughts.

The women who stumbled across these organizations and sought help through them were fortunate. They may have encountered many roadblocks in seeking treatment, but at least they had a clear enough sense of what they were suffering from to know where to look. The others—who went straight to primary care doctors, ob-gyns, or mental health professionals—did not fare as well. If they were given a diagnosis, it was depression.

The social, cultural, and medical understanding of mental illness in the context of pregnancy is largely limited to postpartum depression, and the understanding of postpartum depression is limited to an outmoded, simplistic idea of a sudden onslaught of intense melancholia immediately following the birth of a child, which can so derange the mother that she is driven to kill herself and her child. Postpartum depression suggests a woman who is beaming in photos one day and driving her children off a bridge the next.

This paradigm persists in spite of a robust body of evidence demonstrating that not only is postpartum anxiety far more common than postpartum depression, but what is frequently diagnosed as postpartum depression often does not look like major depression but rather like intense anxiety. A 2014 study from the Postpartum Depression: Action Towards Causes and Treatment (PACT) Consortium looked at data on postpartum depression in women from nineteen different institutions in seven different countries and found five distinct subtypes of postpartum depression: severe anxious depression, moderate anxious depression, anxious anhedonia, pure anhedonia, and resolved depression. Anxiety is the defining characteristic of three out of these five subtypes. Half of all the women studied had either no depression at all or mild to moderate depression; only 75 out of 663 women experienced the "pure anhedonia"—anhedonia being defined as "the inability to feel pleasure"—most commonly associated with depression. In one of the most comprehensive studies done on postpartum depression, only 11 percent of the subjects actually had the symptom most strongly associated with and used to diagnose depression.

The PACT study also confirmed what the advocacy organizations had been tirelessly arguing for years: the vast majority of postpartum mood disorders actually have prenatal, not postpartum, onset. Only 176 out of 664 women had postpartum onset, and only 105 had onset in the first eight weeks, which is likely the only time they will be screened.

Culturally and clinically, however, we tend to view "postpartum" mood disorders as happening immediately after birth. After lobbying on the part of women's health organizations, the fifth edition of the DSM attempted to address the problem of onset by changing "postpartum" to "peripartum," and stating that "fifty percent of 'postpartum' major depressive episodes actually begin prior to delivery." It did not, however, change the maximum time of onset, which remained limited to four weeks. In the DSM's purview, any illness arising more than four weeks after birth is no longer related to the fact that a woman has just built a different brain, grown a child in her body, gone through labor, and arrived back home with a helpless infant in her arms. At that point, "peripartum depression"—still the only diagnosis specific to the perinatal context offered by the DSM—would become "major depression," and anxiety would cease to be a significant symptom.

Meanwhile, both the World Health Organization (WHO) and the Centers for Disease Control and Prevention (CDC) define the full first year postpartum as the window of symptom onset, and many organizations lobbied hard for the DSM to change the onset window to at least six months. The current maximum of four weeks is particularly striking considering that most women are not even screened for depression until the standard follow-up six weeks after birth: two weeks, that is, *after* the DSM cutoff for diagnosis. Many women who experience intense anxiety followed by depression miss this four-week window by months, if not years. A woman has but one opportunity for diagnosis and treatment; that opportunity comes two weeks after she could technically fit the diagnostic criteria, and that opportunity will in any case not include evaluation for the condition she is most likely to have.

In spite of the PACT study, some growing popular awareness and media attention, and the work of advocacy organizations, postpartum depression persists as the sole diagnostic category for any mental illness in the perinatal period. Even one of the country's top experts on perinatal mood disorders, Professor Samantha Meltzer-Brody, who established PACT and was one of the authors of its 2014 study, and who directs the UNC Perinatal Psychiatry Program of the UNC Center for Women's Mood Disorders, dismissed the notion of anxiety as a diagnosis separate from postpartum depression.

"There's sort of suddenly thirty-five flavors," she said of PPD. She used the example of influenza: "We both test positive for influenza A, but you might have horrible muscle aches and horrible fatigue and can't move and it may manifest in me with different symptoms, I may have more GI upset than you do, but we both have the flu." In other words, depression is depression, in spite of its individual variations.

Brody emphasizes that anxiety is a salient characteristic of postpartum depression, and that a clear subset of women have anxiety without any mood symptoms, but she declares this is not so much indicative of distinct illnesses as it is of the heterogeneity of depression, which just like any other illness—she offers AIDS as another example—exists on a spectrum and manifests itself differently in different individuals. However, Brody believes the DSM's characterization of postpartum depression is flawed in its failure to more clearly emphasize anxiety. "Anyone who's taken care of patients for more than two days sees a problem," she told me, "because there's so much anxiety that can be present . . . in women's health in general, but particularly in the perinatal period."

I find Brody's explanations compelling, but as someone who felt no mood symptoms—no overwhelming sadness, no suicidal ideation, no anhedonia—and yet had intense and often debilitating fear, I chafe a bit at the suggestion that I was depressed in spite of not feeling like it. This could be a result of my misunderstanding of depression, but it echoes a long history of women being told that they don't understand what they're feeling, or that they aren't really feeling what they're feeling, or that what they're feeling is not valid.

It also raises the question of how far language can be stretched until it starts to obscure rather than illuminate. If Merriam-Webster's definition of depression is "a state of feeling sad" and "a mood disorder marked especially by sadness, inactivity . . . feelings of dejection and hopelessness, and sometimes suicidal tendencies," and the top DSM criteria for depression are depressed mood, decreased interest or pleasure in daily activities, loss of energy, and suicidality, then to what degree can a person who does not have any of these symptoms be considered depressed? If this definition of depression is too narrow, how much can it be broadened before it loses any real power to define?

The definition of anxiety, meanwhile, seems in many ways to contrast with that of depression: Merriam-Webster's definitions include a "mentally distressing concern or interest" and "a strong desire sometimes mixed with doubt, fear, or uneasiness." Similarly, one key DSM criterion for anxiety is being restless, or "keyed up and on edge." The intentionality and action implied in these definitions is starkly at odds with the passivity of depression. It is clear how one may shade into another over time, or how they might overlap in particular cases, but to fold anxiety entirely into depression seems to miss or belittle anxiety's distinct characteristics of frenzied preventative action, restless reassurance-seeking, and constant, obsessive struggle toward an ideal state of certainty. It also in some ways quietly endorses these characteristics as less problematic than those stereotypically associated with depression, such as melancholia and suicidality. Telling women they're actually depressed, diagnosing them with depression, insisting that their anxiety will be dealt with as a side effect of depression treatment, sends the message that anxiety in and of itself is not an issue: that the real pathology is unhappiness, not fear. Fear is the principal means used to hold women to specific societal standards as mothers; it is the engine of medical control over women and then of women's control over themselves and their children. To question fear would be to question everything, the entire institution of American motherhood.

One day, April woke up to herself. The part of her that had been suffocated by thoughts broke through and surveyed the territory. She had wanted a little girl so badly, and now, she had her. She looked at her daughter and thought, *Oh my God, I'm incapable of enjoying her.* Every time April looked at her all she could feel was fear. This was not the kind of motherhood she had envisioned or wanted.

April turned to Google. She searched for all the random behaviors she'd been beholden to but knew were strange, and she discovered the stories of other women who'd engaged in the same behaviors and written about it on blogs for the organization Postpartum Progress, which raised awareness of postpartum mental illness and how to treat it. April devoured these blogs. *Oh my God,* she thought, *this is me.* She found out that the suffering of the past year, which she had simply taken for reality, for her new self, was actually a condition that could be named in various ways: Postpartum anxiety. Postpartum OCD. Intrusive thoughts.

"When they described intrusive thoughts I was like, *This is all I'm living, this is inescapable.* You can't stop the thoughts, you don't want them there, but they cripple you. And they make you feel like you don't control your own mind, and that's a scary fucking thing." There was immense validation in seeing this process described as a trackable, predictable phenomenon, an illness, characteristic in its symptoms and in need of treatment.

April went to see her GP. She described what she was dealing with, and her doctor didn't really understand it. The doctor had a notion of postpartum depression, but she seemed unaware of any other postpartum disorder. She did offer that April seemed to be suffering from anxiety, and prescribed 50 milligrams of Zoloft. April also found a therapist, who gave her literature about intrusive thoughts as well as exercises to combat them. The therapist would have her write down her scariest intrusive thoughts and then read them aloud, to reinforce the fact that they did not pose a real threat, that they were thoughts, and the brain can think anything. The therapist told her that people have messed-up thoughts every day: *I want to strangle that person. What if an icicle falls off that building?* For a person without OCD, that would be the end of it. A thought, in and out, random. A person like April gets stuck in a rut. *Why did I think that? Do I want to hurt someone? What would I do if the icicle fell?* The thought gains power, then probability, then a semblance of reality.

A month or so into the Zoloft and the therapy, April gazed at Ella and saw her for the first time. More than half a year had passed since her daughter's birth. All those milestones of early infancy, the smiling and the reaching and the cooing, the initial coming into personhood, had passed, and just now Ella's face emerged from the fog of constant worry. Blue eyes, cheeks like risen loaves, a downy fuzz of hair. April was overcome with joy at how beautiful her baby was. This kind of love was an utterly different sensation from what she had been feeling. She sat in her kitchen and time returned, her self returned, her life came back. She wept. "That's when I realized, it can be another way."

April had read online that Postpartum Progress hosted an annual Climb Out of the Darkness event, in which mothers who'd struggled with perinatal mood disorders hiked together on the longest day of the year to raise awareness about maternal mental health. She was just starting to get meds that worked. She was just starting to become the mother she had wanted to be. There was no climb in Pittsburgh, but April said to Alex, "I don't care, we're doing it."

On June 21, 2015, April and Alex left Ella with April's mother and went to Harrison Hills Park in the northern suburbs of Pittsburgh to take a hike. April needed to affirm for herself that the fear under which she'd labored for so long and which she had taken for granted as the condition of motherhood had a name. "When you don't know it's a thing," she told me, "you think it's just you."

Recovery, April would come to understand, was not the absence of symptoms but their management. "Maybe it changed the wiring in my brain," she acknowledged, and so the self that had saved her was now inextricably wound up with the self that had nearly destroyed her. What emerged from all this for April was empathy: she organized another climb in 2016 for more than thirty mothers, and then another in 2017 for more than fifty, raising money for local organizations that support maternal mental health, following up with women, pointing them toward resources and emphasizing the need to seek help.

She is an advocate on Facebook and in her community; when she hears of another mother who has suffered a traumatic birth, a miscarriage, or a rough transition to parenthood, she reaches out. She shares her story. She does not say, "It's normal for new mothers to worry!" Now, she wonders: "If I can have a master's and know about some mental health stuff and be personally not afraid to discuss things and still not be able to know what I'm experiencing and know that it has a name, know that it's an actual condition, know where to actually go to get help for this, and I have all these supports—a wonderful husband, an amazing family that's here—what are the people doing who don't have those things, and what's happening to their kids?"

In October 2015, April got pregnant again. She was having a boy. This time, she felt great, and she felt great about feeling great. Only in the last month did the thoughts start to creep back, but she talked with her doctor and reinforced her plan to start the Zoloft again as soon as the baby was out.

The week before the birth, April got pneumonia. She could barely breathe, she was gagging and choking, she had a high fever. She was briefly admitted to the hospital, where they advised her to count her baby's hourly kicks and to take Tylenol regularly because every time her fever spiked, her baby's heart rate got "tacky." *You know,* they told her casually, *you'll probably break your water from all that coughing.* She went home feeling like she was going to die, and stayed in bed for four days, trying to wrest herself awake from time to time to count kicks. At four a.m. one morning, she woke up coughing and felt wetness. There was blood pouring out between her legs.

At the hospital, they told her everything was fine: she was in labor. She spent the next twelve hours laboring with pneumonia before giving birth to a ten-pound baby boy, who like his sister came out face up. When he was born, there was a collective gasp among the doctors and nurses because he was so big. April, meanwhile, was taking huge struggling sucks of air. She couldn't breathe. Finally, someone turned from the baby and shoved an oxygen mask on her. They pumped her full of steroids to help her breathe, and she was awake and jittery the whole first night.

"It's a miracle that I don't have postpartum shit again!" she told me. But it wasn't a miracle: it was through her own awareness and action. The discrepancy between her two birth experiences is a dramatic illustration of what happens when women's mental health is put front and center and supported. She took control because she knew what to do. She started her meds again. She attended a support group. She spoke her thoughts out loud, wrote them down. She discovered what having an infant could be like when you weren't constantly gripped by dread.

The unwillingness to flag fear as problematic and clinical is reflected in the tools and frameworks used to screen pregnant women for mood disorders. Take, for example, the Edinburgh Postnatal Depression Scale (EPDS), the most widely used screening tool. The behaviors, states, and experiences the EPDS highlights—sadness, disaffection, detachment, low self-esteem, lack of pleasure—are coded as problematic symptoms. The behaviors, states, and experiences it ignores—panicking, ruminating, spiraling off on tangents of obsessive worry, intrusive thoughts, continual checking—are tacitly endorsed as normal or innocuous. There is significant debate about how effective the EPDS or any particular screening tool is in actually diagnosing and treating illness, but regardless of its effectiveness, the test establishes clear parameters for how we imagine the normal versus the dysfunctional in this period of pregnancy and early motherhood. It is impossible for anxiety or OCD alone—even severe, out-of-control anxiety or OCD—to register as a problem on the EPDS. It is impossible, on this most common metric used to distinguish order from disorder, to be too afraid.

The test is composed of a series of ten statements. Only three touch on anxiety: "3) I have blamed myself unnecessarily when things went wrong"; "4) I have been anxious or worried for no good reason"; and "5) I have felt scared or panicky for no very good reason." Even if a woman scores a 3, the top possible score, on each of these questions, she still won't achieve an overall score high enough to raise a red flag. During my own screening I chose "Yes, most of the time," "Yes, very often," and "Yes, quite a lot" for these questions, putting my score at a 9, but answered "Never," "Not much," "Not very often," or "Hardly at all" for the others, which focus on topics like not being able to laugh, feeling unhappy and crying, and thoughts of self-harm. At six weeks, I did not feel depressed. I was sleeping, I loved my baby, I looked forward to being with her. I did not begin to feel depressed until years later, when the anxiety had grown so overwhelming I could barely function. This is a common issue in postpartum women: the anxiety comes first, goes undiagnosed, intensifies, and then beneath it a depression begins to grow like mold. When the woman finally seeks treatment she is told it was postpartum depression all along.

Every practicing psychologist I spoke with told me that it was far more common to see anxiety than depression in the postpartum period, although several specified that a combination of the two was what they observed the most. Dr. Amy Wenzel, a clinical psychologist and expert on postpartum anxiety, who has conducted several pioneering research studies and authored the textbook *Anxiety in Childbearing Women*, told me that the most common case she sees in her practice is a woman who is very anxious about being a good mom and spends all of her time and energy on her baby, magnifying and intensifying her anxiety until it explodes into an existential depression. This culminates in the woman wondering, *Oh my God, I suck at being a mother, and what's the point of being here if I can't even be a mom?*

Dr. Ian Paul, a pediatrician and author of one of the most recent studies on postpartum anxiety, told me, "Any general pediatrician and obstetrician could tell you that it's way more common for mothers to be anxious about their babies and themselves after delivery than it is for them to be depressed. Clearly they're two distinct sort of sets of behaviors. So why isn't [anxiety] talked about or screened for?"

One reason is that depression, the canonical, bearded white male of mental illness, tends to hold towering sway over all other categories of disorder. In the postpartum context, depression offers an example of what psychiatrist David Goldberg calls "the principle of diagnostic parsimony": the medical preference for a single diagnosis. In psychiatry, Goldberg says, "Depression . . . trumps anxiety." According to psychology professor and researcher Stephen Matthey, depression is the "gold standard" of postpartum mood disorders; if women don't meet the criteria for it, they are not considered ill. Women with anxiety disorders scored an average of five points lower on the EPDS than women with depression, meaning that if this were the sole screening tool, these women's disorders would go undetected. Matthey cites a 1982 study that found nearly 8 percent of a sample of 284 mothers of young babies had "pure anxiety," while only 1.7 percent had depression. This study is striking mostly because another study twenty years later came up with almost exactly the same numbers, and further research, however limited, in the past ten years has found anxiety rates more than twice this. Yet the paradigm for understanding and treating peripartum mood disorders has not changed.

In her 2003 study, which has been cited hundreds of times, Dr. Amy Wenzel modified the definition of generalized anxiety disorder (GAD) to fit the postpartum period. Whereas the fourth-edition DSM definition of GAD stipulated that a person must suffer persistent, excessive, debilitating worry—along with at least two other symptoms including restlessness, fatigue, and/or irritability—for at least six months or longer, Wenzel delimited the period to two months. With this small shift, she discovered that 8 percent of her sample of postpartum women met the criteria for GAD, whereas only 1 percent met the criteria for postpartum depression. In fact, depression was the least common disorder in her study: most prevalent was anxiety at 8 percent, followed by OCD at nearly 3 percent. Each of these rates is double that of the general U.S. population, suggesting that this period of pregnancy and early motherhood is a window of particular vulnerability.

A 2013 study in *Pediatrics* found anxiety to be far more common than depression, with 17 percent of women suffering from the former, and 5.5 percent from the latter. This study, one of only a handful in the past decade looking at postpartum anxiety, was conducted by the aforementioned Dr. Paul, a pediatrician and professor of pediatrics and public health at Penn State. When I asked Dr. Paul why he'd ended up doing this research, the answer was embarrassingly obvious: he spends far more time with mothers than they spend with their own doctors. I felt foolish for not immediately seeing why pediatricians would be on the front lines of maternal mental illness, even though I saw my pediatrician upward of twenty times in my daughter's first year, and my midwife only once.

I remember that five-week visit well. It was strange to bring an actual baby to the office where I'd come every month of my pregnancy. After all those apocryphal months of heartbeats and kicks, here she was, a full chunky person in a teal onesie. In the waiting room I looked at the women, their bellies of varying girth, their hands folded on their laps, and I felt nostalgic for that waiting and yet also relieved to have emerged on the other side of it. I sat on the crunchy white paper while Elena slept in her car seat and then my midwife came in and cooed and marveled over her, how big she was, how much hair, and I felt that intense alchemical mix of happiness, sadness, pride, and wonder. I said, "Yes, it's going well," and I was cleared to have sex and then I walked out into the bright July sunshine and was struck by the fact that it was all over. No more visits, no more checks, no more hands on my belly. I cried.

Of course, I was at the very beginning of a journey that was in many ways much, much harder. But I wouldn't walk into that office again for a year.

That month alone, I saw my daughter's pediatrician three times.

I realize talking to Dr. Ian Paul that it is humiliating for women to have to look to a pediatrician to diagnose maternal anxiety. No matter how lovely and thoughtful the pediatrician, the fact that he or she is ultimately left to care for both baby and mother reinforces just how neglected and infantilized the latter is in American society.

"We have to find an adult psychiatrist for a . . . woman who doesn't have the motivation to pick up the phone for herself and call her doctor," Dr. Paul told me, and the tone in which he said this revealed both how frustrating it must be to have to deal with a problem beyond one's area of expertise and also how childlike women seem. I sensed all of a sudden that I was looking in an infinity mirror, and behind Dr. Paul is Dr. Spock and Dr. Freud and on and on and on, each staring with a mix of consternation, concern, and irritation at the hysterical woman in their care. I felt in our conversation—perhaps only as a result of my own sensitivity to this issue—the larger societal judgment that really, for a good mother, who strikes that perfect balance of powerlessness and power, of passivity and strategic intervention, there should be no problem at all, that the existence of this problem is one of a long history of female hysteria and overreaction and noisome *presence*. Mothers should be invisible, should be in control and self-sufficient, and at the same time should patiently and lovingly and studiously absorb a nonstop stream of medical and cultural haranguing about dangers, expectations, needs, and shoulds. They should be able to just *handle it*, just *be natural*.

While many infants in the United States have access to an almost grotesque panoply of resources, from massage to swimming to sensory stimulation class, a mother is left alone with the Internet and a stack of chipper books on the latest bona fide methods for raising a well-adjusted genius. Her well-being is considered only as it relates to the baby's health, and is subsumed under the latter. And while her child will have almost excessive checks on his or her social, cognitive, emotional, and physical development, with intensive intervention at the slightest sign of a problem, a mother shows up once at six weeks to be cleared for sex and is sent on her way. Meanwhile, pressure builds and builds. Dr. Paul's office gets calls at all hours of the night—"my baby spit up," "my baby has yellow poop and the Internet says yellow poop is a sign of liver problems"—and regularly encounters mothers so anxious about sudden infant death syndrome (SIDS) that they stop sleeping.

One researcher who didn't want to be identified confessed to me that no one wants to fund research on postpartum women. He'd spoken with someone at a funding agency who told him that it was much easier to fix a problem when it appears in a child. "If you're going to focus on solving a problem," this person told him, "don't focus on the adult." Fix the kid, who is still open to it, who can be a clear success story, who is allowed and even supposed to be flawed anyway. The researcher explained this to me months before ProPublica broke a major news story about why the United States has the highest maternal mortality rates in the developed world: essentially, the reporters discovered, funding organizations are so busy pouring money and resources into research about babies, and particularly premature ones, that there is little left to study even the basics of caring for mothers.

Struck by how few anxiety questionnaires and screening tests for women in the perinatal period actually focused on worries related to children, Dr. Wenzel designed a screening that focused specifically on these fears. She called it the Postpartum Worry Scale (PWS). The original Postpartum Worry Scale, which Wenzel employed in 2003, was a fourteen-item test measuring mothers' degree of worry in a number of domains related to parenting. Each item was rated on a scale of 0 to 4, with 0 indicating the least intensive worry (not at all/none of the time) and 4 the most intensive (always/all of the time). In 2014, Wenzel and two colleagues decided to revise the original PWS and add six more items specifically related to infant health and development and mother-infant relationships. They administered the PWS to 1,231 mothers of infants.

When these new measures were added, the average response on the PWS was a 2 out of 4. That is, the standard was to be worried 50 percent of the time. This is also the threshold for diagnosis with generalized anxiety disorder. On questions related to the baby's health and development, "the cleanliness of your surroundings," and "balancing your responsibilities," the average response was a 3. The norm in these areas was to worry most of the time. At least according to this study, women who aren't spending a significant or even the majority of their time worrying are the outliers.

When Wenzel wonders whether the anxiety she's discovering in the majority of mothers—in some at high enough registers that it drowns out the rest of their lives, in many at a constant and distracting level of alarm, in most at least a high whine—is normative rather than dysfunctional, she is uncovering the way many women parent now: in perpetual fear. Anxiety has become so common, so pervasive, and so culturally slippery—both protective and destructive, both solicited and ridiculed, both status marker and shameful secret—that we all are just left to muck our way through it.

———————

On a summer night in April's backyard, rain dripped off the eaves, along the tomatoes and raspberry brambles, down the miniature plastic slide. Inside Ella slept in her bed and Oliver, her little brother, in his crib. There was a mesh cylinder filled with moths on the front table: a project one of Alex's grad students had left with him while she went traveling. The suburban Pittsburgh night was quiet. I thought about the time I'd returned from a trip to Mexico I took with my husband and daughter when Elena was just over two. I'd approached that trip with naïve optimism, but my fear raged back, more powerful and crushing than ever, so that I questioned whether I would ever be able to live the life I wanted again.

I'd left Mexico early and suddenly, taking Elena with me, and Jorge had stayed behind. I went from 80-degree sunshine and a city bustling with tourists and parades to an empty house in the middle of Pittsburgh winter. April met me at a city park for a play-date. I was barely keeping it together, but I couldn't tell her that. She looked at me while our kids waited in line for the big concrete slide and she asked, "How are you doing?" There was no pity, no syrupy solicitousness. It was just a matter-of-fact question. "Okay," I said, and it was a lie, but she nodded, and then we talked about Mexico, and she talked about a trip to Michigan when she'd been stressed, and no huge revelations were parsed or intimacies confessed, but that conversation worked like a wedge between me and the fear. I felt immense gratitude for her; I felt seen.

"Anxiety gets you because you fight it," she told me on her back porch. "You fight fight fight fight. You don't want it. But in fact, you just have to float." She undulated her hand through the night, a bird riding currents over the ocean. My heart was briefly in my throat, pulsing, because I knew this truth and could feel it in my body, but it was so, so difficult to live.

"It's there," April said. "It's there."

We let that sit between us.

WHEN ELENA WAS A LITTLE OVER A YEAR OLD, *we moved to Mexico. The first moment I remember from that year is Elena's rapture at the globos: helium balloons that rose like oversized clusters of grapes from the wrists of lackluster vendors. They were all shapes and sizes, hearts and circles, chrome red and frosty mint green, crinkly and glinting in the early morning sun. To a toddler coming from forty acres of woods in rural Ohio, they were nothing short of Wonderland. I took a picture and posted it on Instagram: Elena, fourteen months old, her hair in tiny twin pigtails, pointing as high as she can reach at a flock of globos. Elena was wearing tights and a long-sleeved onesie in spite of the fact that it was likely 80 degrees. I was worried about dengue. I'd gotten it the last time we were in Mexico, when she was four months old, and it had been horrific. Having had it once would not prevent me from getting it again; in fact, a subsequent infection would be more dangerous.* I can never go back to Mexico, *I thought at the time. The fear had already cordoned off vast swaths of my life, and now it wrapped yellow caution tape around this country where I'd spent most of my twenties and where my husband had been born and raised.*

But I couldn't stay away from Mexico; it was central to our lives and identities. My in-laws lived there. When Elena was six months old, I applied for a Fulbright fellowship to study return migration in Oaxaca. I desperately wanted the fellowship, or more precisely I wanted the affirmation of my continued artistic promise, but at the same time I had no idea what I wanted: I'd been cast adrift by motherhood and my fear into a terrain where I could no longer define myself. Like a machine slowing but still moving as its power fails, I went through the motions of my former life.

I applied, I interviewed, and in March I received an email of congratulations: we were moving to Mexico.

This, I reminded myself as I planned our move, was the only motherhood I could have imagined when I was twenty, twenty-five, even thirty: hauling my travel-dazed babe with me around the world, feeding her fried street peanuts and setting her loose on the grimy tile floors of cantinas, swimming with her in hidden bays, cuddling on second-class buses that hurtled down mountains, delightedly giving fuck-all about convention and stereotype. Instead, my motherhood had been mostly long, quiet days in the solitude of Ohio maples and oaks, walking the same loop under changing leaves with my baby on my back.

As our departure for Mexico approached, I tried not to look too hard at the divide between the imagined experience and the actual. With the absurd blend of optimism and denial that characterizes mental illness, I told myself that once we arrived I'd simply have to get over this fear and become that carefree, footloose mother of my expectation. It would just happen, because that was who I was, anyway. It was not yet clear to me that a moat had opened up between my former life, unencumbered by awareness of the danger in every single quotidian experience, and my life now, in which anxiety would forever be a presence. I was still capable of pretending that by the force of sheer will I would just shed this burden, as if it'd been a particularly dogged and silly crush. It was like an alcoholic waking up one morning and deciding to stop drinking. By five p.m., she is cracking her first beer.

The day we arrived in Mexico I was already refusing to let Elena touch any painted surface; I was dabbing the back of her neck with a repellent wipe from one of five jumbo-sized boxes of Natrapel I'd lugged with us. I dressed us both in long sleeves and long pants almost every day. In that country of scorching sun and sweet, dry heat, I bared my arms perhaps once or twice in the course of the year we spent there as a family.

Still, in the beginning, I enjoyed myself. I entered that honeymoon period when the world seems briefly benevolent, or at least harmless in its indifference, and as long as I was reasonably careful it seemed we could live a life somewhat approximating the one I'd nourished in my imagination. We took a trip to a village tucked deep into the Sierra Norte, three *hours up a narrow, curvy paved road and another hour down an even narrower, curvier unpaved road, dust billowing up behind our back tires. I read Elena* One Fish, Two Fish, Red Fish, Blue Fish, *glancing up from time to time at fog-hugged cloud forest and mountains fringed in blue. This was joy. In the village, Jorge, Elena, and I slept together on a twin bed in a room full of the detritus of pueblo life: discarded egg cartons, broken pottery, books that looked as if they'd been whipped around in a hurricane, bits and pieces of toys, dust upon dust. We woke to the vaudeville sound of turkeys gobbling. It was the village fiesta, so the days were a madcap timeless whirlwind of fireworks and basketball tournaments and outdoor religious ceremonies heady with incense and flowers. I took Elena to all of it. I hiked with her to a shrine on a mountain path between villages, saying hello to the old couples who were trekking kilometers with mesh bags of oranges on their backs. One offered half an orange slice to Elena and clutched her hand with affection. This was the life I wanted to live.*

My sense of joy disappeared in increments.

It began with clay. Most of the clay pottery in Oaxaca is lead-glazed, and can be quite toxic if it is old or the glaze has deteriorated. From time to time the government makes a half-hearted attempt to convince local artisans to use lead-free glazes or to fire in different kilns, although within months of the publicized initiative everyone more or less retreats to the status quo. Here is the conundrum of anxiety: it is rational not to want a child to eat from a dish glazed in lead. But what seems like a clear-cut and logical prohibition is quickly complicated by the million unknowns, particular contexts, and unique situations that make life life and not a simple equation solved by yes or no. The memela at the village festival: Was it cooked in barro? Was the barro glazed? Was it old? Was it chipping? What about the soup at the upscale restaurant in the city's Zócalo? What about mole from the market? Quesadilla toppings? The salsas? What about horchata, the most fundamental of all Mexican drinks: where had the rice been cooked, where had the cantaloupe been stored, how traditional did the señora and the little street-side stand seem?

Trying to police this one seemingly straightforward threat—the ubiquitous local dishware—quickly led to a dense and extensive network of prohibitions that could never offer perfect security. I insisted we eat only at three restaurants: an upscale deli run by Spaniards and serving mostly sandwiches; a fancy courtyard serving dressed-up and Europeanized local dishes; and a café where the food was boring but the coffee strong and the staff friendly and tolerant of a toddler's high jinks.

Still this did not placate me. Everything in my path was potentially dangerous. Everything carried risk. I didn't see this as a sign of my own basic, human lack of control, a sign of the futility of trying to achieve perfect certainty. Instead, I became further entrenched. As another therapist would put it years down the line, I ceded more and more territory to my anxiety, until I was living a life the size of a postage stamp, restricted in experience, range, scope, and potential. This was not lost on me. I was often irritable. I sobbed suddenly and intensely. I wasn't sure what was happening to me.

One day we went to eat at a restaurant on the city's periphery road, a place Jorge and I had gone in the past for its traditional plates and its fried platters of snacks that went down perfectly with cold Victorias. My dad was visiting. There was road construction outside, and I could see the dust through the windows. By the time we got the check I wanted to throw up with worry at the thought of it coating our food, our plates. My dad and Jorge decided to go get ice cream. They took Elena. I went back to the apartment, curled up in a ball, and wept. My body shook with the force of the sobs. It was the one and only time I have cried so hard I choked.

I was miserable. I was making myself, and everyone around me, miserable. I was denying Elena a life. I should know better, I told myself. How had I let myself become this? I had no idea, and no way to make it stop.

JAMIE

3

The Risk Society

The concept of risk emerged as part of political philosophy and theory in the seventeenth century, in association with gambling: it elucidated the probability of an event occurring, along with the potential gains and losses following that event. In the eighteenth century, marine insurance agencies used the notion of risk to determine the chance of a ship coming home versus being lost at sea. In each case, risk was a weighing of positive over negative outcomes: the possibility of success versus the possibility of failure. In contemporary language, however, *risk* bears a negative connotation: it has come to refer exclusively to unwanted danger.

Hypersensitivity to risk is not a specific feature of pregnancy and motherhood. Rather, it is the dominant characteristic of what German sociologist Ulrich Beck has called a "risk society." The risk society is characterized by a tragic, ironic paradox: rapid industrialization has given way to a technocracy so complex, so beholden to science and expertise, that its successes ultimately end up becoming dangers it can neither predict nor control. The risk society is safer than any society throughout history, and yet its defining paradigm and organizing principle—indeed, its religion—is risk.

The risks that haunt this society are not the result of ignorance but of an excess of knowledge, and of an understanding of knowledge as partial, contested, and suspect. In the risk society, which Beck first defined and outlined in the 1980s during the peak tension of the Cold War, trust in science and expertise has fallen. No longer do we depend on them to explain our realities to us. In the period from the early twentieth century through World War II, new technologies and scientific developments were celebrated as consummate improvements in quality of life: Frozen foods would save the housewife so much time in cooking. DDT would spare American soldiers the mosquito-borne scourges of the jungle. The affordable car would allow the middle-class white family to get a house with a backyard in the suburbs and vacation at Niagara Falls.

After the apocalypse at Hiroshima, breakneck scientific and technological "progress" came with scare quotes. *Now I am become death, destroyer of worlds,* thought Robert Oppenheimer as he watched a test launch of an atomic bomb in the New Mexican desert: the risk society had created, by virtue of its own dogged efforts of human engineering and intelligence, the ever-looming potential for its own demise.

Nuclear weapons offered the clearest illustration of this new principle, but it crept into everyday life as well. The plastics that give us an infinite variety of affordable toys, toothbrushes, T-shirts, containers, and furniture also poison the oceans and, to indecipherable and varying extents, our bodies. The cars that enable our work and leisure emit chemicals that give us cancer and might eventually smother our planet. The technology that detects deadly diseases in the fetal genome could create superbugs or a eugenic dystopia. Polish sociologist and philosopher Zygmunt Bauman wrote: "[Risk] is now dissolved in the minute, yet innumerable, traps and ambushes of daily life. One tends to hear it knocking now and again, daily, in fatty fast food, in listeria-infected eggs, in cholesterol-rich temptations, in sex without condoms, in cigarette smoke, in asthma-inducing carpet mites, in the dirt you see and the germs you do not."

All of these threats can be identified, and all manner of experts can attempt to measure, qualify, minimize, emphasize, and anticipate their impact, but they all share the fundamental quality of hiding in the scrim of uncertainty and unknowability.

These risks are cultural and subjective: different societies and subsets of these societies envision them differently. In Europe, chemicals are carefully monitored, limited, and sometimes banned; in the United States, the regulation of chemicals is desultory at best and often requires significant evidence of harm, but widespread and extensive action is taken to prevent terrorism. This is reflective of one of Beck's central, ironic principles: in a risk society, "acceptable risks are those which are accepted." The risks that are most effectively highlighted by government, activists, organizations, and/or mass media are the ones most likely to be accepted as valid and organized around. Others are ignored or discredited or minimized, especially if they largely affect the poor. An "objective" risk is really a product of the staging of public perception. Beck explains, "The risks which we believe we recognize and which fill us with fear are mirror images of our selves, of our cultural perceptions." This is not to say that these risks are either more or less real than others that go unrecognized; rather, it is to show that in the risk society, values and beliefs and priorities are expressed in terms of risks.

Risks exist as possibilities, as worst-case scenarios, as unknowable catastrophes, and we expend great societal and individual energy in our generally boring lives trying to anticipate and prepare for them. We have made what turns out to be a terrible peace: unparalleled levels of safety and longevity in exchange for constant anxiety. Without tradition, religion, a spiritual or deeper connection to the natural world, or even "faith in the redemptive powers of utopias," we turn to risk: it becomes the cognitive and perceptual framework around which we define our lives.

"In God's absence," Beck writes, "risk unfolds its fateful and terrible, inscrutable ambiguity." Individuals are left to themselves to negotiate it, and those with the most knowledge are often the most afflicted. They recognize the fallibility of science and mass media and yet must live within these institutions' judgments, frameworks, and rules. They must ask themselves, as Beck put it, "What concerns should one have and in what situations? What are the boundary lines between prudent concern, crippling fear and hysteria?"

The anthropologist Mary Douglas has suggested that in order to understand how risk works in the contemporary Western world, one has to substitute the word *sin* for *risk*. The concept of sin was used to homogenize Christian cultures, to keep potential rebels and iconoclasts in line, and to separate the pure from the soiled. Now, Douglas argues, risk operates in much the same way.

Risk offers a secular cosmology that delineates appropriate behavior, maintains moral order, and prescribes a precise set of values. In the United States, these values include the sanctity of the child, the perfectibility of the child, the sacrificial nature of motherhood, and the responsibility of the individual for maintaining his or her own "wellness." Risk is a way of policing and reinforcing these values. We chart the lines of social purity and transgression with the chalk of risk, and when disaster strikes, we blame the individual for not hewing closely enough to them. Douglas writes of risk as "scor[ing] on [the individual's] mind the invisible fences and paths by which the community co-ordinates its life in common." Risk, masquerading as impartial knowledge available to anyone willing to simply make the effort of education and prevention, is actually a moral order whose censuring of unbelievers and rebels is harsh judgment, banishment, and shame.

———————

Jamie grew up in the "typical, white-picket-fence American family" in Sumter, South Carolina, with a stay-at-home mother and a soldier father. After college, she married one of her brother's closest childhood friends. He took a position at Heinz, and together they moved to Pittsburgh for the job. They knew they wanted kids someday, but they weren't in a rush. They delighted in being far from home, doing what childless twenty- and thirty-something couples with means do: eating out at restaurants and zipping off on spur-of-the-moment trips. "I didn't have a care in the world," Jamie told me. When they started talking about a baby it was mostly because of her age—she was nearing the zone of the "geriatric pregnancy," and she thought perhaps they should get moving.

She got pregnant immediately. They were delighted. "We didn't think anything could go wrong." Jamie pauses. "It"—the "it" being the possibility of a descent into all-consuming fear—"didn't even register."

What did register were the damaging effects of nitrates and the dangers of aspartame. Jamie poured all of her occupational and educational energies into the project of the uber-baby. "I was laser-focused on, like, I wasn't going to destroy my baby by eating a turkey sandwich! I didn't even think to worry about anything with like, me."

It started somewhere in the second trimester. She began to notice herself engaging in strange behaviors, almost as if they were independent of her. She read an article about women who go in for an exam in late pregnancy only to discover that the baby's heart is not beating, and then have to deliver the stillborn baby. Stillbirth became the terror at the center of her world. She fixated on her son's kicks, and he never seemed to kick enough. The doctors would tell her he was fine, but she never believed them. *My baby is going to be born strangled, with the cord around its neck,* she thought. *I'm going to give birth to a dead baby.* She lay awake at night thinking this over and over, then running through the conversations she would have with doctors if and when it happened. She wondered how she would react. How she would get over it.

Jamie started going into her OB's office several times a month, and then several times a week, just to listen to her son's heartbeat. The office employees got to know her so well that a nurse would let her bypass the typical check-in and go straight to an exam room to listen. No one thought to pull her aside and mention anxiety as a potential problem. Nobody said, "This isn't normal." Sometimes they would roll their eyes, telling her, "You're fine, sweetheart! You have a healthy baby, a healthy pregnancy." It was never enough. Eventually, she bought herself a heartbeat monitor on Amazon in order to listen at home whenever she wanted.

Jamie was constantly collapsing in panic. She had a half iced tea/half lemonade from Subway after a doctor told her caffeine intake really didn't matter, and then she read on a blog that caffeine was terrible for her baby. She could barely function for days. She adhered to all the rules—not a sip of alcohol or a slice of lunch meat—feeling like that should quell her anxiety. *If I can just do everything right.* She thought if she executed her pregnancy meticulously, perfectly, obeyed every command from the medical pantheon and every warning on Google, checked and monitored and devoted her total cognitive capacity to her unborn child, she would be okay. But her anxiety reinforced itself, solidifying within her.

Jamie's pregnancy crept past her due date. The anxiety of those final days was excruciating, and finally she went into the hospital late one night with a concern and they agreed to induce her. They broke her water, gave her an epidural. Unfortunately, it didn't seem to work: each time she had a contraction, an electric pain flared in her butt and rocketed down her leg to her foot, as if a long bone there was being forcefully broken over and over. They gave her another epidural. It had no effect: the pain ignited with fresh force whenever a contraction kicked up. At one point she screamed, "I'm being electrocuted!"

No one took her seriously. Her baby weighed nine pounds, eleven ounces, and faced the wrong way, bearing down on her sciatic nerve: the longest and largest nerve in the body, running from the lower back down the legs. This was causing the brutal electric jolts, but no one thought to investigate further: "Everyone thought I was just a snowflake." Her husband told her at one point to settle down.

The baby would not come out. After twelve hours of labor and incandescent pain, she was finally given a C-section. Her baby was born. "The best way I can describe it is: when they took out the baby, they took out my joy. If joy was like a color or a cloud, you would just see it sucked right out of my tummy."

They handed Jamie her son, and she could not have cared less. She had no energy or emotion. "I was a zombie; I was completely empty." After coming home from the hospital, she cried constantly. Three or four days postpartum, she called her gynecologist and said, "Something is seriously wrong with me." The gynecologist said it just sounded like the baby blues but prescribed Zoloft. She said they'd only give Jamie thirty days' worth, and then Jamie would have to meet with a therapist to get more. "What dose do you want?" the gynecologist asked. "I want all of it," Jamie said. It took weeks to take effect.

That first month was an experience of breakdown. She was hysterical every day. She was not producing enough milk, but she refused to bottle-feed because she'd read something that insisted it would harm her son's development. He started losing weight, and Jamie went to the pediatrician's office over and over. A different doctor saw her for each visit, and during each she sobbed. She sobbed when they weighed him. She sobbed when they checked him for jaundice. She sobbed when they took her milk. Her husband or her mother accompanied her for every appointment, because she would not travel alone with the baby; she was terrified to be by herself with him. What if she got in a car accident? What if she had one of those after-pregnancy strokes, what if she was one of the women who have blood clots after cesareans? Finally her mom asked the doctors, "Do you see a lot of women like this? Crying all the time?" Most of the doctors shrugged. One pediatrician said: "No."

Another pediatrician that friends had recommended gave her a worksheet that she remembers as having "a bunch of happy and sad faces." There was a question about thoughts of hurting herself, which she answered truthfully: yes. She never heard anything back.

Meanwhile, she obsessed over her son's breathing. Jamie wanted to do everything in her power to prevent his airway from being blocked. She had two vibrating swings, two Pack 'n Plays, and an assortment of fluffy infant seats in her living room alone. Her goal was to be able to see the baby facing her no matter where she sat. Still, she would check his belly repeatedly to see if it was moving. She'd be in the middle of a conversation and would walk over and lay a gentle hand on his tummy. "What are you doing?" a friend or family member would ask. They'd help reassure her, but a few minutes later she would go back and check again.

The baby slept next to Jamie in a co-sleeper, and she kept her hand on his belly the entire time. It was no better if someone else was watching him while she tried to get some rest. She'd wake up every few minutes and have to check. Her mother and husband got in the habit of yelling upstairs, "Lincoln's breathing! We're check-ing his breathing! Lincoln's breathing!" Jamie did extensive research and discovered a sensor that could be clipped to her son's diaper and that would set off an alarm if he didn't breathe for a certain number of seconds. *At least,* she thought, *I'll wake up if something happens.* Every time she left the house, she packed as if they were going on a weeks-long trip: bags and bags of diapers, extra clothes, medicines, bottles. Her husband protested: "We could get stuck in traffic for hours and the baby couldn't eat this much food!" She countered: What if they were in a hostage situation?

Friends and family teased her for her quirks. Her husband once made a video satire of her preparing for a trip to the store. He feigned a Steve Irwin voice: "Hey mates, we're packing for our journey to the outlets!" He surveyed the gear as if they were explorers on a pioneering expedition.

Meanwhile, Jamie was having intrusive thoughts about suicide. She would go online and research how mothers had killed them-selves. She'd read and reread the stories. Years later, as she was talking to me, she was still familiar with all of them. The one who went to Dick's Sporting Goods right before a birthday party and shot herself and her son in her backyard. "I think her husband started a foundation." The one who stabbed her son and then her-self to death. The one who drove off a cliff. She was awed by their bravery. She idolized them. These women had found their way out of the relentless degradation of fear with decisive action; at least in their minds, they'd saved their children, while she was too chicken. She read the stories over and over again, copying the names and pasting them into Google in quotes to make sure she hadn't missed another from a different news outlet. She circled back to them regularly to see if there were any new comments; she wanted to see if anyone would say, "She could've gotten help here." But no one did.

Jamie developed a plan. If she didn't feel better in three months, she'd throw herself off a nearby overpass.

One day when the baby was one or two months old, Jamie was in the car with him and her mother, returning from a shopping trip. The car was stopped in traffic, and her mother was talking on the phone. Jamie kept looking in the back seat to check Lincoln's breathing, and she started thinking, *Open the door and run. Just open the door and run.* It was a beautiful, sunny day. Her mom was so happy. There was a little grassy strip dividing their side of the highway from oncoming traffic. It would only take a minute to cross it and run into the rush of cars. *Just be brave,* Jamie told herself, *Just do it. Open the door and go. You're such a pussy! Just do it!* She started to count down, *three, two, one, go.* All she had to do was run across the grass and someone would surely hit her. *Three, two, one, go.* She couldn't. Again. *Three, two, one, go.* Then the car rumbled into motion and they all went home.

Human beings' perception of risk is inherently skewed. We rely on systems that are thousands of years old, developed as our human brains were developing, to judge what to fear and how much to fear it. In his book *The Science of Fear*, journalist Daniel Gardner explores the evolutionarily conserved cognitive and heuristic biases that frame our thinking about risk. He argues that in a contemporary world very different from the one in which these biases emerged, they generate irrational judgments. Gardner asks why, as the "healthiest, wealthiest, and longest-lived people in history," we are so afraid, and finds his answer in part in the manipulations of the government, the media, and nongovernmental organizations, and in part in the innate biases these groups play into. The government hypes up risks related to its own interests; NGOs dramatize the problems they address in order to rouse public interest and funding; and the media publishes sensational stories that reflect radical, isolated departures from the norm, which it tries to portray as relevant to a general audience. All of these appeal to our most basic biases.

Take, for example, child "abductions": the vast majority of these are the result of kids running away from home or kids being taken by family members. Most of these kids return in less than a day. In the United States, the number of "stereotypical kidnappings"—in which a child is taken by a stranger—is ninety per year, which puts the risk for the average child at .00015 percent. American parents wouldn't know this, however, by watching an Anderson Cooper segment on abduction, during which Cooper cites a random statistic—invented whole cloth, Gardner reveals—that fifty thousand children are kidnapped each year, and a "family safety expert" warns parents to teach three-year-olds how to pull the wires in the back of a car's trunk to disconnect the tail lights and alert police.

This misrepresentation of risk is particularly true in coverage of crime. Multiple studies have shown that people tend to rate a phenomenon or possibility that is easily recalled as riskier than one not easily recalled. Dramatic stories of crime, however unlikely, however random and far-flung, tend to stick in people's minds. This may have been useful back when people's networks consisted of a series of villages. Now, however, the constant obsessive coverage of crime makes it possible to live in a suburban, gated community in the United States and believe one is constantly at risk of being violently murdered. Even though violent crime accounts for only a very small percentage of overall crime and has consistently dropped in both the United States and the United Kingdom since the 1990s, people continue to believe it is on the rise.

A study by psychologists Amos Tversky and Eric Johnson asked Stanford University students to read three stories about a death: one by fire, one by leukemia, and one by murder. The students were asked to rate the riskiness of twelve different items. The fire story raised their estimates of risk by 14 percent, the leukemia story by 73 percent, and the murder story by 144 percent. This is largely because of emotion: murder stokes people's emotions in a way that fire or cancer does not. Under the sway of emotion, people become "probability blind," according to legal scholar Cass Sunstein. They rate phenomena that have emotional resonance as riskier than phenomena that don't stir up strong feelings.

University of Oregon psychology professor and renowned risk researcher Paul Slovic asked people in a study if they agreed or disagreed that a one-in-ten-million lifetime risk of cancer from exposure to a chemical was too small to worry about. One third disagreed, saying they would worry about this. Very few people, meanwhile, worry about an asteroid hitting the Earth, a risk that is much likelier than the one Slovic proposed. The first example evokes emotion; the second leaves the speculator cold. As neuro-scientist Joseph LeDoux has explained it, the wiring of our brains is such that our emotions are much more likely to flood our "rational-ity" or intelligent thinking than the latter is to tame our emotions.

We are often duped by emotion not only in making conscious judgments, but in unconscious associations. Take, for example, people's tendency to show rash estimates of risk in relation to chemicals but to associate the "natural" with goodness. Chemicals mostly evoke negative emotions—hence the rampant use of *toxic* as a descriptor for everything from dates to politics to personalities—while the natural is commonly associated with health and beauty and vigor. Gardner quotes the biochemist Bruce Ames: "People have this impression that if it's natural, it can't be harmful, and that's a bit naïve." Half of everything tested, Ames points out, is a carcinogen. Coffee, for example—70 percent of the chemicals naturally occurring in coffee are carcinogens in rodent tests. But people practice "intuitive toxicology": the eight-syllable ingredient on the sunscreen label seems cancerous, but coffee grows on trees! In her book *On Immunity,* Eula Biss points out that devastating viruses that may paralyze or kill children are envisioned as "natural," and therefore perceived to be less dangerous than the chemicals used in the vaccines to prevent them.

Emotion plays a crucial role in our evaluations of risk, which seems obvious, but we tend to believe that we're evaluating risks objectively, on the basis of cognitive reasoning. As Gardner explains, Paul Slovic's groundbreaking studies have shown that laypeople are dramatically inaccurate in judging risks. They even underestimate the percentage of the time they are wrong about risk; in a study he conducted, one quarter of participants put the odds of their being wrong in their evaluations at less than 1 in 100, when in fact 1 in 8 of their answers were wrong. Slovic came up with a ranking system that most people use to determine risk:

1. Catastrophic potential: the more catastrophic, the riskier it is.
2. Familiarity: the more unfamiliar, the riskier it is.
3. Understanding: the less we understand it, the riskier it is.
4. Personal control: the less control we have, the riskier it is.
5. Voluntariness: if it wasn't by our own choice, it's riskier.
6. Children: it is much riskier if it involves kids.
7. Future generations: it is much riskier if it threatens future generations.
8. Victim identity: if victims can be identified, it's riskier.
9. Dread: if its effects generate fear, it's riskier.
10. Trust: if we don't trust the institutions involved, it's riskier.
11. Media attention: the more media coverage it gets, the riskier it is.
12. Accident history: the more negative events in the past, the riskier it is.
13. Equity: if some people benefit while others are endangered, it's riskier.

14. Benefits: if benefits are not clear, it's riskier.
15. Reversibility: If it can't be reversed, it's riskier.
16. Personal risk: if it's personally dangerous for me, it's riskier.
17. Origin: if it's man-made versus natural, it's riskier.
18. Timing: the more immediate it is, the riskier.

Of these, a particular cluster—involuntariness, inequity, and catastrophic potential—create a "dread factor" that is the single strongest predictor of people's perception of risk. The "dread factor" doesn't correlate with actual risk: it reflects what people fear the most.

These cognitive and heuristic biases affect us all, but mothers are especially vulnerable. Since stories about the fragility and infinite potential of children and the errors of mothers are so prominent in our culture, mothers' judgments about risk are bound to be off the charts. Becoming a mother is an experience singularly charged with uncertainty and a terrifying lack of control, unfolding under threat of guilt and blame. In this emotionally saturated context, in a risk society both safer than ever and tormented by the possibility of a rare catastrophe, mothers are bound to drown in risk.

The top fears of pregnant women trigger almost all of Slovic's risk categories. Take SIDS, for example. The outcome is catastrophic. Scientists do not understand how SIDS works or why it happens. Besides putting babies to sleep on their backs, which reduces the risk of SIDS, we have little ability to prevent it or to predict its occurrence. It stirs deep fear, earns significant media coverage, is inequitable and involuntary (we cannot choose whether or not to let our babies sleep) and irreversible. It hits that combo triggering Slovic's "dread factor." The actual percentage of babies born each year in the United States who die of SIDS is .0000625. Not 1 percent, not 2 percent: *.0000625 percent*. Yet for many women, avoiding SIDS becomes the single most important focus of their early days with their babies.

In an article for the *Psychological Bulletin* entitled "Risks as Feelings," economist and psychologist George Freud Loewenstein wrote that once the possibility of a negative event passes the zero threshold and becomes a source of worry, subsequent increases in the probability of that event occurring don't affect people's emotions or their choices. That is, once an event becomes possible, it doesn't matter whether there's a .00015 percent chance of its occurring or a 15 or 50 or 85 percent chance, people will still feel intense emotions and act accordingly. Mothers enter into a zone in which risk is the sole framework of their lives, every risk is peak, and each one is equally, imminently possible. Choking. Drowning. Falling. SIDS. Strangulation. Dog attack. Allergic reaction. Food poisoning. Infection. These are feelings as much as they are risks, and the feeling is a terror of harm to one's child. What matters is the mere possibility, not the probability.

It is difficult to fight feeling with information, especially when so much of the information available to mothers is skewed; for example, most medical websites with information about SIDS list only the number of babies who die each year of the disease, which sounds significant, and not the percentage of the total babies born, which is vanishingly small. Yet many women, like myself, nonetheless attempt to become full-time risk managers, embarking on the Sisyphean task of stamping out any and all risk with extreme prevention protocol. Some women devote significant chunks of their lives to this. One acquaintance told me she considered it a relief when she only had to research the best bike helmet for her toddlers for forty-five minutes. Forty-five minutes was for her on the reasonable, shorter end of the spectrum; how much time are women spending in risk research? The irony is that, as Gardner writes, "If an independent thinker really wishes to form entirely independent judgments about the risks we face in daily life, or even just those we hear about in the news, he or she will have to obtain multiple university degrees, quit his or her job, and do absolutely nothing but read about all the ways he or she may die until he or she actually is dead."

Any individual woman could, in theory, buck this culture of

obsession with risk. She could spurn the ubiquitous warnings, turn a blind eye to the grave news stories, be aware of her biases and overcome them. But it is incredibly difficult to turn away from group consensus when the stakes are so high. Gardner details numerous studies in which people, even in anonymous situations when their dissent will not be noticed or punished, even when they can see for themselves that the answer to a question is clearly and obviously true, will go with the erroneous group response over their own instincts. This tendency to go with the group becomes more pronounced the more a particular task is rated as difficult, ambiguous, and important: a task, like, for example, child-rearing.

Even if an individual woman wants to try to make her own decisions, she must fight the overwhelming pressure to conform in a circumstance that is painted as so exceptional and so high pressure. The benefits to this iconoclasm are not easily measured and calculated, and rarely if ever mentioned or celebrated, but the consequences of defying risk are loud and clear: exile from the realm of the good mother.

By the date Jamie had set for her own suicide, the Zoloft her doctor prescribed had kicked in just enough to knock the constant crying down a notch. It weakened the depression and the suicidal thoughts to the point where she could move past them, though they remained present. It did very little for her anxiety, which persisted mostly unchecked and which no one seemed particularly concerned about. The first therapist Jamie saw diagnosed her with postpartum depression, postpartum OCD, postpartum anxiety, and post-traumatic stress disorder, and told her that the fact she had a plan and an exact date for killing herself meant she had "good coping skills." This therapist was confident. "It'll pass!" she said. Jamie found a different therapist, whose treatment consisted mostly of asking Jamie to try to wait for ten minutes instead of three between breathing checks, which Jamie failed to do and found pointless and baffling. In most of the sessions with this therapist, Jamie bawled. Finally, a few months in, she asked if the therapist saw a lot of women like her, and if she would get better.

The therapist was cool. "Some women," she replied, "just don't like being moms."

This therapist might as well have carved out Jamie's heart and tossed it into an incinerator. Jamie left and never looked back. She has never gotten the doubt sown by that comment out of her head.

Jamie had wanted to be a mom. She had chosen to get pregnant. She had waited until later in life, when she had the resources, the stability, the time and desire. She'd selected her moment, the right moment. She had done everything right, damn it. Jamie had plenty of mom friends and knew what being a mom entailed: the lack of sleep, the exhaustion, the frustration, the financial and emotional stress. She did not hate motherhood: she hated being so scared all the time. She knew something chemical, hormonal, and biological was at work, yet she struggled to lift the recrimination of *Some women just don't like being moms.* She had sought help, and what she got instead was a deep wound that scarred into lifelong guilt.

In lieu of therapy, Jamie went to the library. She tried to find every book she could on postpartum depression. Everyone recommended she read Brooke Shields's memoir on her experience with PPD. She'd devoured that book, but it was not enough. She did not find any other books, or even articles, but she did find the organization Postpartum Progress and spent hours on its website. "I read the same comments over and over looking for women who had it too. . . . I just kept scrolling through trying to find the women who say, *Yeah, it will get better.*"

She was so grateful for the camaraderie she found there, for the information and the compassion, that she quit her job and went to work for Postpartum Progress: "They paid like crap, but I wasn't really doing it for the money. I just wanted to give back. Because they truly saved my life. It sounds ridiculous to say that an organization like that saved my life, but it really did at the time."

Over time, her depression abated. If she felt it flaring back up, she would see her psychiatrist, who'd alter her medication. Sometimes, late at night, rocking her son, she would fantasize again about killing herself. She'd lean back, close her eyes, and mentally blow her head off, for hours. She told me, "I had thoughts like that even on a high dose of Zoloft, even when I looked like I was functioning." On the day of her son's first birthday, she went on a binge researching moms who'd killed themselves over the years.

Still, she could separate out the depression from the anxiety and, to some extent, she could deal with the depression better: feel it coming on, halt it, distance herself from it. The anxiety was more pervasive and evasive. The drugs were supposed to help it too, but they never did. It never went away, but no doctor seemed concerned about it. So Jamie learned to live inside the perpetual question, *Is this normal?*

In the seventeenth century, pregnant women who had premonitions of their deaths during childbirth would commission portraits of themselves. To accompany the portraits, they would write "mother's legacy" letters to their children. At that time in history, approximately one in a hundred women died in childbirth.

Today, approximately twenty in one hundred thousand women die in childbirth in the United States. Yet the culture of risk and anxiety surrounding birth remains fervent and charged. Three hundred years ago, there were no cesareans available, no forceps, no IVs and monitors, no recourse should preeclampsia take hold or an infection begin its course. Today the risk is largely imagined, but this imagining shapes the experience of childbirth more powerfully than the reality of its relative modern safety.

Pregnancy is still discussed in a dialect of risk. Women adamant about home birth can recite the litany of increased risks associated with hospital birth; women who want the security of a hospital can cite a separate set of risks related to the home. The goal in all cases is the same: the perfect management of risk and the reward of the perfect baby.

Mothers, writes sociologist Deborah Lupton, are now seen as mere carriers if they are seen at all: Lupton describes how increasingly prevalent images of the fetus floating in serene solitude exclude the mother, emphasizing the fetus's personhood independent of the body that contains it. Lupton argues that as the fetus has become more and more visible through the use of technologies such as ultrasounds, in vitro fertilization (IVF), and prenatal testing, it has moved out of the private, interior sphere of the mother's belly—where it used to exist, in the words of poet Anna Akhmatova, as "the secret of secrets"—and into public space. The fetus occupies a singular category as both individual and public property.

This repositioning of the fetus as a communal concern, whose needs overshadow the mother's, can be seen with disturbing clarity via a survey conducted at an American College of Obstetricians and Gynecologists conference. The survey gave conference participants two scenarios. In the first, a pregnant woman in labor has a cord prolapse at five centimeters. She refuses a C-section for "seemingly trivial reasons." A judge standing nearby will grant the doctor a court order to forcibly perform the C-section against the mother's wishes. Will the doctor do it? Sixty-seven percent of conference participants said yes, they would do the C-section, even though it violates the mother's autonomy and bodily integrity.

In the second scenario, a newborn has a mysterious illness that will lead to death within twenty-four hours without a marrow transplant from the mother. The mother refuses, again for "seemingly trivial reasons." A judge just happens to be lingering nearby and offers to grant a court order allowing the doctor to forcibly take the mother's marrow against her wishes. Will the doctor do it? In the second case, only 38 percent of participants said yes.

The only difference between the two scenarios is that in the second, the baby lives outside the mother's body. In the first instance, when it is in the womb, doctors feel more empowered to act on its behalf, even when this impinges on the sovereignty, health, and well-being of the mother.

Just as the fetus has become an object of public scrutiny, so too has childhood, once a largely private matter of family culture, become the focus of intense public debates. As an editorial on risk and parenting culture by sociologists Ellie Lee, Jan Macvarish, and Jennie Bristow in the journal *Health, Risk & Society* puts it, "What parents feed their children, when they put them to bed, what they read to them, how they discipline them, how they play with them at home and how they let them play outdoors have all become contested and politicized questions."

If at first the concept of the "at risk" child was applied to a select, marginalized group, it quickly expanded to include all children. The more children are envisioned and framed as "at risk," the more significant, specialized, and demanding the task of raising them. The emergence and amplification of this "at risk" classification is due in part to the rise of the risk society. It is also due to the redefinition of parents within this society as "risk managers."

As the processes of childhood development have been reified—babies must now develop a suite of gross motor skills by eighteen months or face intervention, for example—parenting has been reframed as a complex task requiring extensive education, preparation, and nuanced skill. Both the unaware parent, who hasn't done any reading about REM sleep cycles, and the hyperattentive overinformed parent, who refuses to let her child climb a tree or ride a bike, can be equally at fault for placing their children at risk. Navigating risk is a bit like trying to ski slalom on a windy downhill course with little visibility, and it is the main, all-consuming task of the contemporary parent. Parents define themselves and are defined by their perception and definition of risk. Lee, Macvarish, and Bristow explain in their editorial that the relationship between parent and child has become "a key locus for the cultural and political articulation of the idea that society is characterized by the presence of harms."

The grooming of mothers as risk managers begins in pregnancy, with a culture of risk aversion so extreme that upon close examination, it starts to look pathological. In an article for the *American Journal of Bioethics*, ob-gyn Howard Minkoff and bioethicist Mary Faith Marshall explored the implications and the repercussions of this culture and its central tautology: the only acceptable risk is no risk at all. They open their piece with a quote from an editorial in *The Lancet* on home birth: "Women have the right to choose how and where to give birth, but they do not have the right to put their baby [*sic*] at risk." Minkoff and Marshall marvel at the significance of such a claim.

First, they point out that the one major U.S. study that inspired the response in *The Lancet* places the risk of neonatal death in a home birth at 1 in 1,000. For *The Lancet* editorial's author, this risk is unacceptable, and women who take it "do not have the right," or rather, should not. Yet like so many claims of risk in pregnancy and childbirth, this one turns out to be not absolute but relative.

The risk of home birth is double that of hospital birth, which can be made to sound alarming without the qualification that 1 in 1,000 remains a very low risk. The risk associated with home birth is also the same as the risk of neonatal death in a rural hospital. Very few ob-gyns would claim a woman does not have the right to give birth in a rural hospital, yet people who choose to have home births still face stigma and judgment. This in spite of the fact that home births are associated with fewer interventions, C-sections, hemorrhages, and infections, and with lower rates of preterm birth, prematurity, and assisted newborn ventilation.

Minkoff and Marshall question the ethics of using alarmist rhetoric to deny women the nuanced and complex choice between home and hospital birth. They claim this ultimately impinges on pregnant women's bodily and personal autonomy. Plus, they argue, if we follow the logic that "women do not have the right to put their baby at risk," then "a laundry list of anodyne activities would be off limits to pregnant women": going outside during thunderstorms, driving, riding a bike. It is possible to follow this logic down a narrowing path that leads to a paranoid bunker of counterintuitive and illogical risk prevention, and this is precisely what many pregnant women do.

Philosopher of ethics Rebecca Kukla has written extensively about the bioethics of risk in pregnancy and describes an American cultural tendency to fetishize reproductive risk over other types, demanding a purity and absolutism in this context that would be seen as absurd in everyday life. In a report for the Hastings Center in collaboration with the Obstetrics and Gynecology Risk Research Group—an assemblage of bioethicists, anthropologists, and doctors—Kukla argues that the framing of risk in pregnancy is magical thinking, divorced from evidence-based patient care and arising from deeply rooted, historic obsessions with the purity of the pregnant body. In this view, a sip of beer is poison; an allergy medication a silent assassin. Even the word we use for substances that may cause reproductive harm—teratogens—is derived from the Ancient Greek root *teratos,* or "monster." The overtone here is not so much medical as moral. "Risk in the context of contemporary childbirth," writes medical anthropologist and midwife Mandie Scamell, "can be seen to operate more as a moral discipline than a scientific calculation of probability."

Much as the medieval woman struggled for purity by banishing evil, sinful thoughts from her mind lest she imagine her child into a monster, the contemporary mother must banish any and all potential contamination from her body lest she mar the perfection of her unborn child. In this magical thinking, risk acts as a supposedly neutral medical proxy for the moral, social values of abstinence, penitence, and what sociologist Elizabeth Ettore has termed "reproductive asceticism": under the whip of societal shame, a woman must get her body, her psyche, her self into a regimen of obedience and denial in preparation for motherhood.

In pregnancy, as in many other contexts in contemporary American life—environmental sustainability, health and wellness—risk is seen as wholly dependent on the individual and his or her personal choice. Just as individuals are asked to, say, take fewer flights or eat less meat, in lieu of corporations being asked to seek alternative energy sources or build fuel-efficient vehicles, pregnant women are asked to control their bodies instead of corporations, government, or social institutions being asked to mitigate the larger factors that put mothers and children at risk. What should be matters of public concern instead become risks managed by obsessive private vigilance. Searching a modern academic library catalogue with the term "pregnancy," Rebecca Kukla found that 80 percent of subheadings were associated with the toxins an expectant mother must avoid: certain types and quantities of food, alcohol, tobacco, caffeine, and other drugs. Largely ignored in the literature are race, poverty, male violence, and other economic and sociocultural factors that cannot be entirely controlled by the individual pregnant woman and pose far greater risks than a cup of coffee. The responsibility for "making good choices" falls on the pregnant woman, leaving, as Kukla writes, "corporations, fathers, insurers, legislators, and others" off the hook.

Pregnant women are also singled out in ways that other groups, particularly men and fathers, are not. Warnings on alcoholic beverages, for example, admonish that "women should not" drink alcohol during pregnancy, but simply inform that "consumption of alcoholic beverages impairs your ability to drive a car," even though drunk driving is demonstrably more dangerous than light-to-moderate drinking during pregnancy. Kukla points out that pregnant women are held to higher standards of risk management, presented with stronger and more prescriptive warnings, and assumed to be responsible for the fetus in ways that fathers, in particular, are not; to return to the alcohol example, male violence toward women increases by a factor of eight on days when men drink alcohol, and pregnant women have a 60 percent increased risk of domestic violence, yet no warning exists about fathers' alcohol consumption and its risk to both the mother and fetus.

The navigation of reproductive risk rarely challenges existing social structures and power dynamics. The esteemed all-female authors of the Hastings Center report entitled "Risk and the Preg-

nant Body" pointed out that there are certain scientifically documented risks associated with sex: orgasms and prostaglandins in
sperm could cause contractions, and, in the case of placenta pre-
via, intercourse could cause bleeding. Yet very few doctors would
define sex as unsafe, though a considerable number would tell
women to cut out all caffeine in spite of the fact that no risk at all
has been associated with two cups a day or less (and the risk associated with more is derived from studies on women who drank
upward of eight cups of coffee daily throughout pregnancy).
"Which trade-offs strike us as acceptable and which as reckless in
the context of pregnancy," these authors write, "may turn in part
on social relationships, power dynamics, and who, exactly, is being
inconvenienced or burdened."

Even government acts that seem to claim public responsibility
for risk in fact often shift the burden onto the individual pregnant
woman. This is on blatant display in California's Proposition 65, a
1986 law mandating that businesses post a warning if their buildings
or products contain any of nine hundred listed chemicals known
to cause cancer or reproductive harm. Incredibly, the law does not
demand that businesses actually test for these chemicals, nor does
it ask them to state which ones are present and in what quantities. It simply asks them to post a warning sign, now ubiquitous in
California, stating the possibility of reproductive harm. The onus
is then on the pregnant woman to make an "informed decision."

However, as Kukla argues in an incisive article for *Health, Risk &
Society*, this is impossible when the signs offer neither quantitative nor qualitative information. The pregnant woman is left only
with the warning and the *possibility* of reproductive harm, and her
choice—as in so many other areas, from the most minor decisions
to the most powerful ones—is reduced to a simple yes or no. This
dichotomy is not only reductionist, it is frequently nonsensical. A
woman can avoid any and all objects and institutions with Prop 65
warnings without ever knowing whether or not she is actually
preventing any harm, and without knowing whether having used
those objects or entered those buildings might have actually con-

ferred benefits greater than any risk of harm. One of the buildings with a Prop 65 warning is the prenatal clinic run by the University of California at San Francisco. Should women avoid this clinic because of the sign, therefore forgoing prenatal care or seeking it elsewhere at a clinic of lesser renown? Is this a smart calculation of risk or a bizarre, unnecessary trade-off? This is risk as maddening labyrinth.

These omnipresent Prop 65 warnings, Kukla writes, "entrench an implicit and impossible ideal of zero risk"; they suggest that a woman can and should avoid any and all possible danger, even though this is physically impossible. But just as no one is measuring the actual chemicals in the buildings and objects that might contain them, no one is studying how creating an obsession with the total eradication of risk might carry its own significant risks to both the mother and her child.

Insisting on zero risk to the fetus may actually cause harm to the mother. In another article by the Obstetrics and Gynecology Risk Research Group, the authors cite the examples of doctors who refuse to take diagnostic X-rays of sick pregnant women despite significant scientific evidence that shows no effect on the fetus from a single X-ray, and doctors or insurance companies who won't allow a vaginal birth after cesarean (VBAC) because of a .00046 percent risk of uterine rupture. In the latter case, the risk is the same as that of a woman giving birth vaginally for the first time, but slightly higher than that of a typical second birth. This slight statistical difference alone is the impetus for the decision. Women's values and experiences are ignored. The quest here to reduce risk to the vanishing point actually becomes neurotic and absurd, looking much like mental illness. In this light, a woman's desire to hide all her knives, to refuse to let her child touch animals, to never allow a single food additive into her child's body, starts to look not crazy but reasonable.

If any risk at all is too much, no caution is too extreme. A risk becomes synonymous with inevitable disaster, blurring any and all context. A friend of mine attended a class at a local hospital called "Dogs and Babies," thinking it would give her useful pointers. Instead, the class was composed of a sequence of horror stories. It began with the instructor asking people what kind of dogs they had. One man raised his hand and offered, "Husky," and the instructor said, "Number one killer of kids."

Another woman, pregnant with her third child, mentioned to an OB at her practice that she'd like her four-year-old daughter to be present at the birth. The OB, she told me, closed the door and harangued her for more than half an hour about the insanity of this decision. "This is a *medical procedure*," the OB said, as if my friend were a child imagining fairy tales and not a mother who'd already given birth twice. "You could go into cardiac arrest on the operating table. Do you want your daughter to see that?" The woman made a list of all the risks the OB had tried to scare her with: tearing, hemorrhaging, her daughter being traumatized by witnessing "blood and fluids," her daughter being traumatized by seeing her mother naked, her daughter reporting the experience to all of her friends at school and traumatizing other children, her daughter seeing the baby covered in vernix and fluid and being disgusted and unable to bond with the baby.

In a formal letter of complaint to the hospital, my friend pointed out that the risk of a woman going into cardiac arrest during labor is less than .001 percent, and the risk of severe postpartum hemorrhage is approximately 1 percent. The four-year-old daughter's witnessing birth, witnessing her baby brother's first breaths in the world, might have become one of the whole family's most powerful shared memories. My friend, passionate about women's rights and about making women's lives visible, cares deeply about sharing with her daughter the epic significance and struggle of birth, but the OB did not seem to care about this. She cared about the remote possibilities of disaster that she blew up to larger-than-life dimensions. She cared about *zero* risk.

The women doctors, anthropologists, and bioethicists of the Obstetrics and Gynecology Risk Research Group point out, "It is the physician's obligation not to eliminate risk, but to help patients weigh risk, benefit, and potential harm, informed by best scientific evidence and guided by a patient-centered ethic." But this obligation, otherwise in evidence in patient-doctor relationships—as doctors try to help patients decide whether or not to go on certain medications, for example, or whether or not to undergo certain procedures—vanishes in the context of pregnancy.

———————

The room where my daughter Elena had her checkups at our pediatrician's office had a poster tacked to the door of a baby sleeping next to a giant butcher knife. "Every week in Ohio, three babies die in unsafe sleep environments," it announced. This statistic is presumably derived from the number of sleep-related deaths per year in Ohio; in 2015, 471 infants died sleeping in areas considered unsafe. These areas could include adult beds and couches as well as car seats and playpens. Over half of these infants were born prematurely; a quarter were born before twenty-four weeks. This means that around 240 full-term infants died in unsafe sleep situations throughout the year, or about .1 percent of all infants born that year. Still, our pediatrician told us that co-sleeping is "extremely dangerous."

I pointed out that I'd done my research and set up my bed specifically for co-sleeping—a firm mattress, no blankets or pillows or toys, not even my husband—and that both the baby and I slept much better this way. I pointed out I wasn't using drugs or getting drunk or smoking. I pointed out studies that showed that sleep-related deaths are actually much lower in countries like Japan where co-sleeping is the norm and that co-sleeping has long been the norm around the world. She insisted I was endangering my baby's life.

I didn't point out that many co-sleeping deaths happen precisely because of the fear-mongering in the United States around sleep: exhausted parents, too frightened to co-sleep, keep trying to get their baby down in a crib or bassinet until, finally, groggy and overwhelmed and unable to think clearly, they pull the baby into bed with them or fall asleep in the rocking chair. The U.S. obsession with safety can have an effect opposite to its intentions: by stoking parental misery, it ultimately creates dangerous environments for children.

In a rare mood of defiance, I continued to co-sleep and did so without guilt for the first several years of my daughter's life. By the time Elena was two months old I was getting decent sleep. By the time she was four or five months old, she was going to sleep at a fairly regular hour and sleeping "through the night," albeit with the help of breastfeeding on demand, which was easy enough when I was lying right next to her in bed. This single point of defiance on my part against the medical establishment may have spared me some anxiety at this vulnerable postpartum moment, and in fact those first six months after Elena was born were some of the most achingly beautiful ones of my life. Some of the wisest decisions I made as a parent stemmed from a direct disobedience of fear-stoked cultural norms.

In 2018, when my daughter was three, NPR published an article titled, "Is Sleeping with Your Baby as Dangerous as Doctors Say?" The answer was no; the risks had been grossly inflated. The piece notes all the warnings from the American Academy of Pediatrics—no parent should ever co-sleep at any time—and then cites the actual statistics, which show that the risk of death from SIDS while co-sleeping is 1 in 16,400; for comparison, the risk of being struck by lightning is 1 in 13,000. It highlights what I discovered in my own research: the studies on co-sleeping have failed to discriminate between many different types of co-sleeping, including situations in which the mother is drunk or has been smoking, situations in which mother and infant are sleeping on a huge over-stuffed couch or chair, situations involving premature infants sleeping under blankets, and situations in which infants born at term sleep on stripped-down mats with breastfeeding mothers.

This conflation of circumstances denies mothers and babies significant benefits and arguably confers harm. Co-sleeping provides measurable benefits for the child: sleep studies have shown that a breastfeeding mother creates a little nook for her baby in the bed, regulating its heartbeat and breathing, calming it throughout the night.

In this case, a pattern can be seen that governs almost all of women's choices in the context of reproduction: a minimal risk, which can be made almost nonexistent with the right precautions, is exaggerated and applied equally to all women and all babies, with the explanation that women will not be able to parse any differences in risk by themselves and so must be counseled to avoid a situation entirely. Meanwhile, this extreme interpretation of risk can actually damage mothers and babies in subtler, more insidious ways, not so easily measured by science, or which science is not particularly interested in measuring.

4

The Risks Not Taken

One way Jamie measured normal versus pathological was by asking friends and colleagues. She went through a spell where she was obsessed with the news stories about people leaving their children in hot cars. She could not stop thinking about her husband leaving her son in the car. So she asked her boss, "Is it normal that every time I pull in my driveway, I have a pit in my stomach that I'm gonna look in my husband's car and my son's gonna be there?"

"No," her boss said, "that's not normal."

But in the end, it didn't matter: she was sick to her stomach every time she pulled in the driveway anyway. She mentioned this particular fear once to her psychiatrist and he said, "Zoloft could help that," but she'd already been on Zoloft and it hadn't done anything for the anxiety. She didn't want to be on it again. So she just endured the anxiety, the way people endure drought or rain or frost.

Jamie became ultra-vigilant about hoodies. Her mother would buy her son adorable, expensive little shirts with hoods and Jamie would say, "Thank you so much, that's great!" and hang them in her son's closet and never let him wear them. The babysitter would put him in an outfit with a hood and immediately, Jamie would take him out of it, saying, "It's too hot for that."

"I had excuses for everything," she told me. It is possible to get really, really good at excuses. It is possible to squander almost all of one's creative resources on inventing them. Still, after a while, excuses grow threadbare: people start to glimpse the madness like the swirly sheen of a pearl.

"Why are you taking him out of his clothes?" friends would ask Jamie.

"It's a safety thing," she'd reply, like it was plain and simple, and they'd push, and then she'd feel trapped, because she knew she couldn't fully explain without sounding, well, crazy, and on some level she knew it *was* crazy. Listening to Jamie's story part of me thought, *Wow, that's crazy,* and then another part of me was instantly ashamed, because I realized that yep, that was probably crazy, and that it was the exact same kind of crazy I am, only the details of my craziness differ: I might not let my daughter touch fences. Garden hoses. A restaurant crayon. My kind of crazy was as finely tuned and all-consuming, just of a slightly different species. Surely there are women who will read about mine and Jamie's and think, *That's nuts!* And then they will go home and sterilize every one of their children's toys, or Google the health effects of sodium benzoate until their eyes are bleary, or lock all of their electric cords in a hidden compartment. It is so easy to feel smug about another person's crazy—*wow, really?*—and at the same time remain completely, blindly enthralled to one's own.

One day, Jamie was walking by a playground near her house when she noticed a sign: it had a drawing of a hoodie with strings, and it displayed a warning about hoods getting caught in playground equipment. She was ecstatic—her anxiety was not crazy! She took a picture and sent it to everyone she knew and said, *Look, hoods are a threat!* To this day, she does not let her six-year-old son wear hoods.

Jamie tells me: "When I say it out loud I know it's ridiculous, but it's no skin off my back to not put him in a hood, so why not?" Why risk it?

Jamie used the refrain I hear over and over from pregnant

women, and that I only paid attention to once my OCD therapist pointed out how frequently I myself recite it: "Why take the risk?" Most of these gestures are fairly small. How long does it take to pack some extra Benadryl? To cut off a hood? To wash a child's hand? How hard is it to forgo an iced tea? A salmon roll? A beer? Such a small detour is an extra five minutes, a little bit of diverted attention. Until one day, a woman sits down and makes a list of them all, the way I did in the therapist's office in downtown Pittsburgh, and discovers that there are not enough lines on the page for every act of prevention or protection performed in the name of risk avoidance every single day.

Why risk it? The question is rhetorical; no respectable mother has to answer it. The rhetorical givenness doesn't start to seep out of it until one asks it over and over and over: *why wear this, why eat that, why try this, why go there, why drive, why fly, why,* and then the repetition becomes so wearying that it is possible to see how this refrain grinds a life down to its smallest, saddest incarnation, to a hard little kernel of fear.

I have discovered that it is possible to live a life in a frantic, zigzagging scramble, dodging risk after risk, all creative energy and vitality funneled into a pages-long litany of tedious, precautionary acts. The amount of attention that can be poured into such rituals is stunning and tragic. But there is no reward for the mother who says, *Fuck this, I'm going to take the risk.*

The paradigm of zero reproductive risk is most glaring in the context of drinking. Most of those who provide women with care—even supposedly crunchy, establishment-wary midwives—recommend total abstinence from alcohol in pregnancy. No issue better illuminates the problematic ethics of negotiating reproductive risk than the question of safe alcohol use, and more specifically, the fear of fetal alcohol syndrome (FAS).

In her extraordinary book *Conceiving Risk, Bearing Responsibility,* sociologist Elizabeth Armstrong tells the story of how FAS first came to light as a rare birth defect, gradually took hold of public and medical imagination, and eventually became "demedicalized," transitioning from a clinical diagnosis affecting a subset of severely alcoholic women into a social and moral issue that threatened all babies.

Armstrong first looks at the history of beliefs about alcohol and pregnancy, which have swung wildly from grave warnings about alcohol's danger to claims of its benefit to the fetus. Into the nineteenth century, Armstrong explains, it was believed that children were indelibly marked by the moment of conception. The parents' state at that fateful moment would shape the child's personality and health. Thus, parents who were drunk while conceiving children would produce offspring "wont to be fond of wine." Both parents were seen as responsible here. A passage in Plato's *Laws* stated that "when drunk, a man is clumsy and bad at sowing seed, and is thus likely to beget unstable and untrusty offspring, crooked in form and character." The state of drunkenness—sloppy, sickly, morally suspect—would somehow seep into the child's soul.

For most of recent history in the West, it was believed that the quality of a man's sperm—rather than a woman's egg, health, or pregnancy—determined the heartiness of a child. In the late nineteenth century, the sperm's mystical life force was referred to as the "germ plasm": scientists posited that via the germ plasm, a certain set of essential qualities or characteristics were passed on from generation to generation. Doctors warned that alcohol could poison the germ plasm, affecting not only an individual child but the whole stock of a race. Worries about alcohol became implicated in eugenics. Armstrong quotes one early-twentieth-century doctor declaring that alcohol use would result in the "wholesale poisoning of civilized and semi-civilized races."

At the same time, in the opening decades of the twentieth century, a contingent of eugenicists began to promote the idea that alcohol was actually a "fool-killer"; drunkenness would weed out degenerates and "weak stock" and breed temperance in successive generations. Those exposed to alcohol in utero would develop immunity to it, as if it were a type of vaccine. This theory was based on the dubious observation that so-called civilized races—"Jews,

Greeks, Italians, South Frenchmen, Spaniards, and Portuguese"—
had drunk abundantly for centuries and remained relatively sane
and peaceful. As one American eugenicist put it, "the enlightened
nations are the inebriate nations."

The medical consensus veered back toward the adverse impact
of alcohol in pregnancy when women began campaigning for suffrage and higher education. Medicine, writes Armstrong, "functions as a form of social control"; when anxiety rises about women
defying traditional norms—entering male-dominated spheres of
work or study; engaging in political activism; refusing to have children or having them later—medicine can step in to act as a cor-
rective, reinforcing women's "natural" role as selfless, sacrificing
mothers.

In the late Victorian era, doctors speculated that alcohol, carried
in maternal blood, might act as a poison on the fetus in pregnancy.
Certain studies on alcoholics suggested that the children of incar-
cerated alcoholic women—who were forbidden from drinking in
prison—fared better than the children of those who were free and
drank to excess in pregnancy. But more powerful than the find-
ings of these studies was the growing belief that pregnancy was a
period of risk and significance, and that the mother, more than the
father, held responsibility for a child's health. Just as women were
fighting to break free of the bonds of Victorian social norms, they
were reminded that they were the "divinely appointed guardian[s]"
of not only their own pregnancies, but of society.

Then, in the relatively freewheeling 1920s, when women's new
rights had settled in and become familiar, the social tide shifted
again. Drinking in the 1930s and '40s and into mid-century was seen
as fashionable, and women increasingly drank at the same rates as
men. Temperance was prudish, passé. Meanwhile, older epidemio-
logical studies were revealed as outdated and flawed, and the medical establishment rejected the notion of alcohol as a teratogen. In
1942 the editors of the *Journal of the American Medical Association*
wrote, "In human beings it is difficult to prove that alcohol has a
deleterious effect on babies in utero, even when large amounts are

taken." Armstrong cites a 1942 book by two researchers at Yale's Center of Alcohol Studies, the country's leading research institution on alcoholism, deriding the notion that alcohol was a poison, calling it a "social condiment" and insisting that there was "no acceptable evidence" of alcohol's having any effect on the fetus. Doctors' main concern about pregnant women's alcohol consumption was excessive weight gain. A 1953 *Clinical Obstetrics* textbook warned, "Probably the most serious effect of drinking these beverages comes from the calories they, and the hors d'oeuvres which usually accompany them, carry."

In fact, doctors were forcibly intoxicating women in order to prevent and stall preterm labor. This procedure, developed in the 1970s by a doctor whose wife went into labor in her seventh month of pregnancy, involved the intravenous application of pure alcohol, getting women so blitzed that "they smelled like a fruitcake." Armstrong details nurses' complaints of outrageously drunk mothers lashed to their beds. Some women received this treatment regularly for months. At mid-century, and until the late 1970s and early 1980s, doctors were as confident about alcohol's innocuousness as doctors today are of its harm.

In 1973 and 1974, a group of doctors at the University of Washington School of Medicine in Seattle published a series of articles in *The Lancet*. These articles described a pattern of birth defects in children born to chronic alcoholic mothers, and introduced a new diagnostic classification for these defects: fetal alcohol syndrome. The articles were based on eleven case reports, all taken from non-controlled, retrospective studies, but they would form the basis of a new understanding of alcohol use in pregnancy that would radically alter women's lives.

The societal tide was shifting again, with new uncertainty about not only gender roles but also technological and scientific development. Armstrong describes how chemicals, those former emblems of glorious modernity, were now suspect. The environmental movement was creating a new awareness of the fragility of the natural world in the face of rampant development. Meanwhile, a series of high-profile international epidemics of birth defects was drawing attention to the vulnerability of the unborn fetus. In Europe, thousands of women prescribed the drug thalidomide for morning sickness gave birth to babies with severe birth defects, including shortened and deformed limbs and defective organs. In the United States, an outbreak of rubella, which causes devastating effects in the womb, left thousands of babies deaf, blind, and severely cognitively impaired. These high-profile horrors led in part to the formation of the particular group of doctors at the University of Washington who studied and catalogued birth defects, addressing a rising societal preoccupation with the impact of teratogens. They also helped inspire one of the most significant Supreme Court decisions of the twentieth century: *Roe v. Wade.*

Women were entering the workforce in record numbers. They were wrenching themselves free of the "feminine mystique," as defined and derided by Betty Friedan in her eponymous 1963 book. They were postponing pregnancy or suppressing their reproduction with birth control. At the same time, fetal alcohol syndrome colonized the medical and public imagination. FAS, Armstrong argues, became a new and potent weapon of social control under the dubious auspices of science.

Starting in the 1980s, clinical textbooks in midwifery and obstetrics began to augment and intensify their warnings against alcohol use, initially stating that chronic and excessive alcohol use posed a danger, then that moderate alcohol use could pose a danger, and finally that no safe level of alcohol use is currently known. Public health organizations followed suit, culminating in warnings in the 1990s from the CDC that all pregnant women or women considering pregnancy should abstain from alcohol. By the start of the twenty-first century, Elizabeth Armstrong found that the medical consensus had become that no alcohol at any time during pregnancy is safe, even though many of the doctors Armstrong interviewed personally puzzled at this: one tells her, "Back in the 50s and

60s, women were drinking every night at cocktail parties. We were all drinking. We all should have been affected, but we weren't, so why is that?"

Fetal alcohol syndrome itself is exceedingly rare, affecting less than 5 percent of the children of heavy alcoholics. The initial studies that first ferreted out and defined the disease looked at twenty-three cases of maternal alcoholism and found only six instances of FAS—this among women who were drinking so heavily they experienced delirium tremens and cirrhosis of the liver. The rates of FAS are generally estimated at about 2 in 10,000, with higher rates for the most at-risk groups: up to 30 in 10,000, for example, for Native Americans. The actual risk of a woman who does not drink excessively—that is, upward of four or five drinks per day—having a baby with FAS is extremely small.

Doctors, however, describe FAS as a spectrum under the umbrella of "fetal alcohol effects" (FAE). This diagnosis can essentially be given to any child with learning disabilities or issues whose mother had any exposure to alcohol in pregnancy. The possibilities of such a categorization of disease are alarming: by dodging the diagnostic criteria for FAS, which include specific facial malformations of the eyes and lips along with a host of other factors, doctors construct a preventable cause for myriad complex problems. A clinical issue takes on a moral tenor: any mother whose child suffers and who has not followed the most extreme model of risk aversion is a target of blame.

The slipperiness of diagnosing FAS and FAE can be seen in the CDC statistics, which place the number of babies born each year with these disorders between 1,300 and 8,800: an enormous range, and even at its uppermost end a very small number, considering that 150,000 babies with birth defects are born every year. The causes of the vast majority of these cases are a mystery. Fetal alcohol syndrome and fetal alcohol effects can be seen as ways to demystify many birth defects with no identifiable cause, which may be why 71 percent of FAS cases reported on birth certificates are said to be false positives, and why some doctors classify FAS as a "rule-out" or a "trash-basket" diagnosis.

One striking paradox of FAS is that the women most likely to drink—highly educated, well-off white women—are also the least likely to have children affected by FAS. Drinking increases with age, education, and social status, and is less common among minority women—yet poor, uneducated minority women are the most likely to have babies with FAS.

One study looked at women who had three or more drinks per day in pregnancy, and found that among low-income women 71 percent had children diagnosed with FAS, whereas only 4.5 percent of high-income women did. The diagnosis here, a subtle but crucial point, also included "alcohol-related effects" (ARE). The study measured FAS and ARE on the basis of a number of factors: birth weight, head circumference, failure to thrive, congenital malformations, and developmental delays, all of which were much higher among the low-income women. Seventy-seven percent of these women were high school dropouts (compared with 3 percent of high-income women); 27 percent had learning disabilities (compared with none of the high-income women); and 100 percent—100 percent!—had at least one alcoholic parent themselves, compared with 36 percent in the high-income group. The low-income women also had a much poorer nutritional status, which the authors hypothesized may have contributed to their much higher rates of cirrhosis and to the health effects on their babies.

How much here can be attributed solely to alcohol? It is incredibly difficult, as numerous studies have stated and a number of doctors acknowledged to Armstrong, to separate the effects of alcohol from other factors that have a negative impact on the fetus: poor nutrition, smoking, stress, poverty, and advanced age. The earliest reports of FAS failed to take into account any of these factors on birth outcomes in alcoholic women, operating instead on the presumption that alcohol was the clear and single cause of defects. Since only a small percentage of heavy drinkers have children with

FAS, it is possible that alcohol itself is not the teratogen, but rather acetaldehyde, a highly toxic by-product of alcohol as it is broken down by the body. Women and children with a genetic mutation that inhibits the rapid processing of acetaldehyde could have a much higher risk of either passing on or developing FAS. Yet very few studies have investigated this, or any of the complex social factors that might be driving a woman to drink excessively while pregnant. The simplest solution is to warn all pregnant women against drinking at all.

Armstrong ultimately blasts this policy. She claims that it does "double damage by targeting the entire population of women unnecessarily while neglecting the women whose lives are most adversely affected by drinking before, during, and after pregnancy." Painting the situation of women with intransigent alcohol addiction related to abuse, trauma, or poverty as one of individual responsibility ignores and denies the social realities of addiction, wealth inequality, a broken health care system, and unequal access to resources.

FAS is often presented as "the leading preventable cause of birth defects," a claim that Armstrong debunks as circular reasoning: FAS is totally preventable in the cases of women whose risk is so low they require no real preventative strategies, but extremely difficult to prevent in the case of women with long-established patterns of destructive drinking that have damaged significant portions of their lives and relationships before pregnancy. One doctor described to Armstrong the only case of FAS he'd ever seen: a mother who sat on a barstool for nineteen hours a day next to one daughter suffering from FAS before she gave birth to another.

The tragedy of this woman's situation is as acute as the naïveté of those who believe she simply needs to be told by a doctor not to have another drink. These mothers don't need a colorful infographic from the CDC. They need major social interventions. Here we are in the full throes of madness: risk is generalized, exaggerated, and extended to all pregnant women, transforming in the process into the moral principle that, as Armstrong writes, "the greater the freedom offered to women, the greater the purported threats to the fetus."

This principle is particularly entrenched in the United States. Most of the small body of literature around the bioethics of risk and pregnancy comes from the rest of the anglophone world. Academics in Australia, Canada, Britain, and New Zealand have authored research that critically examines the implications of extreme attitudes toward reproductive risk. Much of this research has analyzed Britain's policies regarding alcohol and pregnancy. Colin Gavaghan, an associate professor of law at the University of Otago in New Zealand, examines the rhetoric behind the British Department of Health's decision to change its official policy from advising women to limit alcohol to 1–2 units a week to advising them to abstain from alcohol completely. He quotes Britain's deputy chief medical officer explaining that they "strengthened" their advice to "ensure that no one underestimates the risk." The Department of Health has acknowledged that the new advice "is not a result of new scientific evidence" but is more "straightforward." Adult women who are in fact about to be in charge of the full-time care of a young child are perceived to be unable to understand the concept of limits—the notion that some, but not an excessive amount, of alcohol is safe.

Gavaghan quotes the British General Medical Council's consent guidelines: "For a relationship between doctor and patient to be effective, it should be a partnership based on openness, trust and good communication." Yet there is no openness or communication when doctors withhold or misrepresent fundamental information in the name of "straightforwardness": Gavaghan points out that a meta-analysis of publications on the subject of alcohol and pregnancy between 1970 and 2005 found no adverse effects from "relatively low amounts of alcohol and infrequent occasions of binge drinking." In fact, this analysis found that children of light drinkers did better than children of total abstainers: girls born to the former had fewer emotional problems than their peers, and boys had higher cognitive ability test scores than their peers. A similar study cited in another British article on the country's alcohol abstinence policy found that babies whose mothers had low-to-moderate alcohol intake actually had better growth outcomes.

Pregnant women, however, are not only never informed that there might be a benefit to light drinking, they're told unequivocally that any alcohol will harm their child. Gavaghan argues that in most domains in medicine, it is no longer acceptable for doctors to make decisions for their patients without informing them of both risks and benefits, but "a paternalistic exception is permitted in the case of pregnant women."

When so many of these prohibitions pile up on top of one another—coffee, alcohol, turkey, Tylenol—they suggest a sexist and unethical system more intent on morally enforcing gender roles than on preventing actual harm. They also demonstrate how the obsession with zero risk begins to engender a much bigger, unseen, unmeasured risk: the dramatic delimiting of women's lives by anxiety. Women becoming mothers are in the process of learning the excruciating lesson that everything is terrifyingly uncertain. There is no bigger unknown than the birth and development of a baby into its own human being. Meanwhile, policy makers, in the words of British sociologists Pam K. Lowe and Ellie J. Lee, are "formalis[ing] a connection between uncertainty and danger."

Why risk it? Dr. Janet Williams, a professor of pediatrics at the University of Texas–San Antonio and one of the lead authors of a 2015 American Academy of Pediatrics report advising total abstinence from alcohol in pregnancy, was quoted on CNN.com saying, "There are so many other factors one can worry about, so how about one less concern?" Why not just this one little sacrifice? Except, as Gavaghan points out, "when the risk is non-existent . . . the sacrifice becomes pointless."

This is the brutal rhetoric of reproductive risk: every choice is presented as being simple to make, so simple that it is not really a choice at all. The disorientation and pressure produced by this simultaneous casualness—*it's so easy*—and grave insinuation—

damaged for life—is so disconcerting that it seems outrageous for a woman to exercise any defiance.

As Dr. Williams puts it, *How about one less concern?* Who can turn that down, at a time riven by uncertainty? *Just take a shower instead of a bath. Just spend the extra $3 on organic. Just check his breathing. Just make her walk slowly on hard surfaces. Just don't let him pet dogs. Just prevent her from hanging on monkey bars. Or jumping on trampolines. Or climbing trees.*

The irony is that this logic of *one less concern* is never-ending, feeding on itself, so that the second one concern has been "controlled" another rears its head and whispers, *look out,* and like whack-a-mole it has to be smacked down, and then ten more pop up. It is possible to spend an entire life like this. This should be far more terrifying than having a drink.

Jamie's constant uncertainty and ongoing anxiety were hard on her marriage. Her husband seemed to her very laid-back, not anxious about anything. He trusted the doctors to know what was going on; if they didn't seem to think she had a problem, then he didn't think she did, either. Only once did he voice some doubt and hesitation; a colleague of his had committed his wife to a psychiatric ward after she gave birth, saying that she needed sleep and professional help. Jamie's husband told her he wished he'd been brave enough to seek help for her in that initial postpartum period.

At age two, Jamie's son was diagnosed with autism. I didn't find this out until Jamie and I had already had several conversations. She never mentioned it in all of her initial talk of anxiety. It came up as an aside long after we'd established a relationship. I wondered how much that diagnosis had contributed to her anxiety, assuming that it had. But the autism, she said, was the least of her worries. In some ways, the diagnosis was a relief.

"It was almost like one less thing I had to be anxious about. . . .

Once you have an autism diagnosis, even though so much of it is unknown . . . we can plan, we can look at the resources, we can do the research, you know." She told me she felt it was doing her son a disservice to blame his autism for her anxiety, which had peaked when he was too little to show any real signs of the disorder. And her anxiety, I observed, had revolved around safety, not autism. It was as if the hypothetical and far-fetched scenarios the anxiety conjured up for her—strangulation by hoodie, hypothermia in suburban Pennsylvania—were far worse than the actual difficulties of living with a special-needs child. When she talked about finding a school for her son, about figuring out how to get intervention and be a strong advocate, she sounded calm and in control; when she spoke of safety kits and news stories about hot cars, she sounded jittery and uncertain.

Anxiety, Rollo May says in his landmark work *The Meaning of Anxiety*, is a "profoundly irrational phenomenon." It thrives on the unknown, the unreal, the far-fetched. It diminishes in the face of actual threat. In his book *My Age of Anxiety*, Scott Stossel talks about how Jewish people who were deeply anxious before the Holocaust completely shed their anxiety during the horrors of their internment. Real fear orients us, sharpens the senses. Anxiety dulls, numbs, petrifies.

Anxiety also requires choice. As psychologist Barry Schwartz has put it, choice is a paradox: more choice means more freedom, but more freedom means more anxiety. Middle-class white American mothers have an unparalleled amount of freedom. They tend to employ it by vigorously, obsessively embarking on the quest for what writer Heather Kirn Lanier calls a "SuperBaby." In an essay entitled "SuperBabies Don't Cry," Lanier wrote, "I ate 100 grams of protein a day. I swallowed capsules of mercury-free DHA. I gave up wheat for reasons I forget. I kept my cell phone an arm's length away from my belly to avoid damaging my SuperBaby with electromagnetic waves. I did not own a microwave."

She made all the "right" decisions by a certain cultural protocol. She was an enthusiastic member of the club that demanded the achievement of perfection. Her daughter was born at term weighing just four pounds. In a post on her blog *Star in Her Eye*, Lanier looks back at a photo of herself from when her daughter, Fiona, was a newborn, and recalls the mindset of the kind of mother she was then: "She believes her baby will catch up in weight. She believes if she keeps finagling the limp, four-pound-something body to her breast, if she keeps recording every feeding attempt, and if the intervals between feedings never exceed two hours, then the giant worry that is the baby's weight will lift. She believes in normal, and she believes she and her child will reach it."

Lanier's daughter was ultimately diagnosed with Wolf-Hirschhorn Syndrome, a rare chromosomal disorder. This meant countless medical visits, diagnoses, interventions, and the real, perpetual fear that her daughter might suffer a massive seizure and die. One day in the shower, as Lanier was mentally scrolling through all that she had done to make her SuperBaby—the care to never hold her cell phone to her body, the non-GMO corn—she thought, *I failed. I have utterly failed at this.* Acknowledging this failure, she told me, "I got kicked out of the club." She gave up chasing milestones.

Lanier gives voice to a built-in paradox of motherhood that I had not yet recognized: "You're loving somebody that you're kind of constantly urging to change." Once Lanier realized that she could not change her daughter, she moved into a new phase of her motherhood. In a post about several other children with Wolf-Hirschhorn Syndrome who had recently died, Lanier writes of her daughter, "Every day with Fiona is not a promise but a gift." Not a promise, but a gift: not what may be, could be, should be, with enough risk prevention, but what is.

William James wondered if anxiety was a luxury: something only people who had never endured trauma could indulge in. I don't believe this is entirely true, but I think anxiety can be a way of avoiding having to acknowledge just how mysterious, precarious, and brief our lives are. In the places we are forced to accept this, we are not anxious; in the spaces in which we can deny it, anxiety takes over.

People constantly joke with Jamie, "You can't put Lincoln in bubble wrap!" But her son is six now, and arguably their lives are still hugged tight. Jamie admits she constantly asks herself, "Is this normal anxiety, or is this I'm-just-super-overprotective-and-love-my-kid-so-much anxiety?" She knows the answer. But she can't change it. The knowing makes little difference in altering the behavior. When as a culture we so often associate crippling worry with care, and excessive risk avoidance with smart decision-making, Jamie can always justify refusing to lessen her iron grip on her son's life. Intense, constant, debilitating anxiety like Jamie's can still be fairly easily accommodated into the typical middle-class American lifestyle, and the woman who suffers it can pass as normal.

"[Anxiety] is so low on the totem pole," she told me. "You may have crazy thoughts all day long but . . . get over it, it's like nobody cares." She said, "I wish that people would figure out how to treat it or maybe even talk about it." She shared with me her reasoning, which gave me a dark glimpse of the way so many mothers live now: "Do I wish that it would go away? Absolutely. Do I lose sleep over it, do I have heart palpitations? Absolutely. Am I up three or four nights in a row thinking of all the worst things that could happen? All the time. But do I keep trucking?"

Yes. She does.

In her 2005 book *Perfect Madness*, Judith Warner called the obsession with perfectly managing any and all risk "controllable private nonsense." It is the realm of the mother who frets about whether the sippy cup with a straw is going to inhibit her child's speech ability, or whether it will encourage greater tongue flexibility to get her baby up to the twenty words she needs to hit by next month. Mothers believe, not always incorrectly, that they can control their children's bodies, their minds, their vulnerable little hearts. Mothers have had it constantly hammered into them that they and they alone are responsible. And to be responsible is to learn to live in an extremely narrow space of constantly shifting best practices designated by experts. To be responsible is to stamp out any uncertainty, any disorder, any randomness.

In *Savage Park: A Meditation on Play, Space, and Risk for Americans Who Are Nervous, Distracted, and Afraid to Die*, an exploration of risk through the lens of a Tokyo adventure playground, Amy Fusselman quotes Hitoshi Shimamura, the International Play Association regional vice president in East Asia: "It seems that Americans have always had problems with risk." Americans are terrible at accepting, acknowledging, and living comfortably with uncertainty. Fusselman points out that a British aristocrat touring American playgrounds in 1965 called them "an administrator's heaven and a child's hell." She continues: "American playgrounds that are designed to adhere to the regulations of the Consumer Product Safety Commission and that are subject to reviews by certified playground inspectors and that have instructions for uniform installment of playground equipment that are specific down to the half inch—these kind of structures are fantasies for adults, fantastic fortress images we built to reassure ourselves that death will not happen to our children there. They are temples to that idea."

The playground is fear manifested in soft rubber and rounded plastic. It was my favorite place to go with Elena when we moved back to the United States and Jorge's least favorite. It seemed insulated from the potential danger I sensed nearly everywhere else. Little by little my life inched into these kinds of spaces, clean and bright temples of consumer control—Targets and chain restaurants and Starbucks, places so predictable as to be dead.

"It seems that the first obligation mothering places upon a woman," writes psychoanalyst Jana Malamud Smith, "is the demand not just that she attempt to keep the child alive, but that she accept the fact of living closely with death." American mothers tend to respond to this inherent fact by going into overdrive on the American belief that death can be fought with righteous fervor:

with organics, sustainably made wooden blocks painted with non-toxic vegetable dyes, a 4–1 preschool teacher ratio, bathtub spout covers.

What is lost, thinking always of risk, aiming always for zero risk, is not measurable. There are no statistics, no charts, no metrics. There is a gecko in a cage with a heat lamp for a sun. There is a dog who has never been let off leash. There is no rain in the mouth. There is no solitude, no wandering to the edge of the woods at dusk. There is no unwashed fruit eaten with dirty hands. There is no mess. There is no staking of oneself, one's small life, against the hugeness of the world. There is no sharing a meal with a stranger.

Jane Hirshfield wrote, "As water given sugar sweetens, given salt grows salty/We become our choices." The greatest deception of the obsessive pursuit of zero risk is that we have no choice. We choose, often under immense pressure. And when we choose imagined safety every single time, we gradually give up what makes life worth living.

WHITNEY

5

The White Advantage

Whitney grew up in Timberlake, North Carolina, one of three girls in a happy tight-knit family. She went to college at Duke, where she met her husband, Charles. They were married shortly after graduation. At twenty-five, Whitney discovered she was pregnant—not a complete and total accident, not exactly planned. She was surprised and delighted.

From the start, Whitney wanted a home birth. Her grandmother was appalled. "We were poor," she told Whitney. "We had our babies at home. But as a Duke-educated woman, that is beneath you." Whitney's mother and father knew little about home birth and worried that it was irresponsible. They were skeptical, but she was insistent. She decided on a birthing center, which seemed a compromise between home and hospital.

While she was telling me this, Maverick, her youngest at age two, interrupted. "Mommy!" she shouted. "Waffles?" In the fuzzy distance came the voice of Samuel, the oldest, at five. He asked for a peanut butter sandwich. Whitney told him his daddy would make it for him. Jelly? "We don't have jelly, buddy, Isaac broke it. I'm sorry." These brief interludes made for a sweet, poignant collage during our talks.

Whitney chose one of the few birthing centers in North Carolina and went through her first trimester there with no problem. Then, at her twenty-week appointment, she mentioned that she was feeling something odd. The midwife offered to check her and discovered that her cervix was opening. They sent her immediately to the local hospital, where she was admitted and would stay for the next forty-eight hours. From there, she said, "the care changed." She became a patient.

They did an ultrasound and there was the baby, kicking. They kept asking her questions: no one knew what was going on. So many questions, and tests. They told her they wanted to do amniocentesis, to see if there was an infection. This involved risk: it could trigger a loss. Whitney and Charles decided not to do it. The doctors were dismissive after that. They had nothing to offer her except the grim prognosis of preterm labor at some point, sooner or later. She went home.

Seven days later, she went into active labor. She tried to hold on, to stay away from the hospital. But her mother-in-law, visiting, took one look at her and said, *Whitney, are you not telling me something?* When Whitney knew it was certain, knew she was losing the baby, she cried out.

Everything that followed was traumatic. They called an ambulance. In it, she was upright, which felt uncomfortable in active labor and put pressure on her cervix. Then she had to wait, again upright, for a long time in the waiting room, in active labor. She was finally sent to triage, where she went to the bathroom. Her pee was full of blood.

When the nurse came in to examine her, Whitney told her about the blood and showed it to her. "What is this?" she asked.

The nurse said, "Oh, you've had a bloody show."

Whitney didn't know what "a bloody show" meant. They wheeled her into another room to wait for a doctor. There, a woman came in and asked for her insurance. Whitney remembers laughing. "I did like the crazy laugh, like the evil crazy laugh," she recalled.

"Do you realize," she asked the woman with this mad laugh, "that I'm losing my child?"

The woman left.

Not long after, a white male doctor came in. They hooked her up to a monitor, and it showed her contractions were off the charts. The nurse asked her if she wanted pain medication, and she refused. The doctor sat down next to Whitney and rubbed her knee.

"It doesn't look good for you," he told her. "All we can do is wait it out."

Within a few minutes of his leaving, when Whitney and Charles were alone, she began to feel a bubble between her legs. "Charles," she said, "call someone!" He began pressing the call button, and nothing happened, so soon both of them were pressing, pressing, pressing, over and over, until finally a nurse came on the microphone and asked what was going on, and Whitney told them about the bubble and the nurse came in to check and immediately called a doctor. A white woman came in and said, *Whitney, push,* and Whitney didn't know what to do and started blowing out of her mouth like she'd seen in the movies and the doctor said, *No, bear down.*

They were all doing their jobs, rote, distant, giving instructions, going through the motions, as if they were writing up spreadsheets, as if she couldn't feel or didn't matter or wasn't really there at all. There were moments when Whitney wanted to say, "Y'all, I'm married and I graduated from Duke, and *it's okay.*" By *it's okay,* she meant, it's okay to be human with me. It's okay to see me as a person. I'm not the stereotype in your head.

I repeated this *it's okay* line to Whitney later. She sighed. "I wanted to somehow validate the fact that I'm a good patient," she said. "I wanted them to know that they weren't dealing with someone who had been negligent." She hadn't done anything wrong and yet everything was going wrong. She told me, "Losing felt very counter to all of the things I had done in my life." She had excelled at everything, she'd just graduated from an elite college, and this was the first time she'd experienced the devastating and impromptu blow of loss. Her mother, she said, had been a teen mom. Whitney had grown up hearing: "You don't want to be in that position." She thought if she behaved a certain way, the doctors and nurses would look at her differently, but there was a narrative in place that she couldn't change.

The baby came out in the amniotic sac. She was still kicking when she was born.

They popped the sac and Whitney remembers the doctor saying *oh*, as if making a distasteful discovery. "*Oh*. There was an infection."

"There's nothing we can do," they told her. The white doctor patted her knee. "I'm so sorry," she said.

Whitney held her little girl until her heart stopped. It was March 7, 2011.

"And," she said, "that was it." They sent her home with no follow-up, no questions about her mental health.

In the weeks and months that followed, Whitney remembers a lot of rain. She can't actually remember whether it rained more than usual. She slept all the time. Whenever she woke up, it was raining. "And I constantly felt like I was drowning."

Whitney didn't consider therapy. "In the black community," she told me, "it's not a thing you do. Because I quote-unquote felt fine."

Eventually, it stopped raining. She returned to her life.

Two years later, she got pregnant again. This time, she felt like a walking time bomb. "I couldn't cope mentally." She had found out in a travel clinic, preparing for a trip to the Philippines. She was about to get meds for malaria and she asked, out of curiosity, if the meds would cause harm if she was pregnant. The nurses asked if she was, and she said no, but they gave her a test just in case. She called her husband in shock.

Whitney turned down the meds, and the nurses told her that

with her history, it wasn't a good idea to go to the Philippines. "I immediately felt fear," she told me. "And I was like, *What are you going to do with this fear?*" Her dad called and told her going to the Philippines would be one of the most irresponsible things she could do as a grown woman: "Why would you put this child at risk?"

She chose to go. Her husband at first said, *Whoa, whoa, whoa, what?* But he came around. "When I boarded that plane," she said, "I was like, *This is probably the craziest thing I have ever done.*" She wasn't going on a whimsical vacation. She had promised a friend that she would use her expertise to help a group of women start small businesses, and she wanted to stay committed to that project. Part of her had been deeply suspicious of the medical model of pregnancy all along, and her trip to the Philippines reaffirmed that suspicion. "Witnessing Filipino women go through pregnancy and birth changed my life," she told me. In the United States, she had access to the latest medical technology, the hospitals and the tests, the top doctors and the most nuanced and detailed information about risks and outcomes, procedures and dangers. The Filipino women she witnessed at a rural birthing clinic didn't have much or any of that. But the woman who ran this clinic, the American daughter of missionaries, who had spent her whole life in the Philippines, described Filipino mothers as "resilient." Whitney marveled at this. "Resilient was definitely not something that I was equating with pregnancy. To this day I've never heard a woman describe herself as *I was resilient.*"

The birthing center was secluded, in a jungle. The women would walk in: no wheelchairs, no tiered bureaucracy and admissions. There was no screaming, only the occasional low moan.

At this rural clinic, the American doctor offered to give Whitney an ultrasound to check on her pregnancy. A lot of thoughts went through her head: *Maybe this isn't the best idea, is it going to be the same type of technology, the same level of cleanliness?* "But then," she told me, "something in me was like, *girl, please.* Get over yourself."

The doctor set Whitney up and wheeled in an antiquated ultra-sound machine. They chatted while the doctor began the exam. After a few minutes, she said, "Whitney, I can't find the heartbeat." Whitney tried not to panic, asking what that meant. The doctor said it could mean she was just very early in the pregnancy—nothing to worry about. Or it could mean, she said, that this was a phantom pregnancy: Whitney was experiencing the symptoms and signs of pregnancy without an actual baby. Whitney felt sick with worry. *I made this all up,* she thought. She wouldn't be back in the States for weeks. The doctor called in her whole staff, and there in that room in the jungle birthing clinic, they prayed for Whitney. She was incredibly touched that they cared, though she felt awful immediately afterward. Then they did something that "redeemed so much of the pain." They invited her to help out with another woman's ultrasound. This woman was Filipina, also very early in her pregnancy. During the ultrasound, the doctor revealed that the baby's due date was in February. There is a belief in Filipino culture that babies born in February will be deficient in some way: they will come up short, like the shortest month of the year. This woman was incredibly distressed at this prospect, and so, as they had done for Whitney, the staff prayed over her. They prayed for her to find peace. Whitney joined them. In this, Whitney felt her own agony lift. In the echo of another woman's pain, she was able to distance herself from hers, to put it in a much larger framework, to join in a mystery larger than herself. Afterward, they all shared a meal, and then they went back to helping women. There, in the Philippines, "it was a constant letting go." There was nothing she could do. *If I'm going to lose, I'm going to lose,* she told herself, *and there is no use running to the hospital, because I can't do that here. That doesn't work here.* "I had to let go of a lot of stuff," she said. "American safeguards. I just let it go."

Whitney broke through the wall of control behind which many women barricade themselves: the illusion that neonatal intensive care units, ultrasounds, tests, bans and rules, the research, will maneuver and logic away the possibility of devastation. In some cases, this may be true. Women and babies may die more frequently in places with fewer resources. In the instance of a complication, a high-risk situation, that infrastructure may be life-saving. But it might not—and it might not do anything for the many women whose pregnancies are uncomplicated or whose bodies don't fit narratives of received medical wisdom or those who are just as likely to be misinterpreted and oppressed as recognized and rescued. In the United States, all women are forced to labor under the influence of this system of risks and the infinite technologies to forestall them, all women cling to its promises and the darker side of its constant warnings, and no one considers whether or not this is truly safe, what safe really means for a woman and her child. Whitney told me, "We are wired to feel like because we have all of these things at our fingertips, we're better off." And Whitney had come to recognize that "especially as a black woman, this is a façade."

Every day she got up and went out into a densely populated foreign city. She worked with other women. *Whitney,* she told herself, *this is beyond your control. You're gonna have to believe one thing or the other about yourself. Which do you choose? I'm not going to choose to believe my body is behind the eight ball.*

———

Here are the statistics:

In the United States, black women are three to four times more likely than white women to die of pregnancy-related causes.

Black infants are twice as likely to die in their first year of life as white infants. This is true for infants born to black mothers at every education level.

The white infant mortality rate drops as white mothers' education rises, decreasing from a little over 15 in 1,000 for white mothers with only some high school education to below 5 in 1,000 for white mothers with a doctorate or professional degree. For black mothers, the opposite is true: black women with doctorates or professional degrees have dramatically higher infant mortality rates than those who are less educated. Black mothers with an eighth-grade education or less have an infant mortality rate of a little under 15 in 1,000. Those with a doctorate or professional degree have an infant mortality rate near 30 in 1,000. Black women with doctorates have double the infant mortality risk of white women who did not finish high school.

For white women who grew up in poverty, increased family income in adulthood reduces the risk of low birthweight by half. For black women who grew up in poverty, increased adult family income does not reduce the chance of having a low birthweight child.

White women smoke at double the rate of black women during pregnancy and use alcohol at the same rate, yet they have consistently and significantly better birth outcomes.

After adjusting for gestational age at delivery, maternal age, income, hypertension, and prenatal care, African American women are three times more likely to die in childbirth than white women.

At all income and education levels, black women have a three times greater risk of severe maternal morbidity—life-threatening complications during delivery—than white women. In one study of severe maternal morbidity in New York City, black women accounted for 35.6 percent of all cases, despite comprising only 21 percent of live births. White women made up only 16.8 percent of severe maternal morbidity cases, but 30.4 percent of live births.

Black women with normal BMIs had higher rates of severe maternal morbidity than obese women of all other races and ethnicities.

The rate of preterm births among black women is 14 percent; among white women, it is 9 percent.

"Do you know the statistics?" black women asked me, over and over again, on the phone. I interviewed midwives, mental health providers, mothers. They talked about the statistics as if they were a bundle, a basic set of information like the name, address, and phone number that schoolchildren memorize and recite on demand.

Genetic or biological differences have been discredited as a potential source of these outcomes; studies on first-generation African immigrants have shown they have similar birth outcomes to white women in the United States. After one generation in the United States, however, their children have outcomes on par with African American women. The dominant explanation for the dire situation of black motherhood in the United States is the accelerated deterioration of black female bodies under the perpetual stress of racism. The weathering hypothesis, as it is known, was first introduced in an article in the *American Journal of Public Health* in 2006 by University of Michigan health behavior professor Arline Geronimus. It posits that black women in particular experience physiologically toxic levels of stress from systemic racism and medical neglect and mistreatment; these stress levels wear down their bodies over time, making them more susceptible to illness, which is compounded by unequal access to health care and a medical system that is often skeptical of their pain.

Geronimus and her team measured these stressors in terms of allostatic load: a term defined as the body's "cumulative wear and tear owing to repeated adaptation to stressors." Allostatic load is measured by two categories of biomarkers. The first are substances the body releases in response to stress: norepinephrine, epinephrine, cortisol, and dehydroepiandrosterone sulfate (DHEA-S). The second is the effects of these substances: elevated systolic and diastolic blood pressure, glycated hemoglobin levels, cholesterol levels, and waist-to-hip ratio. Each biomarker that is over or under a particular threshold gets one point. The points add up to an allostatic load score, with a maximum of 10.

Previous studies on allostatic load had been on populations that were homogenous in age and race. Using data from the fourth National Health and Nutrition Examination Survey, Geronimus compared scores according to race. She found that black people scored higher than whites in every category, and black women scored consistently higher than black men, whereas white women and white men were parallel throughout almost the entire life course. By age forty-five, half of black women had a high allostatic load score—greater than 4—and by age sixty-four, 80 percent did. In comparison, half of the white population didn't approach a high score until fifteen years *after* black women—at age sixty—and the number of white people with a high score never rose above 60 percent. Middle- and upper-class blacks were also more likely to have higher scores than poor whites. Among middle- and upper-class respondents, black women of all ages had twice the odds of a high score as white women.

The weathering hypothesis is borne out by an increasing number of studies that have examined the relationships between perceived discrimination and the risk of preterm birth, low birthweight, or postpartum depression in black women.

Perceived discrimination affects black women's health outcomes across all levels of socioeconomic status, income, and education, and may in some cases impact women with higher status more acutely. One 2017 study on chronic worry about racial discrimination, which drew on a sample set of 2,201 black and 8,122 white postpartum women from a California statewide representative survey, found a strong correlation between chronic worry and pre-term birth among black women. Nearly 40 percent of the black women in this study—compared with only 5 percent of white women—reported chronic worry about racial discrimination, with even higher rates among women with more education and greater income. After adjusting for a long list of potential covariables—high blood pressure, prenatal care during the first trimester, health status, smoking, binge drinking, poverty, depressive symptoms, and major stressors from homelessness to divorce to job loss—this study concluded that black women with chronic worry about racism were twice as likely to have a preterm birth.

Another retrospective study also found that black women reporting high levels of racial discrimination were five times more likely than women reporting no racial discrimination to deliver low-birthweight infants. This held true even taking into account depression, net pregnancy weight gain, and alcohol and tobacco consumption.

In North Carolina, a research team found that African American women had higher levels of depression than white women, were less likely to be living with a partner, were more likely to live in unsafe neighborhoods, and were more likely to report experiencing racial discrimination. Of all of these factors, only racial discrimination proved to be a statistically significant risk factor for preterm birth: women who experienced more perceived discrimination had double the risk. In Los Angeles, clinical professor of social work Tyan Parker Dominguez found in a study that African American women's higher levels of perceived racism across a lifetime, and the amount of perceived racism they vicariously experienced as children, accounted for the fact that they experienced much higher incidences of low birthweight than white women, even after controlling for medical and sociodemographic covariables. In fact, the strongest predictor of low birthweight was racism vicariously observed as a child.

Another set of studies by Northwestern pediatrics professor James W. Collins compared groups of case subjects whose babies had been born with very low birthweight to groups of control subjects whose babies were born at normal weights. The first study found that perceived discrimination in one domain doubled mothers' risk of having a very low birthweight baby; discrimination in three or more domains tripled their risk. This association was strongest among college-educated women. The second study found that perceived discrimination among African American women during pregnancy doubled the risk of very low birthweight. Finally, a study drawing on data from a randomized controlled trial on prenatal care in New York City hospitals and health centers suggested that for every one-point increase in everyday discrimination, the birthweight of black infants decreased by approximately forty-nine grams.

Perceived discrimination also significantly increases African American women's risk of postpartum depression. One big study in the *Annals of Epidemiology* drew on data from two prospective cohort studies in Boston. The first, the Asthma Coalition on Community, Environment, and Social Stress project (ACCESS), included participants from public clinics who tended to be younger than thirty, unmarried, and have incomes of under $10,000; the second, Project Viva, drew subjects who were mostly married with higher education levels and incomes.

Fifty-four percent of the ACCESS participants and 78 percent of the Viva participants reported racial discrimination in one or more domains: the most frequent were service in stores or restaurants, and on the streets/in public settings. The Project Viva participants also reported more unfair treatment in schools and the workplace. The significantly higher rates of reported racism among the more educated and well-off cohort are consistent with a body of evidence that suggests that black women actually experience increased stress as they achieve social and economic gains; they may become more aware of racism, confront it more often in predominately white spaces, and have to handle more pressure and engage in more code-switching as they navigate among familial, interpersonal, cultural, and social spheres.

Twenty-five percent of the ACCESS participants and 13 percent of the Viva participants experienced a clinical level of postpartum depression as measured by the Edinburgh Postnatal Depression Scale. For ACCESS participants, each uptick in racial discrimination—from 1 to 2, or 3 to 4—indicated a nearly 50 percent increase in the chance of suffering from postpartum depression. The same was not true for Viva participants, where no correlation was found between discrimination and depression.

The study's authors hypothesized that for more disadvantaged women—without partners and with few social supports, living in poverty—discrimination may have a disproportionate impact on mental health.

Estimates of black women's rate of postpartum depression have varied, but most studies place it at double or triple that of white women; one study of nearly two thousand mothers given a questionnaire on depressive symptoms at twenty-seven weeks found that black women's risk of antenatal depression was five times that of white women's. The most regularly cited statistic, from the CDC, is that 38 percent of low-income mothers and mothers of color will develop postpartum depression. That's 1 in 3 mothers. And yet, as professor of social work Robert H. Keefe put it in a paper on the challenges of intensive mothering for African American women, "PPD researchers have largely neglected the needs of low-income mothers and mothers of color." The vast majority of the studies I looked at on anxiety and depression in the perinatal period—in themselves limited and tending to focus predominately on depression as measured by the EPDS—included only middle-class white women.

Finally, racial stereotypes of black women become particularly charged and oppressive during pregnancy. In her classic *Ain't I a Woman: Black Women and Feminism,* bell hooks outlines these stereotypes. First, the black mammy, portrayed as a "passive nurturer, a mother figure who gave all without expectation of return, who not only acknowledged her inferiority to whites but loved them . . . Her greatest virtue was . . . her love of white folk whom she willingly and passively served." Her own children might die of neglect as she nursed white babies; they might be sold out from under her. But her motherhood of her own children was unrecognized and denied.

The second, in hooks's formulation, was the Sapphire, or the Jezebel, the woman who male anthropologists always seemed to discover in their ventures into black neighborhoods, conceived of as hypersexualized, a siren for helpless white men and a pathological cultural force.

And finally, the matriarch, who is imagined as highly fertile, with too many children, and dominating of her family and culture in an unhealthy and emasculating way.

In a widely cited article on unique sources of stress for black American women, psychologists Lisa Rosenthal and Marci Lobel write, "[These] women are faced with two directly contradictory social pressures: that in order to be real women, they should have children, and that as Black women, others resent when they have children and attempt to prevent them from doing so." As Tope Fadiran Charlton put it in an essay for *Time* on being confronted again and again with racial stereotypes as a black mother, "Being expected to embody 'traditional' femininity, it turns out, is its own strange sort of privilege."

Rosenthal and Lobel point to stereotype threat as a powerful stressor for pregnant black American women, particularly women of higher socioeconomic status, who may live and work in neighborhoods, jobs, and educational settings that are predominately white. For these women, pervasive stereotypes may become much more palpable as they become mothers. Stereotypes have real consequences: Black American women are less likely to report sexual assault or rape, to have their cases filed by prosecutors, and to obtain convictions compared to white women with the same experiences; perpetrators convicted of sexual assault or rape of black women receive shorter sentences than those who are convicted of these crimes against white women. Studies have shown that black patients are less likely to be believed than white patients and less likely to receive adequate treatment for their pain, and also that more than half of white doctors believe at least one false statement about black health ("Black couples are significantly more fertile than whites" and "Blacks have stronger immune systems than whites").

Meanwhile, the "superwoman schema," or the "strong black woman" role as it is sometimes called, has emerged among black women as the historical result of being forced to navigate oppression and triumph in spite of it. Kristy Holloway, a professional counselor in Douglasville, Georgia, who has given numerous presentations on the superwoman stereotype, told me that many of her clients confessed to her, "I'm not allowed to fall apart." These were women, like Holloway, who were used to working at top speed, round the clock, to prove themselves. Black women, Holloway explained, "face so many extra burdens, extra layers; all the stigma bears down like atmospheric pressure." Holloway saw a strong desire in black women to adopt the superwoman ideology as a sort of "badge of female glory," but found this to be wishful thinking. She cited the example of "black girl magic," an alluring concept, but also an illusion: "I'm human; I can't wave a magic wand and make these things go away." Whenever someone called her a superwoman—she has a doctorate, her own practice, and small children—she would say, "Don't put that on me!"

Professor Cheryl L. Woods-Giscombé noted in an analysis on the superwoman schema: "The legacy of strength in the face of stress among African American women might have something to do with the current health disparities that African American women face." In her study, Woods-Giscombé found that the participants she interviewed constantly reiterated the need to be the best and to work doubly hard in order to do so. They refused breaks and sleep and help or support from others, worked late, took on extra responsibilities, sacrificed their health. One college student tells Woods-Giscombé, "They're all ready to write you off. They're all ready to tell you what you're going to be. They're all ready to tell you how far you're going to get in life. And so I felt like that added to a lot of stress, because I refused to be another statistic." The women Woods-Giscombé interviewed refused to be vulnerable.

This suppression of vulnerability contributes to and reinforces a powerful stigma in the black community against therapy and mental illness. All of the black women I talked to cited this. Katrina Pointer, a counselor who runs her own practice in Atlanta, told me that therapy was seen in her community as "something only crazy people do." When she told her family she was going to be a therapist, they thought she was nuts, imagining her dealing with the kind of patients depicted in movies about mental hospitals. In lieu of therapy, women she knew were told to pray, or told that their people had suffered far worse circumstances and gotten through it, so they should shape up and stop being weak. Her clients, predominately black women, often hid their therapy from their loved ones. Katrina also saw a lot of women striving to conform to the superwoman persona. "Hold on a minute, hold on a minute," she would say. "Let me just give you the permission to say, *This shit is hard.*"

To have access to what white women come into via the architecture of privilege, women of color must often make superhuman efforts. Even then, these efforts are not always recognized as the kind of good mothering ratified by middle-class white standards. The asylum seekers from Honduras who carry their children thousands of miles to escape gang violence are not seen as good mothers. Many black single mothers work long hours to keep their children warm and fed but are received with suspicion and judgment, while stay-at-home white mothers in the suburbs who Instagram their toddler's finger-painting are bathed in a warm congratulatory glow.

In an article for the *Journal of Family Issues* entitled "Being a Good Mom: Low-Income, Black Single Mothers Negotiate Intensive Mothering," Sinikka Elliott writes: "The ideology of intensive mothering reflects a version of privatized mothering that is not conducive with the constraints placed on low-income, Black single mothers, and instead increases their burdens, stresses, and hardships while providing a convenient explanation for these very difficulties: mothers are to blame."

Yet middle- and upper-class black women, who do have the resources to achieve this standard, still find it out of reach. In her essay for *Time*, Charlton writes, "I could never be the Good Mother; I knew this long before I had a child." She writes of the constant assumptions she fields as a mother about whether the baby's father is "in the picture," observations about her daughter's skin color, vague castigations in the form of anecdotes about the behavior of other people of color. "It is not," she concludes, "the myth of the Good Mother, but that of the Bad Black Mother, that renders my motherhood at turns invisible and suspect."

When Whitney returned from the Philippines, her worry came on like a familiar weather pattern. She had bureaucratic issues with her insurance that prevented her from being seen by her doctor for several weeks, during which she agonized about whether or not the baby was alive. She felt marooned and unsettled, casting around for insight and information. She contacted a midwife at the birthing center to see if she could possibly have a home birth. The midwife told Whitney there was no way she could deliver her, because of her previous loss, but that she'd be happy to chat with her throughout her pregnancy. The midwife said to her, "Every pregnancy is different. I've seen women with no cervix at all from cervical cancer carry a child full-term, and you can too." This faith nourished Whitney.

When she finally got in to see the doctor, the baby was fine, and though she was relieved, she never got back to any sort of normal. Because of her previous experience, the doctor began talking to her about a cerclage—a stitch to keep the cervix shut. This carries a risk; if she went into labor too early and too fast, the cervix could fail to dilate normally or might be lacerated. "That's what you *don't* want," Whitney said, in a bit of an understatement. She declined.

At eighteen weeks, Whitney had a routine ultrasound. The sonographer discovered her cervix was opening. The sonographer was black, one of only two black women who attended to Whitney during her four pregnancies. This black sonographer was Whitney's single most influential provider.

"She," Whitney told me, "believed that pregnancy *worked*." I thought for a long time after this conversation about how subtly revolutionary such a statement was, just like Whitney's insight in the Philippines about resilience: for someone swimming upstream against a wash of warnings and tests and measurements and judgments, the simple belief in women's own innate control over their bodies stood out.

Whitney and Charles were devastated to get the news about her cervix. *Here we go again,* they thought. The sonographer, seeing the looks on their faces, told them, "You must not know my God." She had seen women in all kinds of desperate circumstances, and she said to them, "The thing you should not do is let go of your faith."

In response, Whitney and Charles cried. *Who is this woman?* Whitney thought. The sonographer texted Whitney regularly to check up on and encourage her, and she and Whitney became close friends; now, they talk almost every week. In her subsequent pregnancies, Whitney returned to this clinic just to see the sonographer: "It was the only place I felt safe."

Whitney was sent straight from her eighteen-week visit at the clinic to the hospital at Duke to see a perinatologist, who "ran the gamut" on her. They gave her whatever they could to slow down or stop whatever was happening; no one really knew. They held her in the hospital for a week and then released her with the admonition to return immediately if she saw blood.

"From that point on," she said, "I was in bed." Hitting that midway point and once again experiencing contractions jarred her so much that she hardly stood up or moved for the remainder of her pregnancy. This was her decision, not a medical suggestion. It was an exercise of control, determination, and commitment. She allowed herself one shower a week for five minutes. She went in for her cervical checks every two weeks. She was having contractions every hour, which she could feel. She was drinking a gallon of water a day, because she'd heard that dehydration could bring on labor.

Whitney describes herself as a "go-go-go" type. "I do not like to be inside all day," she told me. Still, for a little over fourteen weeks, she forced herself to lie in that bed. She Googled natural ways to keep the cervix shut and came across the advice that pregnant women should only sleep on their right sides, because sleeping on the left could somehow compromise the baby's heart. Whitney doesn't remember how. The specifics didn't matter. For four months, she slept on her right side. She had overwhelming pain on her right side by the end, but she would not switch. She Googled, *Are seven contractions in an hour bad? Should I be checking my cervix?* She had a counter on her phone and she meticulously tracked her contractions. She noted the amount of water she drank.

"It just took over," she said—the fear, the worry, the checking. "Everything that I did, I was concerned that it would end up being the wrong decision."

At night her contractions picked up, and she would cry. Sometimes she had five contractions in an hour, sometimes six. "There's nothing to describe the feeling that you could be just one contraction away from demise. *Just one,*" she said.

Whitney's husband took four months off work to attend to her full-time. He cooked for her, read with her, sat by her, took her to appointments. She also found a support group online for women who'd lost children and who were either trying to conceive again or were pregnant. It felt strange to sign up for the support group, but it often buoyed her through the tedium and the worry. They cheered each other on: "Whitney, you made it to twenty-three weeks! You should be really proud! The chances of your baby surviving are greater than last week!" They'd celebrate as a group when a woman went off bed rest, when a woman had a healthy birth.

When she felt scared, she also reached out to the midwife for support and advice. Otherwise, she was without any formal or institutional help.

At twenty-eight weeks, Whitney went for a cervical scan, and they discovered she was having contractions every ten minutes.

They asked her if she was feeling them, and she said no. She was sent to the hospital, where her contractions picked up. A doctor came in to examine her.

"Her name was Dr. Doom, and she was the worst." Now, Whitney can laugh at the absurdity. Dr. Doom. "My contractions increased, I'm not kidding, when she stepped in the room." Dr. Doom was utterly cold. "You're not going to make it," she told Whitney. She wanted to do a magnesium drip. Whitney had endured one of these before, and described it as "fire going through your veins."

Faced with this choice, Whitney felt completely paralyzed. "These are the people who are supposed to know better than you, who have more information than you do," and yet she felt they were wrong. *This* was wrong. Whitney looked at her husband, and seeing her face, he ordered everyone out of the room. He took her hand, looked at her, and asked, "Whitney, where are you?" She told him she was terrified. And he asked, "What do you want to do?"

"I want to leave," she said.

Dr. Doom was disapproving. She insisted that Whitney was about to have the baby. But it was the end of her rotation, and as Whitney deliberated, another doctor named Dr. Samuel came in. He gave off a completely different vibe, and he said to Whitney, "I think you're okay. I think it's a good idea to go home." Whitney told me, "We always mark that moment as totally pivotal." Leaving the hospital might very well have saved her baby's life. Later, when her son was born, she and her husband named him Samuel.

In the nineteenth-century American South, a woman in labor inhabited, in the words of historian Kelena Reid Maxwell, "a shadowy place somewhere between life and death." Her midwife was her guide.

Until the mid-twentieth century, almost all pregnant black

women in the United States had their babies delivered by midwives. These midwives were known as "granny midwives"; the first had come over from Africa on seventeenth-century slave ships, and they passed down their traditions from generation to generation. The most trusted and revered midwives tended to be older, with extensive experience and a spiritual understanding of their work. Sociologist Keisha Goode has argued that the granny midwife label became a racist way of diminishing the midwives, depicting them as ignorant and backward, and thus she argues for referring to them as "grand midwives."

A grand midwife had to have, first and foremost, a calling. She would bring forth life, stave off death, and sometimes ease a soul's transition from one to the other. Midwifery was no minor undertaking and had to be summoned by God. Yet midwives often refused to take credit for successfully managing a difficult birth, acting instead as mere channels for a greater good. In her study "Birth Behind the Veil," Kelena Maxwell quotes one early-twentieth-century midwife who responded when asked about what she did during the birth, "Honey, I don' do nothin'; I jus' lights my pipe and waits."

To become a grand midwife, a woman had to have strong nerves, a firm and deep sense of spirituality, extensive mentoring experience with other midwives, attendance at many births, and a code of moral behavior. Midwives often had a long family lineage of the profession. They were community figures united with the mothers they served in what Maxwell calls "a loose sisterhood." These women shared the "spiritual language and practice" of childbirth.

This language and practice was "syncretic, eclectic, and dynamic." For midwives and their clients, there was no contradiction between bringing out the Bible to quote Jesus during difficult moments, using teas to sooth nerves, and applying salves and creams. African Americans in the U.S. South mixed folk practices, traditional and modern medicine, and organized religion into their own unique healing techniques.

The grand midwife was revered not only or even predominately for her experience, but for the rituals she carried out. One of the most popular was putting a sharp object under a laboring woman's pillow to cut pain, or tucking pieces of the husband's clothing under the bed so that he would help her bear the contractions. A midwife would read the Bible and pray. One woman explains her mother's practice to Maxwell: "Prayers is the most important thing, more than anything else, prayers can do anything. She would always say a prayer." Midwives might also wash, condition, and braid a client's hair; bathe her; massage oils into her skin; and sprinkle her with rose water.

After the birth, the midwife took care of the placenta, which had to be salted and buried. Some midwives would tie the placenta with nine knots, and/or say nine prayers, and almost all would dig the burial hole themselves, measuring a precise number of inches into the ground. The placenta was given the respect that would go to the woman's body when she died.

Midwives also performed abortions, and Goode argues that the acts of delivering and aborting were not seen as contradictory—"both," she writes, "were acts of healing." Finally, midwives washed and prepared the dead for burial, a duty that endowed them with an aura of awe in their communities. It is difficult now to imagine the power midwives held.

One midwife, whom Maxwell describes as "part of a long line of secret doctors in Louisiana," told her, "Back in the olden days that's all they use was herbs and faith."

It is likely that "herbs and faith" actually played a highly significant role in women's outlook, stability, and health postpartum. Following the delivery, the midwife would ritually escort the mother and the baby outside for the first time. This ritual involved some variation on walking counterclockwise around the house and stopping at the four corners. It sometimes involved carrying a thimbleful of water, then drinking it. The idea was to thank God for a safe delivery, to pray for the health of baby and mother, and to mark the threshold the woman had just crossed between birth and death. It is not hard to imagine what these rituals must have meant in a time and place when black women were the recipients of very little care.

For African American women of the South, as Maxwell puts it, "a midwife-assisted home birth was accepted as the natural and undisputed choice from the time of enslavement through the first half of the twentieth century." Physicians were often unavailable to black women, and in the Jim Crow era, black people were banned from most (white) medical institutions, so midwives were the best, and often the only, option. Many black women were also rightfully suspicious of medical institutions and doctors.

The field of gynecology was established largely from experiments on enslaved women; J. Marion Sims, the "father" of modern gynecological surgery, made his breakthroughs by purchasing women and performing surgery without anesthesia on them. There is debate about whether or not these women gave their consent; they were suffering from fistulas, a debilitating condition in which a hole is torn between a woman's vagina and her rectum or bladder during childbirth, rendering her incontinent. Some scholars have argued that the women would have been willing to endure any number of surgeries to escape the misery and stigma of a fistula. There is also debate about whether anesthesia was actually available; it came into widespread use not long after Sims did his work. Undoubtedly, however, Sims participated in and solidified a long tradition of experimentation, often coerced or without consent, on black bodies, and the modern backlash against him—a statue next to Central Park was removed after protests—reflects the lingering pain of this American reality. Needless to say, black women were not eager to run to the medical establishment for care.

One striking example of this comes from Isabel Wilkerson's classic book on the Great Migration, *The Warmth of Other Suns*; Ida Mae, one of her three main characters, takes a long and arduous train journey from Milwaukee back to Mississippi in order to give birth with a midwife. Wilkerson writes, "She didn't quite trust whatever it was they did to people in hospitals. She had never been inside one but had heard that they strapped women down during delivery, and so she decided to surrender herself to a Mississippi midwife as she and everybody she knew had always done."

Most white women were also using midwives in the nineteenth century, but Maxwell points out a crucial distinction between black and white women's choice of care: "White women trusted midwives because they performed like doctors when they were with them, and black women trusted midwives because they did *not* perform like doctors when they were with them." This may very well be because white doctors performed differently around white women, as well as because white women's relationship to expertise, the state, and established institutions was very different from black women's—it was also because, by virtue of black women's exclusion from the mainstream realm of medicine and power, they developed strong connections to a realm of ritual, belief, and community.

At the start of the twentieth century, as medicine was becoming more "scientific," lucrative, established, credentialed, and specialized, obstetrics was struggling to free itself from a reputation as an inferior field, in which doctors might gain experience before moving on to more esteemed work. Obstetricians needed patients, but most women at the turn of the century still had their babies delivered by midwives. Doctors were eager to distance themselves from female "lay healers," and to imbue their work with the authority of science: exact, impeccable, modern, rigorous with expertise derived from laboratories and institutions. The rise and positioning of germ theory as the dominant explanation of disease allowed doctors to claim that methodical cleanliness was the only safe alternative to the midwife's potentially disorderly practice; this in spite of the fact that for nearly a century, doctors had been systematically killing pregnant women with puerperal (childbirth) fever by inserting their unwashed hands into the birth canal, and women had a far better chance of surviving with midwives.

Flaunting their pretense of institutional and societal validity, doctors launched aggressive campaigns against (mostly immigrant and black) midwives. A popular series of photographs of midwives at the time features a grand midwife next to a "typical Italian midwife" and an Irish American midwife—each awarded her own sardonic, racist caption, with the African American's being "ignorant and superstitious, a survival of the 'magic doctors' of the West Coast of Africa." These photos were distributed by doctors and intended to scare women into the white-gloved grip of modern medicine.

Midwives in the South were depicted as a "necessary evil"— necessary because there weren't enough doctors willing or able to deliver black women, and evil because their practices seemed antithetical and dangerous to burgeoning twentieth-century medicine. Goode quotes J. Clifton Edgar, prominent obstetrician and author of the widely used textbook *The Practice of Obstetrics*, declaring that midwives are "except in some rare instances . . . dark, dirty, ignorant, untrained, incompetent women." Edgar explains, "She is evil, though a necessary evil, and must be controlled."

Goode points out that in spite of their presumed incompetence and evil, midwives remained the providers of choice for most women at the time, and that while midwives were required to attend many births before they were allowed to practice, many obstetricians in the late nineteenth and into the early twentieth century graduated from medical school without having observed a single birth.

Obstetricians and medical professionals' push to claim the territory of birth coincided with white women reformers' efforts to reduce high infant and maternal mortality rates at the turn of the century. In 1915, the first year that such data were recorded, six white women, and eleven black women, died for every 1,000 live births in the United States; for the same number of births, 100 white infants and 181 black infants died.

As historian Eileen Boris writes, "Everyone was touched by child and infant mortality," including the women who would go on to lead the influential Progressive movements that would reshape child and maternal health. Jane Addams, the famous Progressive leader, peace activist, and founder of the settlement house movement, was two years old when her mother died in childbirth. Julia Lathrop, who went on to head the Children's Bureau, one of the twentieth century's most significant efforts to foreground the lives and health of mothers, had a grandmother who died in childbirth and an aunt who died in early childhood. A female doctor who worked with Lathrop had experienced the death of two children before they reached age four. Boris cites correspondence between Lathrop and one of her patients in which they wrote of their fear of dying. This fear is not totally unknown today—particularly for mothers of color—but it is not, for most women, a prevailing worry about childbirth. At the turn of the twentieth century, it was.

Maternalist reformers led by Lathrop successfully lobbied the federal government to establish and put them in charge of a Children's Bureau focused on reducing infant and maternal mortality. The Children's Bureau ran large-scale studies and produced the nation's first set of statistics on infant and maternal mortality in 1915. They distributed infant care brochures to mothers, established a correspondence system in which mothers could write to Children's Bureau professionals for help and guidance on care, encouraged the systematic registration of births, and pioneered the "well check" or "wellness visit," in which a health professional observes a healthy child and provides the mother with a "score card" of the child's progress.

The Children's Bureau had to fight an uphill battle for funding and legitimacy from a predominately male political establishment skeptical of "women's" issues and skittish about perceived federal involvement in the individual's domain. It was a measure of the Bureau's popularity and success that Lathrop and her compatriots managed to get the sweeping Sheppard-Towner Maternity and Infancy Protection Act of 1921 passed in Congress. The act, written by Lathrop but titled after Texas senator Morris Sheppard and Iowa representative Horace Towner, allocated more than a million dollars to the Children's Bureau annually for five years to distribute to states for the establishment of prenatal clinics, the health education of mothers, and the training and supervision of midwives.

Sheppard-Towner forever changed midwifery in the United States, paving the way for a medicalized midwifery model, a tiered system of distinct classes of midwives—divided by certification level and medical prestige—and a transfer of power to obstetrics and its emphasis on risk and pathology in managing pregnancy. It also stigmatized grand midwives as ignorant, backward, and dangerous, largely eliminating black women from midwifery.

Whitney spent her time at home Googling her seemingly incessant contractions. Everyone in her support group did this and they all encouraged each other to do it less, but it was so hard. "There was some form of relief that I found in reading about the doom," Whitney observed. "That is not . . . normal."

The midwife came over at around thirty-three weeks to give Whitney something like a private birthing class. She promised to be Whitney's doula. At one point, she told Whitney: "It's really amazing that you're able to do this, but I want you to know that studies show that bed rest doesn't actually prevent premature labor." She explained that it makes sense to get the pressure off, but that the scientific evidence doesn't demonstrate any benefit to lying down all day. "Whitney," she said, "you made it this far because you were going to make it this far."

Whitney felt immense gratitude for this moment. She understood then that the midwife had let her do what she needed to do, which was to lay herself down and take the only control she could. Whitney had felt firmly and intuitively that her body needed this, and she had done it with all of her strength and commitment. The midwife could've intervened to say that *the studies show you don't need to do this,* but instead she had observed, understood, waited. She had held out until the very end and then she'd framed her insight in terms of awe for Whitney's determination. When she left, Whitney said to herself, *I'm going to lie here until the thirty-four-week mark.* And then, at thirty-four weeks, with the same certitude and control with which she'd lain down almost four months ago, she stood up. She almost fell over. "But," she told me, "I walked around kicking it and moving and shaking it until thirty-nine weeks."

On the day Whitney went into labor, the midwife checked and discovered that Whitney was six centimeters. At this point, the midwife had an insight. She told Whitney, "I think this is just what your body does. Some women contract the entire pregnancy. It doesn't mean there's anything wrong with you."

"She said that to me and I was like, *Thank you!*" Whitney told me. "It was huge for me."

At the hospital, Whitney discovered that a black midwife, Cheryl, was on call to deliver her, and this made her feel safe. Her labor dragged on, however, and the baby turned transverse. Cheryl stepped out to give Whitney some time to labor, but as she did she mentioned that Whitney might want to consider "plan B" and "other options."

When she came back in, Cheryl offered to try to turn the baby, and Whitney agreed, eager not to be sent to surgery. During the next contraction, the midwife reached her hand up into Whitney's cervix. "Imagine," Whitney told me, "someone just reaching all the way up there. *Natural* labor." The midwife did this three times, breaking Whitney's water the last time, which helped.

Whitney labored for another ten hours, pushing long and hard. And then her baby was born, and suddenly all the chaos of labor quieted.

"It was just very calm," she said. Not blissful, not terrible, just calm. It didn't last long. The baby's breathing was rapid, so as Whitney's tear was being stitched, they took him from her for examination.

She and her husband stayed in the hospital for four days. The doctors were giving her son antibiotics, testing his blood sugar, equivocating about what to do and whether he seemed stable. Finally a nurse came in and said to Whitney and her husband, "Your son is fine. I'm going to do everything I can to get you out of here." The nurse devised a plan: Whitney was to give the baby a bottle and the nurse would check his glucose immediately, so it would look like it was up. His glucose numbers had been dropping by only .1, by .2, tiny increments, but the doctors hedged and refused to release him. Whitney and the nurse literally plotted her escape.

Whitney regrets not insisting on leaving right away, but she didn't know that all of her children would have rapid breathing when they were born; the midwife later explained to her that this was normal, and that allowing babies to lie on their mother's chest for thirty minutes or an hour would calm the breathing down. Whitney had just come out of a mentally and physically demanding pregnancy, fighting for her son in the womb, then fighting for him as he was being born, and now, fresh and raw from labor, she was tired of fighting.

At home, Whitney focused intensely on breastfeeding. The doctors advised her to pump to get her milk supply up, so she was waking up around the clock to do so. She wasn't eating well, wasn't sleeping well, and she felt all the unpreparedness characteristic of a new mother on top of the lingering pressure and tension of the pregnancy and birth. "I hadn't had a mental break. I just went from fatigue to more fatigue to no-sleep fatigue to not-eating fatigue to when-was-the-last-time-I-brushed-my-teeth fatigue." Whitney said what so many other mothers have told me: after everyone being so excited and upbeat about "you're having a baby!" the grimness of the fog in which she found herself was startling.

It was lonely and stressful. Whitney cried sometimes out of desperation. There were days that felt endless, hopeless. She was alone while everyone was at work—just her and the baby. She wanted to crawl into someone's lap and have her head rubbed. "I felt like I wanted to be a baby sometimes." But she was the mother, a super-woman, alone.

6

Reproductive Rights

In spite of significant evidence to the contrary, in the early twentieth century, Lathrop, the Children's Bureau, and prominent politicians and health professionals blamed high infant and maternal
mortality rates on midwives. As part of the Children's Bureau's
early work, Lathrop commissioned extensive studies on the causes
of these high rates. None pointed to the use of midwives as the
driving factor. Numerous studies from the time found a direct link
between a father's low income, a mother's work history, and infant
death. Black women often worked right up to delivery and returned
to heavy labor within days or weeks of giving birth. The historian
Kelena Maxwell cites the example of a North Carolina mother of
five who picked forty-five pounds of cotton the morning after her
baby was born. Another significant 1922 study by doctor and New
Jersey State Department of Health consultant Julius Levy found
that most infant deaths occurred in the first three hours of life,
and that mortality on the first day for babies delivered in hospitals
was three times that for babies delivered at home. Levy found that
mortality overall for babies delivered by physicians was four times
as high as that for babies delivered at home. It could be inferred
that mothers who went to hospitals simply had riskier pregnancies and births, but Levy's data found that cities and counties with

more practicing midwives had lower neonatal death rates. Statistics
from major cities consistently supported the safety of midwifery
care. In Washington, D.C., infant mortality in the first day, week,
and month of life increased as the percentage of births reported
by midwives shrank. In Newark, a midwifery program in 1914–1916
maintained a maternal mortality rate of 1.7 in 1,000 and an infant
mortality rate of 8.5 in 1,000, but in Boston, where midwives were
banned, the maternal mortality rate was 6.5 in 1,000 and the infant
mortality rate 36.4 in 1,000.

In spite of this evidence, Lathrop concluded that the problem
was a lack of "skilled care." In 1920, she declared, "Twenty percent
of white mothers, and eighty percent of colored, depend upon
dirty, ignorant, negro women for care at a time when they should
have the most skilled attention." It was impossible to do away with
midwives entirely, however, so the next best option was to train
them, in the words of a Mississippi nurse, in the "white folks' way."

In 1921, Laurie Jean Reid, a U.S. Public Health Service nurse, proposed a plan for training midwives to the Mississippi State Medical Association. Reid conjured for her audience of white southern
male doctors the specter of "illiterate, ignorant, negro women,
without the knowledge of the first principles of ordinary soap and
water cleanliness, who are daily attending at the birth of some precious baby." Reid pointed out that the three to four thousand midwives in Mississippi were largely operating on their own, without
official supervision, training, or regulation. They had to be brought
under the umbrella of the state-run health department and the
moral yoke of public health. Folk practices were to be stamped
out. The proposal passed.

The training midwives received from credentialed nurses and
doctors was informed more by racialized middle-class ideas about
how providers should look and behave than by scientific advances
that might improve women's birth outcomes and save lives.
Because white cultural understanding of blackness was deeply
tied to ideas of dirtiness, disorder, and impurity, and because being
black was itself seen as a pathology, cleanliness became the main

preoccupation of training programs. Midwives were scrubbed into submission and gowned in white. One iconic image of the time featured a nurse leading a training of twelve "mammies," as they were labeled in the photo, "each," as Maxwell describes, "resplendent in garb of snowy cap and gown," and each proffering her bag for inspection.

In order to maintain their licenses, African American midwives had to submit to inspections. Public health nurses arrived at random times at their homes, scrutinizing their bags, their equipment, their living situation, and even their bodies and clothes. The aseptic techniques they were to use in births were also to be applied to their persons and surroundings. Meanwhile, they were interviewed to see how tightly they adhered to sets of obligatory procedures: silver nitrate drops were to be put in the eyes of all newborns to protect against blindness in the case of a mother's STD, doctors were to be called at any sign of complication, births were to be reported and registered, specific instruments were to be always on hand.

The training focused most intensively on what midwives were *not* to do, on the limitations of their abilities and expertise. They were to embody the modern and scientific best practices of the time, yet they were not actually taught to do anything, lest they tiptoe into the terrain of the doctor. They received no instruction in alleviating pain, speeding up stalled labor, or stopping hemorrhaging. As numerous historians have pointed out, the point wasn't to foreground the midwife as a competent health practitioner but to put her in her place, racially, socially, and medically. Midwives who defied the new standards—who intervened in ways reserved for physicians, or who carried forbidden folk objects in their bags, or slipped a knife under the pillow of a patient—risked losing their licenses.

There was no room in emerging obstetric practice and ideology for tea, for a walk around the house in the newborn's first hours, for what might provide comfort and mooring to women and how that might influence their and their children's health. The reigning presumption was that everyone would be better off in a sterile hospital room with a nurse clad in bright whites. Certainly, setting standards for cleanliness, for proper procedure—such as eyedrops and vaccines and birth certificates—was an important public health measure. But the practice of training and licensing African American midwives overlooked the real and measurable benefits of midwifery in favor of white middle-class "scientific" ideologies.

———————

The Sheppard-Towner Act that established the Children's Bureau was repealed in 1929, a mere eight years after its passing, because of concern from the medical and political establishment about its "Communist" overtones (the American Medical Association referred to Lathrop and the women at the Children's Bureau as "Bolsheviks"). This was a common refrain applied to public health initiatives that threatened the sovereignty and superiority of private physicians—for example, removing the child's well visit from the physician's practice and making it the provenance of nurses or social workers—and that made "radical" claims about the government's obligation to meet the needs of all women and children. Six years after the demise of Sheppard-Towner, the Social Security Act established a stratified tier of social services that privileged entitlements for white male workers and stigmatized aid to poor women and children as charity.

Sheppard-Towner was radical in its claim that mothers deserved federal programs dedicated to their and their children's health, but its beneficiaries were mostly rural white farm women. For them, infant deaths dropped from 76 per 1,000 in 1921 to 69 per 1,000 in 1928. Among women of color, these deaths stayed almost steady, decreasing only slightly from 108 to 106.

The Act, combined with aggressive lobbying on the part of male obstetricians, was successful in eliminating grand midwives by way of licensing and training programs and social pressure. It established the Certified Nurse Midwife (CNM) credential and as such paved the way for the future revival of midwifery among white women.

Sheppard-Towner was not solely to blame for the decline of black midwifery—the black middle class, the NAACP, and black doctors also encouraged black women to seek hospital care from obstetricians, particularly after the Hill-Burton Act of 1946, which provided funds for the construction of hospitals in rural areas. For many, scientific care, starkly distinguished from tradition and myth, signified progress.

At the same time, studies from 1930 to 1960 showed that, even in less than ideal conditions of poverty and potential risk, women who gave birth at home with a midwife had better outcomes than those in hospitals. Similar studies today have consistently shown that for women with low-risk pregnancies, home birth provides better outcomes than hospital birth. The largest study of home births, conducted in the United States from 2004 to 2009 and looking at nearly seventeen thousand women and their babies, found that home births had lower rates of interventions for mothers and babies, no increase in adverse outcomes, and greater health benefits for mothers and babies. Still, by 2012, 98.6 percent of all U.S. births occurred in hospitals, and 92 percent were attended by obstetricians. Today, black women make up less than 2 percent of the country's fifteen thousand midwives. There has been a mild uptick in the rates of home births; 90 percent of this increase comes from white women.

The "revival" of midwifery began around the time of the natural birth movement in the 1960s and '70s, as a response to the dehumanizing practices of hospitals and as a faction of the rising women's movement. Its guru and chief spokeswoman was Ina May Gaskin, whose Tennessee farm became a kind of mecca for midwifery—a place where women could go to have orgasmic, empowered, natural births. In response to increasing demand for midwives and activism against hospital policies, professional organizations formed: the biggest of these are Midwives Alliance of

North America (MANA) and the National Association of Certified Professional Midwives (NACPM). Both have specific groups for midwives of color, but black women often reported feeling isolated within the organizations.

The midwives Goode interviews in her 2014 study, "Birthing, Blackness, and the Body," consistently point to midwifery's race problem. One midwife tells her, "You can't keep talking about wanting and needing more midwives in this country without talking about race." Others identified problems with mentorship and indirect discrimination; one woman was told by her white mentor that she would have to get rid of her dreadlocks if she wanted to attend births, because they might upset white women. Another talked about how isolating it was to be the only woman of color in her program. This midwife's experience was transformed by the presence of a black receptionist. "She got me," the midwife explained. "She knew what it meant to be black in a white institution." In talking about her midwifery program, one of her strongest memories of love is for the black receptionist.

Black midwives today struggle to establish themselves as figures of medical authority; one midwife pointed out that black people, too, had internalized stereotypes and were skeptical of midwives' capacity to provide care.

> "I have to teach people, more often than not black women, that I am not there only to rub her back and feet. . . . I am capable, I am your provider, you know?"

The most powerful revelation of Goode's study is the intense bond that these midwives often feel with their clients. One woman tells Goode, "We black women, we simply do not have many opportunities for power in this world. But . . . power in birth gives them a feeling of power they will have for the rest of their lives. . . . It's an achievement, a unique experience for black women in our society. It's such an honor to bear witness to this." Another explains, "When I see another black woman giving birth . . . I am there with her. . . . I know her and I relate to her like I can't other women. . . . I know how it feels to be a black woman in this world . . . walking down the street, at work. Stupid stuff people say. The way stuff makes you feel. That small stuff. I also know what it feels like to be a black mother in this world. I know what we've been through as people and what that means for her and her baby." Another calls this "cellular knowledge," and says, "Every time a black baby is healthy and enters this world, it's a miracle."

In 2012, six members of the Midwives of Color section of MANA resigned, citing racism. Their public Facebook post on the resignation is a contemporary reiteration of the recent history of black midwifery in the United States:

We acknowledge that the midwifery history taught in most midwifery programs and promulgated at conferences fails to bear witness to the fact that midwifery history is, in the United States, largely a history of midwives of color. A history of direct-entry midwifery that begins in the 1970s with the "white revival" describes only the thinnest of top layers on a great foundation of centuries of work by African American, Native American, Latina, Asian-American, and ethnically marginalized immigrant midwives. Similarly, a history of nurse-midwifery that begins with the differentiation between professionalized nurse-midwives from (women of color) lay midwives does not acknowledge the truth of midwifery history. We recognize that the process of licensing and certifying midwives after the 1960s in many cases served to marginalize and exclude practicing midwives in communities of color. We recognize that in many cases our legitimation as providers rested on deliberately differentiating ourselves as "better educated," more "hygienic," and/or more "scientific" than these midwives of color, while at the same time excluding them from these paths to "legitimate" practice. We posit that white midwives' failure to acknowledge this history while laying claim to "traditional knowledge" from the 1970s onward is an act of violence, erasing midwives of color from the past and creating an "innocent" present for white-dominant midwifery.

In 2012, Certified Nurse Midwives attended 7.9 percent of all U.S. births. Black women accounted for 13 percent of these. This means that in the United States in 2012, black women were attended by CNMs at approximately 1 percent of births. Certified Professional Midwives (CPMs), whose care is not covered by insurance in many states, attended the births of approximately 4 percent of black women; most of these took place in hospitals, in contrast to the CPM-attended births of white women, most of which took place at home.

All women can gain from the Midwives Model of Care. This model, a copyrighted set of guidelines from the Midwifery Task Force, identifies the following principles:

- monitoring the physical, psychological and social well-being of the mother throughout the childbearing cycle
- providing the mother with individualized education, counseling, and prenatal care, continuous hands-on assistance during labor and delivery, and postpartum support
- minimizing technological interventions and
- identifying and referring women who require obstetrical attention.

A narrative review of all qualitative and quantitative research on black women and antenatal care published in peer-reviewed journals between 2006 and 2017 highlighted several advantages to the midwife model: women who received prenatal care at birthing centers staffed by midwives were less likely to have a preterm birth or a C-section, and they spent more than double the amount of time with their providers during each visit than those who saw ob-gyns. The topics they covered during their visits were much broader than the topics covered in the OB visits. Black women who used midwives for prenatal care also reported feeling more empowered.

The bigger takeaway from this review, however, might be the shocking lack of research on midwifery and black women: the authors found only seven studies that looked at midwifery, and only one that mentioned black midwives. That one focused on the narratives written by black midwives or doulas on their websites, and didn't involve actually speaking to any black midwives or patients.

A 2018 study, meanwhile, found that the states that had the largest numbers of credentialed midwives and higher levels of midwife integration into their health care systems had significantly better outcomes, and vice versa. This disproportionately affects black mothers: the states with the lowest levels of midwife integration and the fewest midwives, including North Carolina, Alabama, and Mississippi, have significant black populations and some of the poorest outcomes.

Jennie Joseph, a Florida-based midwife and the founder of Commonsense Childbirth, a nonprofit whose mission is to change the broken maternal health care system and eliminate racial and class disparities in perinatal health, told me she regularly confronts myths among fellow professionals at conferences and elsewhere. I asked her about the biggest myth she had to address. She thought for a minute. "That there's something wrong with black women," she told me. She gathered steam. "Their attitude. Their food. Their weight. The angry black woman. They're not as good as whatever anyone else is doing. You don't need to listen to them. They can tolerate pain better. They're looking for drugs." She sighed. She consistently had to point out that it wasn't the women who were the problem. "The ways we're doing what we're doing around black women give us this outcome!"

Maternity care, Joseph told me, is the same everywhere you do it: Check the blood pressure. Check the urine. Measure the baby. Check the position. "The difference," she explained, "is the support and the listening and the compassion. Everything else is the same."

But this wasn't a change the U.S. health care system was interested in: instead it was more money, more hospitals, more data, more drugs.

She told me that women who came to her clinic were sometimes moved to tears because they felt they'd been listened to for the first time. One woman said to her, "No one told me that I could be treated like this."

Nine months after she brought her first child home, Whitney found out she was pregnant again. She was shocked but happy. She said to herself, *I am not going to have the experience that I had with Samuel.* She decided she was going to have a home birth. Edie, her midwife friend and former doula, agreed to do the home birth if Whitney's cervix looked fine at eighteen weeks.

For this pregnancy, she saw Edie for all of her care. They would have two- or three-hour appointments, discussing her fears, how her body felt, what was going on in her life. "I got everything out that I needed to get out," Whitney said. The appointments were at Edie's house. Whitney took urine samples in her bathroom, and then Edie would show Whitney exactly what she was looking for in the sample. Whitney would weigh herself on the scale beside the toilet. Whitney learned about everything that, had she gone to a clinic, she would've simply endured as protocol without explanation or understanding.

She progressed well, until she started to feel contractions at twenty-one weeks. She contemplated bed rest, but she had to care for a one-year-old running around. Bed rest simply wasn't an option. So, like most mothers of toddlers, Whitney endured her second pregnancy in high gear. Her contractions ramped up starting at around thirty-four weeks, which made her nervous, but she called and texted with Edie regularly. The midwife always left it up to her. "If you want me to come, I'll come," she'd say, although if the baby was preterm, she wouldn't be able to deliver Whitney. She gave Whitney tips about rotating her hips, making sure the baby was in the best position. He dropped very low, intensifying her contractions. Before she was pregnant with Isaac, Whitney had dreamed that she was going to have a baby on August 31. It turned out this was her due date—the day she'd reach forty weeks exactly. On the night of the thirty-first, with some pressure but no clear signs of labor, Whitney felt tremendously disappointed on so many levels, everything coalescing around this sign. "Girl, go to sleep!" her friends told her. She slept. In the morning, at forty weeks and one day, she woke up and went to the bathroom, and as soon as she was done, "that was it, he was coming." The moment she emptied her bladder it was as if he slid down, engaged, and kicked everything into motion.

This time, Whitney felt completely in control. Her husband called Edie and dragged out the birthing pool, already blown up. He had started to fill it when Whitney hobbled out and put her arms around him and said, *"Oh my God,"* and he yelled, "Get back on the toilet, get back on the toilet!" Instead she stumbled into the pool and collapsed on all fours. She reached down and she felt the head.

"I feel the head," she said, and Charles yelled, "No, what, no!" He called the midwife and put her on speakerphone. She said, "Whitney, I'm on my way," but Whitney's body was doing what it needed to do, pushing, pushing: "It was incredible the amount of force I felt pushing him out." Whitney draped herself over the side of the pool and felt the immense pressure of the head and bore down, and Charles shouted, "Don't sit back!" She yelled, "Be *positive!"* and then she flipped over and pulled Isaac out of the water and held him in her arms.

"It was a euphoria that you can't explain." Whitney took a deep breath. She cradled her son. She felt so happy. Her body had done this. She had done this. After everything that she had been through, she had just made it on her own.

The midwife showed up fifteen minutes later. Whitney was in

the pool cradling baby Isaac. There was no blood in the pool, sig-nifying that there had been no tearing. "Whitney," Edie said, "that was great labor."

It was, for Whitney, "so much affirmation."

They put a clean set of sheets on the bed. Edie told Whitney, "I'm not going to check him or weigh him, I'm just going to let you do what you want. There's going to be a point when you say, *Okay, I'm ready.*" When that point came, they weighed Isaac and he was eight pounds, three ounces.

"All of it," Whitney told me—the labor coming one day late as a little trick, the swiftness of it, the intensity, the thrill—"was just so Isaac." I asked what Isaac was like. "Right now," she said with a laugh, "he's standing up on the kitchen chair, his pants are down, and he's mooning everybody. So yeah, there you go." Then: "Isaac, please get your butt off the table. You are sitting in your pasta!"

Whitney's postpartum period this time was calmer. Not ideal, but more stable. Edie convinced her to do placenta encapsulation—the practice of dehydrating the placenta and making it into pills to be consumed—which was for her "extremely crunchy," but the mid-wife said it could be really helpful for milk production and mental health. Her milk supply overflowed, and she never had to pump. Seven months later, she felt empowered enough that she and Charles decided to leave the United States and move their family to the Philippines.

I asked her about the impulse behind this big move. "It felt like going home," she told me. She had formed such strong bonds when she was there, and she loved how moms took care of other moms. She said, "They just really love children, and I don't feel like we have that here in our country. I feel like there's a hatred toward mothers, a hatred toward children."

I asked her, gingerly, if race figured into it. She thought for a moment. Yes, she told me. "Not that it's not a thing there—there's a lot of colorism, a lot of skin bleaching. . . . The indigenous people of the Philippines who live in the far south are very dark, with big chunky curls, and short, and there's a lot of racism toward them. But as someone from here . . . it was definitely a relief to be away from it."

By *it*, she meant the racial climate in the United States. It wasn't all breezy in the Philippines: people would stop and stare at her and Charles on the street, and sometimes ask to take photos. But she observed that a lot of Filipino culture mimicked or reflected black culture and felt very familiar to her. People wore fashions popular in black culture in the nineties, and she thought, *No one wears that anymore!* She laughed as she recalled it. But she liked the resonances and similarities.

She went on, changing tones a bit, "I also have this—we have this belief in our house that . . . the only way we can eradicate ignorance, even within our own family, is to expose our children to cultures. And we're not afraid to do that."

Growing up, she said, her parents would invite different people to their dinner table. "I would love," Whitney mused, "for my kids to be at other tables. So they arrive on the scene with a lot more empathy and a lot more grace toward people."

She convinced her husband that they should buy the tickets and go. They'd start out by working with her friend's organization building small businesses. They began getting everything ready. Around this time, Whitney noticed that she was gaining a little weight—*I am eating* good *these days*, she thought. Just in case, she took a pregnancy test. Isaac was nine months old, Samuel two years. "I remember," she told me, "I came out of the bathroom and my husband was on the bed waiting for me to tell him the results." She dove onto the bed facedown and started bawling.

"I knew you were pregnant," he soothed her, "and it's gonna be okay. It's gonna be fine." She berated him through her tears, "That's easy for you to say. The whole nine months, I don't know if I'm going to lose."

———————

"American culture," writes Dorothy Roberts, "reveres no Black madonna." Ideal motherhood in the United States has always been white and has aligned with shifting conceptions of the ideal white woman, as she stands in contrast to the ideal white man. Black motherhood, set in opposition to this white female ideal, has been stigmatized, devalued, degraded, and pathologized. Black women's reproduction has also been systematically controlled by the state; as Roberts puts it in her groundbreaking book *Killing the Black Body,* "Regulating Black women's reproductive decisions has been a central aspect of racist oppression in America." The racism that has denied black women basic reproductive freedoms and dignity, and that presents their motherhood as warped and lesser, is tightly helixed with the sexism that tells white women there is only one special kind of good mother, and that any deviation from this spells danger.

The dehumanization of black mothers, the control of their reproduction, and the brutalization of their bodies began in slavery. A pregnant slave would be whipped while lying over a hole in the ground made just big enough to fit her pregnant belly. She could thus receive her flogging while her fetus—a valuable future slave—would in theory be spared. This didn't always work. Moses Grandy, who authored a narrative about slave life in 1843, writes, "One of my sisters was so severely punished this way, that labor was brought on, and the child was born in the field."

Roberts calls the relationship between enslaved women and their children "the first example of maternal-fetal conflict in American history." An early American law dictated that the children of slave mothers and white fathers remain slaves, under the ownership of their fathers.

Enslaved mothers were treated as products or animals. Roberts quotes slaveowners' reports noting that a "breeding woman is worth from one-sixth to one-fourth more than one that does not breed," and boasting, "I own a woman who cost me $400, when a girl, in 1827. . . . She now has three children worth over $3000. . . . Her oldest boy is worth $1250 cash, and I can get it." The ban on importing new slaves after 1808 made the reproduction of female slaves increasingly valuable. Roberts cites an instruction Thomas Jefferson gave his plantation manager in 1820: "I consider a woman who brings a child every two years more profitable than the best man on the farm."

Enslaved women who did not have children might be rounded up and flogged, as they were under one North Carolina planter, whom Roberts quotes as threatening to beat a group of childless women to death, declaring, "Damn you . . . you don't breed, I have not had a young one from one of you for several months."

This emphasis on childbearing did not spare black women the crushing labor that their male counterparts were required to perform. They worked in the fields throughout their pregnancies, and immediately after birth. Their infants were either left in the care of elderly or infirm slaves who couldn't work or they were taken to the fields. Fewer than two out of three black children survived until age ten. Roberts describes one particularly horrific incident in which new mothers, forced to work and without options, had dug a long trough in the ground, where they put their infants. A sudden rainstorm struck while the mothers were at the opposite end of the field. As a former slave described it, by the time the mothers had rushed back "that trough was filled with water and every baby in it was floating round in the water, drowned."

Slave children were put to work by age seven; those who disobeyed were whipped, without their parents' say or control. Girls were frequently assaulted. Many children witnessed the brutal beatings of their parents. Children were also used as collateral by slaveowners to prevent female slaves from fleeing, or to lure escaped slaves back. Roberts points out that only 19 percent of the runaways advertised in North Carolina between 1850 and 1860 were women.

But remaining on a plantation was no guarantee of safety for children, who could at any point be sold to other plantations and masters. The son of activist and abolitionist Sojourner Truth was sold by his owner, John Dumont, and sent from New York to a plantation in Alabama. Truth had fled Dumont in 1826 after he promised to free her—the buying and selling of slaves was abolished in New York in 1799, and slavery was gradually phased out—but later refused. She took her infant daughter with her, but had to leave her other children behind, hoping to rescue them later—a brutal calculation many women were forced to make. Not long after she'd left, Dumont sold Peter, the five-year-old, even though this was prohibited under an 1807 New York law. Truth appealed to her former white mistress, but as she wrote in her autobiography, the mistress's reply was, "A fine fuss to make about a little nigger!" Truth insisted to her, "I'll have my child again," to which the mistress replied, "And what have you to support him with, if you could?"

Truth found the support of Quaker abolitionists and became one of the first black women to sue a white man for the release of her child. The legal battle immersed her in public debates about slavery and emancipation, and marked her initiation as an activist. She won Peter's release, but when he returned, he at first refused to go to her, insisting instead on returning to his northern master.

This echoes in eerily precise ways the experiences of Central American mothers in 2018 who were torn from their babies under President Trump's family separation policy and then reunited months later with catatonic, traumatized children who barely recognized them. Central American mothers found plenty of white mothers who rallied and fought for them, but they also faced an invisible caucus of white women who, much like some slave mistresses, failed to understand them or their children as human. Roberts writes, "The notion that a white mother and child were separable entities with contradictory interests was unthinkable," and it remains so today, but the same principle has never held for non-white mothers and non-white children.

All enslaved women lived with the perpetual fear and reality of rape. In her sweeping treatise *Women, Race, and Class*, Angela Davis writes, "Rape was a weapon of domination, a weapon of repression, whose covert goal was to extinguish enslaved women's will to resist, and in the process, demoralize their men." The rape of slave women, by either their white masters or fellow enslaved men, was not a crime under the law. Dorothy Roberts points out that 10 percent of the slave population by 1860 was classified as "mulatto": most of these children, she asserts, were the result of white men forcing themselves on enslaved women. Rape was used as a weapon to subjugate the entire black community, continuing into the twentieth century, when the Ku Klux Klan used the rape of black women as a violent means of intimidation.

Meanwhile, the rape of a white woman by a black man was a capital offense. Black men were frequently lynched for the slightest sexual insinuation toward a white woman, as in the famous case of Emmett Till. In 1955, Till, a fourteen-year-old African American from Chicago, traveled to Mississippi to visit his family. There, he allegedly whistled at Carolyn Bryant, a twenty-one-year-old white mother of two. Bryant's husband, Roy, and Roy's half-brother J. W. Milam, dragged Till into the woods, beat and shot him, tied a one-hundred-pound cotton gin fan around his neck with barbed wire, and threw him into the Tallahatchie River.

Roy Bryant and J. W. Milam's trial took place after Mamie Till Bradley, Emmett's mother, insisted on an open casket at his funeral and solicited the support of the NAACP in creating a national outcry around his death. The trial featured competing stereotypes: Mamie Till as a single black mother, incompetent and incapable, and Carolyn Bryant as the woman deeply wronged. To garner sympathy, Mamie Till Bradley had to render her humanity visible. As historian Ruth Feldstein writes, she had "to emerge as protective of Emmett, yet not emasculating; fashionable and well-groomed, yet not ostentatious and luxury-laden; hardworking, yet not ambitious; and 'universal' enough to attract the sympathy of whites without distancing herself from the black community." She was largely successful at this, arriving everywhere flanked by men, insisting that she'd raised her son "correctly."

But Carolyn Bryant by her mere existence evoked greater sympathy. Mamie Till Bradley never had a chance. As Feldstein explains, the defense turned the trial into a referendum on the white nuclear family, and the white nuclear family always wins. The all-male jury deliberated for sixty-seven minutes before delivering a verdict of not guilty. Segregationist southern publications at the time described it as a "happy ending," and a "signal for Roy Bryant and his half brother J. W. Milam to kiss their wives." The women— "each the mother of two small sons"—were "smiling radiantly," and the men lit cigars.

As black journalist and feminist Ida B. Wells put it, "White men used their ownership of the body of white females as a terrain on which to lynch the black male." Bell hooks described the hierarchy that endures in American life today: "white men first, white women second, black men third, black women last." "The rape of a white woman by a black man," hooks wrote, was "seen as infinitely worse than if thousands of black women [were] raped by one white man."

The Victorian era cemented white women's status as ideal mothers and solidified black women's reproduction as a threat and a foil to that of white women. Black women's motherhood was seen as other and pathological. It became both a way of instigating white women to conform to gender and racial norms, and a tool that white women could use to negotiate greater power from white men. "Natural," iconic white mothers were to be delicate, demure, frail, weaker and humbler and less intelligent than men yet simultaneously responsible for their moral development. There was little room in this ideal for a white working-class woman, although she could draw on it if necessary, as Carolyn Bryant did during Emmett Till's trial. There was no room at all for black women. Angela Davis writes, "Judged by the evolving nineteenth-century ideology of femininity . . . Black women were practically anomalies." The rigid norms that sent white women into hysteria or that inspired their weeks-long internments on diets of soft foods were created out of a racial narrative: what historian Laura Briggs has called a "doubled discourse," in which white women were "weak, frail, and nervous," while non-white and poor women were "strong, hardy, and prolifically fertile." Obstetrics and gynecology emerged as a field in response to these categories: white women were to be cured of "uterine disease"—convinced to stop studying or writing novels and instead to have babies—while black women's bodies were to be exploited for scientific and medical experimentation.

White women's hysteria was peaking in the late nineteenth and early twentieth centuries, while the United States was establishing colonies in Hawaii, Cuba, the Philippines, and Puerto Rico, wresting vast swaths of western land from Mexico, and enacting Jim Crow legislation across the South. Immigration was also at a high point. The theory of cultural evolutionism, which posited that human groups evolved through a series of stages from "Savage" or "Barbarian" to "Civilized," emerged out of the race anxiety of American elites and dominated scientific discourse. Hysteria fit right into this theory by depicting white women as excessively civilized; they represented the peak of what human groups might achieve, and in fact they might have tipped a little too far past the desirable point of refinement and were now so delicate they could hardly even pick themselves up off the daybed, much less have sex. "Savage" women, meanwhile—a group that could include natives of colonized countries, black women, and poor Appalachian women—were seen as hypersexual and as able to give birth easily and without complaint.

Scientists in the United States obsessed over the pathology of hysteria, railing against the evils of women's education and confiscating women's notebooks and pens, while European imperialists returning from Africa displayed black women's genitals in museums. These two fascinations—with "over-civilization" on one hand and "savagery" on the other—took on eugenic overtones: if white women didn't have children, their race would be endangered.

A serialized study of childbirth published in the *American Journal of Obstetrics* from 1880 to 1882 by a male author concluded that among "primitive peoples" in the United States—a group that included African Americans, Mexicans, Native Americans, and Appalachian whites—labor "may be characterized as short and easy," rarely lasting more than a few hours and with few complications. Meanwhile this founding member of the American Gynecological Association claimed that while white women suffered from "the so-called blessings of wealth and refinement," black women and Irish immigrant women merrily went about heavy physical labor in good health, immune to "uterine diseases."

George Beard—the neurologist who is credited with popularizing the term "neurasthenia," a blanket diagnosis that referred to virtually any psychological ailment in women and included physical symptoms like heart palpitations and headaches—asserted that women in Africa, Asia, and Latin America did not suffer from hysteria. This pseudo-scientific depiction of non-white and poor women as being somehow immune to pain and mental suffering justified their use in scientific experiments. If black women were closer to animals on an imagined scale of cultural evolution, then performing experimental gynecological surgeries or involuntary sterilizations on them was not of the same consequence as it would be for a white woman.

This gendered and racial discourse prevailed, in sometimes subtle and sometimes insidious ways, throughout the twentieth and into the twenty-first century. Black women's procreation, framed as abundant and threatening, was pitted against that of white women, framed as precious and imperiled. Medical, governmental, and social interventions to curb the former, pathologizing black women and excluding them from motherhood, simultaneously enshrined the latter, rendering motherhood the most valued and important identity for white women.

The experience of many American black women, who must perpetually fight against the assumption of pathology and accusations of wrongdoing, should reveal to white women the oppressive illusion that they can and must get it right—that, as "supermoms" or Insta-mommy-bloggers or crunchy homeschoolers, they just might be able to beat the culture at its own game. The game is rigged: mothers never win.

———————

Whitney and Charles ultimately decided to hold back their trip to the Philippines. Edie was not available for this pregnancy, but she recommended another midwife around her age who had as much experience. That midwife had several apprentices, and as Whitney talked at length during her appointments, they would chime in with their thoughts and experiences, a setup that felt like a mini–group therapy. Whitney wasn't quite as connected to this midwife, but she felt even more empowered in this pregnancy than she had when carrying Isaac. Only at one point did she start Googling with paranoia, researching how the spacing of pregnancies can affect miscarriage rates, but she quickly pulled herself out of the nosedive.

At thirty-seven weeks, in the heat of a North Carolina summer, she took her kids on a walk through the neighborhood to a park. Her husband had the car, so she pushed her two boys uphill in the stroller in the stultifying southern heat, feeling proud. She never would have done that with her other pregnancies.

Baby Maverick came in a rush at thirty-nine weeks and six days. Whitney was lying down, and she needed to pee, and again, the instant after she'd peed it was *BOOM*. She made it back to bed, saying, "Charles, call the midwife." He equivocated—she puts on a whispery voice here—"Oh really, are you sure"—so she just stood up and called the midwife herself. "You really sound calm," the midwife said. "Are you sure?" Yes, Whitney was sure. Her boys woke up, and she went to the kitchen to make them oatmeal. There, she collapsed on her knees from the pain. "Mommy," Samuel asked, "what's going on with you?"

"Samuel," Whitney said, "I'm about to have the baby."

She made her way back to bed, where she lay on her side, trying to work against gravity. One of the midwife's apprentices showed up. "She looked a little shell-shocked," Whitney explained with a laugh. She was rubbing Whitney's back, saying hold on, hold on, *hold on* as Whitney let out low, deep moans. Whitney felt like her pelvis was splitting open. Another midwife who lived on the next street and was friends with Whitney's midwife came over to help. She told Whitney, "You'd better get in the pool or you're having this baby on the bed." Whitney moved to the pool. Charles's hot morning breath was in her face. Samuel shouted, *Mommy, you pooped in the water!* This time, she was so in tune with her body, without any fear, that she could feel Maverick vibrating down the birth canal. Descending, descending with exquisite pain, and then, before her midwife had time to arrive, less than half an hour after labor had begun, Maverick flew out in a rush in the water, and they swept her up, unwrapping the cord from her neck and placing her on Whitney's chest.

"That was it," she told me. "Maverick was here. And it was beautiful." They wiped Whitney down. She didn't tear; there was no blood in the water. They changed the sheets and she lay down in bed with her baby. "I wish," she told me, "I had thought about all the crazy things that I was scared to do, because in that moment I was determined to get them done." She felt limitless. Fearless. "There's absolutely nothing holding me back from doing what I aspire to do or from [being] who I aspired to be. It felt like legit triumph. Like winning an NCAA championship or an NBA championship. I won, I made it to the end, and not only that, I had a safe delivery that was not conventional. Something about that made me feel so in control. . . . Literature and the current culture around maternal health makes it seem, or as I interpret as, women are so *not* in control. I felt the opposite. Like I'd owned it."

For the next several years, Whitney stayed home with her children. She breastfed Maverick just as she had her two boys. She finally sought therapy for her first pregnancy experience. She weaved in and out of a borderline depression, feeling criticized for her choices: most of the men she knew wondered why she wasn't going back to work. "Having done something totally miraculous," she told me, "I'm still not good enough." Her dad reminded her that Google had once reached out to her about software development. What was she doing with her life? *You're out of the game,* Whitney heard. "Everyone who knows me knows I'm not the type to sit on my hands. There's not a lazy bone in my body. I have an excuse, a really good one: I just had three kids in three years."

Whitney stuck with her decision. "I want to stay home with my kids. . . . It wasn't a good financial decision but I stood my ground. I look back now and I know I did the right thing." She told me, "I needed to know and see and learn about them, but learn about myself, too." She had never felt like a natural mother, and she didn't while she was staying home: "I had those moments, but they weren't consistent. They were few and far between." But that was almost beside the point. She did it. Looking back at this time, she said to me, "I made it," and then she was quiet, thinking about this, before she added a soft, firm "Yeah." She had made her own choices, owned them, come through them, raised her babies, transformed herself.

Sometimes, Whitney told me, she'd get looks as she was wheeling around three kids by herself while her husband was at work. "These little microaggressions—'Are you eighteen, are you nineteen?' No, I'm thirty!" I asked her whether she felt that most of that came from white people. She equivocated a bit.

"My midwives are white and I'm just hyper-aware, most of the care has been white, so it's hard. . . ." she said. "You almost get tired of trying to prove what you feel like you have to prove." She had gotten used to constantly referring to her set of credentials— where she'd gone to school, the fact that she was married—because she could tell it made a difference. I thought of the writer Dani McClain on the podcast *The Longest Shortest Time,* explaining how she wore her engagement ring to all of her prenatal appointments, how she was very careful with how she dressed and did her hair.

"I would have loved loved loved to have a black home birth," Whitney told me, with a gust of emotion. "The one thing I didn't get from the two white [midwives]—they didn't really connect with me, other than the baby and stuff we had very little to vibe on." Her sister had a midwife of color, a Pakistani woman, and "they got the same jokes, it's different." While she loved her midwives, there was a certain place she could not go with them, a certain guardedness she still had to have.

Today, Whitney is working to design an app for pregnant women of color. She isn't sure yet how it will look, but it will involve integrated care with midwives and doulas and advocates, and it would attempt to "reintroduce joy and sacredness in this time through technology. To re-educate us." The goal, as Whitney explained, would be to "equip women with the tools they need to own their pregnancies. So if I'm a black woman and I'm meeting a white male obstetrician who's feeding me B.S. I know enough about myself and my body to be able to say something." She wants to draw forth "a collective of wisdom from birth workers," wisdom that had been lost as midwifery became a predominately white field. "We're looking at generations of mothers who are no longer able to instill that wisdom into their daughters! We're losing." Many of her friends had harrowing experiences of pregnancy and childbirth. "We're looking at educated women from top-tier universities, and we're looking at traumatic birth experiences," she said. Others were just starting to have kids, and would come to her: *What's this ache? What's this pain?* She found it ironic that she was the one they came to when she'd been as hands-off as possible with her own pregnancies.

"In our country," Whitney said, "all the articles are doom and gloom." Whitney's sister was pregnant and talked constantly about her fear. Her sister, a product designer at Facebook, pointed out that it didn't matter how much money she made, it didn't matter that she had a degree, it didn't matter that she wasn't high-risk because of age or health or any other factors. Black women are 243 percent more likely than white women to die of pregnancy and childbirth-related causes. Whitney's sister had been inspired by her example to have a home birth with a midwife and to hire a doula. But still—she knew the risks.

By the time we were wrapping up our conversations, Whitney's app had a website: the-renee.com. Renee was inspired by the French term for rebirth.

Whitney began to lead "jam sessions," in which she invited a handful of women of color "who've experienced pregnancy and have an opinion about it" to come hang out and talk. The idea was to begin drawing on this collective wisdom, to design a product that was informed by the people she was making it for, and to create a community for them.

The first jam session was held in Durham, where she lives. There were five women: a physician, a doula, a vegan chef, a writer, and a waitress. Whitney asked the women to go through their experiences of pregnancy, and as they talked she listened for "pain points": *The doctor gave me the wrong information; I had an ectopic pregnancy; I had a miscarriage.* Whitney scribbled them on sticky notes and stuck them up on a whiteboard. By the end, she had sixty or seventy. Together, the women narrowed them all down to five. They stood staring at them, and one woman noted that the common denominator was a lack of support.

Whitney gave everyone a sheet of paper and asked them to draw or write or convey in some way the solutions that they felt "would help or would change the lack of support for women of color through pregnancy, postpartum, birth." As Whitney watched, "people were drawing out amazing things, like re-education, and integrated care, more presence of doulas." They had a whole whiteboard full of solutions. Whitney gave everyone little sticky dots to go vote on the solutions they felt would work best. And when they were done and had all placed their dots, there was an overwhelming consensus. There were scattered dots on a bunch of different solutions, but a constellation on just one: prayer.

When Whitney said this, I got chills. I prayed throughout my pregnancy, even though I had been raised without religion and had never been religious. I thought I was praying because I was worried, crazy, or desperate. But I kept praying long after I gave birth, when I felt calmer and more stable. I would run to the top of a hill on my parents' farm and stand still for a few minutes and let myself gaze up to the left at an oak, to the right at a poplar, and pray. It felt like my small self was an energy running into the ground and merging with something larger. It felt like letting go. This was clearly not the solution to all of my worry, but it felt paradigm-shifting. I never talked about doing this, perhaps because I didn't take it seriously, because it didn't fit into any cost-benefit risk-analysis matrix. It was about faith, about believing in myself and in women.

At the jam session, Whitney was floored. She laughed and said, "I don't know what I'm doing here." She was completely out of her depth.

The group of women gathered was not religious. They were all of different backgrounds, with different incomes and experiences. They described praying as about believing in a higher power and having faith, faith in their own ability to go through pregnancy, their own ability to be there for themselves if and when the system failed them; they described it as a force they could channel to uplift themselves. "But it was also interesting," Whitney said, "that everyone agreed that prayer is not only praying for yourself, but is being able to do this for other people."

She had no idea how to address prayer in her app, but she was excited, and she was grateful. In the next month, she held more jam sessions in Raleigh, New York, and Boston.

Whitney recently accepted a job, her first since her babies were born, with a San Francisco start-up. I asked her how she'd balance the job and the app, and she told me with no hesitation or equivocation, "The job is just to fund [Renee]. I don't feel like waiting for VCs who see a woman of color, a woman, a *mom*, who don't want to give me [money]. I don't have time for it. There are way too many people out here who are hurting all day every day."

Listening to women's stories could be overwhelming. "The issues," Whitney told me, "are almost too big to swallow." But she firmly believes that "when we focus on the women who are struggling, when we focus on the really high numbers of black and Native women, we're taking care of all women."

That, Whitney said, is her calling.

Women's struggle for rights and reproductive justice in the United States has historically been divided along racial tracks. White women advocated for a wider array of choices to be made available—for abortions, fertility drugs and options, birth control. Black women fought to wrest their bodies from government control and to obtain even the most basic standards of support and care.

Birth control, while embraced as a welcome necessity by all women, has often justified cultural ideologies and state policies that limit and control black women's reproductive freedom. Margaret Sanger, the celebrated feminist leader who devoted her life to providing accessibility to birth control, began her quest arduously committed to the emancipation of women. Working as a public health nurse in New York in the early twentieth century, Sanger witnessed women sinking under the burden of having too many children. She witnessed botched abortions. The Comstock Law of 1873 made sending any information via mail about contraceptive devices a crime. (The United States wouldn't rule until 1965 that prohibiting married couples from using birth control was unconstitutional, and it wouldn't lift the prohibition on use among single people until 1971.) Sanger was fiery and devoted and took great personal risks. In 1916, she founded the first contraceptive clinic in the United States. Ten days after its opening in Brooklyn, the clinic was raided, and Sanger was arrested and ultimately released on bail. She was later arrested again and sentenced to thirty days "in the workhouse" for distributing contraceptives.

Sanger struggled to find support among contemporary feminists, who cringed at the mention of women's sexuality. Men, meanwhile, were skeptical of birth control, thinking it would encourage lasciviousness and prevent white women from bearing children. Margaret Sanger found her allies and a set of powerful arguments for birth control in the eugenics movement.

Eugenics swept into popularity in the early twentieth century on a tide of pseudo-scientific literature about the supposed innate biological superiority of the Nordic race. As Dorothy Roberts details, the president of the American Psychological Association, the resident anthropologist of the American Museum of Natural History, and a cabal of Ivy League academics published studies and literature asserting the inferiority of all other races, from the "Alpine and Mediterranean type" to the Negro. One book, by University of Illinois professor Dr. G. Frank Lydston, which had the "skull of a Negro murderer" on its title page, advocated for the forced sterilization of criminals, epileptics, and "the insane." Another described racial intermarriage as a "social and racial crime of the first magnitude." It was hailed as recommended reading for all Americans by President Theodore Roosevelt.

Margaret Sanger did not, as Roberts and other scholars have argued, agree with the core eugenicist notion that biology led to unfitness, that the poor were poor because of heritable and immutable characteristics tied to their race. But she did believe that excessive fertility led to social problems like disease and criminality. She thus promoted, as Roberts explains, "two of the most perverse tenets of eugenic thinking: that social problems are caused by reproduction of the socially disadvantaged and that their childbearing should therefore be deterred."

Sanger's firsthand experience of the devastating effects of uncontrolled fertility—poverty, hunger, desperation—dovetailed with eugenic ideologies of racial fitness. Sanger started a foundation, the American Birth Control League, that worked hand in hand with eugenicists to finance projects to distribute birth control to poor black people, and promoted rhetoric that explicitly referenced white mothers' "responsibility to the race" in bringing children into the world. The result was that, as Angela Davis framed it, "What was demanded as a 'right' for the privileged came to be interpreted as a 'duty' for the poor." In 1919, Margaret Sanger declared, "More children from the fit, less from the unfit—that is the chief issue of birth control."

This campaign for birth control was enacted in lockstep with a series of eugenic measures that targeted immigrants, poor people, the institutionalized, and people of color in other ways. By 1913, twenty-four states and the District of Columbia had laws that prohibited marriage by "genetically defective" people: these included, as Dorothy Roberts listed them, "epileptics, imbeciles, paupers, drunkards, criminals, and the feebleminded."

Beginning in 1907, many states passed involuntary sterilization laws, which allowed for anyone deemed socially unfit to be sterilized without his or her consent. The Nazis later modeled their sterilization laws on these American eugenic decrees.

In 1927, in the case of *Buck* v. *Bell*, the U.S. Supreme Court gave the green light to doctors and states to undertake the involuntary sterilization of people deemed unfit to reproduce. The case centered on Carrie Buck, a young white woman who had been committed to the Virginia State Colony for Epileptics and Feebleminded by her adoptive parents after being raped at seventeen and becoming pregnant. The colony approved her sterilization, and the Supreme Court upheld it, arguing, in the words of Justice Oliver Wendell Holmes, "It is better for all the world if . . . society can prevent those who are manifestly unfit from continuing their kind."

The court's decision inspired an enthusiastic embrace of sterilization as a cure-all social policy. Thirty states passed compulsory sterilization laws in the wake of *Buck* v. *Bell*, extending their application from the infirm and institutionalized to any young women deemed unfit to be mothers. Many women earned their "unfit" categorization because they had sex outside of marriage. They would be labeled "feebleminded," admitted to an institution for sterilization, and subsequently discharged. Roberts quotes the superintendent of the Massachusetts School for Feeble-minded Children declaring that feeblemindedness in girls had to do with sexuality rather than intelligence: the girls were "often bright and attractive," but if left to reproduce freely would "become irresponsible sources of corruption and debauchery in the communities where they lived." One report on sterilizations in California found that a popular impetus to sterilize a white girl was her failure to display "the normal aversions . . . to a colored man who was perhaps nice to her."

It did not take long, in a country that had since its inception depicted blackness as aberrant and less than fully human, for compulsory sterilization practices to target black populations. Long after the eugenics movement had been discredited because of its adoption by and association with Nazi Germany, its underlying logic and policies persisted via mass sterilization campaigns that began in force in southern hospitals, which had opened up to black patients after the dismantling of Jim Crow laws, and in prisons. Male patients in these institutions were not only sterilized; many were castrated, with the justification that it rendered them docile.

As late as the 1960s and 1970s, black women were given hysterectomies as a form of birth control and social punishment for being poor or on Medicaid or having illegitimate children, and to provide doctors with surgical training. These procedures were performed by doctors operating under the tacit and sometimes overt encouragement of the government. Roberts cites the example of a 1958 bill introduced by Representative David H. Glass into the Mississippi Legislature, which would have allowed courts to order the sterilization of single mothers. The bill passed in the House but failed in the Senate. Similar bills were presented elsewhere. In Louisiana and Mississippi, it was against the law to have more than two illegitimate children.

The reproduction of poor people of color was represented as the cause of all social ills, with the assumption that if these people could be forcibly prevented from having children, those ills would be cured. Angela Davis cites the example of a Health, Education, and Welfare pamphlet distributed to Native American families. The pamphlet contained two sketches: one of a family with ten children and one horse, and the other of a family with one child and ten horses. "The drawings are supposed to imply," Davis wrote, "that more children mean more poverty and fewer children mean wealth. As if the ten horses owned by the one-child family had been magically conjured up by birth control and sterilization surgery." By 1976, at least a quarter of all Native American women of childbearing age had been sterilized.

By 1970, two hundred thousand U.S. women had been sterilized; by 1980, that number was seven hundred thousand. Most of these women were women of color. In the South, after women were subjected to postpartum sterilizations or sterilized without their knowledge or consent after entering the hospital for other reasons, a hysterectomy became known as a "Mississippi appendectomy." Fannie Lou Hamer, the leader of the Mississippi Freedom Democratic Party, went to the hospital for the removal of a uterine tumor in 1961, and, without her knowledge or consent, was given a complete hysterectomy. Later, in a speech in Washington, D.C., she stated that 60 percent of black women in Sunflower County, Mississippi, had been sterilized without their consent.

The situation was hardly better in the North; Roberts writes that in 1972, a group of medical students at Boston City Hospital blew the whistle on their colleagues, claiming that hysterectomies were frequently and unnecessarily performed on black women without their knowledge or consent. The *Boston Globe* published a front-page story on the issue, citing the example of a teenage girl who was twelve weeks pregnant and came to the hospital for an abortion; a hysterectomy was performed instead. When a medical student asked why the operation had been done, the resident explained that the doctor wanted the experience.

The director of obstetrics and gynecology at a New York City municipal hospital reported, "In most major teaching hospitals in New York City it is the unwritten policy to do elective hysterectomies on poor black and Puerto Rican women, with minimal indications, to train residents." This was also true in Los Angeles, according to a study of Los Angeles County Hospital that concluded doctors were "cavalierly subjecting women, most of them poor and Black, to surgical sterilization." Some doctors would also threaten to take away black women's Medicaid benefits, refuse to deliver their babies, and deny them medical treatment unless they agreed to be sterilized.

In 1973, the Southern Poverty Law Center filed a class action lawsuit in federal court demanding a ban on the use of federal funds for involuntary sterilizations. The suit was filed on behalf of twelve- and fourteen-year-old sisters Minnie Lee and Mary Alice Relf, the youngest of six children in a black family living in Montgomery, Alabama. Nurses from the federally funded Montgomery Community Action agency had asked Mrs. Relf for permission to admit the sisters to the hospital for injections of the contraceptive Depo-Provera. Mrs. Relf was illiterate and signed the consent form with an X. The girls were admitted and sterilized. When the family found out, they turned to the Southern Poverty Law Center for help.

A judge ultimately banned the use of federal funds for involuntary sterilizations and the practice of coercing women to consent to sterilization by threatening to withhold treatment or deny Medicaid benefits. The district court declared that the regulations of the HEW—now the Department of Health and Human Services—on sterilization were "arbitrary and unreasonable"; the court demanded new regulations and mandated the informed consent of patients.

Meanwhile, white women found it almost impossible to obtain sterilizations. While one group of women activists responded to the massive problem of forced sterilization by forming the Committee to End Sterilization Abuse, developing a set of guidelines for health care practitioners—including requiring informed consent, a thirty-day waiting period between signing the consent form and the procedure, and the prohibition of soliciting consent immediately after childbirth or abortion or under threat—another group of activists, and the one whose fight would dominate the national conversation, pushed to eliminate any roadblocks to voluntary sterilization. This group, which came to include the National Abortion Rights Action League (NARAL) and the American Civil Liberties Union (ACLU), sued hospitals for refusing to perform elective sterilizations. The plaintiffs were white women whose doctors had denied them sterilizations.

The fact that these two battles could be waged simultaneously, and at cross-purposes—one to make sterilization easier and remove barriers, the other to put standards in place to restrict the caprices of doctors—speaks to the enormous gap between black and white experiences of motherhood in the United States. Dorothy Roberts writes, "Black women's struggle against the most degrading repression has been left out of the official story of reproductive rights in America. But it is their struggle that highlights the poverty of current notions of reproductive freedom. It is also their struggle that can lead to a more radical vision of reproductive justice."

In the United States, Roberts declares, we have a negative view of reproductive liberty: that is, we recognize it as the right to be free from state interference in "private" decisions, individual choices. We don't see it as a positive liberty: one that obliges the state to provide the resources necessary to prevent procreation or to promote healthy mothering. In this way, we erase social context and government and political responsibility, imbuing "choice" with an almost mystical power, as if it were a wand a woman could wave. As I've talked to so many women about their stories of pregnancy and birth, I've been faced again and again with the reality that choice is one of the greatest American illusions. Americans may be able to choose among fifty-seven brands of potato chips, but they are often hardly able to choose their health care provider, therapist, or whether to work or stay at home with their children.

The midwife Jennie Joseph was born and raised in England and moved to the United States at age thirty. She now runs pioneering birthing centers and clinics for low-income women in Florida. Joseph labeled this illusion of choice a "cognitive dissonance." She told me, "We have duped the American woman, all women, into this confused way of thinking about their reproductive health and life and their agency inside of it." Women spend all day worrying about their babies, about what they might have done wrong, about getting seen by a doctor, about getting seen by the right doctor, about "good insurance"—she laughs at this, incredulous—and the whole system is, in her words, crazy. "Then we've also undermined it by having it be [the women's] fault that they're depressed and anxious and overwhelmed and confused."

Joseph told me she had struggled with endometriosis for a long time as an adult, and an OB she worked with as a nurse told her he could cure it with surgery. Four surgeries later, she was in so much pain she needed a hysterectomy. She was thirty, married, with a three-year-old. While the doctor was performing the hysterectomy, he decided to also remove her ovaries, without her consent. She woke up without them. "Both ovaries. Gone," she told me. She went into menopause at thirty-one. "Blindsided." The experience practically destroyed her marriage. "The levels of depression, anxiety, misery, pain," she said. "What do you do with all that?"

Most women feel isolated, with few policies or governmental programs to support motherhood (particularly working motherhood), and few if any systems in place to address maternal mental health. "We've lost any sense of our power around our bodies," Joseph told me. We often talk about choice as if it is the be-all and end-all, as if it is something possessed by certain women and not others, as if it is a simple solution, when all of our choices exist within a warped system that denies both maternal power and maternal vulnerability. "Reproductive freedom," Roberts writes, "is a matter of social justice, not individual choice."

All our fates are connected even as we live in this matrix that creates risk and then outsources responsibility, that celebrates inconsequential private "choices" instead of real, collective liberation. "This system," Joseph told me, "is so entrenched in these original ways of being, and we're holding on to them because they're so lucrative, and we're all miserable."

In an essay entitled "Racism and Patriarchy in the Meaning of Motherhood," Dorothy Roberts concluded, "In late twentieth-century America more and more white mothers will occupy social positions that were defined by Black mothers." That is, she foresaw, more mothers would have their reproductive rights curtailed and infringed upon, more would struggle to survive as single mothers, more would flail in isolation, more would labor to meet an ideal that becomes increasingly unobtainable.

By recognizing that a lack of choice on one side and an abundance of often superficial choices on the other are reflective of the same core problem, we get a glimpse of the scope of the trap and the reality that radical connections between women are the only way through and out.

SAMANTHA

7

A Woman's Role

Samantha is the only person I know, and perhaps one of only a handful of people alive, who voluntarily moved from San Diego to small-town Ohio. Her mom was concerned about her choices. "What if you meet the man of your dreams and he's from Ohio?" she asked. Samantha did meet the man of her dreams, and he was from Ohio. They settled in Steubenville, which Samantha loved and found beautiful.

Samantha was eager to be a mom. She waited to get pregnant until she was in the last semester of her senior year of college. Then, she went straight from being a full-time student to being a full-time mom. Her first daughter, Sophie, rarely cried and learned early on to entertain herself. Settling happily into motherhood, Samantha got pregnant a little over a year later with her second daughter, Cora, who was born in February 2016, in the middle of winter. Cora was not so easy. When she was upset, she screamed a full-throttle, angry scream. It set Samantha on edge. She had believed that she was a decent mom, but with Cora she started questioning herself. She resented this new baby and thought, *This is your fault, you're a difficult kid*. Then she was flooded with guilt and chastised herself. *It's me. I should be able to handle it, and I can't*.

With Sophie, she had gotten irritated, but "there was never this element of rage, where it was almost unbearable." Motherhood began to slide toward the edge of the manageable. Samantha felt that she was endlessly having to finagle solutions to perpetually shifting problems. She became terrified of falling down the stairs while holding Cora, and she would squeeze the baby too tightly. One day, she put the TV on for Sophie so that she could race upstairs and feed Cora a bottle, but Cora kept refusing to take it. Sophie grew increasingly impatient and fussy downstairs as Cora denied the bottle upstairs, until finally, frustrated, furious, wondering how she'd ever thought she could manage two children, Samantha threw the bottle against the wall. It exploded. Cora screamed. Samantha stood in the bedroom in shock, pummeled by guilt, wondering what had happened to her, milk streaming down the walls.

Inner dialogues stormed through Samantha's mind during the long hours she was home alone with her babies, until they began to give way to what she thought of at the time as "visions." These were not mirages or delusions or hallucinations, but intrusive thoughts. Samantha, however, didn't have the vocabulary to describe them as such at the time. She defined thoughts as intentions—just one shade away from action—and there was nothing intentional or wanted about what was popping into her head. So she labeled them visions. The first came one time when Cora screamed without stopping. Samantha and her husband had bought a little teepee for Sophie to play in, and to flee the noise Sophie had retreated in there with a book. Samantha could not figure out what Cora wanted. She tried nursing and rocking on endless repeat. Into Samantha's head popped a vivid image of grabbing a sofa pillow and covering Cora's face, "not because I wanted to hurt her but just because I wanted the screaming to stop." Instantly, Samantha recoiled from herself. She was terrified. It was "like an out-of-body experience." *I'm a bad mom,* she thought, *but I'm not a murderer.* Like the vast majority of women who suffer from intrusive thoughts, Samantha immediately saw them as alien, absurd, and upsetting.

It was clear to her that what was happening was outside of the realm of normal postpartum worry, but she had no idea how to define it. It couldn't be postpartum depression: that was when women killed themselves and their families. She even went and looked up PPD to be sure. Postpartum depression, she read, meant that a mother didn't want to be around her baby, had no energy, didn't want to eat or interact. That wasn't her. "I was going to the park, eating better, exercising more, getting out to see friends—because everybody said you need to get out—going out of my way to make playdates!" She was screened with the EPDS at her OB's office at six weeks and her score was not significant. She wasn't having trouble sleeping or dreading events.

At night, as she rocked and rocked while Cora screamed, she'd have thoughts of throwing her daughter against a wall. She was so shaken that she said to her husband, "I think I'm actually going crazy."

On the day Samantha realized she needed help, she was trying to get the girls ready to go to the park. Cora was screaming, and Sophie came up to ask her to put a show on TV. She told Sophie to hold on a sec. Sophie grew more insistent: *Mom, Mom, Mom.*

I can't do it, Samantha thought. She didn't hit. She didn't yell. She didn't cry. She did exactly what she was supposed to do: she called her doctor.

On the phone, she explained that she was upset, that she'd had a baby three months ago, and that she thought she was having symptoms of postpartum depression. At the hospital where she'd given birth, they'd told her that if she had any struggles they'd start her on an antidepressant and go from there.

The doctor's office told her to come in. She asked her husband's aunt to come over and watch the girls. Samantha thought the appointment might involve her crying, which could scare them. "I'll be back in an hour," she told the aunt.

Motherhood is both the dominant weapon of patriarchy and the chink in its armor, by dint of a single fact: men cannot be mothers. The edifice of oppression that boxes mothers into a stifling, isolated, fear-ridden niche, warning them to stay calm and gentle and quiet, offering syrupy promises of fulfillment, is constructed upon men's desire to contain what they cannot possess.

Our contemporary ideas about motherhood and its relationship to femininity have been firmly entrenched by a long, arduous, and violent campaign—sometimes intentional, sometimes unconscious—to confine and usurp mothers' power. Like most historical processes perpetuated by those who hold the power, the drive to seize mothers' fundamental authority has over the centuries accrued the taint of inevitability, of simple biological destiny. Peeling back the layers of how this unfolded, it becomes possible to imagine a different kind of motherhood, fierce and frightening, free and bold, of female camaraderie and knowledge that could reshape cultural, social, and political paradigms.

Paleolithic cultures from France to Siberia to Mesoamerica worshipped religious icons of naked women in late stages of pregnancy. These icons can be seen in museums of ancient art: vessels shaped like pregnant women, with voluptuous bellies and breasts. In ancient Mesoamerica, caves were imagined as the origin of life and the abodes of ancestors, and were compared to wombs or vaginas. Paleolithic peoples carved pregnant women holding bison horns out of the limestone walls of caves, built shrines to them, and buried their dead in the fetal position. "Vagina symbols," writes psychologist and author Shari Thurer in *The Myths of Motherhood*, "may have been the phallic symbols of the Paleolithic."

Pregnancy must have seemed an awesome and formidable force, an invocation of the divine in everyday life, and as such inspired religious fervor. Mothers had to be appeased, worshipped, carefully attended. They might bring forth new life, or they might unleash havoc and ruin. This worship was not the vain kind of mother worship we know today, saccharine and empty like the adoration of kittens. It was born of genuine fear: mothers were seen to have a power both exquisite and terrible. Thurer writes that there was a strong association "of the divine woman with the mysteries of death."

Over time, as human cultures grew more sedentary with the advent of agriculture, these Paleolithic icons morphed into goddesses of the ancient world: Kali, the Hindu "black" goddess of death and time and sexuality; Isis, the ancient Egyptian goddess of love and fertility and death; Ishtar, the Mesopotamian goddess of fertility and war. The whimsy and ruthlessness of these mothers was unparalleled; they were the terror of creation personified. "Just as they were associated with fertility," explains Thurer, "so were they associated with death and decay. They were terrible, and, worse, they were terribly necessary." Men had to mollify and appease them. But as villages evolved into cities, men took to the plow and ox, women were hemmed into household spaces, and a hierarchical social structure emerged, male gods came to subjugate and slay these volatile goddesses. There was, in Thurer's words, "a shift in magic, ritual, and imagery from the womb to the phallus." The phallic was imbued with the dark and the light, while the womb was another daily task of women.

The elemental facts of motherhood hadn't changed, but men came up with ways to co-opt and suppress it. Elaborate taboos developed around pregnancy and menstruation. Menstruation in particular was seen as possessing devilish capacities: all the world's major religions have at some point depicted not only the menstruating woman's blood but also the air surrounding her and anything she touches as dangerous. In many religions, including Catholicism, the Eastern Orthodox Church, and the Shinto religion in Japan, women were forbidden from entering churches or temples while menstruating, and in the former two she could not receive communion. A 2017 essay in *Aeon* magazine entitled "The Taboo of Menstruation" quoted Roman author Pliny the Elder, born in A.D. 23: "If a woman strips herself naked while she is menstruating, and walks round a field of wheat, the caterpillars, worms, beetles, and other vermin, will fall from off the ears of corn. . . .

Bees will forsake their hives if touched by a menstruous woman." This piece points out that the word *period* was not used in a television commercial until 1985.

The poet Judy Grahn has speculated that the blood rituals associated with men—from circumcision to Christ's seeping wounds—were attempts to hijack the frightening, innate power of menstruation.

Men have struggled to claim for themselves the reproductive powers they could not cordon off or suppress with taboos. For many millennia the central task of male thinkers and scientists who addressed human reproduction was to explain how pregnancy was actually the project of men. Aristotle wrote that the male sperm "cooks" female "residue" and creates the child. The ancient Greek playwright Aeschylus asserted that "the mother of the child that is called hers is not really its parent. She just nurses the seed that is planted within her by the child's true parent, the male." In the early Enlightenment, scientists declared that they'd made microscopic observations of fully formed human embryos inside of sperm. The woman was an incubator, a warm, dull animal belly in which a complex male project would unfold.

Darwinism built on and reinforced these claims. So radical and heretical in its assertion that humans were not simply created by God but evolved in response to their environments, Darwinism largely pinned women in place: weak, fawning, and hopelessly beholden to the project of carrying men's children. Darwin's theory posited that as men responded dynamically to their environments, competing to survive and outmaneuver one another, they also evolved literary and scientific masterworks and then built on the scaffolding of these masterworks to achieve higher greatness. Women, however, according to Darwin, were focused on the basic function of attracting men. He wrote, "there seems to me to be a great difficulty from the laws of inheritance, (if I understand these laws rightly) in [women] becoming the intellectual equals of man."

Each generation of men reinforced men's tendencies toward

brilliance and hearty exploration, and each generation of women reinforced the primal female desire to be noticed by a man. Darwin is celebrated as a genius; his ignorance of and unconcern for women's bodies is often forgotten or left out of his story. Darwin's French translator, Clémence Royer, entirely self-taught and the first woman scientist in France to be elected to a scientific society, wrote,

> Up until now science, like law, has been exclusively made by men and has considered woman too often an absolutely passive being, without instincts, passions, or her own interests; a purely plastic material that without resistance can take whatever form one wishes to give it; a living creature without personal conscience, without will, without inner resources to react against her instincts, her hereditary passions, or finally against the education that she receives and against the discipline to which she submits following law, customs, and public opinion.

———

At the doctor's office, the nurse practitioner gave Samantha a test. It was the EPDS, which Samantha recognized. This was when she realized how delicately she would have to play her cards. *There is a spectrum,* she thought, *between having the baby blues and being a homicidal maniac.* She did not want to place herself too close to either end. She was disturbed by her symptoms and recognized them as symptoms, and she wanted treatment, but she did not want to be treated like someone who was out of her mind. She sensed how hard it would be to hit that sweet spot, in which her illness would be taken seriously but wouldn't sound alarms that could plunge her life into chaos. She wanted it to be acknowledged with empathy, understanding, and the assumption that she was both a vulnerable human being and a competent woman and mother. She did not know then that the spectrum is much, much smaller than it appears. In many places it is not a spectrum at all, but an abyss: one step away from "normal" and you fall into the darkness of the system.

She worried over the conundrum of having already taken this screening and passed it, with none of the questions really registering her experience or concern. If she answered the same way she had last time, they might just tell her motherhood was hard and send her home. She had to find a way to use this ineffective tool as a cry for help. She needed her dart to land in exactly the right place.

The last question asked whether she had thoughts of hurting herself often, sometimes, or never. She circled "sometimes."

"This," Samantha told me, "is how I got myself into trouble."

The nurse came back and scanned the exam, then stopped and read it again, carefully. She asked for clarification about the last question: was Samantha thinking of hurting herself? Samantha explained that she was having visions, and that they were very upsetting and she didn't want to act on them, which is why she wanted treatment. She was careful to use the word "visions," since thoughts sounded to her too premeditated and deliberate.

The nurse stood up and announced that she'd be right back, but before she left, she called in another nurse to stay in the room. A little alarm bell went off in Samantha's mind. Samantha waited silently with the second nurse. The doctor never came in. Instead, the first nurse came back and said, "I've called an ambulance, and they're going to take you to the ER."

Samantha tried to remain calm. She explained that she and her husband were young, they had two children, and they could not afford an unnecessary ambulance ride and an ER visit. The nurse was unwavering. Samantha would not leave the building, she said, unless it was in an ambulance. "This is normal," she told Samantha. "This is how we handle all these cases. I know it seems scary, but it's really, really routine."

Samantha felt this could not be right. At the same time, she had no idea what the norm was. She called her husband to tell him that she'd gone in to see the doctor about potential depression and was now being taken to the ER. He was both angry and concerned.

In the ambulance, the EMTs bombarded her with questions: *Have you hurt yourself? Are there wounds we have to address?* If she hadn't been so stressed, she might have found this funny. "No, no, no," she answered, "I came here expecting to walk out with a prescription for Zoloft." Where were her kids? the EMT asked. "I'm a responsible adult," she answered. "I found a babysitter."

At the ER, the nurse checking her in asked a similar set of questions: wounds, desire to hurt herself, history of suicidality. She was puzzled by Samantha's answers. "You don't seem suicidal to me," she said.

"That's because I'm not," Samantha replied. The nurse left to go talk with the EMT. When she returned, she was no longer friendly.

"They said you're suicidal," she insisted.

"I'm not suicidal!" Samantha struggled to restrain mounting frustration. "I went in for an appointment to talk about postpartum depression. How am I sitting in the ER right now?"

The nurse went to look for the doctor. Ages went by, in a hospital gown, in socks, not knowing what her children were doing, what was happening to her, why, if this was normal, and how could it be normal, but these people should know what they were doing, so maybe she should just go along with it, but something was off, why, and what should she do, what could she do? She'd been away for two or three hours when she'd told the aunt that she'd be an hour at max. Was Cora screaming? How would Cora eat?

When the doctor arrived, Samantha dissolved into tears. "I came seeking treatment and you aren't giving it to me," she half accused, half begged. "This is a waste of time."

The doctor became uneasy. "Being a mom is hard," she said. "Have you ever heard of Brooke Shields?" Samantha nodded. "She had postpartum depression," the doctor offered.

"Yes," Samantha said. "I think that's what I'm experiencing." She asked for a referral to a psychiatrist. But Brooke Shields was as far as the doctor's commiseration went. She too ran through the questions about self-harm and suicide, and when she'd heard Samantha's answers, she turned to the nurse and said, "Either she's one hundred percent fine, or she's lying."

Samantha pleaded, desperate at this point just to break free.

"Please," she begged the doctor, "just give me a referral and let me go home to my babies. It's been five hours!"

"Oh, you poor thing," the doctor said to her. Then, she left. Samantha sat in the room and sobbed. Her husband arrived and stood quietly by, unable to make eye contact with her. This, finally, forced her to pull herself together. "I need you to suck it up," she told him. "Shit is hitting the fan and I need you on my team." They steeled themselves. They were ready to fight.

When she returned, the doctor informed them that Samantha's only option was to voluntarily admit herself to behavioral medicine for inpatient psychiatric care. She and her husband were given a sheaf of papers. Together, they read that she would not be allowed to leave without a doctor's permission. She would not be allowed to have her phone. Her possessions would be confiscated. She had no idea when she would be released, or how she would contact her family.

In a burst of inspiration, Samantha recalled a moment from *Law & Order* in which someone had asked for a packet of patients' rights. She demanded hers. To her surprise, the nurse produced papers outlining them. As she read through the papers, it seemed clear that what was happening to her was violating her rights as a patient. She zeroed in on one point: the patient had the right to choose and meet her doctor before any treatment was performed. She called in the nurse and held up the consent to inpatient care in one hand and the description of patient rights in the other, pointing out that they directly contradicted each other.

At this point, the hospital brought out the big guns. In her room at various points were the nurse, the head nurse, a hospital administrator, and the doctor. Their warnings grew ominous: it was much better, they told her, to be committed voluntarily than involuntarily.

Samantha held firm. It had been eight hours since she'd left home. Her breasts were engorged. She asked multiple times for a breast pump, but was never given one. She asked to see her children, but was told this was not allowed. She asked to see a social worker, someone who could give an evaluation and determine whether or not it was safe for her to be around her kids, but she was told there was no social worker available on hospital staff. She had texted friends and family for help and advice. A friend suggested she ask for a patient rights advocate; the hospital should have one available to help with the legal process. Samantha asked for one. The hospital staff claimed they did not have one.

Finally, her husband—a calm, shy, conflict-avoidant man who had mostly stood in the background—stood up and announced, "I'm taking my wife." He and Samantha started to leave. The staff threatened to call security. The nurse told her, with a voice that had lost all persuasive sweetness, "It really doesn't matter that you're fighting this, because you're either going to sign the papers, or we're going to commit you involuntarily and we'll have to use the restraints."

Later, an ob-gyn told Samantha she should have called their bluff and simply walked out. But at that point, she said, "I [didn't] know. I didn't think they were capable of doing everything they'd already done. I didn't know what else they were capable of and I wasn't willing to risk it."

The game was up. Samantha signed the papers.

———

Women have a long history of subversiveness; they have never existed wholly within the dehumanizing confines of the "second sex," even as social and political and medical forces have conspired to keep them there. Men have thus constantly had to invent new categories to control and patrol their behavior. Chief among these was that of the witch.

The witch emerged as a direct response to the invention of

what we now recognize as the figure of the "good mother" in the Renaissance era. The good mother was married, chaste, pious, fertile, and was, in the words of Thurer, the Virgin Mary "minus appeal and magic." Whereas the medieval Virgin had been a mystical, quasi-sexual figure, defined by her virginity and her titillating spiritual purity, inspiring the unrequited love of knights and the emulation of women who committed themselves to nunneries, the Renaissance virgin—the *mother* Mary—was a humble matron of the home. She was meant to reinforce a new moral order.

As the bourgeoisie expanded, capitalism supplanted feudalism, and the nuclear family emerged as the ultimate social unit and moral ideal, the home became the center of a nascent social order. The loyalty that in the past had been granted to clan or noble was now intended for immediate family. Instead of sleeping in the same spaces with servants and workers of the same gender, families now slept according to family relationship. Workshops were separated from domestic spaces. The home gained doors and privacy; it gained a threshold, dividing it from public space, which belonged to men. Women, carried over that threshold and dropped into the domestic, would have a very difficult time crossing back. The feminine was stagnant, the masculine, dynamic; the feminine interior and the masculine exterior; the feminine nurturing while the masculine was aggressive.

The mother, contained in the house, was confined and defined by this feminine sphere. The qualities she was allowed to possess were delimited, and those deemed unacceptable were cast onto witches, who posed a threat to this new order. While mothers tended house and minded children, epitomizing soft, asexual obedience, witches were copulating with Satan, boiling babies, sending down hail and thunderstorms, rendering men impotent and women infertile, creating illegitimate children, and stealing penises. The witch, Thurer writes, "soaked up all the loathsomeness that could have poisoned the good mother's purer being."

The lure and power of witches was immense in the eyes of the men hunting them down. In their book *For Her Own Good*, Barbara

Ehrenreich and Deirdre English cite statistics estimating that from the fifteenth through the seventeenth century in Europe, millions of women were executed as witches. In Toulouse, they write, four hundred were killed in a single day. After slaughters, some villages were left with only a handful of women. The crimes they were accused of were not only devilish cavorting, but healing: Ehrenreich and English quote early modern witch hunters dividing witches into the "good" and "bad," with the former delivering babies and offering salves, and the latter engaging in most of the copulating and penis-stealing. The former, "good" witches—mostly midwives and female lay healers—were considered the more dangerous lot. They possessed real intellectual and social power and challenged male control. Medicine was just beginning to establish itself as a venerable male profession in Europe, and midwives and lay healers were the more trusted, more knowledgeable competitors of male doctors. They were exterminated in a campaign of terror, which was then justified and rewritten throughout history as the natural forward march of progress.

In reality, Ehrenreich and English assert, the "expert" techniques of male doctors were often grossly misinformed, grandiose gestures that justified high costs, whereas midwives and female healers drew on a rich body of historical and local knowledge. They write, "A patient would have done better with an illiterate lay healer than with an expensive regular doctor who could write out prescriptions in Latin." In fact, millions of women died of puerperal fever at the hands of doctors in the eighteenth and nineteenth centuries, as these men—ignorant yet of the roots of infectious disease—passed infections from patient to patient in hospitals.

In the United States, the full-scale transition of medicine from the domain of female lay healers and midwives to that of male experts did not take place until later, in the nineteenth century. Then medicine became a distinguished profession, from which it was possible to make a considerable profit and to differentiate oneself from the masses and the lower classes with "scientific" training. Doctors went on "grand tours" of Europe in order to better emulate the gentleman doctor, who might wear a wig and carry a gold cane and refuse to do surgery on the grounds that it was "base." Medical treatment was an elite privilege for which one should pay, not a routine and intimate relationship. The "unscientific" ignorance of women healers was denounced as dangerous, and yet the prescribed cures of male doctors were rarely based on actual science: "A frequent treatment for leprosy," write Ehrenreich and English, "was a broth made of the flesh of a black snake caught in a dry land among stones."

Emerging modern medicine derived its authority, then, not so much from legitimate knowledge but from male superiority and upper-class status. As women were pushed out of obstetrics and gynecology—by 1930, midwives had been almost totally eliminated in the United States, either harassed or outlawed out of practice— women "fell under the biological hegemony of the medical profession." Witch hunts were no longer needed. Women's "femininity" could be reinforced, and their reproduction controlled, through the supposedly neutral authority of science and (male) expertise.

The standards of femininity, meanwhile, grew more stringent through the eighteenth and nineteenth centuries. By the Victorian era, the home had been elevated to a citadel of respectability and moral order, pitted starkly against the amoral vagaries of the capitalist marketplace outside. The divide between white men and white women was starker than ever: men were economic creatures, acting out of self-interest, engaged in competitive struggle, whereas women were domestic beings, selfless and giving, their identities one with those they cared for. Ehrenreich and English described the ethos of the Victorian era as "a cozy dream in which men are men and women are—mercifully—not men." This divide had to be legitimized, policed, and reinforced.

The energy that in the past had been devoted to developing ritual taboos around menstruation and excluding the female body from evolution and hunting witches now went into "cures" for white women ill at ease with their "femininity." White women deemed inappropriately feminine according to the standards of the time—excessively delicate, deferent, and virtuous—were seen as damaged outliers to be repaired with heroic interventions. In the nineteenth century, male doctors believed that the ovaries and uterus governed a woman's femininity and therefore her psychological state. Damage to them would result in "nervousness," a catch-all ailment that covered what would now be known as anxiety and depression as well as countless other illnesses. The ovariotomy, or "female castration," was a routine procedure to cure women of ailments including "eating like a ploughman, masturbation . . . erotic tendencies, [and] simple 'cussedness'"—once the ovaries were removed, the belief went, the troubled woman would become calm and obedient.

If removing the ovaries didn't solve the problem, the uterus was the presumed culprit. In the nineteenth century, the prevailing medical opinion was that the female body could not perform two major functions at once. The uterus and the brain were envisioned as in constant competition with each other; a woman who spent too much time developing the latter would neglect the former, to the detriment of her health. Parties, flirtations, hot beverages, and novels could all stimulate the brain and wreak havoc on the uterus: romantic novels were depicted as "one of the greatest causes of uterine disease in young women." And not only would consuming these novels damage the woman: it could later harm her babies, having deprived her reproductive system of the singular focus it needed.

The woman who insisted on satisfying her brain without regard to her essential feminine nature and reproductive purpose was not only reckless: she was selfish.

Revered psychologist and first president of the American Psychological Association G. Stanley Hall blasted this type of woman, writing, "She has taken up and utilized in her own life all that was meant for her descendants. This is the very apotheosis of selfishness from the standpoint of every biological ethics." A popular medical textbook of the nineteenth century, which went through seventeen editions and was written by Harvard professor Dr. Edward H.

Clarke, declared that education would cause women's uteruses to atrophy. Women were to live quietly, without disturbing or stimulating themselves. In fact, the most famous cure prescribed to "nervous" women at the turn of the nineteenth century, developed by Dr. S. Weir Mitchell of Philadelphia, was the "rest cure," in which women were to lie in a dimly lit room for six weeks without reading, speaking to anyone, or moving. They would eat soft, bland foods and be given daily massages. White women traveled from all over the country and paid exorbitant prices to see Dr. Mitchell; his clients included the writers Charlotte Perkins Gilman and Virginia Woolf, both of whom excoriated his treatment in later works.

If the rest cure was not an option, doctors might attempt to fix the uterus, usually by injecting a "cure" directly into it. These cures consisted of just about anything: water, milk, linseed tea, marshmallow. Yet with marshmallow injections and weeks of silent wallowing in empty rooms, women did not get better; they got worse. They became hysterical, throwing themselves into fits, fainting, beating their chests, tearing out their hair. And the more hysterical they became, the more frustrated doctors became with them, sometimes suffocating them to stop their fits or slapping them with wet towels.

Hysteria demanded a new and different cure: psychoanalysis as pioneered by Sigmund Freud. "Psychoanalysis," as historian Carroll Smith-Rosenberg writes, "is the child of the hysterical woman." Freud pioneered the acceptance of hysteria as a mental disorder that could not be resolved with physical or medical interventions. Instead, he provided a talking cure, in which he'd encourage a woman to acknowledge repressed desire in order to make peace with her femininity. His methods were different from those of his predecessors, but his end goal was the same: to usher women out of the charged sphere of the intellect back to the carefully constructed confines of their feminine destiny.

For millennia the story of motherhood has been the story of men systematically trying to co-opt, repress, pathologize, or otherwise explain away what Adrienne Rich has termed "the primacy of the mother." What this campaign has left in its wake is a motherhood parched of power, richness, danger, and authority, squashed into the flat category of femininity.

Rich finds a representation of the transformative power of motherhood in the goddesses of ancient history. "Out of her body," she writes, "the woman created man, created woman, created continuing existence. Spiritualized into a divine being, she was the source of vegetation, fruition, fertility of every kind. Whether she bore children or not, as potter and weaver she created the first objects which were more than objects, were works of art, thus of magic, and which were also the products of the earliest scientific activity, including the lore of herbs and roots, the art of healing and that of nurturing the young."

Rich was writing in the seventies, when it was still permissible to talk freely about goddesses as feminist idols without too much snark; now, the word *goddess* has largely been co-opted by late capitalism and calls to mind a woman with angelic tresses luxuriating in $59 facial cream in a California wellness spa. The term urges women to "spoil" themselves, which in turn reinforces that they must normally operate in a realm of austerity. The decline of the goddess illustrates how a realm in which women had power as women has disappeared, been smothered by an idea of the feminine created and aggressively perpetuated by men. For Rich, the crucial distinction between the goddess of pre-patriarchal life and the contemporary mother is that the former was "a transformer," with tremendous power and potential, whereas the latter has a largely passive function.

Today, pregnancy and maternity are biological phenomena that simultaneously define a woman and have nothing to do with her. In American society in particular, a mother's predominant power is the power of prevention—shielding her baby from harm. She pursues this quest largely in isolation, expending tremendous amounts of energy on expelling any resentment or negativity or darkness from her feminine life, keeping her intellect and passions and self separate from it and directed only at male realms of work and civic society.

Rich has argued most famously that the female body and its potential, its knowledge, are "the terrain on which patriarchy is erected." For her, men have tamed what they will never be able to possess by creating the "institution of motherhood," into which most American mothers are inevitably ushered and which few are able to escape: a ubiquitous, invasive institution of extensive prohibitions and equally extensive mandates, of carefully codified behaviors, largely confined to the home and defined wholly by the project of building the perfect child. Fear is the impetus for this societal setup as much as power and domination; Rich quotes Joseph Campbell explaining "the fear of woman and the mystery of her motherhood have been for the male no less impressive imprinting forces than the fears and mysteries of the world of nature itself."

———————

They took all of Samantha's clothes. All of her belongings. She was given a hospital gown and socks. At one a.m., they came for her. Everyone else in the hospital was in bed. The doctors were gone. The lights were off.

An ambulance transferred her to inpatient care, where a nurse did yet another intake exam in the silent middle of the night. "Have you ever served in a war zone?" she asked. "Have you ever been in a serious car accident? Have you ever been in a natural disaster? Have you ever had a life-threatening illness?" Samantha kept asking, *When can I see my baby, when can I see my kids, when can I see my husband,* and the nurse responded, "We don't get moms in here. I don't know." The nurse ran through the protocol, reminding Samantha that if she lost control she'd be restrained and sedated. Samantha's breasts, which had been slowly filling with milk for ten hours, were enormous, leaky, and painful.

She was finally led to her room, which she shared with a roommate who, behind the thin curtain partition, was withdrawing from cocaine. All night long the roommate cried and groaned in agony; at one point she was screaming, "Let me out!" Samantha sobbed herself to sleep.

The next morning, they returned her clothes, which had been washed in heavy-duty cleaning solution and smelled of chemicals. The nurse came in early on her rounds and asked, as she would every single day, if Samantha was feeling suicidal or homicidal. "No, I need to get home to my babies," Samantha replied.

The bathrooms had no locks. The furniture was bolted to the floor. Samantha visited the nurse's station to retrieve her hand pump, since she was not allowed to use an electric one, and then began the tedious process of trying to extract milk by hand while nervous, sleep-deprived, self-conscious, and stressed out. She managed one meager bottle, which she returned with the pump to the nurse's station for her husband to pick up later.

From there, she set out to do reconnaissance. She met a few older female patients who were friendly, and laughed as they told her, "Don't worry, honey, you're not crazy." It began to dawn on her that most of the people in the ward had been institutionalized multiple times, and that the vast majority were dealing with drug addiction as well as other mental health issues. As in many rural communities across the Midwest, in Steubenville the main mental health crisis was addiction. Samantha quickly discovered that nearly every small group, treatment plan, and interaction in the behavioral health program was geared toward addicts.

The first order of business in the morning was medication; everyone was ushered into a conference room and given a paper listing the medications they were already on. She was on none, though that would soon change. They were told to list symptoms and side effects of each and to discuss their treatment plan. "My treatment plan is that I need to go home," Samantha said. Later, she would read in her medical records, "patient is angry, patient is frustrated, patient keeps demanding to go home."

Samantha started to worry that by angering the staff, she might be prolonging her stay. She felt she had to show them that she did not belong here, and paradoxically that she was getting well enough here to be released.

At breakfast, a social worker introduced himself to her, saying of her and her roommate, "So you're my two new girls!" She asked him about the form she'd signed voluntarily admitting herself into the hospital. They'd told her she could be out in seventy-two hours. Had that time period already begun? Was the clock ticking? She smiled.

The social worker assured her yes, sure, of course, if she'd signed the paper, she was all good. This reassurance cemented her resolve: she could be out in three days if she just grinned and okayed her way through it.

After breakfast came morning group therapy, run by the social worker. Everyone went around the room and shared their names and stories. There was a man with multiple personality disorder whose voice changed in cadence and pitch as he spoke. A woman with four children whose husband had left her and whose mother had had a heart attack and then died in her arms. Many people struggled with drugs or alcohol; some had been brought in after nearly fatal overdoses. Samantha told her story—going to the OB, being put into the ambulance and delivered here in the early morning hours. As she spoke, she grew newly frustrated with her situation and declared that she shouldn't be here, that it was wrong, that this was not treatment. But the social worker simply maintained the preternatural calm of a parent dealing with a child in meltdown.

After the group therapy she wandered over to the TV room, a communal space at the end of the hall. She discovered that patients had an abundance of free time and very little to do with it other than watch TV and stoke each other's bitterness. There was a stack of magazines crowned with an issue that had Brad Pitt and Jennifer Aniston on the cover. Board games missing half the pieces. Crayons. She asked about books and was directed to a tiny room where a few forgotten bookshelves sat empty, save for one shelf of old thrift-store paperbacks. Later, after she'd finally been discharged, she would fight her traumatic association with this place by returning once a month with a huge stack of adult coloring books, novels, magazines, and colored pencils.

In the TV room, she resigned herself to coloring alongside a huge tattooed man who'd been in group therapy. The patients who'd been in multiple times were friendly with the nurses and would ask them to print out coloring pages from the Internet. Samantha got to work coloring a fish as Dory to give to her daughter Sophie. During her stay, she would pass these meager coloring pages to her husband, who would give them to Sophie as a gesture of connection and reassurance.

She and the man chatted. The patients were predominately men: "people who used to work in the steel mills," Samantha explained, "or farmers, or [on] boats carrying coal down the Ohio River, big blue-collar worker guys." Most of the men were friendly and sympathetic. One man showed up and introduced himself only to announce that his wife had just called and told him she'd run off with their three children. Samantha didn't see him at all for the next three days.

In the afternoon was a second group therapy. She wasn't going to attend, but the others warned her that if she didn't it would be noted in her chart that she was resisting treatment. She went. A different social worker kicked off the session by saying, "Most of your mental health issues are stemming from addiction, so let's talk about addiction."

In the middle of the group therapy session, a nurse arrived and announced that it was Samantha's turn to see the doctor. Her heart soared. Finally! Someone rational was going to recognize how wrong it was for her to be in here!

The doctor was a South Asian woman who introduced herself with a joke about the difficult pronunciation of her name. Samantha made sure to laugh. She sat down and the doctor asked her why she was here. "Well," Samantha began, "I really don't think I should be here." She said this lightly, as if it were a silly mistake, as if she'd somehow ended up in Paris, Texas, instead of France.

"I'll be the judge of that," the doctor replied, and Samantha's hopes collapsed. It was as if an invisible force warped everything she said, and she couldn't get anyone to see her. She felt her cheeks bloom with rage, which she suppressed, launching into an explanation of how ever since her second daughter had been born she'd been scared of irrational things. She'd been irritable—"I mean, I don't get mad at my kids!" she scrambled to explain, though that wasn't true, not of her or any mother alive. Then she added, emphatic, that she'd never thought of hurting herself or anyone else.

She was trapped in a cycle of feeling scared, angry, guilty, and depressed; scared, angry, guilty, and depressed. Samantha felt better voicing this. The doctor was typing and looking at her computer as she spoke. When Samantha finished, she looked up and announced that Samantha was suffering from classic symptoms of postpartum depression. For a second, Samantha felt a flood of relief, as if naming this illness would finally resolve things and free her. The doctor told Samantha she'd put her on 10 milligrams of Lexapro, and wait a few days "to see how it goes."

Samantha begged to see her children. She begged to see her family doctor. Her mother had flown in from California to help out, her mother-in-law was nearby, she had plenty of help.

Children were not allowed in the unit.

Samantha pleaded: her baby was three months old; she was nursing. Please.

Maybe tomorrow, the doctor allowed, but not today. Samantha couldn't help herself:

"I'm here voluntarily," she said. "Why can't I leave?"

"No one leaves without my approval," the doctor said.

Samantha stood up to go, and as she was walking to the door, stinging with fury, the doctor asked her a question that would haunt her for years, a question that would later prompt her to look into legal action.

"Tell me," she asked, "do you think you would have any more kids?"

Yes, Samantha replied, disarmed and honest, she and her husband wanted a big family.

The doctor looked at her and said, "I would stop having kids if I were you."

Samantha felt as if she'd been slapped. She did not reply. The nurse came and escorted her away. Back in the common room where everyone was coloring, she grabbed a crayon. On the back of any available piece of paper—her intake "welcome" packet, coloring pages—she began documenting her experience: the names of all the nurses and doctors, and everything they had said and done. She was going to sue them. This doctor had no right to tell her she should not be a mother.

One of the older women asked, "So now do you get to go home?"

She shook her head.

8

Institutionalized

The twentieth century was dubbed "the century of the child" by influential Swedish feminist Ellen Key. Birthrates were falling, as was infant mortality, and family sizes began to shrink from ten to seven to three or four. Whereas in the past the child had been an economic asset, a little adult who contributed to the family work and income, by the Victorian era, children—like their mothers—had to be protected from the vagaries of the industrial economy. The child—the white middle-class child, that is, for working-class children and children of color were worked to exhaustion in fields and factories—was portrayed as innocent, precious, and full of potential. Childhood became a discrete period with its own stages and characteristics. At a time of dizzying industrial growth and societal change, children were imbued with the potential of forging a vastly different future. With the right expert training, they could bring forth miraculous scientific and technological progress that hovered just on the cusp of the imaginable. If coaxed and trained and stimulated appropriately, any child could grow up to become the president—or a serial killer.

There was one glaring problem with this new, optimistic fascination with childhood. A child's potential depended on an actor who made experts very uneasy: the mother. Ehrenreich and English write, "The discovery of the child was, in one sense, a discovery of the power of women." As the century of the child began its bloom, the male solution to female reproductive power was experts. If the child was to depend on the mother, then the mother was to depend on male experts. The latter offered stern and often contradictory advice on feeding and bathing and sleeping and thumb-sucking, beseeching mothers to act as their laboratory assistants.

Every basic biological need and development of childhood could be and was rationalized: feeding and napping were to take place on tight schedules; height and weight were to be carefully mapped; cognitive and motor skills were to emerge at the appropriate times. In the new industrial era, children could be programmed like machines. One formula ad at the time promised to "build up that tiny body into a strong, sturdy piece of human machinery." Ann Hulbert, who documented the shifting tides of this advice in *Raising America: Experts, Parents, and a Century of Advice About Children*, has written that the early-twentieth-century mother was expected to "walk—and speak—ever so softly, and carry a big chart."

Arnold Gesell's studies on early childhood development at Yale in the 1920s developed a timeline of "milestones" that is still, as we near the second quarter of the twenty-first century, the signature measurement of a child's physical, cognitive, social, and emotional development. Based on small studies of white middle-class children, these milestones—which now track minutiae including "reaches for object with one hand using the raking grasp," "shows interest in a stuffed animal by pretending to feed," and "can draw a person with at least six body parts"—became major nodes of anxiety for mothers.

Suddenly there was a prototypical "normal" infant who hit all of these targets, an exceptional one who surpassed them, and a dysfunctional or damaged one who missed one or several. Apgar scores, IQ tests, growth charts: all engendered both the intense need to meet a precisely defined standard and varied ways of somehow falling short of that standard. Even while expert advice differed and shifted dramatically, from the behavioralist exhortation to never kiss a baby to the attachment parenting mandate to keep one's baby on one's person at all times, women became increasingly beholden to that advice. To ignore it was deemed not only ignorant but irresponsible. This shift toward scientific, expert-guided mothering meant that, as historian Jodi Vandenberg-Daves writes, "Anxiety was the lot of the well-informed modern mother."

In the mid-twentieth century, the rationalist, rigid scientific parenting that metaphorized babies into machines gave way to what came to be known as "permissive parenting," which focused less on systematic auto-programming of children and more on nurturing personal ego development and self-esteem. Permissive parenting was obsessively child-centered and even more rigorous in its demands on the mother. While expert advice became increasingly exact in its prescriptions—precisely how many hours of napping a two-year-old needs; how many tablespoons of peas to feed an infant—it also demanded that the mother act with infinite deference to the uniqueness of her individual child. *You may need to offer a vegetable multiple times before your child will accept it!* warned advice manuals, along with dozens of other elaborate tricks or variations mothers might attempt in order to adhere to the rules without impinging on their children's quasi-holy identity formation and freedom.

The child, Sharon Hays wrote, "[was] now to train the parent." This unresolved paradox would become the source of infinite varieties of maternal anxiety. One mid-century mother wrote to pediatrician Dr. Benjamin Spock, whose *Baby and Child Care,* first published in 1946, is still a best seller today and is the defining work of the permissive parenting era, "It is because I want [my child] to be so happy that I am so distraught and incompetent."

Whereas from Puritan times until the prewar era children were rigorously molded to religious, societal, and cultural standards, in the permissive parenting of booming postwar consumer culture, "the natural development of the child and the fulfillment of the child's desires," writes Hays, "are ends in and of themselves." This era was mobilized by all of the same concerns of the scientific parenting age—milestones and development and scores and charts and measurement and perfection—along with a new mandate to see children as precious beings at perpetual risk of psychological scarring, who had to be constantly tended with infinite individual attention. The definition of a "good mother" intensified further from one who carries the big chart to one who is, in the words of Shari Thurer, "ever-present, all-providing, inexhaustibly patient and tactful," and "who anticipates her child's every need." Thurer concludes, "Mother has become baby's servant."

New advice ordered women to nurture their child's independence by providing choices (What color of shorts would you like to wear today? Which box of crackers?), by facilitating free play, and by acting as emotionally imperturbable, mystical guides through the vagaries of emotion ("It sounds like you're feeling frustrated!"). This was not the heavy-handed Betty Draper of yore, demanding little Sally keep her dress clean and sit still, but Kristina Braverman from *Parenthood,* shaping a child in the way a therapist might shape a difficult patient: with unshakable equanimity, self-assuredness, and patience in the face of the fits of human temperament. The permissive mother provides the perfect emotional framing of every situation, employing her expert training—more a necessity than ever—in the facilitation of the child's distinct personal growth. She is, Ehrenreich and English explain, perpetually "encouraging certain behaviors and discouraging others, with inexhaustible patience and always through indirection." But she never strays far from expert guidance.

This new child-rearing mandate was an outgrowth of the incipient phase of late capitalism, in which individual personality and choice reign supreme. In 1951, the National Education Association and the American Association of School Administrators announced in a study that "the basic moral and spiritual value in American life" was "the supreme importance of the individual personality."

"From now on," write Barbara Ehrenreich and Deirdre English in *For Her Own Good,* "the energies of mothers would pour into the job of nurturing the kind of American youth who, from the cradle on, would fit the mold of the consumer society." Middle-class childhood was a training ground for the playground of choice that defines privileged adult life. *Would you like the blue ones or the red ones, Henry? You don't want green beans? How about carrots, then?* The child was both consumer and product, intricately molded according to scientific doctrine into a supreme individual who possessed the confidence, ego, desire, and vigor to consume his or her way to happiness.

Permissive parenting gradually deepened into what today is known as "intensive parenting," a moniker that finally gives up the freewheeling pretense of "permissive" and accepts full-time, all-in commitment as a badge of honor. The mother in this context applies scientific technique to decoding her child's behavior and compares it to precise developmental charts; stimulates a diverse range of abilities from empathy to pincer grip; monitors her own behavior—*No fighting with Dad! No sharp language! No blank staring at the phone!*—and converts every moment of joy or frustration into a verbalized lesson in self-awareness. Historian Jodi Vandenberg-Daves analyzes the Mama Bear in the Berenstain Bears books for evidence of this creeping trend: she writes that while the Mama Bear mostly hung around in the background in the sixties and seventies, by the eighties she was "applying sunscreen, keeping the cubs from watching too much TV and eating too much junk food, and lying awake at night while Papa slept, worrying about children's troubles, from bullies to stranger danger."

Sociologist Sharon Hays first introduced the term "intensive parenting" in her 1996 book *The Cultural Contradictions of Motherhood*. She defined intensive mothering as "expert-guided, child-centered" as well as "emotionally absorbing, labor intensive, and financially expensive." She also portrayed it as conspicuously at odds with American society's core value, which she identified as the "instrumentally rational" pursuit of self-interested material gain. The glaring discrepancy between the national mandate to consume and accumulate wealth and the pressure on mothers to be entirely self-sacrificing and nurturing beyond all reason or efficiency drove Hays to the conclusion that motherhood is a way for American society to try to compensate for its materiality. Mothers, she proposed, were meant to save us all from the moral void of the market, and they were meant to enjoy doing so, to find their deepest satisfaction in it. Mothers should evade capitalism's amoral vices and spare their children as well, while also training them— via the constant inquisition and fulfillment of their desires—to be productive capitalist citizens.

The harshest and most paradoxical axiom of contemporary intensive mothering is that micromanaging every aspect of a child's life, being constantly hyperattuned to the slightest blip on his or her emotional radar, and perpetually seeking out the optimal experiences for his or her development is both fun and *natural*. In the 1960s, when technological and scientific progress began to seem more suspect, motherhood embraced the "natural," without shedding any modern pressures. Contemporary intensive-parenting philosophy often rides on the claim that this is just what parents have been doing for millennia, albeit aided by white-noise classical music and baby math class. This admiration of the natural is evident in the way scientific studies are often mixed with exhortations to look to the behavior of so-called "primitive" cultures. Dr. Sears, one of the preeminent baby advice experts, refers vaguely on his website to a host of scientific studies that supposedly prove that babies carried in slings—like those worn by indigenous women in Mexico—are smarter, calmer, and more empathetic, while pointing out that anthropologists "know" this is true from casual observation of non-Western cultures.

While these experts promise mothers that they are simply doing what comes naturally, following their innate instincts to feed their one-year-old exactly two ounces of light dairy protein per day, they also imply that if mothers err from a "natural" course they could forever harm their children.

The major surge in intensive parenting happened as mothers

were heading to work in larger numbers: women made up just over 37 percent of the U.S. labor force in 1960, 45 percent by 1975, and more than 50 percent by 1980. In a direct relationship repeated throughout history, as more fluid gender roles gave women more equality and freedom in the workplace, their responsibilities as mothers intensified. As Vandenberg-Daves put it, "While often working more, [mothers] also needed to be ever vigilant, continuously emotionally available, creative, and even fun." This fun stood in stark contrast to the expanding set of horrors that could harm children, from day care to abduction to food poisoning to hot cars in the summer to amusement parks and the failure of a parent to introduce a certain number of words by age two. A review of parenting advice by Susan Douglas and Meredith Michaels in their 2004 book *The Mommy Myth* summed up the paradox as such: "Childhood is filled with peril, but motherhood is fun, fun, fun."

Thus, while under intensifying pressure to raise their children according to a set of specific "natural" standards defined by ever-evolving scientific studies and cultural norms, mothers had to recognize mothering as self-actualization, and deeply enjoy it. Mothers should need their children as intensely as their children needed them, and neither should need anyone else. If this was not fulfillment enough, the mother was inadequate, perhaps ill, certainly dangerous. The message of mutual fulfillment renders "natural" the vigorous demands and sacrifices of motherhood, pathologizing ambivalence. Thurer declares that the tension between expert advice and the constant assurance that it all comes naturally has created "a degree of anxiety and guilt in mothers that is unparalleled in history."

For what is at stake is fundamentally a woman's femininity: just as the white Victorian woman unhappy with a life of petticoats and socializing might have had her uterus injected with tea in an attempt to bring her in line with the ideal female of her time, the twenty-first-century mother who is struggling to stay steeped in ever-patient love and fun might need psychiatric internment to accept proper intensive motherhood. Thurer summed up the progression of the twentieth century nicely when she wrote, "[Experts] have invented a motherhood that excluded the experience of the mother."

———————

Despite her reservations, despite her fury, Samantha stuck with the good girl's strategy of compliance. When a nurse in a group therapy session told Samantha that she should set a timer for ten minutes and give her toddler undivided attention even if the baby was screaming, Samantha did not respond by telling the nurse "it stresses the toddler out to hear the baby scream," or "it's a major trigger for me to hear my baby scream." She nodded. When the nurses suggested she just "go for a walk and relax!" she nodded. Only one nurse, much younger than the others, asked her if anyone had given her any resources on postpartum depression. Samantha said no. This nurse printed out some papers from the Internet— basic information Samantha could have found with a Google search, but nonetheless a gesture Samantha appreciated.

Samantha passed each day in anticipation of her brief visit with the doctor. On Friday, her third day, the stakes were particularly high: if she didn't get out that day, she would be in all weekend. When the doctor revealed that no, she wasn't being released, Samantha hardened.

She demanded to see her kids. The doctor refused. Samantha dug in her heels. The doctor agreed to a brief visit on Saturday.

The visit, for which Samantha had risked her good reputation and which she feverishly anticipated, is what most haunts her about her experience in the psych ward. She and her children were carefully supervised by nurses. Sophie, her toddler, was scared, and Samantha could tell she was struggling to put on a happy face and act normal for her mom. Samantha tried to nurse Cora, the baby, but Cora refused her breast; she'd taken to the bottle. Samantha was devastated. Nursing had been the one activity that bonded her to her new baby. She was too traumatized, unable to produce enough milk, and Cora was no longer interested.

When it was time for them to leave, Sophie asked why Samantha could not come with them. After Samantha had gone behind the door into the unit, Sophie threw herself at it, crying. Samantha's voice still shakes three years later as she recounts this part of the story.

That weekend, Samantha stewed. She wanted out as quickly as possible, and that meant cooperation. But she also wanted information in her medical record that stated she'd objected to the treatment. She was thinking of going to court and didn't want it to seem as if she'd just happily acquiesced the whole time.

Samantha hid in her room and sobbed, not wanting anyone to see her distress. But in a group therapy session over the weekend, it finally burst through. One of the social workers mentioned that Samantha had been quiet.

"I am *trying*," she said, and the words took flight. She wanted treatment as much as or more than anyone else here, and she couldn't get it, she couldn't get the right treatment, and did they understand how inapplicable this was to her life, how devastating it was to be separated from her kids? She wouldn't be able to breastfeed because of this!

She let loose and could not stop herself. When she was done, the man whose wife had left him and taken their three kids began to rant. "This is a lawsuit right here!" he said. The social worker tried to shut him down. "This is a miscarriage of justice!" he raged louder. By the time he was calmed, Samantha was unsure whether to sob or laugh. From then on, the others in the ward started calling her "Justice."

On Sunday, she felt better. No matter what, she'd be getting out on Monday. Her seventy-two hours would be up. She asked the nurse how it worked: did she have to stay and see the doctor first, or would she get out first thing in the morning? The nurse was evasive. Samantha pushed. "I'll check," the nurse told her.

It turned out that the social worker who'd reassured Samantha on the first day that the seventy-two-hour clock was ticking had been wrong. Samantha had needed to sign an extra form in order to set that clock in motion, and she hadn't signed it. She hadn't known it existed. If she wanted to sign the paper now, the seventy-two hours would begin on Sunday night.

"I was," Samantha told me, "SUPER-PISSED." No one—not the nurse in the ER, the intake nurse, none of the nurses at the facility, the doctor—had told her about this paper. "It didn't matter that I said all the right things, asked all the right questions, it didn't matter how careful I was." All of her strategic calculation had amounted to nothing.

Samantha was used to having choices, questioning authority, taking charge of her care. This was why she'd picked up the phone in the first place, to be proactive in seeking help. She figured if she knew the limitations of the hospital's power, if she knew her rights, then she could control her situation. But here her imagined individual authority ran aground before the vast structures that patrol, contain, and discipline mothers.

Samantha was so infuriated that the nurses called in the director of behavioral medicine, who, instead of addressing Samantha directly, gathered the group of patients in the TV area. In a conciliatory tone, he said, "I heard some of you are confused about the seventy-two-hour rule." Samantha raised her hand. "I'm not confused about it. I completely understand it. You withheld a piece of paper for me to sign." "I'm sorry," the man told her, "that you misunderstood what the social worker told you."

"No," Samantha said. "There's no misunderstanding." The director smiled. He explained that she was confused. He revealed that the clock was only ticking on the seventy-two hours when the doctor was in, so weekends did not count toward that time. This riled up all the patients, who hadn't known it, and it set everyone to protesting. Samantha pointed out that she'd read the patient handbook from cover to cover and it said nothing about weekends not being included in the seventy-two-hour window. Finally, one of the nurses pulled Samantha aside and gave her a warning. There was a possibility she'd get out tomorrow. She was taking the medication. She had been compliant. If she signed that form now, the doctor would keep her in for seventy-two more hours just out of resentment.

"I can tell you've been playing the game," the nurse told her, "and I think that's your best strategy." Samantha called her husband, who was devastated. She talked to her mother, who was enraged. No one knew what to do. Her mother advised her to trust the nurse and heed her advice. That day was the twenty-second, and her daughter Sophie's birthday was the twenty-fifth. They'd planned a huge party, a birthday for Sophie and a baptism for Cora, with the whole family coming. Seventy-two more hours would mean running the risk of not making it. Samantha didn't sign.

On Monday, when Samantha got in to see the doctor, she announced that she was happy with Samantha's progress on the medication, happy with the notes the nurses had taken over the weekend, and it would just be a couple more days.

"I don't understand," Samantha said. The doctor explained that Samantha was perhaps on a high now, and they couldn't tell if she was going to have a low, or an adverse reaction to the medication. She had to stay.

On the phone with her mother, Samantha wept. Her mother called the hospital multiple times demanding information but couldn't get anywhere. Samantha's husband also called, to no avail. He decided to come in personally and confront the doctor, in spite of the fact that he was painfully shy and hated the idea of it. When he got to the nurse's station, he announced that he was there to see Samantha's doctor. The nurses told him to wait outside the unit, so he posted himself right in front of the door.

In Samantha's chart, there is a brief note stating that the patient's family requested to meet with the doctor, and the request was passed on. Samantha's husband waited for hours. Samantha finally called him from inside the unit to ask what was going on. He didn't know. Samantha pressured the nurses to figure out what was happening, and one finally went out and told him that the doctor had left through a back door. Her husband went home and, with repressed rage, painted all of their kitchen cabinets.

Samantha's mother-in-law contacted lawyer after lawyer, trying to get Samantha out, but they all told her they couldn't do anything. Samantha's mother found a group called Disability Rights Ohio that worked with patient rights advocates, but no one knew who the patient rights advocate of the hospital was. "It was a wild goose chase." That night, Samantha went to bed more depressed than ever.

On Tuesday morning, a nurse came in and announced, "I have some good news!" Samantha did not thank the nurse. She did not celebrate. She signed all the papers. She noticed her diagnosis was "major depressive," in spite of the fact that the doctor had told her she exhibited symptoms of postpartum depression, and she thought the two were distinct. Plus, she felt her diagnosis should have been anxiety, not depression. Still, she signed.

She had to wait until the afternoon to see the doctor one last time, and when she did, the doctor smiled and asked her if she was in a great mood now that she was going home. Samantha thought, *You want me to say thank you?* At the same time, she did not want this pulled out from under her at the last minute. She smiled. One of the nurses escorted her to the parking lot. "You're not really home free until you get into your vehicle," Samantha told me.

At home, Samantha was swamped by the cognitive dissonance that would define the next several months. Her mother had flown in and was ecstatic to see her, and everyone celebrated as if her release was occasion for a party, as if she'd accomplished something. Part of her wanted to show everyone *I'm fine! Look how fine I am!* and another part of her knew she was still sick, perhaps even sicker. The shame of it burned. She held her daughters for a long time. Sophie would not let her alone, crying and clinging, panicking whenever Samantha left her sight. The scene of Sophie fighting to get to the door of the unit as it closed played over and over in Samantha's mind.

Samantha began by trying to get access to her medical records. This involved a surprising amount of bureaucracy: phone calls, voicemails, arguments. She contacted lawyer after lawyer. She found a counselor through a friend who was not affiliated in any way with the hospital where she'd been admitted, but that counselor seemed to know very little about postpartum mental illness. She kept saying Samantha was just overwhelmed and needed "me time": "Why don't you go shopping and treat yourself?" It was all Samantha had, so she went with it.

That office also had a nurse practitioner who could manage her medication, though Samantha hated him from the start. He told her that she might be upset with the hospital, but they'd done the right thing. He screened her for bipolar disorder, despite the fact that she'd already been screened for it and never shown any signs. She realized that most people she encountered in the mental health system wanted to shove her into a familiar diagnostic category— major depression, bipolar—because they had no idea what postpartum illness was or how to deal with it.

But Samantha attended her sessions, managed her medication, and tried to take legal action against the hospital. Lawyers were extremely reluctant to take on a case that involved one of the two biggest employers in the region. When she found a lawyer who expressed interest and sympathy, she waited months while he reviewed all of her records: from inpatient care, the ER, the ob-gyn, and her notes. He then told her it was highly unlikely she could win a suit against the hospital. Her chart didn't clearly represent her circumstances: some entries from group therapy and her discussions with the social worker noted that she'd had thoughts about harming her baby, but other entries stated simply and plainly that she wanted to smother her baby with a pillow. There was no way, the lawyer told her, that she could convince a jury that her thoughts were mere thoughts or that a nurse or doctor had lied in filling out the records. "Doctors are good guys," he said. The hospital would drag her through the mud, make her look psychotic, homicidal. It would be devastating for her and her family.

"What happened to you is horrible," he told her. He would fight it with her if she really wanted to, but it would be ugly. Samantha gave up on legal action. She did write a letter to her old OB, recounting what had happened to her and how damaging it had been. She never heard back.

Her mother learned about a support group in Pittsburgh, and Samantha went to check it out. She showed up one Friday afternoon at a small yoga studio and prenatal education center on the main drag in Lawrenceville. When it was Samantha's turn to share, she introduced herself and told her story. The thoughts. The OB. The ER, the psychiatric hospital, and now, the nightmares. Now, her daughter Sophie developing nervous tics, refusing to be separated from her even for a minute. When she was done, she waited for the recriminations. She waited for a woman to cluck and say, *Well, the doctors were just doing what they thought best.* Instead, someone said, stunned and bold, "That's fucked up!" There was a raucous chorus of agreement. Samantha burst into tears. She had finally found her healing.

Samantha went religiously to the support group for the next several years. The counselor who led it suggested that she was suffering from PTSD. It was the first time anyone had mentioned that possibility to her.

A year after her hospitalization, a friend of Samantha's offered her a job at a nonprofit, acting as an advocate for victims of sexual assault. Samantha was skeptical at first—she didn't feel equipped to handle her own trauma, let alone other people's—but her friend assured her that her own experience would help her empathize with others, and that her clients' experiences were different enough from hers that she was unlikely to be triggered. She would have to negotiate between sexual assault victims and the hospital, asking for rape kits and reports. She'd had no one to advocate for her, and now she could be that person for someone else.

Samantha's third baby was due on April 17, 2018. She drove to Weirton, West Virginia, to go to a hospital there for her OB visits, although even entering a hospital as a pregnant woman gave her panic attacks. A midwife there was sympathetic to her needs and told Samantha that anytime she thought she might panic, she could go outside for as long as she needed and still be seen whenever she came back in.

Samantha got a doula and practiced hypno-birthing. She felt calm and confident, even as she recognized that she would always carry her symptoms and the scars of her experiences with her. They were the bittersweet legacy of a system unable to process complex maternal feeling and experience, a system in which "better safe than sorry" can end up being both unsafe and deeply sorry for mother and child.

In the last week leading up to her due date, Samantha's panic attacks returned. She couldn't shake the sense that this baby was a test: would he heal her or break her? At forty weeks, she asked to be induced. The midwife sent her to the hospital and hooked her up to a drip of Pitocin, a synthetic version of oxytocin used to stimulate labor. Samantha brought recorded self-hypnosis meditations with her for the birth and played them in the delivery room. She was self-conscious but firm, telling her husband and the doula and the doctors, "This is going to sound really stupid to you guys, but please don't laugh at me, just let me do my thing."

The baby's going to birth itself, the meditations intoned. *My body was made for this. I am not afraid.* The nurses thought this was bizarre, but Samantha gave birth in nine hours with no medication. Most important, she stood up to the figures who'd cut her down so much last time. The doctor on duty during her birth insisted she needed an epidural. *Give me some credit,* Samantha thought, *it's my third child.* She refused the epidural. Then the doctor wanted her in bed, hooked up to monitors, but there were no apparent problems with the baby. Samantha refused. The doctor wanted to put an internal monitor on the baby: a small device that would be thrust up into Samantha and screwed into the baby's tiny scalp. *By the time you get this in, it's gonna be go time,* Samantha thought. She told the doctor the baby would be coming soon.

"I just checked," the doctor said. "You're not going anywhere."

Samantha started pushing anyway, and in the intensity of the pain, as the doctor tried to talk her into monitoring, Samantha started yelling, "You are not getting it!" The doctor was so taken aback that she recused herself, telling the nurse that she was sending up another doctor and that she'd be seeing other patients. Samantha was triumphant. The last time around she'd perpetually told herself, *Well, this person is a doctor, they're doing what's best, and it doesn't feel right, but I'll go with it,* and now, she told me, "It's my birth, it's my body, I should be able to call the shots."

The new doctor who came in said, "You're having a baby!" and let her go at it. She felt her baby emerge, the surreal sensation of his body coming through hers. She was ecstatic. "He was just a total angel," she tells me. "I know that sounds ridiculous." They named him Logan. He was the calmest of her three children, and for the first two weeks he hardly cried at all. His birth was a rite of passage for Samantha. She decided to sleep with him in spite of vociferous warnings. Even those who knew about her anxiety tried to nudge her: *It's not anxiety to worry about suffocating him, it's just being smart.*

"I understand there are real risk factors," she told me. "If you obsess over every single risk, and you try and calculate every choice you make, you're going to end up ten times more exhausted than you already are. I really had to be at peace with the decisions I was making and trust that I have a motherly instinct. I need to trust the choices that I make for my kids."

Logan didn't move around a lot when he slept, and he was often right near the cool air vent, so she put a blanket next to his bottom half. Some people she knew gasped at this and told her she had to use a sleep sack. "Am I going to freak out about this, or am I just going to go to sleep?" she asked me. "He randomly could kick the blanket over his head one night and that is a risk, but I think this is safe. And also, this is what I need to do to function."

I recognized in Samantha's voice the language I practiced using with my therapist, the language that too often mothers have to come to after being nearly crushed by fear. The language they should have from the beginning: *I am making this choice because I believe in myself, and nothing is without risk. Terrible things could happen, but I refuse to live in constant fear.*

"Last night," Samantha told me, "I tucked him in, I laid him down, and I put the little blanket up over his bottom and I'm like, what if he did suffocate?" But then, she checked herself: "Why am I thinking like this? All because I put a blanket on my kid's legs?" She laughed, but the laugh was knowing, not easy. The symptoms were still there. She still goes to counseling every other week. She's on medication. She has a routine.

"I forget to give myself some credit," she said as we chatted one afternoon when Logan was six months old. Her husband reminded her that she used to call him, begging him to come home from work early. She hadn't done that in years. "Now, if I'm feeling a little stressed . . . I have the language and the ability to communicate what I need." She learned this, she pointed out, from the other women in her support group, who had been the first to validate her, the first to tell her unequivocally, *That's fucked up.*

———

Motherhood, Rich writes, used to be revered as the essence of life. "The words for mother and mud (earth, slime, the matter of which the planet is composed, the dust or clay of which 'man' is built) are extremely close in many languages: mutter, madre, mater, material, moeder, modder." As mothers have been isolated from the churn and swirl of society, as their identities as anything other than mothers have been cleaved from their maternal selves, as their sense of community and meaning has been shriveled by a society in which parents and children live apart from other adults, as they have been perpetually warned and reprimanded and "educated" by medical professionals and a media culture of excessive fear, the tremendous power of motherhood has been reduced from flame to burnt ember. Rich writes, "In transfiguring and enslaving woman, the womb—the ultimate source of this power—has historically been turned against us and itself made into a source of powerlessness."

How to reclaim it? I envision a world in which to become a mother is something like, as Louise Erdrich put it, "being initiated into high priestesshood": a world in which motherhood is a creative, generative force that shapes society's myths and trajectory. This requires understanding motherhood not as an exercise of passivity, shrinking back from one's self and life in a sentimental wash of childlike murmurs and infinite patience, but as the active acquisition of power, the mother's chest inflating with the breath of creation like that of an old God on a church ceiling. It means acknowledging that mothers don't just nurture: mothers can also destroy, remake, sabotage, resist.

I learned this when I buried my daughter's placenta. The placenta, envisioned as the baby's twin, soul, spirit, or guardian, is buried in many cultures as a sign of honor and respect, and to tie the baby to the land. I kept it after Elena's birth, and for three years, the placenta sat in a freezer in my dad's storage room, nestled among butchered deer and cows. I was going to bury it when she was three months old, but I was too tied up with trying to keep a small helpless being alive and myself relatively together to go through with it. Then, one day in spring when my daughter was two, my stepmom was rummaging around in the freezer when she came across the heavy plastic bag containing a round tub, and she asked my dad, "What's this?" to which he replied, "Sarah's placenta." I was given an ultimatum. The placenta had to be in the ground by the time Elena turned three.

My family are not really the placenta-burying kind of people. My stepmom did have a home birth. But, even with her astrological leanings, she was revolted by the notion of eating one's placenta, dehydrated into innocuous vitamins or not, and she did not hang on to hers. My sister birthed each of her kids with no medicine and no midwives as if she were going for a brisk 10k, and was back at work three months later. Had you told me in 2004 that in twelve years I'd be lovingly cradling one of my own bloody organs, I would have laughed in your face. Yet becoming a parent showed me how little I knew about myself, how malleable and vulnerable and also how brave I could be.

On my daughter's third birthday, Jorge retrieved the tub containing the placenta from the freezer and Dad had the insight that we should probably run it under warm water for a second, lest the placenta had stuck to the edges. So I held the tub in the sink, looking at the writing on top: SARAH MENKEDICK, 07/08/82 (31 YEARS OLD), and the nurse's name, and the time the placenta was plopped in here and frozen—15:03, 6/4/2014. All these numbers, dates, and times, tremendously evocative of the most powerful experience of my life.

Just before 15:03 the midwife had asked Jorge to cut the cord, then showed me my placenta, raw and bloody on the uterine side, and on the side facing the fetus veiny and deep purple, the thick branches of the "tree of life" rising from the white trunk of the umbilical cord. I marveled over it, without a real understanding then that the placenta had been the initial and ultimate invasion of my body and self, more so even than the baby.

In the earliest stages of pregnancy, the fertilized egg begins to divide, and after about five days it has formed a blastocyst, characterized by an inner mass of cells that will become the amniotic sac and the body of the fetus, and an outer wall of cells—called trophoblasts—that will become the placenta. These trophoblasts are incredibly invasive: they burrow into the woman's uterine lining and siphon from her blood supply, harnessing nutrients for the growing embryo. They are so aggressive that researchers compare them to cancer cells, and if they attach to the wrong spot—the fallopian tubes, another part of the abdomen, or a part of the uterine lining that is too thin or scarred—they can rupture organs or cause the mother to bleed to death. To quote a 2014 New York Times article on placental research: "[Trophoblasts] shove other cells out of the way and destroy them with digestive enzymes or secrete substances that induce the cells to kill themselves."

This is what is happening while mothers are being told to imagine their babies as kidney beans. Their bodies are being violently appropriated: their blood flow tapped, rerouted, and flooded with hormones and messages to keep the body from rejecting this new, demanding organ; their nutrients and resources channeled entirely into building a placenta that will be larger than the baby for half of the pregnancy, weigh more than a pound at birth, and contain thirty-two miles of capillaries. I spent the first trimester of my own pregnancy nauseated, exhausted, and depressed. I slept for fourteen-hour stretches, ate a lot of bagels, cried, and drank tea religiously for the first time in my life. At twelve weeks, when the placenta had established itself and provided a blood supply for the baby, I was finally hungry and able to run again.

The placenta is the baby's advocate. Its aim is to get as much as it can for its charge, to deposit the latter's waste and excess heat into the mother's bloodstream, and to filter out any dangerous toxins in the mother's blood. When the fetus lacks a gut, lungs, skin, a liver, kidneys, and an immune system, the placenta does the work of all of these. It mediates between the mother and the baby, trying to draw the best from the former to nourish the latter.

My placenta was the link between me and my daughter, the last remnant of her birth and of our lingering physical connection. On the day of its burial my family strolled through the pastures to the tallest oak tree on the farm, just inside the welcome shade of the woods. Jorge carried a ten-pound rock with an engraving that read LA FAMILIA SANTIAGO, JULY 3, 2010, a gift my cousin had given us for our wedding as a way of reminding us that we were now a unit. We would place the rock atop the hole we dug for the placenta.

Unexpectedly, in spite of the awkwardness and wariness of my family, I began to cry as I extracted the placenta from its tub, smearing her blood and my blood all over my hands. I cried as I placed it in the small hole my dad and Jorge had dug, and I cried harder when my daughter hugged me. I'd wanted to say something big and sweeping to her, but in the end I was a bit overcome with embarrassment and emotion, and so I just looked at the delicate features of her little face and said, "Thank you." She kissed me, with the gentle understanding that she is doomed to spend a lifetime with a mother who sobs over symbolic rocks at rural ceremonies.

Elena and I placed flowers and handfuls of earth atop her placenta. I felt a wrenching mourning for the end of her babyhood—not because I missed her milky smell, or swirling a finger around the tenderness of her soft spot, or her marshmallow baby fat—but because that period demanded more of me than any other time of my life. Because it was when I had to be the bravest and most vulnerable person I have ever been. I dropped fistfuls of Ohio dirt on top of the placenta and one thought looped through my head: this birthing and early mothering was the hardest thing I have ever done. *This was the hardest thing I have ever done.*

That Sunday night of Elena's third birthday, I wept beside her in bed. For her, but more, I believe, for myself: for a resilience I never knew I had, and that I believe all mothers possess, however they choose to express it. We are not soft, sweet, docile icons, mute and passive virgins: we are fucking fierce. Motherhood requires a tremendous bravery that I never recognized or celebrated before I was forced to come into it, shaking and stunned. It leads women to march, to protest, to fight, to enact change, to persevere at great risk to themselves, to challenge the very foundation of society.

After the placenta had been buried, we set the rock atop it, and we all walked back to the house. Elena jumped on a mini trampoline, my niece went to recover from all the overwrought midlife emotion on the couch, my parents made lunch. A summer breeze stirred the pear tree. I washed the blood from my hands, thinking about the oak, the rock, the placenta. Buried there is the truth of what it feels like to be so susceptible and broken-open, and also to say: *I can do this. I will do this.* I contain this, thirty-two miles of capillaries, a new tree of life. Mutter, madre, mater, material, moeder, modder: the mud, the material, the making at the heart of everything.

WHEN WE RETURNED *to the States from Oaxaca, I was on the brink of major depression. I was buoyed only by the hope that Pittsburgh might be safe for us: a possibility quickly blown up by news stories of lead in Pittsburgh's water and a notice from the city that the house we were renting had lead service lines.*

The first therapist I went to see specialized in postpartum mood disorders and had an office in a converted hotel next to the river and railroad tracks downtown. The therapist was kind, simultaneously matronly and tough. I tried to come off as intelligent, too intelligent to have any real mental illness. I dreaded her sympathy. I filled out some intake forms. We talked a bit about work-life balance.

"OCD is a beast," she said suddenly. A massive wave of emotion swelled from whatever recess I'd been forcibly, exhaustedly cramming it into. I held it back with all my strength. I will not cry here. I will not break down. *But the burning urgency of the tears, and how difficult it was to repress them, revealed to me that I was in fact utterly captive to this beast. I saw the magnitude of the struggle: how hard it had been and how hard I'd been trying not to see it.*

"It takes an enormous amount of energy to do what you're doing," she told me, meaning to live with the weight of constant worry and to also live as though it is not a big deal, as though you are a normal person going about a normal life. Each day involved navigating a titanic amount of fear and repression, all the while doing the dishes and cheering the baby on her tricycle and dancing to "Shake Your Booty." The therapist saw through my calm, smart veneer to the subconscious noise I was constantly muting and briefly unmuted it, and the impact was deafening and shattering.

At the end of my session, I descended the escalator and crossed the park-

ing lot to my car and sat there for a few moments all shut up in the heat, the river coursing in front of me, the skyline beyond it flat and pretty as a postcard. I rested my forehead on the wheel and sobbed.

The therapist told me that I should really seek specialized help for my OCD, and she wasn't qualified to provide it: a rare act of professional integrity and honesty I would come to appreciate.

I found my next therapist eight months later. He had the couch and the requisite Pittsburgh cityscapes decorating his walls, but he treated OCD as if it were a bothersome skin infection, not a tortured and complex afflic-tion of the mind stemming from a deep psychological wound. I talked a little about my past—living and traveling overseas, then coming to Pitts-burgh for an MFA program, then leaving again for Mexico and coming back again—and a little about how early motherhood had made me scared of so many things I hadn't even flinched at or known existed years ago. He used none of the parroting empathetic language I'd been prepared for— "That sounds exhausting!" Instead, he settled his tidy laptop on his lap and launched into a battery of matter-of-fact questions: Did I count? Did I check? How many times? How often? Did I wash my hands? How many times? How often? Did I have a clean hand?

"A clean hand?" I asked.

"I think you know what I'm talking about," he said, and I turned a deep crimson. I did. Often, when I touched a surface or an object I thought might be contaminated—a windowsill, say, or a piece of old jewelry—I considered that hand to be dirty, and for the brief spell before I could get to a sink, the other one was clean. I laughed. He knew OCD like a hunter stalking his game. I felt seen in a way that was at once horrifying and embarrassing and gratifying.

Okay, I thought, here it is in all its absurd, debilitating craziness. What I'd taken to be signs of my particular intelligence or vigilance were actu-ally familiar symptoms. Hand-washing, check. Magic numbers, check. Elaborate prohibitions, check.

In each of the many questions the therapist posed to me, I recognized what I'd taken simply to be careful mothering as instead, or also, a symptom. Did I have to order things? Did I feel the need to seek reassurance? Did I constantly feel that something might happen to someone I loved because I wasn't careful enough? Did I repeat actions over and over until they felt right? *There were a few negatives, to questions that clearly corresponded to religious, violent, or sexual OCD. But for the most part, after having sailed through the other questionnaires for depression and bipolar on steady no's, I found this one offered a clear diagnosis. I was almost in awe. I scored in the second-to-highest category of OCD: severe. Suddenly the hours of my day I'd spent Googling, checking, washing, obsessing, crying, and reassuring myself bloomed bright red as evidence of illness. Straightening pillows, adjusting towels, organizing dishes just so: all of these habits and rituals were revealed as symptoms, simultaneously vivid in their strangeness and mundane in their predictability.*

It was confounding, it was a relief, and it was also terrifying: how in the world had I gotten so sick? It was as if I'd been converted to a harsh evangelical religion without even noticing, and now I had no idea how to undo the conversion; it had wormed into me, belief I couldn't un-believe, language I couldn't unlearn, ritual I couldn't bleed of its potent dogma.

The therapist did not find this fascinating. To him, I was another patient who would go through the same process grappling with the same mental blocks; I was programmed and programmable. He did not see me as a mystical, fucked-up bohemian who was complex and difficult and unique, which I thought might be the only upside to all of my misery. I thought about how absurd it was that I had been toiling with this thing, this straightforward and trackable and checklist-able thing, all along, and I had thought it was simply myself. By then, of course, it was my self, bound up with my personality in countless ways I'd start to track, and exorcising it—or at least diminishing it—would also mean starting anew with my own understanding of who I was, what I believed, how I wanted to live my life.

I was given a chart on which to track all of my rituals, and told to make a hierarchy of my fears. We would begin exposure response prevention, or ERP, right away. "You have to give it a fight," said the therapist. "This is the start of a new life."

"Exposure," write the authors of The Mindfulness Workbook for OCD, *"means that you are opening up to something, as a camera lens*

*exposes to light." In exposure, you let the fear in. And you try not to react
to it. Recovery in the world of anxiety is often about not doing: not acting
on a thought, not repressing it, not explaining or responding. Recovery
is about learning to be still and to be aware and to be without control or
certainty. It is about opening oneself up to the worst, most frightening
possibilities, the darkest side of our minds and selves and lives, and then*
doing nothing. *There are few concepts more anathema to the American
way of life.*

I found myself asking over and over as we did exposures, But isn't that
dangerous? *To which Dr. S would laugh with delight and say,* "YES!
Yes, it's dangerous! That's why you have to do it anyway!" *The exposures
may or may not have actually been dangerous, depending on whom you
ask. I painted my daughter's nails with cheap drugstore nail polish. I
walked past construction sites billowing smoke. I didn't wash my daughter's hands before she picked up an apple. They did not fit on any traditional hierarchy of danger, which is what made them specific to OCD, and
I would argue, specific to motherhood.*

*Every mother has her own hierarchy: she may be unperturbed by the
preservatives in Chex Mix but terrified of the germs on a public restroom
hand dryer. Another may not let her child near an electronics cord but allow
the same child to climb ten-foot concrete structures. I remember overhear-
ing two women chatting in the kids' section of a Cincinnati bookstore: one
said, "I wouldn't take my daughter to the park, there are animals there,"
and the other agreed, "So many germs!" I almost laughed, until I realized
that I had lied to the counselors at my daughter's summer camp about her
being allergic to sidewalk chalk because I worried it had lead in it.*

*The idea with exposure therapy is to start with a fear at the bottom of
the hierarchy that causes stress but not the highest level. The exposure—
which may be physical, such as painting nails, or imaginary, such as
writing a story about a feared scenario—has to last long enough to make
the fear become mundane. I grilled Dr. S about why, if I'd been in theory
exposing myself to my fears for years—seeing lead pottery everywhere
in Oaxaca, for example, or walking past construction sites—they had
not become mundane? Dr. S explained that an exposure has to involve a
sustained period of time and concentration in which anxiety peaks and*

then levels off on its own, without my acting on it. What I'd been doing previously is feeling my anxiety peak, desperately performing some sort of ritual to bring it back down, and repeating this ad infinitum. This process had only strengthened the associations between anxiety and whatever set of objects I feared.

Take, he said, riding an escalator. If you're scared of riding an escalator, and you have to ride one for five minutes at the mall, you'll squint your eyes and breathe heavily and rush your way through it, thinking as you get off, Thank God that's over. *If you have to ride the escalator up and down and up and down for two hours, by the end you'll be bored enough that you'll be daydreaming about what you're wearing to work tomorrow. Do this every day for weeks and the escalator becomes just another fixture of daily life.*

"Look," Dr. S told me, "there's always a grain of truth in it." Lead is super-toxic. Germs can kill us. The American government is not very reliable about limiting the use of pesticides or toxic emissions. *It's not as if all of my fears are invented out of whole cloth. But what becomes pathological is the excessiveness and the randomness of the steps I take to create what Dr. S calls a "force field of okayness." How I will rearrange my entire life to avoid a paint chip and then drive through a blizzard on snowy country roads. How I refuse to get gas while my daughter is in the car, but I encourage her to fly down a huge cardboard slide on her stomach because I want her to know adventure. It's the lack of proportion and the hunger for absolute certainty that distinguish my anxiety from "normal" fears, allowing it to develop a logic that perpetually reinforces itself.*

Because, I tell myself, I don't let her play with sidewalk chalk, she hasn't been poisoned. Because I only feed her organic non-GMO food pouches, she hasn't gotten the flu. But instead of certainty, I am always left with more anxiety. If my constant patrols and controls for threats worked, Dr. S told me, "you wouldn't be wasting your time driving down here twice a week for therapy." He's right, of course. And yet this is the only way I know how to mother. Who wants to say, as Dr. S tells me to repeat to myself over and over, The bad thing might happen. The bad thing might happen. The bad thing might happen, but I'm going to do it anyway because I want to live my life.

Exposure means opening up to anxiety and refusing to look away or seek reassurance. It means waiting out the wrenching and overwhelming urge to make it all okay until eventually the anxiety drops. Then it means repeating this again and again.

This is how I found myself walking around my kitchen listening to my own voice softly narrate my own worst nightmares. I scrubbed crusty eggs out of bowls, I made banana muffins, while voice memos describing my fears played on repeat: ominous and gut-wrenching until they diminished slightly and became just another narrative muttered to myself during downtime. Forty minutes or an hour of listening later, and with a sort of futility rather than fear, I would take out my earphones and eat Cheez-Its and watch a documentary with Jorge. I often felt nauseous and weary after these exposures, the way I felt after a big fight or an intense spell of sobbing. But I tired myself out with them until they no longer spun my stomach or set my whole body tingling. I listened to myself say over and over It might not be okay *and* You have to accept that it might not be okay.

I won small victories. Once, when Elena was with me at a therapy appointment, she went digging around in my tote bag and unearthed a gummy bear. It was covered in hair and grit. Elena was still young enough to actually ask me, with total earnestness, if she could eat it. I looked at Dr. S. He said, soberly, gravely, "Sarah, this is a test."

My pain must have been palpable. There was a moment of silence. "Please?" Elena begged.

"Go ahead," I said, and into her little mouth went the crud-covered gummy. She wiggled around with happiness on the couch. I felt a full-body cringe. Dr. S leaned forward, elbows on knees.

"Sarah," he said, "you have to accept that she lives in a world that is mildly dangerous. You have to let her live in that. You have to let her have mildly dangerous experiences in the world. And you have to accept that it might not be okay. You have to say to yourself that it might not be fine. But you're going to let her do it anyway because that is how you want to live your life."

Years later, when I'd grown accustomed to Elena snatching up bits of discarded food from the dog-haired, dust-covered black hole behind the couch, I'd wonder how that moment could ever have struck such fear in me. At the same time, I was sobered by the fact that this trigger—a gummy bear gross with dirt and fuzz—could easily be replaced with a fresh trigger now and the same process would unfold. I asked Dr. S once if it would ever go away. He launched into one of his little anecdotes. "I always talk about the chipmunks," he said. "You know the ones with the high voices? It's like one of those. It's still there, but it shrinks, and it has a funny little voice, and you learn not to pay much attention to it."

JACLYN

9

Psychoanalysis

Many of our accepted ideas about motherhood come from its relationship to psychoanalysis. For psychoanalysts, mothering has long
functioned as both laboratory and metaphor. The mother-infant
relationship has been imagined and studied not only as the groundwork for psychological health or dysfunction, but as a parallel of
the analyst-client relationship. Mothers, writes psychologist Adam
Phillips, were used by British school psychoanalytic theorists "as
though they were a genus, to provide descriptions of what psychoanalysts were supposed to be doing."

Particularly in the years following World War II, British
psychoanalysts—notably, Anna Freud, Melanie Klein, and D. W.
Winnicott, some of the most respected and influential of their
generation—conducted observational studies of infants and very
young children. Infant-mother relationships provided them with
templates for the development of a healthy or pathological psyche,
and for the ideal relationship between analyst and client. The
infant—new, needy, transparent in its desires—was a formidable
subject, for psychoanalysts could watch naked patterns of emotion play across its face and project all manner of interior sources
or exterior consequences onto them. The infant was a blank slate

being written on in real time by its mother, with the psychoanalysts charting and speculating on the significance of each mark.

Psychoanalytic theory has long drawn on infancy as a prototype for adult psychological health or neurosis: in the psychoanalytical purview, the obsessions, losses, fears, repressed desires, and relationships formed during this time harden in the growing brain, then sink down into the subconscious, where they shape the decisions and ideals of the full-grown person. Thus to observe an infant interacting with its mother in real time, being coddled or ignored, reprimanded or pacified, was to witness the adult psyche in formation, a live feed of the emerging pathologies and behavior patterns the analyst might assess later in the day in her office. Each small detail in this observation indicates a potential path to future harm or prosperity, and even though these were scientific studies, artificial in countless ways, we have inherited this fixation on a direct cause-and-effect relationship between a child's personality and behavior and a mother's most minute actions.

The introduction to the inaugural issue of *The Psychoanalytic Study of the Child*, a journal founded in 1945 that featured many of the psychoanalytic pioneers and luminaries of the day, declared that the future of society depended on children's capacity "to withstand the ever mounting tensions in the world" and that psychoanalysis was the essential tool for studying and developing this capacity. The introduction highlighted some of the important work psychoanalysts were doing to save children from future psychological debility. For example, one study of "the nursing situation" had revealed that if, when the infant was nursing, the mother proffered "a breast but not a maternal smile," the infant would not be able to establish both the necessary oral and visual connections and proper object relations, all of which would have "uncertain consequences for adult functioning." The absence of that one crucial element—the maternal smile—could lead to a lifetime of struggle.

Observing the infant would also, psychoanalysts argued, provide an opportune context in which to study themselves; alongside meticulously documented observations of what was happening minute-to-minute between the infant and his mother, the psycho-analyst was to note his or her own state of mind. Then, reviewing the notes, the psychoanalyst could discern the smoke trails of trans-ference and countertransference: the projection of unconscious mental processes and structures from the infant to the analyst (or the mother), and the analyst's projection back. The observations gleaned through "a privileged entry . . . into the terra incognito of this infant-person's private internal world" could teach the psycho-analysts to become psychoanalysts.

At the same time, they were developing enduring theories about the nature and meaning of motherhood. Imbued with a notion of infancy as the most critical life stage, psychoanalysts mapped onto their observations all manner of potential hazards. Intensely identified with the infant, they experienced any minor inattention to his or her needs as painful.

In a 2006 article on psychoanalysis and infant observation for the *International Journal of Psychoanalysis,* Margot Waddell notes the observations of a psychoanalyst named Paola, who followed an Ital-ian family for months after the birth of their second child, Giulia. The mother gave Giulia a bath that was too cold, and the baby shiv-ered and cried; Paola was "all but overwhelmed by the painfulness of the situation, by the impact of her own identification with the baby and by how that identification affected her capacity to remain a sympathetic and disinterested recorder." Paola saw herself as the child. Her expectations as she observed, recorded, and interpreted the relationship between mother and baby were not the pragmatic expectations of a fellow adult with complicated needs and respon-sibilities but the expectations of an adult imagining herself into the helpless innocence of an infant.

This is a natural human tendency. All mothers have felt it observ-ing other people's children: a tug in the gut when a mother yells at her little boy at the grocery store, a feeling of revulsion and twisted sadness if she pulls his elbow harshly with a grimace. It is almost impossible, witnessing the power imbalance, the vulner-ability, not to feel aggrieved for the child, not to wish for perfect empathy on the part of the mother, even though all mothers have at many points yelled at their children, tugged them by the elbow, sent them to their rooms alone, or zoned out from boredom or exhaustion. Psychoanalyst Adam Phillips has written that these twentieth-century observational studies have produced "canonical fantasies about mothering"; over time, these fantasies were reconstituted and presented as the healthy norm. It is taken for granted that the mother is and should be her children's primary caregiver, alone most of the time with an infant, all-sacrificing, and meeting her child's every need before it even gains coherence.

Psychoanalysts, writes sociologist Nancy Chodorow, "reify relationships in which women provide exclusive care," assuming that these are natural and universal, and that their lack is devastating. Chodorow notes with irony that even as these influential twentieth-century psychoanalysts took for granted the primary importance of the mother, they often mentioned in asides that they themselves and the children they studied had been raised mainly by nannies—a longtime and widespread European practice for the privileged that eluded psychoanalytic observation.

Nowhere is this reification of the exclusive care of the mother more evident than in the central notion of "attachment." Take, for example, the mid-twentieth-century work of Mary Ainsworth, whose pioneering "strange situation" studies developed today's principal measure of infant attachment. In these studies, a mother and infant sat in a room, observed by researchers behind a one-way mirror. The infant would be subjected to a number of scenarios: a stranger would come in and join the infant and her mother, then leave. The mother would leave the infant alone with the stranger, then return. The mother and stranger would leave the infant alone, then the stranger would return, and then the mother would return.

The infant's reactions to these varying scenarios determined her attachment style: secure, insecure avoidant, or insecure resistant. Healthy infants were secure: they would show perhaps a short, brief upset when mothers left or when strangers appeared, but would quickly readjust. Damaged infants were insecure resistant or avoidant: in the case of the former, they would be too upset when the mother left, crying and fussing, and in the case of the latter, they'd be insufficiently upset, showing little emotion at the mother's departure or return. A good mother had to be swiftly responsive to her infant's needs—building the confidence necessary for the infant to be separate from her—without being overbearing, which might lead the infant either to welcome her departure or to wail in distress. Here, as everywhere, mothers were to walk an extremely fine line.

Ainsworth conjured the three-minute strange situation into a litmus test of the mother's mothering—delicately and perpetually involved but not overly so—and the infant's corresponding psychological vigor. Ainsworth and other psychoanalysts, in the words of Rozsika Parker, "lent the authority of science to representations of the ideal mother as sensitive, measured, attentive, and naturally one with her children." Observational studies like Ainsworth's used hard experimental data—crying time, play behavior, eye contact avoidance—to infer truths about inner states and then to explain how the mother had caused them. "Attachment" garnered a host of powerful meanings that spoke to an invisible psychodrama. "This internalized something that we call attachment," Ainsworth wrote, "has aspects of feelings, memories, wishes, expectancies, and intentions": attachment, in other words, is nothing less than the fire forging the self, with the mother responsible for the associated feelings, memories, wishes, expectations, intentions.

Ainsworth's work has significantly enhanced our understanding of infant development and mother-infant relationships. Yet observational studies like that of the strange situation can generate paradigms in which the mother is all-powerful, and her behavior is entirely determinative not only of her infant's psychological health, but of the entire trajectory of her child's life. Cast aside are genetics, personality, the meshing of the mother and child's temperaments, family size and style, and culture.

The all-powerful mother can be seen as outright dangerous. The psychoanalyst René Spitz, who was born in Austria and came to the

United States in the mid-twentieth century to study child develop-ment, describes the mother as a "disease-provoking agent." Spitz traced infant illnesses to specific "maternal attitudes": the attitude of "Primary Anxious Overpermissiveness," for example, would produce colic; "Hostility in the Guise of Manifest Anxiety" would cause eczema; "Cyclical Mood Swings of the Mother" would drive the child to fecal play; "Maternal Hostility Consciously Compen-sated" would create a hyperthymic child. These categorizations might sound ridiculous now, like a relic of bygone science, and yet the figure of the mother summoned by contemporary attachment theorists like Dr. Sears and T. Berry Brazelton resembles the one conjured by Spitz. We no longer think a mother's mood swings may drive her child to fecal play, but we do believe that if she leaves him crying too long in his crib she might generate ADHD or "poor learning outcomes."

Attachment research illustrates the ways in which observational studies about parenting or childhood often get transmuted into general warnings about maternal influence. Psychoanalyst and attachment parenting pioneer John Bowlby, for example, became interested in attachment behavior after reading studies on geese, which showed that goslings will "imprint" on whichever animal they come in contact with after birth (an unsurprising revelation for any mother who's read the book *Are You My Mother?* on end-less repeat). Bowlby—whose upper-class mother subscribed to the behavioralist belief that paying too much attention to a child would make him weak and dependent, and largely ignored her son as he was growing up—studied delinquent and hospitalized chil-dren. He classified them according to behaviors and types, publish-ing reports on their characteristics. In 1949, he was commissioned by the World Health Organization to conduct a study on the men-tal health of orphans following World War II. The resulting work, *Maternal Care and Mental Health*, was published in 1951. In it, Bowlby argued that children who were separated from their mothers, or who did not have a warm, intimate, loving, and continuous rela-tionship with them, could suffer permanent trauma.

At the time, this was a radical proposition. John Watson's behaviorism had been the dominant parenting theory of the past half-century. Watson, a prominent psychologist, emerged from a traumatic, oppressively pious, poor childhood to found a quasi-religious movement that claimed all behavior is conditioned and results from external situations rather than internal states. Behaviorism demanded rigid routine and discipline and a total lack of emotion and affection on the part of caregivers, in order to condition children into strength and self-sufficiency. A pat on the hand was considered sufficient praise. A kiss was seen as nearly obscene. The claim that not only was affection essential, but that its withholding could cause permanent damage, was thus shocking, anathema, and radical. Bowlby spent his career advancing these ideas, which are now axiomatic; attachment is as integral to the way we talk about parenting as sleep or diapers.

Attachment parenting is not bogus, but when lumped together with intensive parenting techniques and enduring psychoanalytic fantasies about the mother, it is often taken to extremes. There were huge benefits to Bowlby's work, including reforms to European institutions dedicated to caring for children, the end of hospital policies prohibiting parents from staying with their sick babies, and a new understanding of the importance of loving care—not just food and supervision—in a young child's life. Yet there were also important consequences, some inspired by Bowlby himself, and others by the heirs to his work, including contemporary pediatricians who warn mothers that co-sleeping or failing to breastfeed or having a beer could lead to ruin. For his part, Bowlby was a rabid opponent of working mothers. He listed "full-time employment of mother" as a situation on par with "social calamity—war, famine" in terms of the damage it could cause a child. His work was distributed as a warning to women looking to enter the workforce.

Many studies that warn about the perils of maternal neglect are derived from such extreme circumstances: infants whose mothers have died, infants in understaffed orphanages or war nurseries, infants in child-care centers for women prisoners. Their lesson, however, is not specific but general: *any* neglect on the part of a mother can be catastrophic. Combined with observational studies of "normal" infant development, they craft a powerful fantasy of perpetual hyperattunement, haunted by the danger of a wrong move. This is the legacy we've inherited from psychoanalysis: watching infants as if their every gesture might signify potential genius or failure, watching mothers to see if they are perfectly adept, perfectly responsive in a way that quiets our deepest fears and ignites our most profound fantasies about protection and love.

Attachment derives from the most pervasive contemporary mothering myth: the belief that it is possible to eradicate oneself and one's own particular desires to disappear completely into another's experience, all the while administering this experience with a meticulous scientific level of management and finding ecstatic, natural fulfillment in the process. Babies and mothers are supposed to be in sync, physically, biologically, emotionally, while the mother simultaneously shapes the baby's physical, biological, and emotional self. The mother here is not a person; she is a function. She has been compressed into a therapist. It is impossible to see mothers, feel them, know them as people, just as it is impossible—and improper—to see and know and feel a therapist. "Midcentury psychoanalytic thinking," writes psychoanalyst and author Shari Thurer, "colluded in the obliteration of mothers as persons."

Jaclyn knew she wanted to be a rabbi at age six, when her mother was diagnosed with brain cancer. Her mother was thirty-seven and had just given birth to Jaclyn's younger brother. Jaclyn remembers the conversation: "Mom has something in her brain that needs to be taken out. She's going to have surgery, and everything's going to be okay." Jaclyn was certain her mother was going to the hospital to die.

Her mother recovered and never relapsed. But Jaclyn was forever changed. She learned that terrible things may happen and that people you love may get sick. She left her mother's hospital room feeling that the sole power she had was prayer. *Please make my mom better. Please do whatever You can to get her out.* She became possessed by the conviction that there was "something bigger than us, something bigger than the here and now."

Jaclyn's parents had both come of age Jewish in New York in the 1960s and 1970s. In that world, the Holocaust was a vivid event in recent history and memory, present in people's minds and lives. Jewish identity was important and central. At the same time, even though they went to a conservative synagogue, Jaclyn's parents were not particularly religious; that is, they were not strict about the observation of Jewish laws and codes of behavior. Everyone they were friends with was Jewish; their neighborhood was Jewish. Her parents married in 1974, and five years later they moved to California. Their first priority there was to join a synagogue. They had Jaclyn in 1984 and sent her, and later her brother, to Jewish day school.

In 1997, Jaclyn had her bat mitzvah, an event that held particular significance for her because of her acute sense of life and death. She describes her adolescent outlook—catastrophic, clear-eyed, and cosmic—and the ritual of the bat mitzvah as going together "like chocolate and peanut butter." As she went through the process, she felt as though this was the most meaningful moment of her life and had come at just the right time.

After high school, Jaclyn went to rabbinical school, where she felt pressure to become more traditionally observant. She had attended a reform synagogue all her life, and thus hadn't had to adhere to all the "persnickety" rules. For a year, she grew very conscious of what she ate, she kept kosher as much as possible, she didn't eat bread during Passover, she tried not to drive or spend money on the Sabbath. It was "a lovely effort to have more quiet," and in that quiet she discovered that, for her, the joy of religion came from a sense of purpose and connection, not from particular codes of conduct. She didn't need a formal description of God.

She felt Him there in her singing. She wanted to be a good person, and Judaism seemed "the most sensible, approachable, beautiful blueprint for how to be a good person in the world."

Whenever she met people who were agonizing over failing to be more observant, who didn't feel they were devout or serious enough, she reassured them. *Let me tell you,* she'd say, *about the year I grew up.* She'd talk about how she'd been very strict and followed all the rules and how it felt good, how it gave her insight, but how in the end it didn't elevate her spiritually. In seeing people's reactions when she told her story, she discovered a truth that would later become core to her life: saying *This is what I went through* is a powerful, vulnerable experience that changes lives. "What is religion supposed to be?" Jaclyn asked me. "A form of connection in a very dark world to something bigger than the individual alone."

Jaclyn met her future husband, Josh, on Jdate, a Jewish online dating service. They were married in June 2013 and she got pregnant right away. This was ironic, considering that they'd had long, weighty conversations about the possibility that they might not conceive immediately. They knew the deep-rooted stigma against infertility in the Jewish community. They were so hyperaware and conscious of fertility issues that they were almost pessimistic about their hopes of starting a family, and then it happened precisely as it was supposed to. Jaclyn had no idea that another type of darkness might appear for her around the corner. "I was far more aware of the fact that I could have a miscarriage than the fact that I might suffer tremendously after our child was born. Postpartum depression was this thing that I knew existed, but it was so far away—it wasn't something that entered my orbit."

This is a refrain I hear from all of the women I've talked to: postpartum depression is the sensationalist news story, the rare absurdity that afflicts a woman unlike me, a woman unhinged and reckless and unstable. It is distant and pitiable, on the far fringes of society.

Jaclyn had struggled with anxiety at various points throughout her life; at times, it was just a low drone, and at others it was so overwhelming she could not sleep or eat. She downplayed it and never thought it required significant treatment, although a therapist she saw in her late twenties recommended Prozac, which she started and which helped smooth everything out. She even stayed on a very low dose of the drug throughout her pregnancy, after a lot of agonizing and repeated consultations with her OB. Never did the OB, or any doctor, mention to her that she might want to be on the lookout for postpartum anxiety. It never occurred to her either.

Jaclyn's anxiety started at the beginning of her third trimester. It was mid-October and Seattle was sinking into its winter funk: rainy, gray, 40 degrees. The world tilted just the slightest bit and Jaclyn could feel herself sliding. There was a sense of impending darkness. It became profoundly clear that something was about to happen, something was about to change, and "it didn't feel like rainbows and butterflies."

Her anxiety was fueled mostly by the inquiries of doctors. It seemed they were asking her a million questions: *How often is he kicking?* She began counting. *What was she eating? How was she feeling?*

She was already keyed up by the time she went into what she describes as "the longest labor of all time." Her water broke at thirty-nine weeks, following a massage. She waited all day for contractions, which never came, so late that night—a Thursday—she checked into a hospital, where they began administering drugs to kick the contractions into gear.

By Saturday evening, she was still lying in the same hospital room, waiting. Twenty-four hours after she'd arrived, she had received an epidural for the pain. By the time she started pushing, seventy hours in, she could feel the contractions in her hips. She pushed for four and a half hours, and then it was decided that the baby would have to be vacuumed out, and her room flooded with people. She was in a fog, she felt as if she didn't know who she was or where she was, she hadn't slept, she was extremely uncomfortable, she wasn't sure what was happening. It was "a total shitshow." And then Avi emerged from her body and the feeling was simultaneously *What the fuck is this, what just happened* and overjoyed relief and the desire to collapse after labor. She held him, her son, for the first time, thinking, *Oh my God, I just had a baby, oh my God, I made a baby. Oh my God.*

"I guess I was just referencing God," she recounts, surprised.

There was a brief window when her parents came, and together they marveled over the new soul and she felt emotional and amazed. Though she was not in love with her son, she was fascinated by him: *I made this human, and he's cute. He's really cute.* That first night, he slept well.

The second night was "horrendous." He woke up crying, she couldn't soothe him, he was wanting to nurse at short intervals—cluster feeding, as it's called—and her difficulties with breastfeeding became apparent. The next day, rocked, unsettled, she and her husband went home, and she tried to forget about her pain, the discomfort of childbirth, the experience of days and days of labor, to focus on her son. "No one," she told me, "prepared me for how my body was going to need serious recovery time after I had my child." She plowed ahead as if she'd walked into and out of the hospital essentially the same person; as if, as she put it, "babies just fall out of you" and then you keep on going.

Breastfeeding didn't feel right. Something was wrong with one of her breasts. No one could figure out what it was. She underwent an ultrasound and then a mammogram, the latter in a cancer clinic, where she sat terrified and waiting. Meanwhile, she went regularly to a center in Seattle for nursing help, struggling to feed her son. Finally, they discovered that she had a clogged duct and MRSE—antibiotic-resistant bacteria—in her breast. Her son was three weeks old, and Jaclyn was becoming scared and angry and overwhelmed. To her mind, to be even a decent mother she had to breastfeed her baby, she had to love doing it, and she had to be totally available whenever he needed it.

Jaclyn was not playing with her son, not spending time or interacting with him; she was pumping all hours of the day and night. Jaclyn knew people who gave their babies formula and she earnestly believed this was akin to poisoning. She had a friend who fed her daughter formula from Costco, and Jaclyn thought, *She is killing her daughter. She is damaging her for life.* The pressure to breastfeed was so intense she forgot the basic fact that her child needed to eat in order to grow. Jaclyn saw her situation as one of redemptive success or total failure.

This pressure was reinforced everywhere she went in "crunchy-granola-vibey" Seattle. A nurse at her son's first pediatrician's office saw her giving her son breast milk from a bottle and gave her a stark warning about the damage she might do to him.

Everything was, as Jaclyn put it, "turned inside out and upside down." She forgot about God. She forgot about community. She was in pain seemingly all the time. Every two hours, she pumped. She was sleep-deprived. She couldn't recover from her long, excruciating delivery. The only time she remembered her previous life, it was in a wave of panic: *How will I ever be confident enough to string a sentence together in public?*

Every outing was planned around and dominated by the question of breastfeeding. When she went out, she was terrified to go back to the house, as if it were a trap from which she might never escape.

One Monday evening when her son was six weeks old, she went to a new moms' group at a friend's house. Sitting there, listening to everyone, she started to feel like her body was on fire. She felt ill, then almost giddy, then ill again. She came home, unsettled. Her husband had gone to bed; he had to be up early for work. Her son would not sleep or stop crying. He was feeding but could not be sated; he was not getting enough milk. If her motherhood up until then had felt like yarn being tugged from a skein, in that moment it unraveled in one swift yank. She lost her patience. She lost her one and only mooring, her mind, although in another way perhaps she also found it.

At three a.m.—"the worst parts of your life happen at three in the morning"—she looked at the baby in her arms and screamed, "I can't help you, I can't give you what you want! Fuck you!" She was holding him so tightly that she shook him a little, and that minor movement terrified her so much that she laid him gently down, ran into the bedroom, and cried to her sleeping husband, "I can't take care of him, I'm done, I can't do it, you have to take care of him. I've had it!" She could hear her son wailing through the baby monitor, and she collapsed in a heap on the floor. It was the lowest she had ever felt or imagined herself feeling.

Her husband, Josh, jolted out of bed and asked her what had happened and she could only weep, "I shook Avi, we're not supposed to shake Avi." Panicked, he raced into their son's room and picked him up to soothe and assess him. Once it was clear that the baby was fine, her husband switched into high gear. He went downstairs and woke up Jaclyn's mom, who was staying with them to help out. He asked her to watch the baby, and he tended to Jaclyn. Everything came pouring out of her: *I made the biggest mistake of my life in becoming a parent. I don't want to do this anymore.* Her husband promised that the next morning they'd call the doctor and she would get help. *Now,* he said, *sleep.*

She slept. When she woke up, her husband sat down next to her. He'd taken the day off work. They were going to see the doctor.

"He really saved my life," Jaclyn told me.

By ten a.m. they were in her OB's office. The OB said that it sounded like severe postpartum depression, and recommended Jaclyn go to the ER as soon as possible. Jaclyn was resistant. She did not need, she said, to go to the ER. Josh and the doctor both pleaded with her. "Stop trying to think you have it all together," Josh said. "This is not your fault." They told her in many different ways, *This is what is best for everyone; we need you better; it's not your fault.*

Jaclyn fought like hell, but her husband prevailed. They showed up at the ER of the same hospital where her son had been born. Jaclyn felt like a total failure. She had failed the motherhood test. Everything was dirty and chaotic and smelled of bleach. While they sat and waited, frenzied, urgent situations unfolded before them. *Why am I here?* she kept saying to her husband, and *I'm scared,* and *Thank you so much for staying with me*—a "word vomit" as she tried to process what was happening to her. At some point her husband put her on the phone with a friend who had also struggled with postpartum depression. That conversation proved crucial to her acceptance of what was to come. The friend calmed Jaclyn down and told her to let go, to let them help her get better.

They were taken to see a social worker, who within ten minutes told Jaclyn, "I know you." Jaclyn had sat in on this social worker's conversion to Judaism and the woman remembered her. They all had a good laugh at the absurdity, but then the woman said she'd have to find a different social worker and Jaclyn was devastated. The next woman zeroed in on the notion that Jaclyn had shaken her baby, even though Jaclyn insisted she'd only panicked and thought she had, and the baby was fine. Every question returned to shaking the baby, and the social worker insisted Jaclyn had to be admitted to a psychiatric facility. *Please don't do this,* she pleaded with her husband. Her husband began to weep. He was so emotionally drained that he crumbled, and watching him Jaclyn thought, *What the hell have I done?*

Down on the floor blowing bubbles, climbing up and flying down slides, snuggling under the covers of a fort, a mother is childlike. This can be a gift: a furlough from an adult world of productivity into one of presence, clarity, and giddy joy. I have ridden on the carousel for hours with my daughter, up and down on the glassy-green seahorse, dazzled by the whirl and carnival gleam of lights. These are times when I am immensely grateful for an escape hatch from my often dull, limited adult sphere.

Yet as mothers slip into childhood—regressing, as many psychoanalysts have posited—they are expected to be utterly in control as adults. This adulthood is not a complete one. It does not permit a range of passions and desires. Psychoanalyst Rozsika Parker explains that as the child's language balloons with imagination, the mother's becomes imperative; as the child is timeless, the mother is time-bound and hurried; as the child probes moral limits, the mother's morality is overly determined; as the child is vulnerable, the mother is strong. This is evident in the way so many parenting books and articles speak to mothers: as if they are both very young children and rule-following adults.

In *A Life's Work,* an acerbic exploration of motherhood, Rachel Cusk writes of pregnancy literature, "You are offered a list of foods to eat, recipes for how to combine them, and occasionally photographs of the finished result, with captions such as *Salad* or *Bowl of Granola.* You are told, with the help of illustrations, how to get into bed, how to lie in it, and how to get up again. You are told, again with illustrations, how to make love."

The mother becomes, in the words of psychologist James Hillman, "marooned in adulthood," a sad and isolating island of rigidly prescribed gestures, language, and behaviors. In trying to make her child "perfect" and to act so herself, the mother is to bleed herself and her maternal relationship of human dynamism. Parker writes, "Mothers are expected to be containing and cognizant in a culture that curtails the range of feelings deemed 'normal' in them, and constructs a split representation of mothers as either children themselves or their children's therapists."

A mother is unable to acknowledge the range of ardors her children can stir in her; to do so would be to accept that she is not only a bad mother, but an *unnatural* one. She stiffens instead into what we in the twenty-first century would recognize as a *parent:* rationalizing, measuring, studying, advising, and shaping an ideal little postindustrial citizen who will learn empathy through reading and problem-solve his way out of tantrums and develop his cognitive capacities through creative play. Motherhood as relationship, heady with love and hate and struggle and desire, has become taboo and uncouth. A relationship cannot be standardized.

I have seen the psychoanalytic fantasy played out in designated kid spaces all around me: the playground, the Children's Museum, the shallow end of the pool. I have participated in it myself. Parents speak in a cartoonish parent-ese of platitudes and aphorisms, often in the first-person plural, like robots programmed to micromanage for maximum learning potential and minimum drama. There is the playground parent who lets her children know in a restrained singsong that they'll be leaving in five minutes, then four, then three, then two, then one, and "What's the last thing we can do? What can we do to get ready now, so that we can all leave the playground?" The mother at the pool who says: "I really like how you got in the pool the *safe* way, sweetheart, did you see how you did that?" and whose no-no's sound as if they've been dehydrated and sweetened. The Daniel Tiger parents—including me—who bust out one of the myriad educational jingles in the hope that the infinite patience and wisdom of Daniel's parents will have some sort of bearing on real life.

I've heard bearded dads unironically croon, "If you have to go potty, STOP and go right away!" Moms who sing, "When you wait, you can imagine anything!" as if this were truly liberating for a three-year-old. In this parlance everything is a suggestion, but one with only one possible answer that has to come via the most excruciating process of persuasion. This is neither childhood nor adulthood but the robotic contemporary invention of experts.

As psychologist Alison Gopnik has put it, we don't say that we "wife" our husband or that we "daughter" our parents. We don't even speak of "fathering" children beyond the actual physical act of conception. But we do speak of "parenting" and "mothering" as verbs: actions that we undertake for others. Of course, mothers do have to have different relationships with their children than they would with their grown parents or with other adults. There is an aspect of performance to mothering. The mother of a young child can't simply stand up and walk away; she can't reason or plead. She can barely steal ten minutes for a walk or a bath.

There are no equivalencies to the mother-child relationship. The particular intimacy of that closed unit, the immensity of obligation it demands and the surprising difficulty and beauty of that obligation, which for many women is a wholly new form of love—this relationship could lead to fascinating explorations of the human condition via studies of what psychoanalysts have dryly called "maternal states," but mostly, it has not. Psychoanalysis has instead birthed the fantasy of the therapist-mother. This mother is someone, in the words of French feminist Luce Irigaray, "who makes the stereotypical gestures she is told to make, who has no personal language and who has no identity."

Rozsika Parker writes, "Our culture permits flexibility in other activities that involve intimacy, some heterogeneity, some diversity of style, but hardly any at all when it comes to mothering." Ambivalence, above all, is taboo. Parker argues that maternal ambivalence is essential for a nuanced and fluid relationship between mother and child. The term "maternal ambivalence" is slightly misleading here: by ambivalence, Parker is not suggesting a mild indecisiveness, an I'm-not-sure shrug. For Parker, ambivalence is the storm between love and hate. She defines it as "the experience shared variously by all mothers in which loving and hating feelings for their children exist side by side."

Parker profiles a series of women who are struggling with their maternal ambivalence; most of them are unconscious of it and repress the feeling, only to find it seeping out through the seams of their lives in sadness, frustration, isolation. They struggle to live up to a maternal ideal of unity and omnipotence; they believe their child's life should be their life, their child's desires should be their desires. Parker distinguishes this dangerous fantasy of oneness from a different goal of mutuality: shared moments when mothers and children are both happy and satisfied, when neither experiences the other "as a source of either plenitude or deprivation."

I think immediately of the first time I was able to sit on the floor and read poetry while Elena drew, how magical it felt to be able to be close to her and also to be swimming in the still pool of those poems. In both friendship and courtship, there is a point in a relationship when two people are able to be alone together—reading, perhaps, or drawing or working—and this marks the beginning of a new type of intimacy. The moments when Elena is happy playing dress-up while I cook or write in my journal, or when she sits on the bed with Jorge and me and play-acts reading her book while we read ours, are my favorite experiences of family life. To establish this kind of intimacy, a mother needs ambivalence. She needs it to reclaim herself, to find space in which to breathe and grow. Parker writes, "Both mother and child need the mother's affirmation of her own needs, desires, opinions, rage, love and hatred if separateness is to be established—and thus relationship." Without ambivalence, motherhood is an empty performance.

Ambivalence is also essential, according to Parker, because it forces the mother to see her child anew, to understand her more deeply, and to react with a deeper compassion. Parker quotes Freud, "We owe the fairest flowering of our love to the reaction against the hostile impulse which we sense within us." The hatred illuminates just how profound and real our love can be. The hatred has us grit lullabies through our teeth until we laugh and give up and sing. And sometimes, too, it can break us, driving us to moments of deep hurt and shame, just as the love can break us and drive us to intense grief and fear.

Adrienne Rich wrote in 1976, "My children cause me the most exquisite suffering of which I have any experience. It is the suffering of ambivalence: the murderous alternation between bitter resentment and raw-edged nerves and blissful gratification." It is rare for a mother to admit this. Aggression in women is socially unacceptable and frowned upon, and in this context, it is quasi-criminal. The psychoanalyst Barbara Almond has written, "In my experiences with patients I have found that this aggression is both psychologically inevitable and socially unacceptable to a very marked degree." Almond argues that the repression of ambivalence has created a society full of brittle "too-good mothers," who are terrorized by stories of monster babies and terrified of producing one via error or neglect, who second-guess and qualify their instincts with intensive research and effort, who feel they must not only do everything right but must also love doing it. She concludes, "Maternal ambivalence in its most extreme forms, the dark side of motherhood, is today's crime that dares not speak its name."

Denying ambivalence, and the hate that engenders it, denies a mother her personhood. "The mother," wrote psychoanalyst D. W. Winnicott, "hates her infant from the word go." He listed eighteen precise reasons why she hates him: "He is ruthless, treats her as scum, an unpaid servant, a slave. . . . His excited love is cupboard love, so that having got what he wants he throws her away like an orange peel. . . . He is suspicious, refuses her good food, and makes her doubt herself, but eats well with his aunt. . . . At first he does not know at all what she does or what she sacrifices for him. Especially he cannot allow for her hate."

Winnicott is best known for his concept of the "good-enough mother," who is really "good enough" in the way that, say, an organic rosehip macaron with fresh raspberry cream is "good enough" as a dessert. She is exceptionally attuned and masterfully attentive. Winnicott posits that a mother should not act on hate, but that she needs it, the way cookie dough needs salt. Her child needs it, too: the hate permits a separation that makes room for relationship, and the infant's own emerging sense of self.

Hate, Winnicott argued, arises naturally from situations in which one person has an intense, volatile need for another, of which motherhood is the most classic example. Becoming a mother is the process of learning to tolerate this hate: not to repress or ignore it, but to sit with it, much in the way anxious patients must endure their anxiety. Repressing hate causes it to fester, then arise in unexpected places: as fear, fastidiousness, resentment, depression. Winnicott wrote, "A mother has to be able to tolerate hating her baby without doing anything about it. She cannot express it to him. If, for fear of what she may do, she cannot hate appropriately when hurt by her child she must fall back on masochism, and I think it is this that gives rise to the false theory of a natural masochism in women."

It is important to note the subtleties here: Winnicott is not saying that it is acceptable for a mother to inflict her hate on her child. He emphasizes the need to "hate appropriately," to accept the hate and incorporate it into the parenting picture. Instead, pummeled by shame and guilt, women hate themselves for hating, punish themselves for hating, and so on and so on in a cycle. I have lived it myself.

The first time I expressed my hate, my daughter was less than two months old. We had spent the day at nearby Kenyon College with my dad, walking the grounds, then checking out a fishing spot Dad would visit later in the summer. It had been a beautiful day, filled with the green blurs of Ohio fields outside the window, sprays of daisies, and the sunset like steeping raspberry tea. At the end of the day, back at my parents' cabin, Elena would not sleep. She fussed in her newborn way without focus or obvious cause, and after an hour of nursing-rocking nursing-rocking I was seething with barely contained rage. My skin seemed the thinnest of cling wrap holding it back.

I held her on my knees in bed, stared into her eyes, and shouted, "I HATE YOU!" Her tiny face was red and befuddled and her eyes focused on me for an instant. Then she resumed her grunts and squeaks. The statement seemed to have little effect on her, but it destroyed me like a capsule set to fizzing. All of my hate evaporated along with all of my self-respect, and my very sense of self. I have never felt such a profound and destructive failure. I confessed it to Jorge when he returned as if I were revealing the whereabouts of a buried body, I wrote pages and pages about it in my journal the following morning, I treated my baby's body for days with extra care as if I had literally scalded her skin. Yet having released this most unmotherly of statements I also felt freed. I had been returned to the ideal state of endless maternal selflessness. The hate was a separate, evil creature I needed to exorcise and it was gone, dissolved in the acid of guilt.

But of course, it recurred. Of course, there were other incidents of rage, of hate. I did not act on them physically, but they were there nonetheless, pressing their way to the surface of a pond I tried to force into placidity. Gradually I learned to recognize them, to sit through them, and it took me a long time to understand that they made my love more palpable and precious. They left me feeling what I imagine many mothers feel when their children finally sleep at night: a mix of heartache, nostalgia, longing, relief, guilt, fear, and sheer wonder, tracing the tiny crook of the elbow, the filigreed eyelashes, the tender soles of the feet.

Jaclyn gave in. Her husband went home to the baby; she went to one of the antepartum rooms in the hospital and got the best night of sleep she'd had in weeks. The next day, staff psychologists and a psychiatrist visited her. Everyone was nice and understanding and thoughtful; she was at Seattle's top hospital. "Even in my sort of fog, I could definitely tell that this was not their first time dealing with this situation," she told me. They reassured her that she would be fine, that she would get better and be the best mother she could be for her son. The OB she'd seen the day before came over to check on her. She felt supported and more settled. They announced that they'd secured her a bed and would be transferring her to the psychiatric ward at another hospital. Her husband could meet her there to say goodbye. She was put on a gurney and wheeled out to the ambulance. En route, she covered her face with her coat. She had never been so embarrassed in her life.

"My whole life," she told me, "I've seen a psychiatric facility as . . . something that was just such a *shonda*." This is a Yiddish word for an embarrassment. Only crazy people went there, people who tried to kill themselves.

She arrived at ten-thirty at night and had to turn over most of her belongings: shoelaces, power cord, razor. When they took her breast pump, Jaclyn was overcome with a sense of regret; clearly this had all been a mistake. She asked, "How long am I going to be here?" The night nurse stared back blankly and replied, "Well, you could be here for a couple of weeks!"

Oh my God, I'm going to die here, Jaclyn thought. *I am fucked.* She was taken to her room. Every hour, someone came by to check that she was still in her bed. Somehow, after several checks, she fell asleep.

Her first encounter the following day was with the occupational therapist, who took Jaclyn aside and quietly informed her that she was a member of Jaclyn's synagogue and wouldn't reveal anything about meeting Jaclyn in here. Jaclyn froze. She had no idea what to say. She was terrified, resistant, vulnerable, and this woman *knew* her.

There were nine beds in the facility. There were people who'd attempted suicide, people with schizophrenia, people who needed electroshock therapy, bipolar people, severely depressed people. There was one woman who came in talking about being pregnant, and for an instant Jaclyn thought, *I can be friends with her!* but it soon became clear that the woman was incoherent, rambling about having had an abortion, interrupting people to make inappropriate comments. There was a woman who would not leave her bed and who screamed randomly throughout the day.

There were no locks on the doors. Jaclyn was terrified; she was a mess. The staff acknowledged that this was not the ideal setting for her but insisted she play by their rules to get out. She had to be stabilized, and first that meant medication. The psychiatrist she saw was "the sweetest guy," who kept apologizing for her being in there, saying things like *I know this is not ideal. I know that this is really not where you should be. If we had a perfect world, you'd be in a place specifically for mothers with PPD, but we don't have that. Thank you for being a trouper. I know you're going to be okay.* This was tremendously soothing for Jaclyn. Later, Swedish Hospital, where she delivered in Seattle, would open the Swedish Center for Perinatal Bonding and Support, in which women suffering from postpartum mood disorders could get treatment with their babies. Clearly, even with a lack of resources at that moment, there was an understand-

ing and a recognition about what kind of care women in this particular situation needed. The psychiatrist took her from 10 to 40
milligrams of Prozac a day, which helped very quickly.

Jaclyn would wake up, pump, get breakfast, and then head to a
workshop or a seminar on coping skills or anger management. The
psychiatrist would come for one-on-one meetings. There would be
art activities and movies. "It's sort of like camp!" Her husband took
two weeks off work and came to visit her every day. She quietly
accepted her situation, settling into it. She found the staff friendly,
understanding, even apologetic. She was reassured by this.

Near the end of a week, the doctors told her that she had stabilized enough to go. She was ecstatic at the prospect of finally seeing her son. It had taken this distance for her to realize how much
she loved him. "I needed a time-out," she says, matter-of-factly. Up
to that point, she had felt no connection; she wasn't sure she even
liked him. By the end of those six days, the love that had been
buried beneath stress began shining through. She wanted nothing
more in the world than to see her baby.

Being released "was like getting out of prison." She had only
been outside once during her stay, and walking into the fresh air
felt like starting her life over.

She returned home with her husband. Holding her son again,
she cried and cried. "I promise," she told him, "I'm going to work
on getting better." Avi was six weeks old. He was beginning to
smile. At that moment, her life as a mother cleaved neatly in two;
there was the first half, of fear and despair, kick counts, isolation,
pumping all hours of the day and night, *have to get it right,* and then
there was the second half, with the familiar markers of maternal
exhaustion—the diapers, the sleep deprivation, the tantrums—but
with Jaclyn done now with the fantasy, ready to be herself.

10

Maternalism and Momism

In Puritan New England, mothers were considered incidental at best. Fathers shaped their children, and they did so mostly with unsparing use of the rod. A child playing idly might be publicly whipped as an example to his peers. Puritan children had to have the innate tendency to sin beaten out of them, and God's word driven in. Only a father had the perceived moral authority and education to do this; women were powerless not only in the civic and political spheres, but in the home as well. They were imagined as weak and vulnerable to "passions" and "indulgence" and "excessive fondness," grave defects in a place that demanded a steely focus on survival. Women had little time for what we would understand as "child care"—cuddling, teaching, playing—as they went about carving a living from wilderness, making and cultivating the fundamentals of sustenance. Puritan child-rearing advice manuals were addressed to fathers. Fathers dressed children, fed them, taught them, rocked them, and decided when they were ready to begin school and leave home.

This was not the kind of emotionally involved relationship we might imagine now; it more closely resembled the meticulous social control of Gilead in *The Handmaid's Tale.* It was a matter of God and survival. In the sixteenth and seventeenth centuries, a third of children died before the age of five. The fiery Puritan preacher Cotton Mather had fifteen children, thirteen of whom died before he did. These children were mourned to varying degrees: some writers of this era described inconsolable sadness at a child's death, while others moved on quickly. The French writer and inventor of the essay Michel de Montaigne described the loss of a child as "not without regret, but without great sorrow." Children were valued for economic contribution rather than for emotional rewards and often began work by the time a contemporary child would begin preschool.

Following the American Revolution, the home became increasingly divided from spaces of work. The lives of white fathers and mothers diverged, and children were seen less and less as tainted beings to be whipped into submission and more as innocent romantic babes born, as Wordsworth put it, "trailing clouds of glory." The work of French philosopher Jean-Jacques Rousseau, which had reshaped European thinking about childhood, began to percolate to the United States several decades after it had taken hold on the Continent. Rousseau argued that childhood was precious, innocent, and sacred, a time of near-divine cavorting in the natural world. He advocated for breastfeeding, the core connection between a mother and child, at a time—the eighteenth century—when many European babies were farmed off to wet nurses for a year or two. He was sentimental and sweeping in his proclamations of the glory of youth, even though he abandoned his own five children to a foundling home. The innocence he glorified did not apply to black children in the United States, who were sent to work at preschool age or sold off under slavery. They were commodities, while white children were becoming priceless.

Moving into the Victorian era, the same "fondness" the Puritans had damned would now allow mothers to raise good, moral citizens. Culture became feminized: as white American men set out conquering and developing, white American women were expected to act as "agents of civilization." Professions associated with this position, particularly schoolteaching and the care of libraries, became the domains of women. The mother, according to a magazine article from 1833 quoted by historian Jodi Vandenberg-Daves, "is forming the characters of the future defenders of our faith, the administrators of our laws, and the guardians of our civil liberties and lives."

For white women, motherhood was a civic task, and gradually it became a political one. White women were offered what Vandenberg-Daves has called a "compromised maternal citizenship." Their identity, work, and responsibility as mothers allowed them to claim a certain degree of power. Starting in the pre–Civil War era, white women imagined they taught men about justice and liberty, kept them free of vice in the commercial and moral realms, and enforced piety and goodness over male reason. Suffragettes also fought against slavery on the grounds that it violated a sacred mother-child bond. They fought for the right to vote with the argument that, as mothers, they had to defend the best interests of girls and women. They fought for access to education by insisting that in order to properly educate their children they had to be educated themselves. By the mid-nineteenth century, Vandenberg-Daves writes, women reformers had "[set] out to mother the world."

In the Progressive era, mother activists fought to end child labor, provide mothers with pensions, and establish settlement houses for poor and immigrant women. Jane Addams, a Progressive reformer, a co-founder of the ACLU, the first American woman recipient of the Nobel Peace Prize, and the "mother" of social work in the United States, asserted that giving a mother the right to vote "would fulfill her traditional responsibility to her children," and she insisted that government needed the input of mothers because they understood better than anyone the conditions and demands of the home. Margaret Sanger, meanwhile, made her argument for birth control in part on the basis that it constituted more responsible, modern motherhood: "Our girls," she wrote, "must be brought up to realize that Motherhood is the most sacred profession in the world, and that it is a profession that requires more preparation than any other open to women."

White women had their own political sphere, using language that spoke to women's experiences and roles. This period came to be defined alternately as "maternalism" or "moral motherhood" because of the way it took for granted a woman's primary role as a mother and her moral clarity, civic duty, and responsibility for nurture arising from this role.

The paradox of maternalism, and the complex legacy it left for feminists, was that while it advocated for broader social reforms on the moral basis of women's maternal roles, it never challenged the institution of motherhood itself, nor sought to liberate women from it. Whereas in Europe, women fought for reforms such as universal day care, which would make it easier for mothers to balance work and home life, in the United States in the nineteenth and early twentieth centuries women's rights activists took as axiomatic the belief that mothers should be the primary caregivers of their children. Reforms that would make it easier for mothers to do work other than mothering, particularly work that did not involve caretaking or nurturing, would have challenged the moral foundation of maternalism.

Some of these early women's activists were genuinely radical: the Quaker abolitionist Lucretia Mott confronted a pro-slavery mob that burned down Pennsylvania Hall. Angelina and Sarah Grimké, abolitionist sisters, toured the country giving anti-slavery lectures, arguing with the men who jeered at them in the audiences, declaring themselves and enslaved women "sisters" and insisting on white women's obligation to work for black women's freedom, arguing that women's liberation and black liberation complemented each other. Many female abolitionists found their footing in this movement, learning fundraising, petitioning, protesting, and other political skills. Many men were less than thrilled: "If the vine," wrote the General Association of Congregationalist Ministers of Massachusetts, "whose strength and beauty is to lean on the trelliswork . . . thinks to assume the independence and overshadowing nature of the elm, it will not only cease to bear fruit, but fall in shame and dishonor into the dust."

The leaders who rose to power in the initial incarnation of the women's movement in the mid-nineteenth century largely ignored the struggles of working-class and black women. They focused on enabling middle- and upper-class white women to access middle- and upper-class white men's power. As Angela Davis points out, the Seneca Falls Convention, the event that marked the formation of the first women's movement, made "not even a passing reference to black women," nor featured a single black woman speaker or audience member. "Even the most radical white abolitionists . . . failed to understand that the rapidly developing capitalism of the North was also an oppressive system," Davis wrote in *Women, Race, and Class*.

These activists leaned on their power as white women to earn benefits for themselves, feigning helplessness when it came to the struggles of women of color. As bell hooks put it, "The whole history of feminism can be justified as 'let's just get THIS done first.'" Much of the rhetoric women's suffragists used relied on the superiority of white women to people of color. "I will cut off this right arm of mine before I will ever work for or demand the ballot for the Negro and not the woman," Elizabeth Cady Stanton declared.

Susan B. Anthony, meanwhile, argued that in every state there were more literate women than men, more literate white women than "negro voters," and more literate American women than foreign voters, so therefore if white women were given the vote, they'd essentially override the votes of all other inferior groups.

At the second state convention of the women's rights movement in Akron, Ohio, white women in the audience tried to override Sojourner Truth's speech by shouting, "Don't let her speak! Don't let her speak!" She spoke anyway; this was the famous speech in which, confronting a male heckler in the audience who declared that women couldn't even jump over puddles or help themselves into carriages, Truth declared, "Nobody ever helps me into carriages, or over mud-puddles, or gives me any best place! And ain't I a woman? Look at me! Look at my arm! I have ploughed and planted, and gathered into barns, and no man could head me! And ain't I a woman? I could work as much and eat as much as a man—when I could get it—and bear the lash as well! And ain't I a woman? I have borne thirteen children, and seen most all sold off to slavery, and when I cried out with my mother's grief, none but Jesus heard me! And ain't I a woman?"

For many white women activists of her era, the answer was no: or at least, not the right kind of woman. Other black women who ran their own feminist clubs were barred entry to the mainstream movement headed by white women. Lila Ruffin, an African American suffragist, journalist, and newspaper publisher, declared in a speech to her black women's club that white women didn't want to be associated with "black female immorality."

In spite of many appeals from black women activists, Anthony and the turn-of-the-century maternalist reformers opted to seek the support of southern white supremacists over solidarity with black women. At the 1903 convention of the National American Woman Suffrage Association, Mississippi delegate Belle Kearney declared, "Just as surely as the North will be forced to turn to the South for the nation's salvation, just so surely will the South be compelled to look to its Anglo-Saxon women as the medium through which to retain the supremacy of the white race over the African." Kearney was the keynote speaker of the convention.

As bell hooks wrote, "The women's rights movement had not drawn black and white women close together. Instead, it exposed the fact that white women were not willing to relinquish their support of white supremacy to support the interests of all women."

Yet the work black women activists were doing at the turn of the century sounds uncannily prescient now. Black suffragists demanded the vote for women on the basis not of their identity as mothers—presented as innately good and moral—but rather on the grounds of the *work* they did as mothers, both in the home and outside of it. By the early twentieth century, 70 percent of black women were earning wages. Black activists organized kindergartens and day nurseries for mothers who had to work. As historian

Eileen Boris writes, "Black women were usually fighting the state, rather than courting it." Whereas white women could and did appeal to white men for support, black women found their support inside schools, churches, and civic organizations, particularly in the South, where the prevailing caste system would have made it virtually impossible for them to negotiate with any established institution. Black women built what anthropologist Nancy Naples calls a "community of other mothers," who labored not only in the workforce but in public and civic spaces for their communities. Naples concludes that 50 percent of Latinas and 50 percent of the African Americans in her 1992 study were involved in community activities, including advocating for child care, fighting school officials to improve education, struggling with landlords and police officials to improve housing and safety, and interpreting for non–English speakers.

White maternalist reformers largely ignored the needs and the situations of women of color in favor of a white middle-class Protestant ideal of motherhood that placed the mother at the helm of a tidy moral home. The maternalist mother could possess delimited public or political power, but only on the grounds of her identity as this white, ideal, full-time moral mother, never as a working mother or as a woman struggling to fit motherhood into a life of complex obligations. This laid the groundwork for the all-or-nothing dilemma that would plague so many mothers at the end of the twentieth century and into the twenty-first: women could either accept full-time motherhood, the whole maternalist ball of fuzzy moral goodness, or reject it, establish careers, and make their way in a white man's world where motherhood had no real value. Many mothers have ended up trying to do both under extreme stress. The paradigm of motherhood largely still functions in these polarizing extremes. Boris writes, "The larger culture substituted paeans to motherhood and child life for any adequate resolution of the conflict between capitalist development and the real needs of mothers and children."

In the mid-twentieth century, the basic tenet of maternalism—that motherhood lent women moral depth and a particular experience and understanding that should translate into public, political power—would be almost wholly reversed, so that motherhood became an entirely private identity and personal quest for fulfillment, irrelevant and almost inappropriate in the public sphere. This transition gave women who were not mothers access to public power and refocused women's rights on professional achievements, but it doubly repressed mothers. Denied fundamental protections and support that would make mothering—and particularly mothering and trying to do anything else—easier, they were also now deprived of unique status and insight as mothers.

The backlash to maternalism began just before World War II. It brought together vitriolic misogynists and incipient feminists under the umbrella of a powerful social critique called "Momism." "Momism" was essentially a charge leveled at the middle-class, middle-aged American women who had gained unprecedented political and cultural power by brandishing their roles and identities as mothers. It attacked these women as sentimental, emasculating, pathological, overbearing, narcissistically obsessed with their own inflated sacrifices as mothers, power-hungry, hypocritical, and lazy. Momism essentially attacked women who held a degree of power that was becoming alarming to men. It is almost unimaginable now to see mothers, particularly middle-aged mothers, as powerful, but at the turn of the century, thanks to maternalism, historian Rebecca Jo Plant writes, "in no other nation had middle-class women succeeded in exerting a comparable degree of cultural and political influence."

Popular writer Philip Wylie's bestselling nonfiction book *Generation of Vipers* introduced the term "Momism" in 1942, railing against a "gynecocracy" of moms who meddled in both politics and their adult children's lives without any genuine authority. Wylie expressed contempt for the prevailing notion that "moms" had endured any particular suffering that demanded obedience or respect from their children. In bombastic terms, he declared that mothers were not morally superior, that they didn't deserve any special status because of their role as mothers, and that they were using motherhood as an excuse to assert ridiculous influence over areas in which they had no business intervening. Worse, they were emasculating men, crushing their sons with their inflated power.

This critique gained widespread cultural traction following World War II, which exposed what Plant has called "a veritable epidemic of mental illness." Millions of soldiers broke down overseas or returned to the United States with debilitating, clinical psychiatric issues. Blame was not laid on nerve gas or the brutality of trench warfare or the impact of witnessing genocide, but on mothers. Mothers who maintained close relationships and emotional intimacy with their adult sons were now scolded as dangerously overbearing and sentimental, and blamed for the psychological crumbling of these sons in the face of war. An unchecked, venerated, demanding mother's love was corroding their masculinity. Psychiatrist Karl Menninger condemned what he called "the vicious cycle": the American boy became and remained deeply attached to his mother, preventing him from becoming a vigorous and sexually satisfactory mate, which forced his wife to turn her energies to her sons, and so on, so generations of enfeebled men couldn't even properly engage in combat.

Momism denied mothers any recognition of their struggles as such; experts even began to scoff at the pains of childbirth. Some psychiatrists attributed the agony of labor to women's "emotional attitudes." Women were meant to bear children and should stop whining about it as if it were difficult. Similarly, mothers should stop demanding emotional obedience from their children for a "sacrifice" that was actually a privilege. Rebecca Jo Plant writes, "Still largely barred from constructing their identities as autonomous individuals, and still prevented from competing on equal terms with men in the workplace and the broader public realm, [mothers] were now also discouraged from constructing their identities as selfless nurturers, whose sacrifices entitled them to certain emotional rewards."

This legacy of Momism is alive and striking today. Take a 2017 *New York Times* op-ed by Karen Rinaldi entitled "Motherhood Isn't Sacrifice, It's Selfishness"; in it, Rinaldi makes the confusing argument that "[b]y reframing motherhood as a privilege, we redirect agency back to the mother, empowering her, celebrating her autonomy instead of her sacrifice." This assertion makes it sound as though one can simply choose between autonomy and sacrifice, and mothers—perhaps in self-pity or entitlement—are choosing the latter. In fact the "choices" women face in becoming mothers— how or whether or not to balance career and motherhood; how to negotiate family life; how to afford family life and where; how to find any time for community or self in the midst of all of this— often don't feel like choices at all but like very imperfect compromises in the throes of a system that tells women to be grateful.

If you just *choose* autonomy, Rinaldi's argument goes, it will magically happen, whether you have to give up your job or unwillingly put your child in day care, whether or not you have community or family support, whether or not you're flailing trying to conform to the pressures of intensive parenting, whether or not your spouse is supportive or you ever get any time for yourself. Rinaldi's op-ed operates as wishful thinking, and, worse, it precisely echoes right-wing rhetoric that asks mothers to stop complaining and moaning about how hard it all is in pregnancy or postpartum, to stop asking for help or special status or recognition, because, as Rinaldi puts it, "tending to our children [is] the most loving yet selfish thing we do."

Who wants to put in place a social or community or government program, to demand a new societal paradigm, for a selfish personal choice? It is shocking the degree to which this discourse expresses the same paradox of the Momism of the late 1940s. Mothers, then and increasingly now, were damned if they did and damned if they didn't: they couldn't fully and autonomously function in a world that pretends motherhood doesn't exist, nor could they expect support, rights, or sympathy for their work as mothers, which, they were reminded over and over, is a simple and beautiful privilege and nothing very special, difficult, or interesting.

Momism shoved motherhood out of public view, where it had once existed as a social and moral and cultural experience that gave women authority, and made it a private act of self-realization. In conjunction with female activists and theorists, male experts, Wylie chief among them, attacked the notion of maternal sacrifice and, in Plant's words, "reversed the trajectory of indebtedness": over time, the mother went from demanding her child's gratitude for her great travail to being forever indebted to the child for providing her with profound personal fulfillment. Simultaneously, she went from asserting a public, political power and voice on the basis of a motherhood she saw as a communal good to celebrating the private bliss of a motherhood she saw as the height of individual achievement.

Motherhood again became a cloistered experience and identity, separate from the (predominately male) realms of culture, art, politics, and society. This was the justification for failing to provide enough social programs to make mothering easier or to incorporate mothers into work life in a functional way; for cordoning motherhood off from any claim to public power; and for rendering mothers' complaints about their difficulties pathological or ungrateful. Mothering, as Ehrenreich and English describe it, "[came] unhinged from any external goals—an end in itself which [would] invite women to enter deeper and deeper into a shadow world of feelings and suspected feelings, guilt, self-analysis, and every nuance of ambivalence."

Momism, with its pyrotechnic zeal for destroying the status quo of the current social order, resonated with surprising allies, especially young white women who did not want to be defined by their motherhood (or lack thereof) and who condemned the maternalist notion that women could only find power and influence via the domestic realm. Even older white mothers, the main targets of

Momism, embraced its tenets, fed up as they were with sentimentality and a confining and belittling Victorian morality.

Yet women who charged Momism made a dangerous bargain that would haunt mothers for centuries: they marginalized motherhood to the extent that women could no longer derive real power or authority from it. Women were expected not to ask for special status or help because of their motherhood, and were left with the choice either to assert themselves in respected (male) realms in spite of being mothers or to embrace motherhood and be excluded from those realms entirely. Motherhood was shoved deep into a conservative zone, where it became associated with a highly traditional and submissive female identity. Thinkers like Simone de Beauvoir and Betty Friedan built on Wylie's critique, deriding the domestic as a prison and painting women who sought power there as repressed and misguided. Friedan even joined in the chorus of voices blaming overzealous, subjugated homemakers for the epidemic of postwar "nervousness."

The historian Mary Beard warned, "If the homemaker does not regain her own sense of . . . her inherited power, she will be the kind of material on which Hitler and other dictators of our age have preyed for their designers." Beard's worry that homemakers would be denied access to their power as women and mothers is eerily prescient in the years following an election in which a man who bragged about sexual assault, openly expressed misogynist contempt for his female opponent, and campaigned on racist hate won 52 percent of the white female vote. Beard, who'd grown up under maternalism, was disturbed to see motherhood shorn of its progressive cred and rendered a private, reactionary affair. Abandoned by feminists eager to ditch the baggage of the domestic, women who chose or were forced to stay home, and who did find a significant portion of their identity bound up with motherhood, were shoved deep into the invisibility of sentimental cliché and shut out of power spheres that only became more stereotypically male: more cutthroat, more ruthless in their demands of time, ambition, and achievement.

In the wake of her hospitalization, Jaclyn switched to formula and weaned off the pump. She relied much more on Josh and her mother's help to intervene when the baby cried uncontrollably. She and her husband hired a postpartum doula to help her full-time until Avi was four months old.

"We spent all of our savings on our doula," Jaclyn told me. After the costs of the hospital stay and the doula, they left Seattle to move back in with Jaclyn's parents in L.A. It took Jaclyn a long time to begin to talk openly about this.

"I am angry," she told me, "that even though we had excellent health insurance and the support of our friends and family and we had so many things working in our favor, the treatment cost a shitload of money," she said. "There is something wrong with our society when even people who have access to all of these things . . . still have to do serious financial recalibrating in order to recover from having their first child." So much, she asserts, comes down to money.

"It's rare for a woman to have a smooth delivery and a smooth postpartum period and a smooth maternity leave," Jaclyn says. And yet "mental health care is not part of our language."

Many women also suffer suboptimal or flat-out traumatic interactions with the medical establishment in trying to access the care that they need. Jaclyn mentions the case of a woman in Sacramento who made an appointment at her OB's office for symptoms of postpartum depression. She was having scary, violent thoughts but had no desire to hurt herself or her baby. She wanted medication and therapy. The nurse called the police. They "escorted" her to the ER—two cars tailing her as she drove—where she waited ten hours with her four-month-old daughter before a social worker decided that she would not need to be admitted for a mandatory seventy-two-hour period of inpatient psychiatric care. In the meantime, her clothes and shoes were taken from her, and she had no place to nurse her daughter. When she was finally discharged, she was given a handful of Xeroxed pamphlets on postpartum depression.

The story this mother posted on Facebook about her experience had more than forty thousand likes and more than thirty-three thousand shares. The thousands of comments read like a litany of the deficiencies in current postpartum health care for women. Some women said they received supportive care from midwives, ob-gyns, or primary care doctors. The vast majority shared insights and stories like these:

"They admitted me and I was held for 11 days without access to my family, my children, or any support person from my life. It took 11 days to see a doctor and after 15 minutes he signed my release and let me leave. Luckily I found the help I needed on my own."

"Thank God for self-help books and a great supportive family who helped me get through. God help those who do not have what I did."

"I'm 2 years postpartum and still have my ups and downs with PPD, when I told my OBGYN she just gave me a prescription with 2 pills did not even explain well and told me NOT to elaborate on my feelings too much because if I did she would be obligated to send me to a psych ward. I instead just shut up and dealt with it."

"I went to see a doctor for what I thought was postpartum depression. No ill thoughts regarding me or baby . . . just crying waaaaay more than I ever should have. Clearly hormones were crazy. The dr seriously told me 'you just need to get over it.' "

"I went to my OB and she gave me meds, had me come back every week and asked how I was. When I said I wasn't better she upped the dose. She didn't even give time for meds to kick in before she messed with it. She got to the point where she told me (after a week of taking meds) that she was overdosing me that's why I was sleeping for 18 hrs a day. . . . I never went back and now trying to deal with this on my own bc I am a stay at home mom and I'm not married so I have no insurance, and the state said PPD was not a reason for me to keep mine."

"I struggled with PPD and said nothing until after my 2nd child . . . out of Fear. So sad. It should have never been that way."

"I am so afraid to talk to my doctor about mine, my son is 8 months

and I just feel it getting worst. I'm just afraid what they will do to me yet alone my son so I just try my best to work through it."

"I went to the ER for my PPD and PPA and they never gave me meds that I desperately needed because I was pregnant. I didn't have health insurance at the time so I couldn't even get meds and be able to afford them. They too gave me handouts that made no sense."

"Brooke Shields got hugs and meds. America sucks for the rest of everyone."

Of course, this is a biased sample. These are women who feel inclined to share and are likely to have had a negative encounter with the health care system. Yet the dramatic response to stories like these, the way they fire up pockets of latent fury around the Internet, suggests that there is an enormous gap between common medical and cultural understanding of the "normal" postpartum period and most mothers' actual experience.

Whether mothers receive help from a medical provider, and whether that help is actually appropriate or deeply damaging, is as capricious as weather—depending on the intersection of region, class, race, that provider's particular training and set of assumptions, and the exact wording a woman uses. Black women are more likely to have traumatic encounters with the medical system. Georgia counselor Kristy Holloway told me the story of an African American friend of hers who'd had a C-section and had severe stomach pain. She kept insisting her stomach hurt and being told, "You had a C-section," until finally when the pain became so unbearable she couldn't even touch her stomach, the doctors examined her and discovered she was bleeding internally. If they'd waited one more hour, she'd have died. Another black woman, a client of Holloway's, had a baby born with an enlarged heart, who was given only a few hours to live. The doctor proposed a series of dramatic interventions and the woman, overwhelmed, said she wanted to wait for her husband to make a decision. The doctor told her, "When your baby dies, it's your fault." Erin Spahr, the founder and clinical supervisor at the Perinatal Mood Disorders Clinic at Johns Hopkins, told me about one of her clients, a black woman with bipolar disorder, who had gotten into a fight with her baby's father at the hospital and who'd been overwhelmed after the birth; Child Protective Services was called, and her newborn was taken from her. "She did get her baby back," Erin told me, "but that was extremely hard."

Jaclyn describes herself as "unbelievably lucky." First, she says, because her husband was so proactive. "He's not perfect, he's a pain in the ass sometimes, but he is a good man." He took action, worked with the doctor's office, and advocated for her every step of the way. His presence alone may have made a big difference: recent studies have shown that doctors are more likely to take a woman's pain seriously, and judge her concerns credible, with a man in the room.

Second, "Seattle has invested enough resources, time, energy, and money into education, advocacy, and treatment around peri-natal mood disorders. It is not a foreign concept for them," Jaclyn said. So, while her experience mirrors many other women's—she was sent to the ER and to a psychiatric facility despite her protestations—her providers were supportive and empathetic to her particular situation. Jaclyn continually emphasized how many people—from the psychiatrist to the night nurse to her OB—told her that this treatment wasn't quite right for her but was the best available, and that simple concession illustrated a deeper aware-ness of the realities of maternal mental illness. Six months after Jaclyn's inpatient experience, the hospital opened their perinatal mood disorder treatment center, where mothers could come with their babies.

Jaclyn was not treated as an outlier or a pariah, even though her treatment was not ideal. She came out of the hospital feeling not shamed and exiled but re-centered, as if she'd been picked up from one path and put down on another. Little by little, "the noise and the darkness and the anxiousness . . . was starting to turn down. The heat just turned down."

When she returned to work, at twelve weeks, she realized just how much she'd missed her community. "I was so pushed off my axis that I didn't even realize that I was not around a community.... God, religion, Judaism: that was not a part of my early weeks of motherhood." The isolation of new motherhood had swallowed her; she forgot she needed people, she forgot God.

She was terrified about going back and not remembering people's names; what if her brain had turned to mush? She had a meeting with her boss two weeks before she was scheduled to come back, and she found herself ranting: "I'm just going to suck. I'm going to be a shit rabbi."

He was calm. "Jaclyn," he said, "I know you."

Coming back to work was like returning to a native habitat she hadn't realized she'd needed. By fourteen weeks, Jaclyn felt as if she had fully returned to herself. Both she and her husband waited for the other shoe to drop. It didn't.

Jaclyn decided to write a sermon about her experience. It occurred to her that this sermon would be perfect for Rosh Hashanah, the Jewish New Year. "The birthday of the world," she described it, "the divine feminine." On October 2, 2016, on Rosh Hashanah, Jaclyn stood up in front of a congregation of more than a thousand at the Temple De Hirsch Sinai in Seattle and laid bare her darkest secret.

11

Empowerment

In the 1950s and 1960s, American mothers were told that they had it all: their own suburban homes, modern conveniences, beautiful children, easy lives in the free world. This was happiness, it was fulfillment, and it was a *lifestyle:* sit back, have a martini, vacuum the living room. The mainstream, ideal white mom was remade in the image of a wife. She was sexy, young, energetic, hip. She was not powerful or formidable; she was to provide the proper antidote of attractive femininity to bolster her husband's masculinity. She was not overly focused on her kids, who should be well behaved and well dressed. She had hobbies, but not political ones, and she was certainly not supposed to work. She was *Mad Men's* Betty Draper. The housewife burrowed deep into the American female imagination.

Meanwhile, the women activists of the 1960s and 1970s were careful not to reference and certainly not to tout their motherhood; instead, they presented themselves as rational beings, the opposite of the stereotypical female (and mother). By the 1970s, it was impossible to imagine a time when middle-class mothers could have inspired such vitriol and fear. Sufficiently reduced in their power and shoved off the public stage, mothers were no longer a concern; men now saved their scorn for women who were directly competing with them.

First-wave feminism of the postwar era grew out of Momism and painted motherhood as a false societal construct of femininity that had to be transcended or evaded in order not to hold women back. The battle these feminists were fighting was to some degree valid: domestic roles were often suffocating and many women had few clear alternatives, drowning in isolation in, as Betty Friedan put it, "the problem with no name." But first-wave feminism ignored the pervasive struggles of black and working-class women, for whom work was often an obligation that barely sustained a family. In an effort to liberate women from "the feminine mystique," first-wave white feminists defined power, control, and self-worth in stereotypically masculine terms of career and self-definition.

Liberated women could not be the ones who cared for others. Yet thinking of liberation as something that can only happen outside the home, in stereotypically male spheres and forms, and seeing motherhood as something that must be set aside, minimized, or avoided, reinforces the dichotomy between public and private spheres, between feminine and masculine, and leaves many women who do become mothers in an awful bind. They spend the vast majority of their time on, and devote a great portion of their identities to, a role that they are expected not to bring into the spheres of power: not the workplace, not the studio or the museum. Their work, their self-actualization, must be split from their mothering.

This early feminist vision also ignored the reality that for many black women and women historically forced to work, the home was the one sphere where they were empowered. For the majority of American women in the workforce, work was degrading, menial, and necessary. Bell hooks points out the irony that white feminists at the time depicted the housewife as a tragic victim, when millions of poor black Americans were being oppressed by the American economy. "Working for pay," writes hooks, "neither liberated [the masses of American working-class women] from sexist oppression nor allowed them to gain any measure of economic independence." In many cases, the domestic and underpaid work of these women—maids, nannies, child-care workers—facilitated the independence and "liberation" of middle-class white women.

While working for pay did offer the middle-class white woman economic independence, it did not liberate her from sexism, as white women would discover over the latter half of the twentieth century. They had fought for entry into a white male capitalist system without challenging its tenets, and then found themselves without maternity leave, without functional work hours, without affordable child care, without places to pump breast milk, and with a whole sea of condescending and demeaning attitudes about motherhood. Hillary Frank, host of the award-winning podcast *The Longest Shortest Time*, details some of these challenges in her 2018 *New York Times* op-ed "The Special Misogyny Reserved for Mothers": pitching and promoting her show, she is told she sounds "like a little girl"; she is asked, "Who would want to listen to this except for moms?"; she is accosted at a conference by a man who says, "You're the baby lady."

I chatted with a young mother in California, a PhD student in the throes of the newborn days. She had never wanted to be a mother and had actually decided against it when fate intervened at the last minute. She told me she had long resented all the power mothers held. "What power?" I asked, incredulous. She cited Mother's Day and all of the normative images of the ideal woman as mother. I knew what she was referring to. I recognize the problematic, sentimental celebration of motherhood as the ultimate achievement of womanhood. But this, I argued to her, doesn't actually give mothers any legitimate power.

The popular celebration of motherhood by politicians and Target cards and cable TV is a cliché, a false ideal of motherhood so ubiquitous precisely because mothers have no real power. Motherhood is over here, at home, a private theater of personal fulfillment via intensive parenting—not supported by the state or social programs, not incorporated or considered in tandem with working life, not a public or community concern—and prestige, power, *life* is over there, serious and ambitious and full of men and women who either aren't mothers or work very hard to hide their motherhood.

This division has forced on women an impossible choice: embrace your motherhood and therefore your femininity, your otherness, your inferiority, and face the tide of outward approval and passive sexist belittlement that entails, or outright reject or minimize motherhood in order to rise above and get ahead, trying to ignore the unquantifiable, deep-rooted complexities and truths of mothering that have no purchase in capitalist culture, conceding that motherhood is just another personal experience that doesn't bring any real power.

It seems impossible to draw attention to and empower motherhood without threatening the women who do not want to enter those realms or who feel oppressed by them. Stony Brook University professor E. Ann Kaplan poses this as an impossible question: "Since patriarchy wants women to want children . . . how can a woman distinguish her desire for the child from that imposed on her?" How can mothering become an experience that holds real civic and cultural power without essentializing women's nature and sensibility? The French theorist Julia Kristeva, who pointed out that mothers are so often left with the choice between a retreat into the female world or a "symbolic" identification with the social and political power of men, argued that women needed to start listening for "whatever remains unsatisfied, repressed, new, eccentric, incomprehensible, that which disturbs the mutual understanding of the established powers."

After my first book came out, I wrote an op-ed for the *Los Angeles Times* lamenting the fact that women feel they cannot or should not write about motherhood. I quoted another woman writer, now famous, who had written a story about her birth experience early in her career. The story was well regarded and put her on the map, but she felt she should stop writing about birth lest she end up on the "birth beat," with the pastel book cover. I understand this rationale. But I marveled in my op-ed that birth should be considered a lesser realm, rather than one of the most significant experiences in a person's life. Many women wrote me after this op-ed sending thanks for legitimizing creative work about motherhood, but the email that really stood out came from a young woman who ranted that I was "taking women back to the stone age." She was furious. "Not everyone wants to give birth!" she wrote. She felt a celebration of birth was a threat to her autonomy: too reminiscent of the oppressive history of women's forced reproduction. Our exchange was just one example of the all-or-nothing framework that depicts motherhood as the ultimate personal fulfillment or the ultimate female oppression. In fact, as all mothers know, it is neither, and it is, at times, a bit of both.

Daphne de Marneffe writes, "Though feminist activism has helped secure for women the public power previously denied them, it has done little to challenge the assumption that women who spend their time caring for children are powerless, un-self-actualized, and at the margins of cultural life." This, de Marneffe speculates, might be why so many women are shocked at how profoundly different their selves and lives feel when they become mothers. Many women write me emails that say something along the lines of, "I can't believe how complex this is." On the one hand, it's impossible to know anything of the intensity of grief or birth or any of these transformative experiences until we're inside them. On the other hand, it's shocking: motherhood has been so successfully reduced to an exercise in banality, boredom, and twinkly love that women can't believe how wholly it can alter their sense of self.

Nearly a half-century ago, Adrienne Rich wrote, "We know more about the air we breathe, the seas we travel, than about the nature and meaning of motherhood. In the division of labor according to gender, the makers and sayers of culture, the namers, have been the sons of the mothers."

Even as increasing numbers of women writers and thinkers have come into their own, occupying more creative space, motherhood remains a somewhat taboo subject. Women who talk or think about it too much are not taken seriously. If they want accolades, they are to turn their attention to subjects of interest to men.

De Marneffe writes that this contemporary motherhood taboo operates much like historic taboos against sex; women must hide their desire for children. I took it as a point of pride in my twenties that I was ambivalent about having children, and I assured myself and everyone I knew that if I did, it sure as hell wouldn't define me. Many ambitious women of my generation think this way.

Of course, some women might become mothers without an experience of powerful transformation. For me, this wasn't the case. Motherhood completely unsettled my sense of self: not only of my own self, but of the meaning of a self, and in fact the meaning of my entire relationship to the world. It was a profound crisis.

In 1957, the sociologist E. E. LeMasters conducted a study measuring the impact of parenthood on well-being. LeMasters posited that the arrival of a child could be considered a crisis in family life. He developed a five-point scale to measure the intensity of this crisis, with one meaning nonexistent, two meaning slight, three moderate, four extensive, and five severe. Then he administered this scale to forty-six couples. Thirty-eight of them reported an "extensive" or "severe" crisis. LeMasters concluded that the remaining eight, who reported only a mild crisis, were "deviants."

These were middle-class, educated, married couples; thirty-five of the thirty-eight pregnancies were desired. None of the group had "neurosis" or a "psychiatric disability." In 1957 LeMasters wrote, "The thirty-eight couples in the crisis group appear to have almost completely romanticized parenthood. They felt they had very little, if any, effective preparation for parental roles. As one mother said, 'We knew where babies came from, but we didn't know *what they were like.*'"

I have heard echoes of this quote from so many women I've talked to. Even as women in the United States have gone on to dominate higher education and move into just about every previously male-dominated field, many wade into motherhood with little to no conception of the actual nature of the event. While most other domains of gender equality and awareness have marched on, motherhood hovers in 1957.

As sociologist Sharon Hays has written, mothers are expected to effortlessly switch between modes of complete self-abnegation and aggressive self-advocacy. In some ways, this divide mimics the persistent conceptual divide between the feminine and the masculine: the former completely giving, private, interior, and the latter domineering, public, exterior. To resist this framework is to conceive of a maternalist politics that is not essentialist, to recognize that motherhood does create a set of particular difficulties and struggles that should be acknowledged and socially supported, and to validate the choices of women who do not want children or to occupy stereotypically feminine roles. Adrienne Rich wrote, "To destroy the institution [of motherhood] is not to abolish motherhood. It is to release the creation and sustenance of life into the same realm of decision, struggle, surprise, imagination, and conscious intelligence, as any other difficult, but freely chosen work."

What would an empowered motherhood look like? It would release motherhood from the bonds of the experts. It would recognize mothering as a way of knowing and understanding the world, a way of seeing, and it would seek to explore this ontology in literature, science, and culture. It would presume the skills and characteristics necessary in mothering would be essential in many realms, and not private or trivial. It would put mothers and children in relationship, lifting the burden from mothers of being robotic micromanagers and therapists. It would privilege community life over family life—that is, it would integrate single and married adults and parents and children. It would dismantle the oppressive notion that children can be cultivated, perfected, prepared and baked like cakes. It would, above all, feature many more mothers' voices, speaking of their own struggles and experiences. Shari Thurer writes, "Virtually all the messages we get or have ever got through reading—subliminal, liminal—have been mediated by a patriarchal sensibility." What does it mean to want a child, to raise a child, to become a mother, in a way patriarchy does not want? Cannot abide? Pushes against with all its might?

In the anthology *Revolutionary Mothering: Love on the Front Lines*, a collection of stories from marginalized mothers of color, writer Alexis Pauline Gumbs declares, "We are making a claim that should be obvious but is often overlooked. In order to collectively figure out how to sustain and support our evolving species, in order to participate in and demand a society where people help to create each other instead of too often destroying each other, we need to look at the practice of creating, nurturing, affirming, and supporting life that we call mothering."

The authors in this anthology, many of them activists who see their motherhood and/or their experience with their own mothers as intricately bound up with the fight for social justice, reclaim motherhood as a "revolutionary" or radical identity. They argue for a new maternalist politics, for motherhood as a political platform articulated as social consciousness that foregrounds those most marginalized by a capitalist system. I think of the mothers I know who drove Central American women across the country from Arizona to New York to reunite them with their children, who'd been pried from them under Trump's family separation policy.

On an unseasonably warm September evening, I heard the writer Rachel Kaadzi Ghansah speak in a small and intimate chapel on the University of Pittsburgh campus. She read from an essay about the mother of Jean-Michel Basquiat, and declared "all black women are engaged in a mothering that extends beyond the biological act." As an example, she offered the time her mother ran into a distressed friend in the supermarket, and how her mother stayed with that friend until she was ready to go. She asked, "Did I not recognize that this was mothering? That this was a woman's work?"

Women have historically struggled to fit into a man's world. When women are criticized for being aggressive or angry or combative, the response is often that women should have the right to act like men: they should be allowed to assert themselves. This is true. But it should be equally important for men to be held to the standards of deep empathy and patience and nuanced care for the other.

We are at a critical moment when American society is in dire need of care, when mothering has much to teach us about how to be human with one another. In the introduction to the *Revolutionary Mothering* anthology, Gumbs offers a new definition of mothering: "Mothering, radically defined, is the glad gifting of one's talents, ideas, intellect, and creativity to the universe without recompense."

"When Charles Dickens opened the novel *A Tale of Two Cities* with 'It was the best of times, it was the worst of times,' I am absolutely certain he was talking about maternity leave," Jaclyn began her sermon. This was the second time she was giving it, and she felt stronger, more confident. The first time she gave it had been the evening before, at the start of Rosh Hashanah, at a suburban campus of her synagogue. She'd been terribly nervous. "Hey, I have mental illness, like, how are you?" she joked in singsong, recounting it. She'd had to tell herself over and over that this was important and she believed in it and she should trust herself. The response had been warm and kind. But tonight would be the bigger test, with a big, feisty urban crowd of people who knew her well: two hundred of them had shown up at her son's bris, or circumcision ceremony, eight days after his birth.

The air in the De Hirsch synagogue was thick and heavy. The building has an architecture like an "upside-down cupcake" in Jaclyn's words; a wide base narrows into a high, dome-like, indigo ceiling, from which hangs a tiered chandelier of gold stars. The congregation sits in midnight dimness before a bimah that glows gold. Dark stained glass adorns the walls; there is no natural light. The space feels contained, its own cosmos, divine. When Jaclyn returned years later, she felt suffocated there. She recognized its beauty but found it oppressive.

Jaclyn stood on the bimah under the astral chandelier. "This past December," she said, "Josh and I became parents to a beautiful, strong, amazing son." Jaclyn paused. "But the truth is," she confessed, "it took us a little longer to get there than most."

She told them she'd been terrified. She told them, "Becoming a parent was not an easy adjustment for me. Honestly, I don't think it's an easy adjustment for anyone. But something happened to me—Ms. Type A, ambitious young rabbi—shortly after our son was born. In a time everyone told me should have been the happiest of my life, I was instead diagnosed with postpartum depression."

The room went dead silent. Normally, she told me, there is a hum: background noise of people shuffling their feet, rustling papers, whispering quietly, flowing out or in. This time, the air was charged, heavy, still.

"Rosh Hashanah," she went on, "is the quintessential pivot point between who we are and who we want to be: between all that's been and all that will be." But to truly achieve a fresh start, she said, "we must be willing to crawl out from underneath the dark and the ugly, and step out into the light."

Jaclyn outlined all the factors that had worked in her favor: she had health care and was able to get treatment, she had the support of friends, family, and her work. She was lucky. She'd returned to work. Then she pivoted: "Unfortunately," she said, "I am the exception, not the rule." Her sermon began to gain force. "Instead of telling new parents the truth—that those early days are really hard for many of us, we tell them, 'these should be the happiest days of your life,' and we amplify their shame. We tell them they're probably 'overtired' or that their 'bad, sad' feelings will pass, even though we expect them back at the office, on average, *two to six weeks of unpaid leave later.*"

Jaclyn announced that 43.8 million American adults experience mental illness each year. Mental illness, she said, "touches every corner of our lives: from disheveled-looking individuals we dismiss as 'homeless' or 'crazy,' who cause us enough discomfort to dodge to the other side of the street, to war veterans returning from Iraq and Afghanistan with severe post-traumatic stress, to our mutual acquaintance with the powerful mood swings who we think might be bipolar, to the cyber-bullied teenager harboring hopelessness and contemplating suicide." In other domains of medicine, she pointed out, when something hurts, when something is broken, we work to fix it. But when it comes to mental illness, Jaclyn said, "We change the subject. We sidestep. We scoff at therapy. We dismiss. We refuse. We hide. We insist that we are fine. But then our pain grows deeper, and our problems—as individuals, as families, as a nation, persist. So many of us—and for a while, myself included—choose not to step forward or share our struggles: that we're depressed, we have crippling anxiety, we've been on antidepressants for over a decade. We choose denial and silence over honesty and empathy. Many of us are afraid of the reactions of loved ones, acquaintances, coworkers, congregants, afraid of the judgment and the consequences. Far too many of us won't acknowledge our pain, or the pain of our loved ones, who have suffered in silence far too long."

Jaclyn told the stories of Sarah and Hannah, the two women who "anchor the sacred texts of Rosh Hashanah." Both women had beloved sons given to them by God; both struggled with madness. These stories, Jaclyn argued, are included in the great narrative by those "who saw in these women's pain an opportunity. They knew there could be value, comfort, and hope in sharing their words and in sharing our pain with one another." The stories of Sarah and Hannah are for her an encouragement and an opportunity for everyone to share "stories of agony, losses and setbacks and secrets that shape who we are and affect who we love."

Jaclyn urged her congregants, "We must talk about the difficult things no one talks about—we must do our part to end the stigma around mental health. We must talk about it with friends and with our children, in our workplaces and social circles. . . . We must work to eradicate the shame and acknowledge to ourselves and those we love that treatment *is* possible. That incredibly holy work begins with talking. Owning. Sharing. For who knows," she concluded, "when you might get the chance to save someone's life?"

There was not a peep in the room. Then, from a far corner, applause. Jaclyn glanced up, startled. Clapping is generally considered disrespectful in synagogue, since services are not supposed to be treated as theater. But people were overtaken. The applause spread until the majority of the room was clapping. People began to stand up. Jaclyn had never experienced this before. She lowered her head, embarrassed, amazed, listening to this "beautiful sacred sound."

Afterward, she saw a woman threading her way toward her through the crowd. She recognized the occupational therapist from the psychiatric ward. The therapist had tears in her eyes, and when Jaclyn saw this she began to cry, and the two fell into each other's arms. "Look at how far you've come," the therapist said. After her came others, holding and hugging her, offering thanks. She received more than forty emails and letters in response to her sermon. Ten days later, at Yom Kippur services, a wealthy congregant whose family had quietly struggled with addiction and mental health problems for years handed her a $1,000 check; he wanted her to give it to an organization that supported maternal mental health. Jaclyn donated it to the new center for the treatment of perinatal mood disorders at the Seattle hospital where she'd given birth.

Two years after her sermon, Avi was a toddler and Jaclyn had made advocating for mental health awareness a central part of her identity and career as a rabbi. Jaclyn told me, "If we're going to take care of human souls, we need to be really honest about what human souls need. That terrible message that having a baby is supposed to be the most magical time of your life, and the pressure we put on new parents not to feel sadness and not to feel exhaustion, spreading that message, working on this initiative: that is my belief in God realized."

IT WAS LATE IN THE AFTERNOON, *high summer. The attack came on as swiftly as a dizzy spell, as the most physical of sensations, except it had nothing to do with my body. Of course, it did, yes, the increased heart rate, the shortened respiration, but the body was an afterthought. If only it could be placed there; what a relief. A leg cramp. A stomachache. The mind processes these and works through them.* This is not me: I will make sense of it. Take some Tylenol. Lie down. *But anxiety comes, or seems to come, not from the body but from thoughts, smuggling itself in disguised as the self. And even if I recognize the disguise, I am helpless before it. I believe its ketchup streaks are blood. I believe its ghoulish face paint is evidence of death. I believe it and I hate myself for believing it.*

Anxiety is made of thoughts, propelled by thoughts, maintained by thoughts, and thoughts *should be something I can control.* Thoughts should be something I, of all people, can whip into shape. It's my job, for goodness' sake. It's my identity. *Yet the cocky little fuckers run roughshod over me, like miniature bulldozers in the brain.*

I sat in the backyard and smoked a rare cigarette. I cried. It was a beautiful day. There, across the yard, was my small brick house with my sleeping daughter inside it. There were my girl and my husband and all my books and my dog and the bed where my daughter braids my hair, and between it and me existed an ocean I could not cross no matter how hard I tried to force my mind. GO. It would not go. It stayed here, on this side, in a storm of my own making. It was a rare moment when, instead of seeing anxiety as a clearer-eyed, more painful version of reality, I understood it as pointless suffering. I was suffering. It seemed the dumbest and vainest and least valid form of suffering, and yet there I was so battered by it I was sucking down a cigarette in the midday sun and sobbing, incapable of sitting still, incapable of thought or vision. The irony finally dawned on me that I was so, so, so scared of suffering, but in running from it, I had created it for myself. Now I could not escape.

I sit in the backyard with the fear and for a moment, on the high of the cigarette's brief clarity, I come into that soft core of tenderness. I think of how many people, if you are persistent and gentle enough with them in just the right way, if you push ever so softly, will give way to their own soft spot and reveal it to you. Will crumple, will weep, or will sit very still. I find here the kind of love I found when I was pregnant and saw everyone as a baby: a powerful sense of the vulnerability every person carries. This is the only relief I can find in what otherwise seems so pointless, so silly, so easily surmountable. It is a rare oneness, with myself, with the pain, with others.

I can see everyone else's crazy. When I hear the stories my therapist tells me of other women, I think, That's insane. But then I bow down over and over to my own fears. The only gift is when I finally break and say, I give up. It doesn't really help. But vulnerability, the alive sense of that soft spot everyone is guarding with more or less vigor and stress, is no small consolation prize. I'll take it; it's the only bridge back home.

I am no longer sure which is more frightening and debilitating: the particular situations that inspire the fear, or my awareness of its persistence, its insatiable hunger. I cannot will it away, think it away, hope or dream it away. It is still there, even after all the books I read, even after all I know. Knowing is in fact completely irrelevant before it.

The body knows the looming of disaster or is convinced it knows in a fundamental way that has nothing to do with statistics or facts or conscious awareness or so-called reality. The body carries within it the constant possibility of betrayal, from within or without.

My brain was bombarded with what-ifs and worries that no amount of intelligence could calm, though I expended tremendous amounts of intellectual energy trying to do so. All of that was in vain. It was a pointless, useless, debilitating experience of running in place, harder and harder, under greater and greater strain. I believed so much in my intelligence that it took me far longer than it should have to get help. I believed both that I was smart enough not to be crazy, and also that if I was crazy I was smart enough to think my way out of it. Fear consumes the self and then takes on its qualities, corrupting individual intelligence. It programs its DNA so completely into the self that even years later, it is there, like an ancient virus lugged around in a contemporary cell.

My intelligence is busy churning out the essential insights that drive my career and my understanding of the world, and my intelligence is also damning me, coming up with surreal magical connections and symbols and stories that suck my life down the drain of madness. My intelligence is like a robot that has escaped my control, misprogrammed, rogue. It can still do what I need it to do but it will simultaneously and just as eagerly set itself to justifying why I need to place all the cup handles facing backward.

It is this that makes the disease so debilitating, so painful. For all of my life, I have privileged intelligence above money, popularity, beauty. In college, I took graduate courses and hung out with grad students and made a big show of sitting in coffee shops reading Nature's Metropolis: Chicago and the Great West. In my years of travel, I read Hemingway in bars and wrote terribly self-important blogs, and from time to time I'd make lists of Great Books or Important Movies or other such-and-such that I needed to master on my quest to smartness. I staked my identity on intelligence. Almost all of my fears revolve around it: I am not scared, for example, of the baby getting cancer or falling off a ledge, but of what can affect her brain. I am terrified of being perceived as ignorant, of making a wrong decision, or a simple, stupid error. My pride and self-esteem are wrapped up in this quality.

And yet having a baby also tempered my reverence for intelligence. I came to understand that there are insights that transcend intelligence, that intelligence can deny and try to finagle its way out of. My aunt wrote me a letter once and in it she complimented my dad: she said that "his strong intelligence is always evident, but it is softened with simplicity and matter of fact reasoning." It had never occurred to me that intelligence might be a mixed quality. That it might be distrusted. That it might corrupt one's relationship to the world as much as enhance it. That it wasn't inherently the truest or wisest way of relating to people.

This sounds naïve; it's not that I couldn't understand how intelligence could be used for malice, or that I thought intelligence automatically engendered profundity and morality. But I assumed that intelligence was the necessary starting point for any sort of insight, depth, inquiry. I could see immediately what my aunt meant about my dad, though I'd never considered it in those terms before. My dad doesn't believe everything he thinks. He knows he is intelligent; he develops critical opinions and makes thoughtful choices, but he is not beholden to his intelligence as a man is bound to a flashlight at night. He makes room for other ways of being, seeing, understanding. He devotes plenty of time—hiking, hunting, meditating, working in his workshop—to presence that goes beyond intelligence. He develops friendships that depend not on the shared sparking thrill of intelligence but on connection, camaraderie, listening. His intelligence is beholden to rather than exempt from curiosity, empathy, and devotion.

"You have to accept not knowing," Dr. S told me. *The sensation of not knowing can be one of fear, at first. But then it feels like nakedness, and then like smallness. Like waking up and having no idea, like giving up on perfection.* "In reality," write the authors of The Mindfulness Workbook for OCD, "perfection is the perpetual state in which something horrible is about to happen."

My anxiety grows more acute the more "perfect" I imagine my life to be. I do not feel I deserve this imagined perfection and fear it will be violently wrenched from me. At Elena's well-check appointments, I was told she was healthy, beautiful, meeting her milestones, and I would think, What did I do to deserve this? *The answer was always nothing. What, I wondered, might be lying in wait, as retribution?*

Seeking reassurance, I would gauge my perfection and merit against that of friends. She has a million-dollar house and a CEO job and lives in a gorgeous world-class city where everyone wants to live and has two healthy children she can afford to send to preschool, so see, my life is not so perfect after all! *I fear losing anything I have—my husband, the advances I have made in my career, my daughter, my family, my relative creative freedom—and at the same time I fear having it. I justify it by telling myself it is really not that much, not that outrageous, should not tempt downfall as much as others whose setup is truly enviable, but it is also true that the people I know who have suffered the most tend to be those who have deserved it the least. The relationship between privilege, success, stability, love, and ethical/personal/spiritual merit is shaky at best, and oftentimes downright inverse. But my mind, my educated mind, the mind on which I have bet all my self-esteem, turns out in the end to be rather naïve. It runs in ridiculous circles around this question of deserving or not deserving, worthy or unworthy, doomed or saved. It refuses to accept that being good, that striving for perfection, won't save me from tragedy.*

Ultimately, I am scared of being happy and also scared of some dreaded situation taking away my happiness. I cannot shake a sense of how precarious and vulnerable happiness is, how threatened simply by the dawning of another day, by whim. It seems inevitable that happiness will fade and, of course, it will; we will all lose everything in the end. This is what makes the happy moments so unbearably lovely.

"Un clavo saca otro clavo," Jorge told me years ago, when we first met, trying to sound like the tough guy he so transparently was not. One nail removes another, the saying goes, meaning in macho Mexican culture that the best way to recover from heartbreak is to fling oneself into another romance. I never found this relevant for relationships, but I do for fear. Perhaps the only benefit of a new, scorching fear is that it can immediately render previous fears tame and ridiculous. In comparison to the threat of inhaling diesel in a taxi for an hour, the previous threat of pesticides on kale seems laughably bourgeois, whereas a day or two ago the threat of pesticides on kale had made the threat of walking past road construction seem laughably bourgeois. Kenneth Koch has a poem called "One Train May Hide Another," which ends like this:

One doctor, one ecstasy, one illness, one woman, one man
May hide another. Pause to let the first one pass.
You think, Now it is safe to cross and you are hit by the next one.
It can be important
To have waited at least a moment to see what was already there.

It is *what-is-already-there* that I can't get to, the deeper fear beneath all fears, vast and heartbreaking, speaking to a loss or a truth I can't articulate. I know it is there; I can feel it beneath me in the everyday, from time to time in the car, from time to time while running, or going to sleep, or walking the dog. I used to feel it occasionally as a child, a bizarre and inexplicable despair when I first woke up in the morning. It lasted seconds, a moment at most, but in its duration the whole futility and absurd sadness of life pressed down on me so hard it seemed useless and impossible to rise. Then, just as quickly, it would be gone, like a mountain cloud whisked over the valley. I never thought much of it. But I have come to think that its potential lies dormant in all of us, and at certain moments in life we sense it there, crouched in wait.

When I hold out against my symptoms, withstanding the urge to chute away from the anxiety into some sort of ritual or Googling or other attempt at relief, I am confronted with sadness. It seeps up like some cold ancient fog through the foundation of fear. I want to fold into it. I sense it in the goodbyes, the ends, the memories of moments so brief and then gone. I find I feel grief. Not for any particular self or person or situation, but for the limitations of my life, the impossibility of doing everything or even anything right and my inability to ever truly know how to best live my life, be happy, keep my child safe. This grief is present in the hug I give my dad when he gets in his car to drive back to the farm; in the ferns and garlands of bittersweet we gather for our Christmas tree; in the press of my mother's cool cheek to my own; in the mess of my daughter's hair on the pillow.

MARNA

12

Welfare

In the mid-twentieth century, the nuclear family, headed by the wage-earning male patriarch, was the standard for social, cultural, and psychological well-being. The "disobedient" mother—single, divorced, or working—was threatening, seen as the source of disorder. As historian Ruth Feldstein demonstrates in her book *Motherhood in Black and White,* the Great Depression and the Second World War buried the relatively progressive maternalist politics of the early twentieth century beneath an avalanche of worries about the state of the nation and the family. Academics, politicians, and architects of popular culture argued that mothers were the cause of a national crisis. "When women misbehaved," wrote Feldstein, "they endangered citizenship, the health of families, and race relations."

John Dollard, a social psychologist trained at the University of Chicago and working for the Institute of Human Relations at Yale, spent five months in the early 1930s immersed in a southern community he dubbed "Southerntown," to produce *Caste and Class in a Southern Town.* The book was widely praised by the top scholars of the day and acted as a template for future academic work. It was innovative in its depiction of racial prejudice as a destructive force for both whites and blacks, and it argued that black people could aspire to the same success and stability as whites in the right circumstances. The rationale underpinning these observations, however, was firmly rooted in the gender stereotypes of the day.

For Dollard, and for the great majority of commentators on both sides of the political spectrum all the way through the twentieth century and into the twenty-first, the problem of racial oppression was pinned on black women. The health of a family and a community was measured by the status of its male breadwinners, and black men did not share the power and control of their white counterparts. Black women worked, and because they worked, they became more independent, and in becoming more independent they created, in Dollard's words, "a weak, mother-centered family," and therefore rendered "the hold of the Negro man on his woman . . . institutionally very weak."

Dollard concluded that because black women were economically dominant, they became sexually dominating as well: "as accessible as animals in heat and always ready for sexual gratification." For this reason, white men found them irresistible, and frequently entered into liaisons with them. When black men in Southerntown insisted to Dollard that white men were in fact raping black women, Dollard labeled these men "defensive" and offered that black women were really seeking pleasure.

The only way for black people to advance, Dollard posited, would be to diminish the role of black "matriarchs," confining them to more conventional and dependent sex roles, thus enabling the men to rise to power.

E. Franklin Frazier, a sociologist whose 1939 book *The Negro Family in the United States* would be a formative work for generations of sociologists, echoed Dollard in warning that ongoing racism was largely a problem caused by black women's "matriarchal" status. Frazier argued that the Great Migration of southern blacks to northern cities destroyed the values of the old generation and unleashed female power from "the simple folkways of . . . peasant folk." Frazier labeled the social structure of the South "The Matriarchate," in which families were centered on black women, whose power was contained by tradition and vast networks of kin. In the North, however, this benevolent matriarchate turned into "Outlawed Motherhood," in which single women loosed from the constraints of rural life became over-sexualized, dominated their men, and degraded the life of their communities. This motherhood was *the* crisis of black life, according to Frazier. It prevented black men from assuming their "rational" masculinity, and it subsequently produced frustration and aggression in these men or, worse, feminine passivity and emotionalism. The black men who'd succeeded in the North, Frazier asserted, had done so because of the appropriate "subordination of the woman in the economic organization of the family."

In the 1940s and 1950s, this take on racial inequality gained popularity, shifting the emphasis from innate genetic or biological characteristics to psychological dysfunction stemming from the behavior of mothers. The family was a microcosm of society, and inappropriate masculinity on the part of the woman and/or femininity on the part of the man in this sphere was perceived to cause larger social problems.

Psychoanalysts Abram Kardiner and Lionel Ovesey's *The Mark of Oppression*, published in 1951, asked how the black man had lost his "magical powers" as a provider. "[The] trouble," Kardiner and Ovesey concluded, "lies in the original relationship with his mother." Men raised in a "female-dominated household" could not practice "healthy heterosexuality": they were too weak or too aggressive, too emotional or too repressed. Kardiner studied under Franz Boas and Freud, and ran an interdisciplinary seminar at the New York Psychoanalytic Institute and Columbia University. His views were establishment.

In *Black Metropolis: A Study of Negro Life in a Northern City*, anthropologists St. Clair Drake and Horace Cayton analyzed the lives of African Americans in segregated urban Chicago. The book, which featured an introduction by Richard Wright, debunked many myths of black life, but largely did so by reinforcing the status quo of white patriarchy. Drake and Cayton assured readers that upper- and middle-class black families "usually follow what might be called a patriarchal setup like that of white families," and embraced "individual competition" as a core value. They chastised black women for dominating their men: "Since she pays the piper, she usually feels justified in calling the tune," they lamented. These canonical works reiterated the assumption that a healthy, functional family and an ordered, happy society required the prosperity and status of white men. As Kardiner and Ovesey put it, "Our constant control is the American white man. We require no other control system."

The preeminent document on the black matriarch was the now-infamous report written in 1965 by Daniel Patrick Moynihan, assistant secretary of labor and director of the Office of Policy Planning and Research under President Lyndon Johnson. Entitled "The Negro Family: The Case for National Action," the report argued that black culture was a "tangle of pathology," and that this was due in large part to the prevalence of fatherless homes. Moynihan wrote, "In essence, the Negro Community has been forced into a matriarchal structure, which, because it is so out of line with the rest of the American society, seriously retards the progress of the group as a whole." Moynihan was particularly concerned that black women paid too much attention to their female children— doting on them, encouraging them to go to school, for example.

"The very essence of the male animal," Moynihan wrote, "from the bantam rooster to the four-star general, is to strut." Any achievements on the part of women, and particularly black women, impeded men's "natural" desire to parade their masculinity around as an achievement. Black men, he urged, should join the military; black men should be given black women's jobs; the state should intervene not to aid mothers but to see "what it takes for a working man to raise a family . . . and then see to it that what it takes is available." Moynihan's argument allowed those who were made uneasy by the demands of the civil rights movement to blame social problems that affected black families on the behavior of black women, thus also exculpating white people and the state.

Bell hooks writes, "Of all the negative stereotypes and myths that have been used to characterize black womanhood, the matriarchy label has had the greatest impact on the consciousness of black people." She points out that while powerful men employed this image to depict black communities as dysfunctional and black women as "immune to pain and suffering," black women "embrac[ed] the label . . . because it allowed them to think of themselves as privileged." Hooks interviewed a woman who was working as a clerk, in near poverty, and who kept referring to herself as powerful, matriarchal, even though "she was nearly having a nervous breakdown trying to make ends meet."

The issues plaguing the black community were not seen or analyzed as the product, in the words of civil rights activist James Farmer, of "an 'orderly and normal' white family structure that is weaned on race hatred and passes the word 'nigger' from generation to generation." Rather, they were the fault of black women: black women who'd failed to heed the standards of the white patriarchal, nuclear family, and whose "disorder," the academics and the policy makers warned, threatened to spill over and tarnish all women. In fact, intolerance and judgment of black women's "defiance" of the suburban norm of working dad, stay-at-home mom, and the kids—a way of life long denied these women in any case by a web of laws and regulations—expanded gradually to encompass all women. Any woman who strayed from ideal motherhood—by virtue of being single, poor, on welfare, LGBTQ, overly independent, overly ambitious, overly defiant of protocol— found herself censured. What began with black women would come for all women, though white feminists often treated their experiences as categorically different.

In a March 2019 episode of the popular podcast *The Longest Shortest Time*, journalist and author Dani McClain talks about growing up with a single mother and negotiating the stigma associated with it. The show quotes President Obama speaking to a predominately black crowd, saying, "We know that more than half of all black children live in single-parent households. Half! We know the statistics that children who grow up without a father are five times more likely to live in poverty and commit crime." Then it cuts to Mitt Romney, extolling the benefits of the nuclear family: "Because if there's a two-parent family, the prospect of living in poverty goes down dramatically. The opportunities that the child will be able to achieve increase dramatically. . . . We can make changes in the way our culture works to help bring people . . . in the American system." The assumption here is twofold: that families composed of a married heterosexual couple and children are stable, happy, healthy, and part of a vision of thriving American prosperity, and that black women could be part of the system if they simply married. McClain calls this an "equal-opportunity myth," appealing to people on both sides of the political spectrum; this has been true for most of American history.

Yet there is little evidence to support this myth. While family structure might have a disproportionate impact on the wealth of white women and children—white single mothers are likely to become poor following a divorce—it does not have much of an impact on the wealth of black women and children. Black women are much more likely to be poor when they are married and also when they divorce, and black children living with two parents, as Dorothy Roberts writes, "are still more likely to be poor than white children in female-headed households."

A massive intergenerational study on race and economic opportunity in the United States, based on tax records from 1989 to 2015 and released in early 2018, confirmed the fact that marriage does not lift black children—and particularly black men, so often the focus here—out of poverty. The income of black men raised in two-parent households was only marginally higher than the income of those raised by a single parent, and remained well below that of whites. A black man raised by two parents each in the ninetieth percentile for income—making around $140,000 a year—earned the same amount in adulthood as a white man raised by a single mother who earned $60,000 a year. As Roberts writes, "Just as marital breakdown is unlikely to be the cause of Black mothers' poverty, so marriage is unlikely to be the solution."

Black women, meanwhile, remain the recipients of social critique. Duke English professor Wahneema Lubiano writes, "She is the agent of destruction, the creator of the pathological, black, urban, poor family from which all ills flow; a monster creating crack dealers, addicts, muggers, and rapists—men who become those things because of being immersed in *her* culture of poverty."

———————

Marna was born and raised in San Francisco but spent many of her childhood summers in her mother's native Arkansas, in the country. She went to college at Clark Atlanta University, where she studied journalism and English literature. Two and a half months after graduating from college and returning to San Francisco, Marna found out she was pregnant. She was twenty-four.

The father was a guy she had met through a friend's boyfriend. She didn't particularly like him at first, but they hung out regularly, in a desultory way. He was honest "to a fault," and Marna liked that. She liked that he would say, "Yeah, I did it," as opposed to equivocating and blaming. She liked that he wasn't going to prettify the world for her. She was someone who prided herself on being able to deal with it.

He came over to her place after she got off work and together they watched all the classic mob movies: *Casino, Scarface, Bronx Tale, Donnie Brasco*. It was "a surface get-along," as Marna explained it, but pleasurable. He wasn't like most of the people Marna hung around, but it didn't matter much because it was a little fling. Marna realized that he didn't have a job, and it was fishy that he still had money to spend. "That's not the type of people I was raised around. I was raised around hardworking people; everybody was getting paychecks," Marna said. One night she finally decided, *This is not the guy I want to be around at all.* She broke up with him.

The next morning, Marna woke up feeling sick. Her stomach hurt. She went downtown and "everything smelled like a sewer." *Oh my God,* she thought. She had that moment: *I think I might be pregnant, for real.* All day, she tried to get hold of him. He didn't reply. When it was late he finally came over; Marna was half-sleeping. She got up and went to take the test.

Coming out of the bathroom, she threw the stick at him.

"I don't understand," he said.

"It's a pregnancy test!" she shouted. "I'm pregnant!"

He asked her what she was going to do, and she said, "I'm keeping it." She hadn't even thought about it. It was clear to her that she'd keep it.

They decided to try and make it work.

She had a little spotting, and she went to her OB's office to see what was happening. The OB asked Marna if she was going to keep the baby. Yes, Marna said, with no hesitation. *Are you sure?* the OB pushed.

Marna was taken aback. The OB's tone shifted. "Everything looks fine," she told Marna, "but that doesn't mean you won't miscarry." The rest of the exam unfolded in silence. As Marna was leaving, the OB tried again. "You don't have to do this," she told Marna. "It's going to be really hard. You need to know what your options are."

It was, Marna told me, "very disheartening, to say the least." It was her first prenatal appointment, and she was brimming with awe and fear at her body and its capacity, but cast over it all was the clear medical message that her pregnancy was not wanted even though she herself very much wanted it. Marna didn't get it. Back home, talking to her mom, Marna mentioned that the doctor "was acting really funny." Her mom perked up right away. "Oh, no no no no," she said. "You're going to have to find a new doctor. We're not gonna do that." *Okay,* Marna thought, *so I'm not crazy.* Her dad explained that some people were just like that. Her parents never used the word *racist.* But the office was in Pacific Heights, an affluent white neighborhood of San Francisco. She was likely their only black client. "I just had no idea," Marna said.

She and her boyfriend went together on the first trip to the new doctor's office. As she waited to get her blood drawn, the nurse reprimanded her. "You need to talk to your social worker!" she yelled at Marna. "You can't just come down here!"

She told me, "I was so oblivious. I was raised in an upper-middle-class family. I didn't know about social workers, Medicaid, and I was like, what?" Her boyfriend straightened it out: "She's got private insurance," he told the nurse in a withering tone. Then suddenly it was all cheery, fine.

Her relationship with her boyfriend began to sour as the pregnancy progressed. They'd start talking, the conversation would escalate and he would get angry, and before she knew it they were in the middle of a war. He wasn't physical, so she didn't think he was abusive. "I didn't know how an abuser operates. I hadn't dealt with abusive relationships before." He goaded, harassed, and insulted her until she got so furious that she wished she could somehow push her stomach to the side and full-throttle attack him. This urge was so far from who she was as a person: normally, she was quiet, peaceful, thoughtful.

She could tell that her hormones were surging, and she feared sending anxiety and anger and stress to her baby. She agonized. Should she give her boyfriend a chance and stay with him? She wanted a nuclear family so badly. She'd grown up in one of those ideal families: her mom and dad had been married for decades, each child planned and prepared for. She clung to this dream like a scrabbly cliff edge, and then her boyfriend called to tell her that because he hadn't gone to anger management classes, he would be sent to jail. Marna was stupefied. She'd never even known this was a possibility. She called her sister from the floor in the bathroom, hysterical, heaving with sobs. She was going to have "one of *those* pregnancies," without a partner. "I couldn't believe that I was so far off the mark of how I was raised."

Marna sank into a funk that she tried to write off: *I chose a lousy boyfriend, it made me sad, I should move on.* "Depression was something other people went through: not me," she said. Nearly two decades later, while she's telling me her story, Marna notes that there was only one other time in her life where she experienced that level of sadness.

Pregnancy was supposed to be the happiest time of her life, and instead she felt trapped in a well. She was twenty-four, and she felt like she was fourteen. Her dad was the most dependable person she knew—if he said he was going to be somewhere, he was there. If he was going to get something, he'd get it. And here she was dealing with someone who was a total wild card. She was alone, so happy to be a mother, sure in her decision, and so lost. "It was like I was dumped into a different dimension."

At the same time, Marna told me in the next breath, "I was very excited to be pregnant. I loved the fact that I was carrying a life inside of me."

Within a week of her boyfriend's telling her that he was headed to jail, Marna was diagnosed with gestational diabetes and admitted to the hospital. Looking back now, she thinks there was a direct connection between the trauma of that breakup and the breakdown of her body. She gained almost sixty-five pounds.

No one asked her why she had gained weight. Why, as she put it, she was "stuffing her face full of food." No one asked her how she was feeling. She told me, "I literally gorged myself through the pain."

Marna's doctors put her on a very high dose of insulin, so she had to give herself multiple shots a day in the stomach. Each time she was terrified that she was poking her daughter. "Of all the times for me to be sticking a needle in my stomach!" She had to wake up in the middle of the night and check her blood sugar. She got on the medical roller-coaster of risk and there was no getting off.

The doctors started worrying about her daughter's heart; they wanted to do an EKG, a stress test. The test seemed okay, but after that her blood pressure spiked, and that marked the beginning of preeclampsia: a dangerous and sudden rise of blood pressure in pregnant women. She was finally released from the hospital with the stipulation that she return three times a week to have her blood pressure checked and her baby monitored.

Marna's mom remembers picking her up from the hospital that day. The look on Marna's face—devastated, scared, rattled—broke her mother's heart. But her mother did not say anything. She did not ask anything. She thought Marna was going through something very tough, and she let her be.

Marna understood that her pregnancy involved risk. "I get trying to explain risk," she said, "and trying to explain the severity of a risk." But the way the doctors did it was so cold and matter-of-fact and, as Marna put it, "above me—I had no say. I didn't know what to ask." Being lectured about risk was like scrutinizing a landscape of shadowy threats without knowing which one was actually imminent and dangerous and which one was distant and negligible. Each visit involved a new dire prediction. Her blood pressure continued to spike, at one point hitting 200.

She asked why she had to come in so often and was told that the longer her pregnancy went on with her gestational diabetes, the greater her chance of a stillbirth. This was the actual word choice they used with Marna eight months into her pregnancy: the culmination of all of the relentlessly negative predictions. Marna's body was stung into alertness. *Now you've gotten my attention here,* she thought. *You mean to tell me I'm going to go through all this pain, this mental anguish, all these problems, all this other stuff, trying to be a trouper, all of this to have a dead baby? NO.* But she had no control, no tools to gain any.

Years later, Marna became a doula, and she found out that gestational diabetes can easily be kept under control. But no doctor mentioned this to her. "They scared me half to death." She thought, *I am the only one trying to be happy for myself in this situation. Nobody is happy with me.*

On August 9, 1935, Congress passed the Social Security Act, which was signed into law by President Franklin Delano Roosevelt on August 14. In lieu of a universal system that distributed benefits to everyone, like Sweden's, the Social Security Act distinguished between old age insurance—Social Security—to which white middle- and upper-class men were "entitled" on the basis of work; and welfare, conceived of as charity for poor women. (Racial and gender bias were not explicitly written into the law, but were de facto: the professions excluded by the act, including agricultural laborers, domestic servants, hospital workers, librarians, and teachers, were typically the province of women and minorities, and anyone whose work was intermittent was also ineligible.) Social Security was depicted as though workers "merely got back what they put in," in the words of historians Linda Gordon and Nancy Fraser, whereas welfare was portrayed as an indulgence, receiving something for nothing.

This distinction rendered the massive federal spending on middle- and upper-class workers, which totaled $711 billion in the 1990s and included corporate tax breaks, child tax credits and exemptions, and government-backed mortgages and housing subsidies— available for most of American history only to the white middle class—largely invisible as an entitlement. It foregrounded welfare, which, in comparison, made up $20 billion in spending at the same time.

The original incarnation of "welfare," called Aid to Dependent Children or ADC, was given only to children, and was an extension of the "mothers' pensions" that maternalist reformers helped establish in the 1920s. Mothers' pensions allowed "deserving" mothers who lacked a male breadwinner to stay home with their children. More than forty states instituted these pensions between 1911 and 1920. They were intended specifically for mothers of, as Florida State University professor of sociology Jill Quadagno, author of *The Color of Welfare*, puts it, "worthy character": that is, white mothers with clean and tidy homes who did not work.

Less than 3 percent of mothers' pensions went to black women. Pensions, and the ADC that later incorporated them, were explicitly *not* meant to foster female independence; they were intended to substitute for a man, keeping docile and well-behaved homemakers afloat. The vast majority of ADC funds went to the white widows of white male industrial workers with young children.

In 1939, Congress passed amendments to the Social Security Act that allowed widows to receive financial assistance through the old age program instead of ADC. The advisory council that recommended this change justified it on the basis that ADC was "insufficient to maintain normal family life or to permit the children to develop into healthy citizens." The question of how non-widowed mothers left to rely on ADC would raise "healthy citizens" in "normal family life" was left unasked and unanswered. These mothers were divorced, single, or married to unemployed men; they were outliers, and stigmatized as such.

Although, as Dorothy Roberts put it, "Americans now view welfare dependency as a Black cultural trait," for the first several decades after its inception, welfare was not available to black people. Southern states in particular systematically denied black women benefits. One major disincentive for granting welfare was the possibility that black women who received it wouldn't be as willing to work the low-paying subsistence jobs under the South's prevailing caste system.

The category of "employable mother" excluded most black women from benefits. But southern states judiciously worked all the angles to ensure the lowest number of black recipients possible: they established "man in the house" rules that allowed social workers to pop up unannounced and search for men cohabiting with unmarried women, they created seasonal policies that kicked women off welfare during cotton-picking season, they denied women on the basis of having more than one child, they eliminated women who took on renters in their homes for extra income, they turned down women whose moral or sexual behavior was considered improper, and they negated benefits when an applicant didn't have a "suitable home." Quadagno cites the first African American elected to Mississippi's legislature in one hundred years: "Should you be able to walk or crawl, then you do not qualify for such programs." Meanwhile, the Social Security Act of 1950 expanded the number of recipients of this insurance by ten and a half million and increased their benefits by 80 percent.

As Social Security became more firmly entrenched as an expensive entitlement program for the middle and upper classes, resistance to ADC as a handout to "undeserving" and "immoral" women intensified. By 1950, Social Security cost the government $290 million, and ADC cost $50 million, but the latter was depicted then just as now as a major drain on the resources of the middle class. By 2017 Social Security cost the government $945 billion, and Temporary Assistance for Needy Families (TANF), the modern-day incarnation of ADC, $16.7 billion.

The mid-twentieth-century rhetoric around ADC sounds uncannily modern; recipients were classified as, Feldstein cites, "shiftless, lazy, immoral, degenerate, dishonest, and radical." The main basis for these judgments was the fact that these women were not married.

Following World War II, a constellation of forces increased the demand for ADC and the number of women in situations that required it: a baby boom; rising divorce rates; the sudden decrease in work opportunities for women, who'd been ushered rapidly into the workforce when men left for war and then shoved just as quickly out of it when the men returned; and the shuttering of the nation's first and only federally run day-care centers, meant to accommodate those working women during the war. Handwringing about the ADC, however, tended to see the program itself as the cause rather than the effect: welfare was encouraging women to get divorced, have scores of "illegitimate" children, neglect them with hypersexual and degenerate lifestyles, and apply for . . . welfare.

The Notification of Law Enforcement Officers (NOLEO) requirement, an amendment to the 1950 Social Security Act, ruled that welfare administrators were obligated to notify police if they gave ADC benefits to families where the father had "deserted." The police would then track down the father, drag him back, and force him into his manly obligations to prevent the state from having to play his role. If they wanted to receive benefits, women were forced to name the father of their children, without regard to whether or not this father might be abusive or hostile. Women who were resistant were coerced to embrace the state's intervention on their behalf. Over the course of the decade following the NOLEO amendment, seven states and eighteen major cities established official investigative processes to track down men who could support women in order to get them off ADC.

At the start of the 1960s, nearly 90 percent of ADC recipients were white. Black civil rights activists began campaigning in the early sixties to change welfare's eligibility rules in order to finally make it widely accessible to black people as well. The National Welfare Rights Organization (NWRO), formed in 1966 and composed of lawyers, welfare mothers, and neighborhood organizations, staged sit-ins and confrontations at welfare offices, demanding increases in benefit levels, access to jobs, and the elimination of statutes that allowed administrators to whimsically deny benefits to women. The NWRO members were often met with violence— including beatings from the police—and racist rhetoric: Senate Finance Committee chairman Russell Long called the activists "Black Brood Mares, Inc."

The NWRO was successful, however. The courts struck down the existing regulations and increased benefits and access. As a result, the welfare caseload in 1967 went from 86 percent white to 46 percent nonwhite, according to historian Gwendolyn Mink. As the program included more black families, they were used to tarnish its reputation. A *Saturday Evening Post* article on ADC depicted black children living "in wretched hovels" with sexually active women. This image was not representative of the vast majority of ADC families, but, as Feldstein asserts, "Charges against ADC affected all women through their discursive relationship with black women": that is, the more black women received ADC, the more it came to be seen as morally compromised.

In the decades following the civil rights movement, program after program designed to assist African Americans was dismantled when white people claimed it infringed on their freedom. As Quadagno explains, the attempt to extend positive liberties to African Americans—to create situations in which they could flourish, raise families, build generational wealth, and become part of the middle-class mainstream—infringed on the negative liberties of whites to not have to do anything that made them uncomfortable. In the end the protection of white comfort generally won, even if that meant keeping black people in destitute conditions and largely excluded from white life. In *The Color of Welfare*, Quadagno offers a book's worth of examples, one of the most salient being the federal government's failure to regulate and integrate the housing market. After decades in which the government at least sporadically attempted to ban restrictive covenants that prohibited black people from moving into white neighborhoods, build functional and integrated housing for blacks whose homes were decimated under "urban renewal," and prevent mortgage discrimination and red-lining policies, Nixon simply gave up in the 1970s and declared that fair housing policies infringed upon "one of our"—as in white people's—"basic individual rights."

It is impossible to separate the history and rhetoric of welfare from the state of black motherhood. The American welfare system was built on the ideal of the patriarchal, heteronormative nuclear family, and black families were denied access to this ideal from its inception. By the 1980s, over half of black families with children were headed by single mothers. The welfare system surveilled their lives, demanding gymnastic procedures of adherence to obscure regulations, insisting they work but cutting off benefits if they worked just enough to reach poverty level. The benefits that sustain and build the generational wealth of the white middle class—affordable mortgages in historically and predominantly white neighborhoods, quality public schools, tax breaks, Social Security, jobs that provide health care and regular hours and maternity leave and salaries—are not available to welfare recipients, and for most of American history were not an option for black people. The inadequate welfare system then becomes one more example of, in Roberts's words, "a racist unwillingness to include Blacks as full citizens."

I began researching the history of welfare around the time I started talking to Ayesha. Ayesha was born and raised in the Bronx. She is one of ten children, six boys and four girls, born to a mother from South Carolina and a father from Saint Croix, Virgin Islands.

"My childhood," she told me, "was really hard. It was so hard. It was really hard." Then she paused. She was living in a house in Coney Island, secured for her family through New York City's PATH housing program.

"I'm going to tell you why as soon as I put my slippers on and walk out to the yard."

I heard shuffling steps, muted conversation, as I sat at my Ikea desk at home, looking out a window at a quiet cobblestone street with a towering evergreen and sycamores. I imagined her on her porch step. I saw my own life as a snow globe, a rarefied little world. My existence in Pittsburgh is hardly the stuff of high luxury; we live in a house in a neighborhood of duplexes and run-down apartment buildings, in a city where it's still possible—though increasingly less so—to find five-bedroom Victorian houses to rent for $2,000 a month. We limit our expenses, and we are hardly able to save. But in comparison to how Ayesha had grown up and the world she lived in, I felt I was in a French castle. Each time I talked to Ayesha,

I was yanked out of my complacency and I saw, anew, my house-plants, the quiet we lived in.

And yet our conversations were equally marked by uncanny similarities. For as disparate as our lives seemed, we worried about many of the same things: providing for our children, having meaningful work, dealing with the negative emotions we sometimes have for our kids. It was this overlap that most struck me. I'm not sure what I expected when we began talking, but perhaps that her life would be unrelatable to mine and vice versa. A sense that the issues she faced were of such a magnitude that my anxiety didn't exist within the same paradigm. And there was some truth to this.

Erin Spahr, the founder and clinical supervisor of the Perinatal Mood Disorders Clinic at Johns Hopkins, works primarily with inner-city women from Baltimore who experience postpartum anxiety and depression. She observed that these clients, often suffering from intergenerational and acute trauma, were extremely overwhelmed as mothers and focused on trying to get a grip on themselves. Whereas white middle-class mothers like myself tended to be highly focused on their babies, "scared of getting anything wrong," as Erin put it, the women Erin worked with didn't have their own needs met, didn't feel safe, or weren't taught to regulate their emotions, and were now in charge of meeting the needs and regulating the emotions of their babies.

But the anxiety of these women is not a separate beast from that of middle-class white women. They are entwined: the lack of support and care for mothers like Ayesha echoes the same old dog-eat-dog American themes in which a woman either pulls herself up—perhaps by relying on an unreliable man—or is allowed to flounder and drown.

Ayesha's story begins on Grove Street in the Bronx. The neighbor had a treehouse in her yard, and Ayesha would play in it with the neighbor's daughters and son. There was a basketball court around the corner where her brothers used to run games with their friends. These years were the best of her life.

When she was six, men came to the door and told Ayesha's family to get out. The eviction was sudden and complete. They had less than ten minutes. They grabbed pictures and videotapes, whatever they could carry, and left. They stayed for a year and a half at Ayesha's grandmother's house. But then she had enough, and told them they would have to go. The family entered the shelters. "From there on," Ayesha says, "it was like a cycle."

They'd stay for a while in a family shelter, find a house through the city intake center known as PATH, then get evicted because they couldn't afford the bills or the landlord was dodgy or for other reasons that seemed murky to Ayesha. They'd go back to the shelters. When Ayesha was ten or eleven, her mother went back to school at Monroe College and got her associate's degree, which earned her a job filing papers in an office, but this did not make a substantial imprint on the family's life other than splitting the kids up with different caregivers while their mother worked. Her father was a barber, but he was in and out of their lives and unreliable at best. "He left us with nothing," Ayesha told me, "no money, no food, nothing."

At a shelter in Queens, through a friend, she met the boy who would become her baby's father. He was twenty; she was fifteen. Everything the boy did, she did too. He bought potent medical marijuana prescribed for an AIDS patient and he and Ayesha each took a handful of pills. Within ten minutes, Ayesha felt like she was about to die. Still, she stayed with him. They drank, they smoked, they partied. It was her childhood.

"He was nice in the beginning," she said. But then, he became controlling. "I don't even dress provocative but nice, classy, presentable, and I was nice, friendly!" she said, defensive, but this was not enough for him. He began hitting her for saying, doing, wearing the wrong things. Her brothers beat him up once when they saw him lay his hands on her, but she stayed with him. When, after two years in the shelter in Queens, the family finally found another home through PATH and moved in, Ayesha thought it could be a way out and a new stability. But there was a dispute with the landlord over bills, and they were evicted. Ayesha ran away to be with the boy.

At eighteen, she got pregnant. She panicked. She thought about killing herself. She couldn't find a job. She dropped out of school. All the women in her life told her to keep the baby. Her father told her to get an abortion and she screamed at him, called him a shit-ass father, declared, "You're supposed to help, this is what real men do!" She stopped talking to him. Ayesha kept the baby. In an attempt to remake her life, she moved on a whim to Albany to stay with a friend, hoping to get a job, save money, and become a cosmetologist. "I want to pursue my dreams," she explained. But the friend was living with a sketchy boyfriend who made Ayesha feel uncomfortable. She also couldn't find a job, and was constantly anxious about money. "I tried and tried and tried to get work," she told me. "I didn't have the right techniques to live comfortably."

Her boyfriend in the Bronx eventually lured her back with promises to take care of the baby. She was four or five months pregnant and wearing a dress. "It was a nice summer dress." She speculates for a moment—"I don't know what it was, if it was my butt because I gained weight?" Her boyfriend grabbed her, talking about her body, pushing her, telling her *change*, holding her by the neck. Then he ripped her clothes off. "How you rip a pair of leather *boots*?" she asked. She left. "Everything nice I had, he destroyed it," Ayesha told me. When she gave up on him, she was hit with the sinking feeling that there was no one for her. She moved back in with her mom in a new shelter. She was anxious and depressed throughout her pregnancy, but her mother told her that she'd had depression with all ten of her children. Maybe it was normal.

At eight months, Ayesha went into the bathroom and discovered she was bleeding. She went to the hospital and spent thirty-six hours in labor; her daughter was born underweight and went straight to the NICU. Ayesha was told her baby would have to stay there until she reached five pounds. "Every time I went to the NICU to see her, I cried and I cried and I cried." This marked the beginning of her motherhood.

By the time the baby was released and Ayesha took her back to the shelter, she was almost hysterical. Ayesha cried when the baby wouldn't stop crying; she didn't know what to do to console her. She didn't know what was wrong. Her mother took over, rocking the baby, patting her back.

At the shelter, Ayesha met a girl named Jeanine who was about her age. She told Ayesha that she sold her vagina for money. "Until you get a job, you can sell whatever you want to," she advised. Jeanine was hanging out with an older African guy. He was nice to Ayesha. "He took me out to eat, and he gave me money, and I was like, *I didn't even have to sleep with him!*" But the next time they went out to eat, they had sex, and "from then on . . . the drugs." One of the girls introduced Ayesha to coke. Her baby was two months old and mostly with Ayesha's mother—"a saint"—as Ayesha disappeared into cocaine, marijuana, and alcohol. At some point, Ayesha tried to stop going up to the Bronx with her new crowd, but "it doesn't matter where you go, whatever it is follows you."

"The main reason why I wanted to do drugs," she told me, "was because I had the child. I can't speak for every woman and every mother but I feel like every day, sometimes every day, we don't want to be mothers. She's always on my conscience, she's a part of me. Even though I am a mom every day, I don't like being a mom every day."

When her daughter turned one, Ayesha and her family left the shelter for a house on Coney Island. Ayesha stopped using hard drugs, although she continued to smoke weed to calm herself down. But her anxiety and depression only intensified. She would go to the beach and sit by the water, thinking, worrying about her daughter. She cycled through ten different jobs, unable to hold one down because of her anxiety attacks. People gave her advice and ultimatums, "It was hard, it was rough pressure." She was desperate for her baby to have a father, but she turned down her volatile ex-boyfriend's sporadic attempts to reconnect. She saw other families with dads and moms and sank into despair and guilt.

Her anxiety peaked one night when her daughter was two. She

was sitting outside on the step with her neighbors, smoking a blunt, when she felt like she was having a heart attack. "Can someone call an ambulance?" she panted, but then worried about going to the ER and what they might do to her there. She rode it out that night, but that prompted her to finally go to the doctor, where she was diagnosed with both anxiety and depression. They wanted to send her to more doctors and put her on medication.

Around this time, Ayesha's older brother died. He'd had a seizure disorder. Her brother's doctors had given him medication for his seizures, and Ayesha has the impression that the medication figured into his death. For this reason, Ayesha doesn't trust the doctors, or the government for that matter, and refuses to take any medication. Instead, she prays and tries to go outside every day. Sometimes when she's irritated at her daughter, she has to walk away and go lie down.

I asked her what the anxiety felt like at its worst. "It feels," she said, "like there's no such thing as a perfect parent. We do the best with our kids." Her response reminded me that we all operate within ranges. We try to do all we can within our range and then we cannot do any more. This is painful to accept, but far more painful when that range is drastically limited.

"I feel like someone is going to pinch me someday, and I'm going to wake up, and I'm going to be married, and I'm going to be happy," Ayesha said. She clung to this fantasy of the nuclear family.

A few months after we started talking, Ayesha went back to school to get her GED. She attended class for four hours in the evenings from Wednesday to Friday. She enrolled her daughter in public pre-K, an offering she was fortunate to have access to in New York City. She wants to go to cosmetology school and open her own business. "I want to do something that I love to do," she told me.

The last time we talked, she told me she thought she was emerging from a midlife crisis. She was twenty-two.

Shortly after my conversations with Ayesha, I traveled to Salem, Ohio, to volunteer as a Spanish interpreter for Guatemalan immigrants detained in a massive immigration raid on a meatpacking plant. I carried diapers back to the house of one mother at least a foot shorter than me, wearing indigenous dress, with a seven-year-old the size of a four-year-old and a wild-haired toddler. She had taken her children on buses across Mexico, then walked through the desert into the United States. She spoke no English or Spanish, only Kiche. Her husband worked as a seasonal agricultural laborer, earning what was surely less than minimum wage. He was gone whenever there was work to be had. He'd been detained in an earlier raid on a nearby gardening center.

They lived in a squalid apartment. The linoleum floors of the kitchen peeled up, the carpet was ancient, the ceiling low, and all of their possessions were piled and strewn about. I gingerly set the diapers down. The mother thanked me by bowing her head. I walked back to the church basement that had become a de facto legal clinic, past peeling white picket fences and limp American flags.

Throughout history, white women have chosen racial solidarity with white men over gender solidarity with women of color in an attempt to gain access to the fruits of capitalist triumph. An alternative to that erroneous path is to choose solidarity with other women, other mothers in particular: to seek the resonances between our lives so that we may begin to repair the gaps. Erich Fromm wrote, "Important and radical changes are necessary if love is to become a social and not a highly individualistic, marginal phenomenon." I asked Erin Spahr of the Perinatal Mood Disorders Clinic at Johns Hopkins what her strategies were for low-income women of color versus upper-middle-class white women. She responded that in all cases, she tried to validate the woman's experience. She tried to provide a sense of safety, to help the woman discover her own fears so that she could be present emotionally for her child. She listened. This is a form of love—a space between people, for confessions and hopes and flaws, and for the seed of solidarity to germinate.

"In our society," bell hooks writes, "we make much of love

and say little about fear. Yet we are all terribly afraid most of the time. . . . Fear is the primary force upholding structures of dominion. It promotes the desire for separation, the desire not to be known. When we are taught that safety lies always with sameness, then difference, of any kind, will appear as a threat. When we choose to love we choose to move against fear—against alienation and separation. The choice to love is a choice to connect—to find ourselves in the other."

13

Solidarity

A day before Marna hit thirty-seven weeks, she began to worry that she hadn't felt the baby move. Immediately the doctors' prediction came rushing to the forefront of her mind: stillborn.

Marna lightly jostled her stomach. The baby moved, but the movements seemed too weak. Marna called her doctor. She went in to the hospital for a check, and they ran the myriad tests they always ran and decided to induce her. Marna didn't know why. "I was just like, okay, I guess they're keeping me." The nurse told her she would be there all weekend.

Marna took a long hot shower. She got on a conference call with five of her relatives who had also recently been pregnant. They talked and laughed and cheered her on and made her feel supported. But the moment she got off the phone, she was alone again. The doctors showed up in an endless rotation of pressure and questions. Did she want an epidural? No. It's going to be really hard if you don't have an epidural. NO. Did she want pain medication? No. They gave her an IV anyway because of her blood pressure. Are you sure you don't want the epidural? Yes. Her mom and her sister hadn't shown up yet, and Marna desperately missed them.

They monitored her daughter's heart rate with external and internal monitors. They put a catheter inside her. Her mother and sister showed up and her labor began to progress quickly. Marna dragged her IV around the room, insisting on moving because she didn't want medication and she wanted to squat and roam and try everything. She told the nurse she knew she was in transition, so the nurse offered to check. Marna was at five centimeters.

"I was like, *Oh my god, I'm only halfway there.*" She started crying.

"Why are you crying?" her mom asked her, and Marna said, "I'm going to have to get the epidural." She sobbed because she didn't want it, and she didn't want medication, but everything suddenly seemed impossible. The anesthesiologist told her he had another epidural and then he'd do hers, and in that interval, the nurse offered to give her fentanyl. She didn't want to "drug her baby up," but the nurse told her it would take the edge off. Marna agreed and they gave it to her through her IV.

All of a sudden, Marna went loose and limp and weak. A contraction would come and she'd lift her head and then feel it drop back down under its own weight. She loathed herself, thinking, *This is the dumbest thing I have ever done.* Then the fentanyl stopped working and she immediately said, *Please give me more.* But they told her they'd have to wait for a certain interval. All of a sudden she felt an intense pain in her back and realized—as she told me in auditory all caps—THIS IS WHAT THEY MEAN BY BACK LABOR. She emerged from the fog of the fentanyl and said, "I need to stand up. SOMEBODY HELP ME STAND UP." She stood up, had a contraction, and felt an intense *whoosh.*

Marna asked what was happening, and the nurses shoved her on the bed and the bed started moving and people came in and the lights flipped on. *Push!* they yelled.

Marna gave four pushes, and her daughter was out. It went very quickly. They whisked the baby away to the NICU without any skin-to-skin contact. Later they told Marna it was because the baby couldn't regulate her temperature, but Marna knew that skin-to-skin could help babies do that. "I don't dwell on it," she told me, "because it makes me angry."

Shortly after they took her daughter, a nurse called and asked if they could give the baby formula because she was hungry. Marna, still in a daze, less than an hour postpartum, said yes. Someone brought her a breast pump and told her to start pumping.

Marna's daughter weighed only four pounds, so she stayed in the NICU while Marna went home. She had a rented apartment above her parents' storefront. Returning from the hospital, she went inside, collapsed, and cried and cried. She was grateful that her daughter had survived, that she had made it through, and she was also terribly sad to be coming home alone.

"Being a doula now," she says, "I look back and, you know, they didn't do any of the stuff that I felt like in hindsight they could've done. When I look at that stuff now, when I attend births now, I personally feel like I missed out."

She told me, "I don't feel like personally I was treated in a way that was prejudicial, . . . but I'm sure that the system, the institution . . . I'm sure they probably considered me a certain way. I was overweight. I'm sure I fed into their stereotypes and they were just giving me what they thought because this is what happens with all these other people that are like me." There had been numerous times when she could tell that "there is an assumption where they know I'm a black person before they've seen or interacted with me, maybe because of a chart, and they're ready to see a particular type of person. And when I don't present that type of person, I see their behavior and their attitude and the way they respond to me change." Marna understood no situation was straightforward. She understood that maybe she was the thirtieth person a doctor had seen, and the doctor was tired, and the doctor had his or her own problems, and then here came this woman who didn't want an IV. "Well for crying out loud!" Marna channels the doctor, "Why not?!" She got it. But at the same time, "They're supposed to make the effort to not do that. . . . You as a doctor are supposed to be trained a certain way. And if they're not trained a certain way, why aren't they?"

Marna drove out to the hospital every day to be with her daughter, but she couldn't shake the sense that this wasn't normal. "You're supposed to be home; you're supposed to be home with the baby." Just like she was supposed to be married; she was supposed to be supported; she was supposed to breastfeed. "I didn't get to debrief," she told me. "As a doula, you debrief [with your clients]. You go over your experience."

Finally, she was able to take her daughter home. After all of the ups and downs of the birth and the NICU and the friction she felt between what-should-be and what-was, she descended into an "immense sadness."

This must be the baby blues, she thought. She found out her daughter's father had gotten another woman pregnant. She struggled to breastfeed. She was shocked when her mother didn't support her in trying, insisting she give her daughter formula. She wanted so badly to be a good mother. "I didn't feel suicidal," she reflects. "I felt this feeling of like, *I wish I wasn't here.*" She went to all of her appointments; her doctors never questioned her, never raised an eyebrow. She didn't have the script or the experience to express what she felt.

She loved her daughter, and thought her daughter was the most beautiful, magical baby. Her daughter would wake up and smile at her, and Marna would take pictures of her first thing in the morning. There was a duality in her life then, the sadness and the love. Sometimes the two emotions would merge in guilt: for not enjoying her child wholly with no negative feelings; for having so many worries; for not being part of the quintessential nuclear family.

Marna's daughter was born in September. She hit rock bottom around Thanksgiving. She had a huge family: thirty-five cousins on her mom's side alone. She was very close with them. But that year, she was miserable. Seeing her relatives who had children made her feel worse. The only person who noticed was an aunt of hers. She pulled Marna aside and asked, "What's going on with you?"

"Nothing," Marna insisted, "I'm just tired." The aunt didn't push further. That night, after Marna went home, was the first time she realized something was actually wrong. But she didn't have the words for it or the resources to make sense of it. "I never got any help," she told me.

Marna found her way out through her community and her faith. The five relatives who'd been pregnant around the same time all had young children and got together often. Her parents loved being grandparents, and her dad in particular loved to take her daughter everywhere. Since she worked with her family, she could bring her daughter to work. She could breastfeed. She could go upstairs to their apartment above the storefront and take a nap. "These things," she told me, "made the difference."

She built a new relationship with God. "I started seeing my divine path, really quickly." She talked about the light at the end of the tunnel—forgiveness. She explained:

"Being angry . . . breeds disease. It breeds depression. It eats at you; it devours you. [I thought], *I have to count my blessings.* I made it through my pregnancy, made it through my labor and delivery, had a quick and easy labor and delivery, I have a daughter who has a wonderful spirit, and I do enjoy being a mom. I have a job where I can take my daughter to work, breastfeed, nap, do all that stuff. None of this is happening the way I expected it, ever, but all hope is not lost. I can be okay. I didn't get everything I wanted and no one ever does, and it's okay. It may not have been what I expected or even what I deserved, but it's okay. I'm okay. If I can take out my pregnancy from all the other stuff, I loved it. I absolutely loved every waking day. . . . The first time I felt her move, and kick, and my stomach started poking out a little bit. I loved all of that. I loved that I had a part in creation. One cell becomes two becomes four becomes a baby becomes a person, and my body gets to be used to create someone else. That's something only God does, and He chose to do it through me. He chose to do it through women." She laughs. "That's a whole 'nother thing! We could get into that!"

Whenever Marna is on a job as a doula, or even whenever she's talking with people who know she's a doula, she talks about depression: "It's not normal," she says, "but it's common." *Pay attention to the pregnant woman,* she tells her clients and her community and friends. *You need to talk to her and you need to work to get some help.* She sees her role as normalizing—"a lot of times," she explains, "in the black community we don't talk about mental health issues."

Marna came into an awareness of mental health only when her daughter grew old enough, around three or four, to begin having real interactions with her father. Marna would bring her back from the court-ordered visitation and her daughter would cry. Marna began reading into what could be happening to her daughter, who was ordinarily a happy child. She found her daughter a therapist, and "it was through *her* journey," she told me, "that I started to look at my own reactions and behavior." Marna sat in on the therapy sessions, and the therapist would ask her questions. She remembers asking herself for the first time at one of those sessions, *Am I depressed?*

Marna went to a mental health conference to learn more about her daughter's anxiety issues, and one of the presenters told her something very simple that has stuck with her for decades, and that she frequently repeats to other people in the black community: "If you have high blood pressure, or gestational diabetes, you go to the doctor. It's very matter-of-fact, but when it comes to your mental health, *Oh, now, they're going to think I'm crazy.* If something's not right mentally or emotionally, and either you see it or you've had someone close question it, there's nothing wrong with seeing a therapist."

Marna didn't end up seeing a therapist until her daughter was older, but she did join a sister circle, in which women of color talked about their experiences. She still participates.

After several long conversations, Marna and I talked frankly about race. I asked her if she felt like she had the "strong black woman syndrome," and this made her reluctant to seek help. I then backtracked a bit and asked her what she thought of the syndrome; if she thought it was a real thing, or a stereotype, or a combination of both.

woman syndrome," and this made her reluctant to seek help. I then backtracked a bit and asked her what she thought of the syndrome; if she thought it was a real thing, or a stereotype, or a combination of both.

"I don't have to be a strong black woman," she said, "but I couldn't be anything but strong." She framed it to me as do or die: "If I don't step up and be the parent and change the diapers and make the money, what happens? . . . It's not a choice, it's something we usually end up having to be. Because of life. And that's even having a quote-unquote good life. You could have everything and . . . maternal health, morbidity, mortality, infant mortality, all that stuff, it doesn't matter, what family structure, what education, what income, it doesn't even matter. That has nothing to do with it."

She takes a breath, and keeps going: "I think that black women are forced to be strong. They're either forced to be strong out of lack, or forced to be strong because they've maybe been pigeonholed or stereotyped. . . . It's like slavery: We didn't want to be slaves. We didn't want to do it. But we had to get up every day and do it and get whipped and smile and *yes ma'am* and love the babies we have. That's genetic. That trauma is passed down. We didn't have a choice."

She continued, "When you have to, that's a crisis. My car has been over the bridge and we're in the river and it's sinking, and we all have to get out of the car. I wasn't *strong* because I had to get everybody out of the car—I had to do it! If I didn't, we die! That's where we live. It's not like, *I see the car sinking and well, okay.* It's like, breaking doors, OUT, EVERYBODY OUT. We're always in a crisis, that's stress, that's cortisol, that's adrenaline, that's always in our bodies. . . . We don't have housing, we don't have food, our kids aren't in good schools. In income, we're probably some of the lowest. And then if you live in a city like San Francisco, the wealth gap is very evident. Am I going to have my job? Am I going to pay my rent, keep my lights on, am I going to have a weird altercation with the policeman out of nowhere and be shot? . . . These are stressors we live with in Anytown, USA. Then if we move out and we don't have these problems, is it going to be assumed that we have a job because we're black? Are we going to get the promotion we're supposed to get? How are people treating me? Am I going to have to code-switch to keep my job? People who have stuff, they have the income, they have the money, they have all the pieces together: they're worried about that. It doesn't matter where you're at; you're forced to be strong."

One day, Marna told me, she was at a birth—"Wait," I interrupted, "What do you mean, *I was at a birth?*" She explained that she was the type of person whom friends would invite to their births, for support and companionship. Marna loved pregnancy. She loved motherhood. She would have been happy to be a surrogate mother if the need had somehow presented itself. "You're *crazy!*" her friends told her. But she was obsessed with birth, and she was a natural—her presence was calming, grounding. At that first birth, even when the pace started to intensify and accelerate and she could see some might panic, she thought, *I can do this.* A friend said to her then, "You know, this is a profession." Marna laughed. "I'm like, like a *job?*"

"It's called a doula," the friend said.

"How do you spell that?" Marna asked.

When Marna first started looking up the concept over a decade ago, she could hardly find any information. "This is San Francisco!" she told me. "If there's anything weird and natural, we're on top of it, so how come I can't find it?" She put it out of her mind, but every once in a while she'd look it up again. Eventually, she found online courses. *This is what I want to do,* she thought. But the courses were expensive, and no financial aid was offered. Then one day about four years ago, she spotted the post of an acquaintance on Facebook: "I just finished my doula training!" The post featured a picture of this acquaintance holding up her certificate with a group of black women. Marna messaged her, and the acquaintance told her about a class she'd taken in Oakland.

Marna called. Shafia Monroe, queen of black midwives,

answered the phone. She invited Marna to apply for a scholarship. Marna did and received $500 off. She took the course.

Now, as a working doula, Marna thinks first and foremost about a woman's history: if she's had anxiety, or depression, she's at risk for it in pregnancy and postpartum. Sometimes women are shy and won't share personal details with her, so she does "tons of pre-natal visits." She tries to see women and their families at minimum four or five times prior to their due date.

Marna told me, "I recognize so much of myself in the women I work with. In so many different pieces." I feel this too in my work, in listening to the stories of others' lives. Marna's voice is gentle and patient, and I can imagine how it holds the women she works with in her care.

Her clients have a lot going on. Perhaps they have been evicted or are being threatened with eviction. They may not be eating enough or eating a proper diet. Marna asked one of her clients, a mother of three, pregnant with her fourth, about her diet and the woman got upset: "I can't eat everything that you're asking me to eat because I'm trying to put food in my kids' mouths!" I get it, Marna says, and she does. She meets women where they're at. She buys groceries. *What do you need?* she asks. *Do you need me to come sit and give you some sleep? I could give you four hours so you can get a nap in.* There have been times Marna has been the only support person in the birthing room.

Many women aren't happy with the treatment and the care they're receiving, but because of Medicaid or insurance they have to deal with it. "A lot of women have sexual trauma that they're not verbalizing to their providers," Marna told me. "How do you support someone, what does that support look like?" One of her patients wanted a natural labor and was doing great during the birth with Marna when one of the nurses said, "We want to start an IV." The woman didn't want an IV. The tension heightened, so Marna intervened for her client: "She doesn't want any medica-tion." The nurse talked over her, insisting on the IV, until finally the woman blurted out, "I used to be a drug addict! All these IVs and needles trigger me!" The nurse relented. A few minutes later, another nurse entered the room and said, "We still need to connect the IV."

"This is what's happening in labor and delivery rooms!" Marna told me.

Marna recounted one particularly harrowing story of a mom she worked with who had a lot of complicated medical needs. She was on a suite of medications. She had her baby, and Marna left, and the next morning Marna got a frantic call from the woman's partner saying they had given her the wrong medication. She was having a reaction and couldn't hold down any food. Marna went to the hospital.

"The lady," she told me, "is just green. She looks absolutely green." She could barely move. Her partner was panicking. Marna noted that the room was stocked with formula, though the woman had wanted to breastfeed. Marna demanded to see the nurse on duty. She ultimately had to go out searching for her, and when she found her, she said, "My client is in there. She's green. Have you seen her? She's *green*. She shouldn't be green. I don't understand what's happening."

The nurse was casual. "We don't want to say it was a reaction," she responded.

"How long has this been going on?" Marna asked.

The nurse shrugged. "I'm not her nurse," she said.

Marna pushed. "You haven't given her an IV to get her hydrated?" She insisted the nurse come into the room and talk to the woman's partner. They decided on a different medication. Marna had another appointment and had to go, but before she did she laid some ground rules.

"She's not well," she told the nurse. "Do you see that she's not well? We need to solve this." Marna ensured that an IV was started before she left.

"[These things] add up. They start to add up," Marna explained to me. "It leads to women feeling less than, or everybody's against them, or they can't trust their medical providers. It's a lot of things that end up leading to that depression, or add to it, or exacerbate it. When you're not treated well, or you're not treated in a way that's comfortable for you, or you have medical providers and people that you can't trust, the odds aren't in your favor to have the best outcome."

Marna was recently offered a position as the program director for an organization that helps black women receive care from black doulas.

"My cure for my depression," Marna told me, "is to get out of myself and selfish thinking." She realized that when she helped people, she was fulfilled in ways she could not explain. She mentioned the hopelessness she had felt while giving birth: "It helps me be really sensitive to that person and let them have their process too. They don't have to be embarrassed or afraid to cry, or feel like things are out of control." She laughed. "You mean to tell me all this crazy weird bad stuff actually made me perfect for these other things coming up in my life twenty years later?"

Marna told me, "I used to think my biggest vulnerability was actually being vulnerable." She'd shut vulnerability down. But now, she said, "Lo and behold, I'm learning that my vulnerability is my greatest strength."

She realized people had to get to a place of physical and mental safety before they could open up. "If we didn't have to worry about certain things, maybe more people would be vulnerable," she told me.

"When I started doing work as a doula," Marna explained, "all of these places, those empty spots, those holes in me, were filled, because I felt like every time I go into a birth, I'm healed through some sort of way."

ANXIETY BEGINS LIKE AN ABUSIVE RELATIONSHIP, with a twisted agenda masquerading as excessive concern. *"Are you sure you want to eat that?"* *"Wouldn't it be better to put those knives away, where you can't reach them?"* *Anxiety takes care of you in the way an abuser takes care, by restricting boundaries until he assumes total control.*

It is tempting to see the anxiety as part of the self. If it's not the self, then what is? The writer John Green, in an interview with Terry Gross on Fresh Air, explained how his OCD had forced him to grapple with his understanding of self-consciousness. He asked, "If these thoughts feel like they're coming from outside of me, and I'm forced to have them, and I can't choose my thoughts, then who exactly am I, you know? Like, who's running the ship here? Am I really the captain of my consciousness, or is there some outside force that's shaping this for me?"

Dr. S, my therapist, asked me to talk back to my OCD. A diminutive man in his late thirties, in nice leather shoes and polo shirts, suburban and neatly groomed, he would adopt the voice of OCD as if it were a Disney villain. "Are you sure that's safe?" he would ask, bugging out his eyes. "Why don't you wash your hands one more time? It'll just take a second!" I pictured the OCD he ventriloquized to be a bulbous black-and-red genie, sometimes huge and overbearing, other times small and mischievous, scampering about my shoulders. It was a comical and embarrassing exercise. So much about mental illness is humiliating. I might be able to write a book or run a marathon, but when a random thought pops into my head telling me that I should wash my hands multiple times to be safe, I am powerless and shattered. This thought—when emboldened by the victory of its transformation into action—births ten more thoughts, which gleefully take over the whole day, maybe the week, maybe the month. OCD is not innocent; its offer of protection is a bait-and-switch, and it crushes me beneath the weight of my own revealed helplessness.

At the same time, the deeper I get with my OCD and treatment, the more I realize that it is also a part of me. It is the part of me I try so hard to repress, the part of me I don't believe is worthy of love, the part of me I judge in other people. It has to be fought, but to some extent, it also has to be placated. I also have to say, I'm not as smart as I thought I was, I'm not as in control, I better not judge these people because *whoo-ee* look at me. *It can't simply be exorcised. It illumines the brittleness and the arrogance of my own precious assumptions about myself: that I am smart, that I am in control because I am smart, that I can do everything just so, that I can do it better. But it also attacks the parts of myself I want to keep: the gritty traveler, the artist who bucks convention, the bold experimenter.* Fine, it says, my thoughts are random, *my thoughts are constructed, my thoughts are only thoughts, but then so are yours:* all of it is a fantasy, dark and light.

Over time I realized that there is a cycle to fear, but that the cycle has a baseline, and the baseline shifts. At times, the baseline is low, and thus when the cycle kicks up its effects are mild, and they dissipate with relative quickness. At other times, the baseline is high—from stress, hormones, any number of factors—and when a cycle kicks in, I am unable to work or to think about anything but potential dangers. It can be majorly disruptive. I am sick to my stomach, and a cloudiness settles over my brain and makes it difficult to talk or listen. Gradually, it fades, over weeks or months.

When it recedes, I think I am making progress. I think of it also as a condition, something to be managed and monitored and utilized in the building of a more conscious life. It is a tool in the arsenal of American self-betterment: I aim to use it as a whip for wellness! Then, when a new cycle comes surging back, it cares nothing for progress, it cares nothing for philosophy, it cares nothing for monitoring or management. There is nothing thing-like about it; it rises from within, as much me as bile or blood.

I realize at some point that I have to abandon the hope of ridding myself of this thing *as if it were exterior and separate. I cannot compartmental- ize the fear, carry it with me like a briefcase, make it into a tidy lesson, although at times the whole of it softens and enlightens and teaches as much as it hardens and narrows and blinds.*

One day I went running in the park, listening to exposures on repeat on my phone. I may have harmed my daughter for life. This one decision could have ruined our lives. *I listened without a break while sycamore leaves drifted along the lazy river of a fall breeze. Shafts of sun- light turned the dark ravine into a cathedral. I wanted to listen to Iron & Wine, to Natalia Lafourcade, or even just to the crickets, but instead I listened to a playlist of my current worst fears. It made me realize that I have lived my life in categories—the good and the bad, the productive and the useless, the beautiful and the ugly, and on and on. I had to let them dissolve. I have to let my anxiety into the moments when I am most con- tent; I have to uncouple the associations I have between worthiness and happiness, between control and certainty. Undoing those, so many others come undone. I can see I've been clinging to a fantasy self.*

The month before Elena turned three, just as Pittsburgh was greening into summer, two friends of ours stopped by the house on a cross-country bike trip. They were intrepid Europeans we'd first met in Oaxaca, when they were biking up a narrow, sinuous, nearly vertical mountain road and we were driving to visit Jorge's parents. When we got to Jorge's house, I told his mom about the bikers and asked her if we could invite them over for pozole; claro, she said. I ran down the road and waved to them as they passed; would they like a warm bowl of soup?

We spent hours at the outdoor table crunching through the slow-cooked grains of hominy, swapping travel stories. I was twelve weeks pregnant. Afterward, they continued their ride over the mountain and down through the tropics of Veracruz, then returned to their office jobs. Several years later they took off on another adventure biking around the world. They were crossing the United States first and wrote us from somewhere in Ohio, remembering we'd said we were living near there. Their route hap- pened to take them right through Pittsburgh.

Seeing them bike up to our house, after a three-year interval in which we'd had a baby, made me feel, acutely, the distance between my life with

Elena and who I was when we first met. We ate roasted vegetables together at our wooden table, and as I listened to their stories about summiting the Rockies and camping in patches of small-town America, I felt a vertiginous nostalgia and a deep sense of unmooring from my own life. They were about to trek overland across Iran and I was going to—what? Clutch my daughter's waist as she pawed her way across the monkey bars one more time? Hike the same small stretch of urban forest collecting acorns? For days after they left, I insisted to Jorge that we should sell everything we owned and move to Thailand. I wondered if my anxiety had grounded us. I wanted to be free, and I wanted to feel like myself again.

The irony was that our Dutch friends were enamored of our Pittsburgh life. To their eyes, our family life involved a mash-up of outdoor concerts with ice cream, National Geographic books read on the couch at night, beers on the front porch, hikes, roasted sausages and vegetables, and morning coffee. It was good. It was not backcountry camping in the wilds of Utah—it was a different species, it belonged to a totally different taxonomic system—but it was good. Still I wondered perpetually whether I was only here because of anxiety, and if absent that particular affliction I would be the dream parent of my imagination who trekked overland through Chile and ate mysterious grilled meats in hovels with her small family. Until finally one day when I brought this up with Dr. S, he shrugged in his nonchalant way, and said, "Maybe that's true. Maybe if you didn't have OCD you would be that person."

It felt as if a dull knife had stabbed me in the gut. I kept pretending that if only I could yank my twenty-seven-year-old self from the grip of a worried, settled mother, I could get right back to my ideal whirlwind unconventional living. But the issue wasn't simply that anxiety had changed me; it was that I liked my life as it was, but my self-conception, riddled with shoulds and stale beliefs, hadn't caught up yet. I clung to this idea that, as Mary Catherine Bateson put it in Composing a Life, "real success stories are supposed to be permanent and monogamous." Bateson's project in that book was to debunk this myth, to show how women's lives in particular are works of art in constant flux. She made the simple and profound claim that "we will live many lives." I came across this book when I was thirty-six, when the train of early adulthood finally dropped me off at the empty plain of middle age. Bateson's book revealed to me the immaturity of my dichotomous understanding of the self. She wrote, "Change proposes constancy: What is the ongoing entity of which we can say that it has assumed a new form? A composite life poses the recurring riddle of what the parts have in common. Why is a raven like a writing desk? How is a lady like a soldier? . . . If your opinions and commitments appear to change from year to year or decade to decade, what are the more abstract underlying convictions that have held steady, that might never have become visible without the surface variation?"

Motherhood is an experience that gave me a second life, akin to the Big Bang in its transformation of my inner cosmos. I sit upstairs each morning on a big wooden chair we rescued from the curb, staring out the window at the massive evergreen across the street. I write my morning pages, per Julia Cameron's advice, trying to clear out the thorny brush from my mind so it won't clutter the day's writing. I note the rain, the winter light, whether or not there is a bird perched atop the tip of the tree like a Christmas star.

"We cannot find our enlightened minds while continuing to be estranged from our neurotic ones," writes Buddhist psychiatrist Mark Epstein. In encountering my neurotic one—indeed, in losing myself in it—I came to understand what it means to be well. Before, I'd imagined wellness as the exhilarant happiness of a new journey. The wide-open freedom of a bus chugging up a remote mountain road—a pure and singular feeling. Now I imagine wellness—or contentment, maybe, not exactly happiness—as an integration of all parts, "crafted from odds and ends, like a patch-work quilt." It is neither the freewheeling joy nor the despair, but a vision pitched between the two, the thread that connects the days, the morning work studying the evergreen, the hours at the kitchen table committed to writing even in all of its maddening insecurities, the bike ride to Elena's preschool under the crowns of the sycamores. "Buenos días, sycamores!"

In his 1960 book Psychoanalysis and Zen Buddhism, Erich Fromm wrote, "For those who suffer from alienation, cure does not consist in the absence of illness, but in the presence of well-being." Fromm uses the term alienation broadly, referring to alienation from society, from nature, and from the self. It is healed by incorporating what has previously been repressed or estranged, what a person continually wants to deny. Here is the clarion fall morning, the twirling leaf in a theater of blue, and here my worst fear played on intimate repeat.

Well-being, I discover, feels like the far side of grief, being aware of all that I have and the fact that I could lose it. It feels like breaking down the borders of my zone of safety, which may or may not wall out imagined dangers but certainly walls out the world. Buddhist nun Pema Chödrön describes it this way: "The mind is always seeking zones of safety, and these zones of safety are continually falling apart. Then we scramble to get another zone of safety back together again. We spend all our energy and waste our lives trying to re-create these zones of safety, which are always falling apart. That's the essence of samsara—the cycle of suffering that comes from continuing to seek happiness in all the wrong places."

When mothers tell me, "It's not all rainbows and butterflies," when women grapple to convey the constant flux between loveliness and terror inherent in mothering, I think they are getting at our slow awareness of the fact that happiness on a yearly scale doesn't often look like we imagine happiness to be when we are young. It looks more like an integration of disparate parts. On any given day, happiness might be a plate of onion rings and a cold IPA or coffee and a novel, but in the larger scope it feels like not clinging, not grasping, not running away from, like just being where I am. It feels like not having to have it all figured out, not trying to come up with solutions to every potential problem or to every mistake, not needing a perfectly coherent self like a flipbook whose every page builds clearly on the previous one into a crisp, precise picture.

Fear has made me unrecognizable to myself, and yet fear also seems to hold the potential for release from so many cycles of dissatisfaction and struggle. Fear disfigures and obscures, swallows my playfulness and openness and ability to see, and yet fear shoves me closer to the burning core of life, its energy and power. Fear hardens, but fear also dissolves all the petty distractions and walls I devise to keep the world out. It offers the hopeful possibility of becoming someone who possesses a powerful, healing love. Chödrön writes, "Fear is a natural reaction of moving closer to the truth."

Shortly after we moved to Pittsburgh, Jorge and I decided to tackle the seven boxes of random belongings that my parents had finally forced us to drag out of storage in their cabin's attic. One was filled almost entirely with doilies I could not bear to throw out after my grandma died. "Are you serious," Jorge said. I could fill a U-Haul with Babysitter's Club books and notes my friend Ellen passed me in sixth-grade science class.

That night I uncovered letter after letter my sister had sent or given me over the years: yellow legal pad pages filled with her loopy, athletic handwriting; birthday cards crammed with compliments and wishes; the pregnancy congrats she handed me at Stauf's Coffee in Columbus, in a gift bag with baby shoes wrapped in tissue paper. Reading these notes, I realized, with a sensation like a hook in the gut, how much I took them for granted. I received them, appreciated them, but never quite recognized them as an aura of love and kindness and tolerance that sustained me. I was absorbed in my travels and relationships and career quests. While I rode bareback across the Inner Mongolian grasslands or snuck across the Colombian border in the middle of the night with a group of drunken Ecuadorians, my sister wrote me letters.

I can see now that my fearlessness was often grounded in self-absorption. My obliviousness to fear was also at times an obliviousness to compassion. This is not to suggest that I do not regularly mourn and long for my old daring. It is impossible for me to imagine myself replicating these adventures now without being utterly riven by fear. For example, chasing a rangy man who'd hired my boyfriend and me to work in the grape fields in France and then refused to pay us. Or, in Patagonia, getting lost on a slope of scree in an impending blizzard. There are too many to list, and so many small ones: eating at certain restaurants, living in certain apartments, forgoing mosquito repellent and vaccines. Even those small decisions are now unfathomable, so dramatically have I swung to the opposite end of the spectrum. And while I miss my carefree self, my fear has also brought a new vision. I have seen in my own gradual shift from fearlessness to extreme fear that to be scared is to care, sometimes too much, sometimes to the point of sickness, but to have no fear is to be carefree, untethered to the fates and concerns of others, unable in some cases even to see them beyond one's assumptions.

I think of the base jumper Jeb Corliss, interviewed by Anna Sale on her WNYC podcast Death, Sex, & Money. Corliss spends his life leaping off cliffs in a thin batsuit-like contraption, his survival dependent on the precise angling of his "wings." In 2012, he crashed into a rock on Table Mountain and nearly died, but after months of painful recovery he was back at it, undeterred. Corliss and people like him are riveting for their extreme fearlessness. But the coldness of his relationship with death—to borrow Sale's chosen adjective—also translates into an inability or refusal to feel. Corliss tells Sale he's had five long-term relationships and "They're all bullshit, you know, it's just total bullshit." He goes on to explain, "I'm impossible to have a relationship with. I'm a very difficult person. . . . People, I think, give feelings, like this, oh they're the most important thing and I think that they're a very ancient, archaic way of dealing with things. I think dogs work on pure feeling."

When I was young, I appreciated my sister's letters when they came, probably even cried with gratitude at really special ones, and I saved them all. But I don't think I understood what it meant for her to write them. I never sent birthday cards. I'm fairly certain I didn't call very often. Once I left a message for my brother saying, "Jackson Samuel I cannot believe you are seventeen already!!" He was eighteen.

This is not to say I was callous, cold, unfeeling, but my capacity for a type of compassion that anticipates the needs of other people different from me—not just a compassion that feels bad for them when they are suffering—was as undeveloped as my fear. I recognize the need I took for granted before, the way someone who has a heart transplant suddenly appreciates each steady beat of this "strange tangled imp," as Dean Young put it, that makes her life possible. My mom talks to me for hours on the phone as I drive through the night on a return trip from Cincinnati to Pittsburgh. She tells me about her adventures doing intakes at the psychiatric department in the ER of Children's Hospital, her voice full in the quiet dark, and I sense how nice it is for her to share these stories and how much I want to listen. I write my niece letters. I cook enchiladas for my parents. I did these things before, but they feel different now. I feel the gift in them. I feel my fear outlining just how precious and precarious these moments and actions are. I feel the decision to be open or closed.

"Love," Joan Halifax writes, "is not merely an emotion. It is a meltdown that reestablishes a more unified space of brilliance, goodness, and sadness."

SONIA

14

The Fruitful Darkness

Sonia's family spent their summers at the beach in Cape May, South Jersey, and there, she sighs, "is where this whole saga begins." She was single, happy, with an established career and a nonchalance about getting married, having children, the whole lot of it. One perfect beach day, she was settled into a low-slung chair, reading a magazine, her fishing pole stuck in the sand beside her. A man came running down the beach. She looked up just in time to see him nearing the fishing line. "Hey, watch out!" she cried, and he stopped and ducked. An intense feeling came over her. He almost seemed to her to glow. He kept on running and then, he stopped. He turned around and came back. She took her line out of the water. "Do you know any good places to eat?" he asked.

Two years later, they were walking along the beach in Cape May together and a small plane flew overhead trailing a banner: WILL YOU MARRY ME? That was September. They were married in April.

They started trying on their wedding night. She was thirty-nine, he was thirty-eight, and they didn't have much time. Over the next year, they kept trying, living their lives without worrying or thinking about it too much, without doing any measuring. Then her husband's mom passed away suddenly, plunging the family into grief. Having a child was put on hold as they grieved. This unexpected halt gave Sonia perspective: it'd been a year, and nothing was happening. She went to get checked out and discovered that she had fibroids.

Fibroids are common, noncancerous growths in the uterus. They can be so tiny as to be undetectable, and they can also be big enough to significantly enlarge the uterus. The doctors were not sure whether these fibroids were causing an issue or not, and decided not to disturb them. They flushed her tubes, made calculations and took counts, poked and prodded. The result of all of this intervention was not a clear diagnosis or picture of her possibilities, but rather a highly medicalized understanding of what it takes to get pregnant. So, when she and her husband started trying again, they brought in ovulation sticks and temperature gauges. Their efforts paid off: Sonia got pregnant. She was excited, really excited, but she didn't tell anyone because she knew she was supposed to wait. At twelve weeks, she started to tell some people, including her colleagues, because she'd begun to feel terribly sick. She was nauseated and throwing up every day.

At fourteen weeks, Sonia went for an ultrasound. The tech took a look and as soon as the picture showed up, her demeanor changed. Sonia knew right away that something was not right. The tech left to get the doctor, and Sonia was left lying on the table, half-naked, her feet up in the stirrups, waiting. When the male doctor came in, he announced, standing over her prone body, "There are some issues."

Sonia tells me this at a café, sitting outside on a balmy summer afternoon. She is beautiful, the kind of beautiful you might encounter in a sepia photo and linger over. Her big brown eyes are expressive, but her expressions are reserved, guarded. When she talks to me about her experience in this small room fourteen weeks into her first pregnancy, she says, "I don't think it was handled very well for somebody who's having their first baby," her eyes glisten with an involuntary sheen, and she stops talking for a moment, looking down.

Her fibroids, she learned, were growing along with the baby and stealing its nutrients. There were two big ones, one in the front and one in the back of the uterus, taking up the baby's space. Instead of learning the size of her baby, Sonia learned that her fibroids were by now the size of an orange and a grapefruit. There was no way, her doctor told her, that she would make it to term.

"So," she says. "We spent a few weeks kind of with that news." She pauses. "The concern was that my uterus could burst, and it could . . . my husband would lose both of us." There was also a chance, she says, that she could miscarry. The doctors told her this with a whiff of consolation.

Sonia's choices were to take the risk and pray for a miracle or to move forward with the medically advised action: terminate the pregnancy. Left to make this decision by herself, Sonia entered the devastating isolation of motherhood, what she calls "the silo." She shut herself in. She gave up hope that anyone could understand the magnitude of the choices a mother must make. She believed this suffering was part of the deal and must be carried alone.

Sonia says, "The baby didn't make it." She and her husband didn't talk about what happened; there was no way to fit it into the pregnancy and motherhood cosmos, or even to that of typical grief and mourning. Neither of them wanted to discuss the agony of the choice with their families or friends. *We lost the baby,* they said. Nearly eight months after I first met with Sonia, we were talking on her couch in the middle of winter, watching her daughter eat a tuna sandwich, listening to Raffi's "Bananaphone." We lingered for a minute or two in silence, until she said, "It still sits with me."

––––––––––

Early in her career as an anthropologist, the Buddhist nun Joan Halifax went to live with the Dogon, a remote Malian tribe, in order to observe an elaborate seven-year ritual that took place every forty-nine years. She spent her days perched on the steep Bandiagara cliffs, watching Dogon women march through the swirling red-gold sand. Speaking to Krista Tippett in an episode of *On Being,* she later said, "I realized, as I was sort of sitting there crouched in this crevice of a cliff, watching this transpire—what in my world, what in my country, allows us to mature?" She could think of very little. "I reflected, and I said: Wars do."

Halifax couldn't think of any other ritual that marks the pain, struggle, and transformation of youth into maturity. She noted, "When a baby is born, [there is] usually no real rite of passage that sacralizes an individual's life. . . . Where our identity changes in a really extraordinary way, again, there's nothing to mark that change in the lives of most of our young people."

Halifax returned to Paris, then to the United States, where she sank into a psychological breakdown. She flailed for years, trying to find ballast in drugs and travel and academic work, until she landed on Buddhism. The rigor of its silences and stillness healed her. She came through what she has come to call "the fruitful darkness." In her book of that title, Halifax explores the significance of this experience via encounters with shamans, healers, Buddhist pilgrims, and medicine men from Tibet and Mexico. The people charged in their cultures with illuminating and honoring the meaning of human life believe that "fruitful darkness" is an initiation: those who emerge from it become medicine men, and the ones who remain in it are sick. Every psychological illness is an initiation into this darkness.

In the cultures Halifax visits, she says, "illness is understood as a loss of the sense of connectedness, of relatedness, of continuity—the experience of a kind of existential alienation. This alienation expresses itself as a divided self, a self that has forgotten the extensiveness of its being." In motherhood, many women discover for the first time an extreme alienation. Not only in hours of solitude with a needy and helpless new human child, not only via a biological experience that cannot be shared with anyone, but through having to confront a way of being that has no bearing or space in American culture: a disintegration of the self with all of its clear definitions, goals, parameters, and achievements, into a love that engenders what Julia Kristeva has called "the slow, difficult, and delightful apprenticeship in attentiveness, gentleness, forgetting oneself."

Americans put so much stock in the self, defining the self by what it has, and how much: we think about our self-esteem, our self-confidence, our need for self-help. The self is a light beamed straight from one's mind, illuminating the path to success. The self is public. It manifests in profile pictures and in tweets and in a million other arenas, in the navigation of academic and professional and creative and cultural and social spheres. So many Americans have grown up with the notion that if they develop a strong-enough, fierce-enough, defined-enough self—one with character, verve, gumption, a handful of qualities honed like muscles—they can persevere through anything.

But mothering takes the self like a big hearty dog takes a stuffed toy and shakes it so vigorously that all the fluff scatters. Mothering plunks women down into a realm that earns no real respect, garners no real interest, amid all the mastery and propulsion of the self. This is the realm of care. The learning therein comes not from work, not from school, not from intellect and the deliberate challenge of tasks, but from time, openness, the kind of breaking down and rebuilding that makes a garden. Thaws, freezes. Thwarted seeds, surprise blooms. It is a knowing that cannot be commodified, bartered, bragged, converted into the currency of the self.

In his 1976 classic, *To Have or To Be?* German philosopher Erich Fromm characterizes the condition of contemporary industrialized societies as one of having: cars, houses, consumer goodies, and also health (what we would now call "wellness"), knowledge, relationships, experiences, and feelings. Having is measurable. It is about craving and then possessing, wanting and then achieving. It is consumed with staking the borders, desires, and claimed summits of the self. It feeds on itself: more begets more. Fromm contrasts this with a mode of being: the capacity "to grow, to flow out, to love, to transcend the prison of one's isolated ego, to be interested, to 'list,' to give." Fromm uses *list* here as it was used in the thirteenth century, meaning "to take a free and active interest in," or "to strive for." Being involves deep listening, real engagement, connection that comes with the desire to get out of oneself. To move into being demands a different notion of fulfillment, one that doesn't have any association with producing anything useful. Being can be scary. Fromm writes, "Most people find giving up their having orientation too difficult; any attempt to do so arouses their intense anxiety and feels like giving up all security, like being thrown into the ocean when one does not know how to swim."

Women who have newly become mothers often feel the wall between having and being crack. A baby is a portal into being. A mother can find herself trapped in some sense between being and having, between, as Daphne de Marneffe puts it, "the possibility of letting motherhood radically reorder one's priorities and continuing with one's other valued goals relatively unaffected." The dividedness mothers often feel, between different selves, or between a self and no self, is a symptom in part of the way the self is defined by having.

The remaking of the self that mothers experience—the struggles of overcoming boredom, fatigue, irritation; of being persistently present; of trying to survive a love that can feel like an ocean one can't swim—is not of great concern to a world focused on having. So, many fall back on a system of rewards, products, and achievements that fits into the framework of success in which they've operated for most of their lives: this is the "Mommy Olympics," as de Marneffe calls it. Or they can resort to clichés, which mask the complexities of individual experience and squash it into a quote to be hung above the dining room table or posted on Facebook. There is no way to articulate and venerate being in a society so focused on having. One of the ways, which we have mostly lost, would be ritual.

Halifax writes, "What were the consequences, I continually asked myself, of living in a culture where change is not marked?"

In a void where few rituals, stories, and symbols are available to mothers, women have responded by conjuring a shadow universe of fear and darkness and loss. The immense passion and confusing energy that motherhood generates gets channeled into a never-ending series of disaster scenarios necessitating vigilant prevention. The wide-open and terrifying potential for being narrows into a relentless pursuit of security.

In a beautiful essay for *Tin House*, Alyssa Knickerbocker recounts how she struggled to work on a novel immediately after having her baby, and instead worked on a Word document she titled "THE BAD THINGS I IMAGINE HAPPENING." She imagines her baby falling from the deck of a ferry. "This is what I did with my imagination," she tells us. She had long assumed that she wouldn't "let" motherhood consume her—"Let it," she writes. "We use that phrase, implying that these women were weak or not vigilant, that they forgetfully left a door open and allowed something in, something that filled up every room in the house, every room in your heart, all the room in your head."

Knickerbocker straddled that threshold between the world in which she had previously lived, where she produces work and is valued for it, and the world she has been thrust into by motherhood, in which she is "able to feel so deeply, to completely dissolve the boundaries between myself and others." She reconciles the two through a Word doc of catastrophes. She tries to define the tremendous feeling, the boundarylessness of early motherhood, as a superpower, because "to label it postpartum depression . . . makes me sad. It is such a small, clinical phrase, reducing the experience itself to something small and clinical." There is no framework for making sense of this transition other than "postpartum depression."

"Anxiety," Kierkegaard wrote, "is a desire for what one dreads." Perhaps because we have no way of recognizing and expressing the transition to motherhood—its particular blend of terror and tenderness, its deep loss and its joy—anxiety pulls us like a magnet. Anxiety offers the illusion of control and meaning. It is a state of awful temptation, of being lured toward the unimaginable incident, the news story of the decapitated boy, the last moments before the mother drove off the cliff. It grows and grows, becoming the entire organizing principle of reality. Women live their lives by the core principle of what cannot happen: prevention becomes a quasi-religious task.

———————

Sonia had surgery to remove her fibroids, and the surgery caused scarring, which further reduced her chances of getting pregnant. She had to wait six months before she and her husband could start trying again, and when they did, "It wasn't fun anymore."

She lost sight of what she was doing and why. "It was back to the ovulation sticks and the temperature taking and charting and getting really vigilant about it because now, I'm on a mission, because it's like, *Screw you, nature, I'm in charge here, and I can do this.*" She had three or four positive pregnancy tests. One pregnancy even proceeded to an appointment that revealed a heartbeat, but at the next appointment, the heartbeat was gone. All ended in miscarriages. She didn't talk to anyone about what she was going through. She didn't want anyone else's opinion. The initial joy had completely disappeared. "Whatever it was in the beginning," Sonia told me, "it became the complete opposite."

Five years after they first began trying, when Sonia was forty-four, she got pregnant with her daughter, Lila. She had made a deal with herself: if she wasn't pregnant by forty-five, they would stop trying. Exactly nine months before her forty-fifth birthday, the test came up positive. When she found out, she told her husband, "I might be pregnant, I'm not sure." The first time she'd found out she was pregnant, she had made a little onesie with their last name on it; she was "all in and so excited." This time, she spent eight months on edge: distant, detached, moving as nonchalantly and emotionlessly as she could through the experience. She was sick the entire time, from week six to week thirty-six, again throwing up almost every day. She refused to take anything but a small dose of Diclegis, the only FDA-approved drug for nausea in pregnancy, lest she harm her baby. She lost weight. She agonized over the myriad prohibitions of pregnancy.

"I'm reading everything. I'm reading every label of everything I'm ingesting: oh, this has more than ten ingredients; I don't know what this ingredient is; oh, I have a terrible headache, and they say Tylenol's fine but I took a Tylenol a month ago, and what if ten years from now they're like, oh, everybody sue Tylenol, join this lawsuit!"

She did not feel depressed. She didn't cry. She wasn't lethargic or sleepless or melancholic. "I was *anxious*," she says, with a *duh* overtone now, "but I didn't recognize it as anxiety. I mean, looking back it's very obvious that's what it was. But I just . . . like how would I know? I can't have a turkey sandwich?" By this she means, if we're legitimately scared of eating a turkey sandwich, and conditioned to be scared of it, then how in the hell are we supposed to recognize anxiety as anxiety?

Sonia considers herself an independent person: she spent most of her adult life single, developing her career. For her, to stand in the middle of her living room debating whether or not she should climb on a chair to change a light bulb was profoundly demoralizing. Pregnancy chipped away little by little at her self-sufficiency, her own instincts about her capabilities, her distinct personal sense of what makes life worth living.

Sonia introduces me to a term that will bounce around in my head for the next year: "the normal bucket."

"It was just so hard. But again, I'm thinking, that might be normal, the normal bucket." In pregnancy, everyone wants to be in the normal bucket. No matter how unconventional, how offbeat and rebellious you are as a person, you want your pregnancy to follow textbook conventions. You don't want aberrations or departures. And for babies, the normal bucket has fairly clear dimensions: sizes the baby must reach at certain points, features that must develop, appropriate ranges for heart rates, proper positions for birth. But for women, or at least American women, the normal bucket is deep, dark, dimensionless. We imagine it is a space we can make sense of and fit in if we do everything right, although there is no end to everything we must do right and so many opportunities to do wrong. We clamor so hard to be in it that we don't realize it's a bottomless well, and we fall down and down and down.

Years later, it's difficult for her to distinguish what is normal from what is destructive or pathological. Of her pregnancy, Sonia says, "It was just completely the opposite of what's supposed to happen."

It is tragic that in the present day, when as a society we are capable of keeping a twenty-three-week-old fetus alive in a hospital, when books are dedicated to explaining to women what is happening to their baby every single day of pregnancy, we still understand so little about what mothers experience, so little that all we have are "glowing and happy" or its dark opposite.

In the middle of Sonia's pregnancy, a cousin she was close to, who was pregnant with her second child, had a stillbirth. "[Her son] was kicking on the way to the hospital when she went into labor," Sonia told me. If Sonia had allowed herself any hope before this, it was quashed at this moment. "I was just waiting for the other shoe to drop."

Meanwhile, no one suggested that she might need mental health support. The only person in her whole community to mention mental health risks to her was her nutritionist. He warned her, "I just want you to watch out for signs of postpartum depression after you have the baby, and let me know if you have it." Telling me this, Sonia smiles. "I just remember telling him, 'There's no way I'm going to have postpartum depression. I've been trying so long and so hard for this baby, and I'm going to love this baby.'"

Sonia knew that her birth would require a C-section. Her fibroid surgery had thinned her uterine lining and increased the risk that her uterus could burst if undergoing contractions. She and her OB planned her C-section for thirty-eight weeks, on January 30, 2015, at eight a.m.

Sonia's family—her parents, her three brothers, and one of her nephews—drove overnight to the hospital early in the morning on the thirtieth. They got there at six a.m., before Sonia did. When she arrived, she was ecstatic to see them. She needed, in particular, to see her mom. She gave her mom a huge, long hug before going into the operating room.

The baby was born at 8:29 a.m. There were approximately ten seconds of silence as the incision was made and the baby was lifted out, and those ten seconds seemed eternal to Sonia; she was waiting with clenched fear. Then, a cry. The doctor held the baby up: it was a girl bellowing with all her force. Sonia was crying so hard she couldn't see.

The worst cruelty of anxiety might be the brief reprieve it offers between spells of fear. For a while, the universe seems, if not quite kind, then blissfully bland, innocuous and unconcerned with you. Then, sometimes only after a stretch of hours, the anxiety comes back.

Sonia's reprieve lasted only as long as her tears. Instantly, she wondered: *What next? Will she make weight?*

The baby looked good and healthy and strong. Sonia had to spend eight hours in the recovery room because the doctors had pumped her full of anesthesia. She felt fine, even though she couldn't move. She felt, in fact, mostly okay in the hospital. She wasn't scared to leave; she was even looking forward to it. The only moment she felt jarred was when they showed her videos: dramatic public service announcements that featured women who dropped their babies from rocking chairs, women who shook their babies and killed them in a single instant of uncontrollable impulse. She had to sign a form saying she'd watched the videos: a signature avowing her commitment to her own terrible responsibility.

When they got home, Sonia was mostly happy. Utterly exhausted, but happy: her baby was here and safe, her parents had gotten the chance to meet her, it had all gone relatively smoothly.

Two days after the birth, per standard procedure, Sonia and her husband took the baby, named Lila after Sonia's grandmother, to the pediatrician to be weighed. They discovered that she had a mild case of jaundice. The doctors and nurses told Sonia and her husband to take her immediately to the NICU. Sonia was baffled by this, unsure how troubled to be. She did the requisite Googling and thought it strange the doctors were in such a panic over a touch of jaundice. "Like, people just used to stick their kid in the window!" Sonia wasn't overly concerned when they arrived at the NICU. There, the nurses weighed Lila, and discovered her weight was way down. The scale at the pediatrician's office had been wrong.

Suddenly, Sonia was sick with guilt. *I've been starving my baby.* They took Lila and put her in an incubator under lights. Then, Sonia says, "It just starts. It starts in that time frame. It starts kicking in: *I'm the worst mother.*"

Anxiety carves out a shadow life, a life unlived. We are all, as psychologist Adam Phillips has pointed out, living two lives: our lived and our unlived ones. Phillips writes, "We think we know more about the experiences we don't have than about the experiences we do have." Randall Jarrell wrote, "The ways we miss our lives are life."

Children intuitively understand the creative process of being and becoming, which psychologist Rollo May declared involves "destroying the status quo of one's environment, breaking the old forms." This is why children seem like different people in the span of six months, a year, two years. May wrote, "In every experience of creativity something in the past is killed so that something new in the present may be born." The toddler kills the baby, and the four-year-old kills the toddler, but the mother all the while is expected to remain the same. Not only that, but she is expected to be an uber-mother, an archetype. The mother's creativity, her becoming, is suppressed and pushed into the nether realm of *what-if, I-can't,* and *no.* She has to maintain everything just so. The mother becomes trapped in what psychiatrist Kurt Goldstein labeled "meaningless frenzy, rigid or distorted expression, withdrawal from the world . . . in the light of which the world appears irrelevant."

While the mother flails in anxiety, children use anxiety as a springboard to self-discovery. Kierkegaard asserted that "the Myth of Adam is re-enacted by every human being somewhere between the ages of one and three." At these ages, children discover that becoming their own human beings will likely necessitate defiance. They become aware of the possibility—and the necessity—of conflict with their parents. Children's identities are forged from the anxiety that arises when they come to understand that their desires and needs may not always align with those of their parents and may in fact have to be developed in that difference. Kierkegaard labels this "the alarming possibility of being able."

"The self," May paraphrases psychotherapist Harry Stack Sullivan, "is formed out of the growing infant's necessity to deal with anxiety-creating experiences." This is not how most of us would imagine a conventional childhood, envisioning instead a bubble of innocence that must be preserved for as long as possible, an idyllic state before fear and uncertainty creep in. Instead, May argues, anxiety makes us; it is the tool that whittles us from the wood of our wombs, our mothers, and our homes. When children do not have enough fundamental security to push through it, their growth is stifled. Women who cannot confront anxiety-producing experiences also experience this stunting of self: they petrify into the outlines of what experts and social norms expect them to be, trapped in unlived lives.

The psychoanalyst Otto Rank has defined the two central human fears as the life fear and the death fear: the former is fear of creation, of forming new selves and relationships, and the latter is the fear of losing individuality and regressing. Anxiety, Rank posited, comes from an inability to balance these fears. Mothers are caught between them, in a morass of paradoxes: between, as Helene Deutsch has framed it, activity and passivity, aggression and masochism, femininity and masculinity, love and hatred. Rozsika Parker describes a pregnant woman's psychic world as defined by "elemental opposites": "birth and death, creation and destruction, order and chaos, big and little, strong and weak, self and other." The mother is tugged by the forces of these opposing poles. Because the darker realm of experience is consistently repressed, mothers are left in shallow denial, their choices only the "normality" of happy feminine self-realization or the pathology of "postpartum." The creativity, the force and insight, that could surge out of this great transitional flux largely gets channeled into frantic rituals of prevention, performed with the dogma of high priests, in failed attempts to expunge what is not allowed.

Halifax quotes Rilke: "Love and death are the great gifts that are given to us. Mostly they are passed on unopened."

———

Sonia's anxiety escalated very quickly. The baby spent several days in the hospital. Sonia slept on a little bed in the waiting room that her husband had made by cobbling together different types of chairs. She started pumping. Everything began slip-sliding. Sonia started having loud thoughts: *What are you going to mess up next? Why did you ever think this was a good idea?* She did not dare share these thoughts with anyone.

When she and Lila finally returned home, Sonia was scared to give her baby a bath, and then scared that her baby would be ridiculed for being dirty and she would be judged. She was terrified of the stairs. She would linger on each step as if she were hovering on the lip of a sheer cliff. *The longer you're on the stairs,* she'd tell herself, *the more dangerous it is,* but her body was frozen. Then defeat would swamp her like a blast of dank air: if she couldn't even walk down the stairs, how was she supposed to be a parent?

She was, in very little time, scared to do everything. One day she had to mail a package at the post office, which was five minutes from her house. Between getting herself ready, getting the baby ready, psyching herself up, driving over, parking, sitting outside the post office, going in, and mailing the package, the task took her more than four hours. *Who's going to go postal while I'm sitting there in the post office?* she thought, with no irony. The whole way there, she worried that a deer would jump in front of the car. She worried that a car was going to stall in front of her. Everything required the strategy and calibration of a nuclear physicist. Her thoughts were so pervasive and intense they blurred out the world around them. Later, when she told her husband how alone she'd felt in those first few months, he reminded her that he had been home with her. She asked, disbelieving, "You were?"

"Yeah, I took twelve weeks off of work," he said, and she asked, "You *did?*" He had gone through an entire bureaucratic process at his job to take paid leave under the Family and Medical Leave Act. He got the time and spent the full twelve weeks at home. She remembered none of it. "It was just such a fog."

Sonia checked the baby monitor every two minutes; she'd put it down and then immediately pick it back up, holding it close. She was terrified of dropping the baby, of hitting Lila's head on the corner of a sharp object. "I wanted to just live in a padded bubble." She would sit awake at night, holding Lila, thinking they were finally safe when it would occur to her that a plane could crash into the house, or a meteor, or a satellite from 1962 that had fallen out of orbit.

Sonia was screened for postpartum depression at her six-week checkup. She looked at the questions and thought, *If I circle this, they're going to get the wrong idea.* She toned down her answers. It was true that she didn't want to harm herself or her kid. It was less true that she rarely felt down, but she didn't want them to think she was depressed. It only occurred to her later how scared she was of having her child taken from her. "Where did I get that fear from?" she asks me.

Meanwhile the common refrain she heard, plucked from the Rolodex of appropriate casual comments and recited as unthinkingly as a nursery rhyme, was, "Can you believe how much you love her? Isn't it amazing?" And she would feel terrible, thinking, *Why don't I love the kid more than anything, like everybody is saying I should?* It never occurred to Sonia that she needed help. Instead she blamed herself. She felt the guilt and the fear like a physical pain in her chest. It wasn't, she specified to me, that she didn't care: "If anything, I *overcared.*"

This phrase jostles me. I remember when I visited my first therapist, I filled out a questionnaire about my relationship to my child that included the phrase "overly attached," with the option to check the corresponding box. I checked it, gobsmacked by the thought that too much attachment was possible. It was like someone telling me, after a lifetime of dietary doctrine, that one had to be careful not to eat too many vegetables. And yet at the same time it made sense. My baby was everything, and the everything that she was could so quickly turn into nothing, to a loss so entire it would obliterate my life. This translated into an experience of motherhood that was, as Sonia put it, "just constant worst-case scenarios."

She told me, "People would say, 'Can you just believe how much you love her? It's so overwhelming!' And I'm thinking, *Yeah, it's overwhelming. . . . This is bananas, that I have to raise this tiny human who can't even see three feet in front of her.*"

Sometimes after these encounters she would get so angry with herself that she'd galvanize a whole bunch of energy and, say, sign her kid up for music class. She tried with all her might to be the kind of mother she thought everyone was, a normal mom, in the normal bucket.

Sonia finally sought help only because of her disintegrating relationship with her husband. She had no idea what to expect from motherhood, so she didn't know whether her isolation and fear and sadness as a mother were normal. She knew, however, from having been married for years that what was happening between her and her husband was not normal. After eight months, she went to see a therapist about her marriage. It was there that she found out she had what the therapist simply called "postpartum." She was told that the screening test she took "read more anxiety than depression," though Sonia learned to identify what she had as postpartum depression and this is how she describes it to me. The therapist recommended a combination of therapy and medicines, along with a support group.

It took her a few weeks to muster up the courage to attend the group. *I'll go one time and see what happens,* she told herself. And there, in a narrow boxcar of a room lined with yoga mats and birthing balls, "is where the healing began." She felt ambivalent about the impact of medicine and therapy, but she knows for certain that her conversations with other mothers truly helped.

Sonia got better. She feels more comfortable as the mother of a two-year-old than as the mother of an infant. But she is wise enough to know that it's not over, and that maybe her fear and anxiety and depression will never really end. "I can't say, well, I'm not in this postpartum depression anymore, because I don't even know." There is no normal to return to. As Sonia puts it, "My old life is gone, my old self is gone." This happens regardless of a woman's particular experience with motherhood, whether it is traumatic or joyful. Her old self is gone. Her notion of what a self is and how it's defined, its steadfastness and purpose, is forever changed.

I recognize in Sonia the same tenderness that I discover in myself just after the worst bouts of fear. My conversations with her remind me that the most powerful gift of this descent into darkness is humility, and the healing of listening to other women. When I left Sonia's house one winter afternoon I felt immense gratitude, as if we had both tended to an invisible consciousness—the weight and worry of grief and loneliness and uncertainty—that we alone could see.

The following spring, I gave a reading at the Carnegie Library as part of the Pittsburgh Arts & Lectures series. I told a number of friends, and only one showed up. People had their busy lives and schedules; it was a beautiful, warm evening with buds shining on the trees. But there, in the back of the room, was Sonia. She'd heard about the event, found child care, driven in from the outskirts of the city, found parking. She sat and listened to me. Afterward she waited for a minute behind a small group of people, shy, waving hello and goodbye, and I beckoned her to stay. When the room cleared out, I gave her a hug and I felt my throat tighten and burn. I said, *Thank you, you didn't have to do this.* She said it was nothing. Maybe it was. But to me this connection, this storytelling, this showing up, was everything.

Paula Nicholson, a psychologist who has studied women's transition to motherhood, makes the case that it is taboo to mourn in the postpartum context, though motherhood can be many women's first experience of grief. Whereas death or divorce or other life changes usually involve a culturally and socially sanctioned period of mourning, Nicholson argues that mothers are not allowed to experience loss, and if they do, they are pathologized.

"So strong is the taboo," she writes, "that women themselves frequently fail to admit their sense of loss in a conscious way." Motherhood, the ultimate "happy event," Nicholson declares, seems antithetical to loss. And yet Nicholson lists a whole host of losses inherent to having a child: loss of autonomy, identity, work, time, friends, relationship patterns, sexuality, health, comfort. Each woman may experience any one or several of these. Nicholson makes the somewhat radical claim that "some degree of postpartum depression should be considered the rule rather than the exception. It is also potentially a healthy, grieving reaction to loss." Postpartum depression might be the only ritual American mothers have to express their grief.

In the book *Freedom from Obsessive-Compulsive Disorder: A Personalized Recovery Program for Living with Uncertainty,* which I bashfully check out of the library, psychologist Jonathan Grayson describes loss as an essential part of the process of recovering from OCD. Grayson tells sufferers that before they can attempt treatment, they have to ask themselves: *Am I willing to live with uncertainty?*

The question seems infantilizing. We all live with uncertainty in a million ways every day, as Grayson points out. We don't know where our loved ones are at any given second, yet we assume they're not spies for the CIA. We can't be entirely certain we won't sprain an ankle if we go for a run, slip on gravel during a bike ride, be harassed on the street, or get lost in a new place. We navigate uncertainty every moment of every day.

But Grayson is referring to an existential uncertainty about whether or not we can protect ourselves and our loved ones from danger, about whether we are living our lives in the right way, and about whether we are good people, whether we are loved. He is referring to the terror of being abandoned, of failing our families, of violating our most sacred principles. This is the kind of uncertainty that desperately seeks to ground itself in information, in reassurance, in plausibility, in prevention—and never can. To live in that uncertainty means that every time you feel that vertiginous love, that teetering-on-the-cliff-edge love, you have to look down and see how close that love is to disaster. You have to stare down until you feel your whole life plunging into the canyon, shattered, and you have to keep staring until you are ready to go home and live as though eating scrambled eggs on the front porch, slicing an apple, drinking a cup of tea, are the absurd blessings of the now, and all you can ever really count on.

Committing to the process of living with uncertainty, Grayson says, means confronting an unexpected loss. It is not the loss that the quest for certainty constantly tries to prevent: the disease, the death, the mistake. Rather, it is the loss of the fantasy world that this quest maintained, a fantasy that may have long remained hidden behind the fervent need to preserve it. The fantasy of the bohemian uber-mom. Of the perfect marriage. Of the unwavering activist, the pure artist, the impeccable religious devotee. For mothers, it is often the loss of the mother they imagined themselves being.

There are a million versions of this ideal mother: the one who can breastfeed in public, who can take her baby on transatlantic flights like trips to the coffee shop, who can coach a winning soft-ball team, who will never stray from fierce dedication to her career. For me, I wanted to be the kind of mother who was a nonchalant nonconformist, all nerve and bold experience.

Occasionally, I have been this mother, and the delight of those rare moments is immense and heart-exploding. But mostly I have been a quiet, interior mother. I have been a mother who spends hours on the concrete steps of the front porch writing in my jour-nal while my daughter develops elaborate games with markers and paint. I have been an excessively cautious mother, washing or wiping my baby's hands dozens of times a day, refusing to get gas when she's in the car, bringing her own dishes to restaurants. The mother I thought I would be, the mother I have been forced into becoming by anxiety, and the mother I actually want to be have all blurred and made me more unknown to myself than ever. All I truly know is that I feel the loss of the mother I dreamed of being.

What do we make of that "big squeeze," as Pema Chödrön calls it, between who we believe we once were, who we imagined we would be, and who we have become? Motherhood is often the first true test of self in a woman's life: how much holds up, how much crumbles, how much mutates? A friend and I were talking once about how it seems impossible to know what one would do in a life-or-death situation until one is actually there. My friend refer-enced a time when she'd been at a public park and heard gunfire. Instead of running away, as she had thought she might, she held still and crouched down. It had seemed utterly surreal to her to be crouching. In decisive moments, when expectations vaporize amid vivid reality, we are often not who we had imagined being. Mother-hood is this shift made permanent.

I was surprised by how much I loved breastfeeding. I loved the intimacy of infanthood. I could have watched my baby for hours as she puttered on the ground with a leaf. I had no interest in my career or in ambition. I never would have imagined this.

Later, I could not bear to set my daughter down on the filthy tiles of a cantina, to take her along streets thick with diesel fumes, though years before I'd lauded the friends who let their children do all these things, and silently derided those who did not.

Now, I do not know who I am. I have never not known with more conviction in my life. I find myself writing in my journal each morning, "I don't know. I don't know. I don't know." How much of what I have lost or given up has been to the disease of my anxiety, how much to the nature of motherhood, how much to the simple fact of time? I can't begin to work through these questions until I first accept the loss of the mother I thought I was or could be.

I believe, I hope, that on the other side of this loss is a love that I have found in connecting with other women. These women have, in the words of Joan Halifax, found "the gold of compassion in the dark stone of suffering." I have never loved women or needed them the way I have since I became a mother. Occasionally I find myself so grateful for a woman that I want to curl up in her arms and write her gushing fan letters. I have called women sobbing. I have sat with them on hot afternoons and absorbed their confessions. I have read their books and then held these books in my hands as if they were talismans, threads connecting my often-untethered life to other lives. I have had beers with women and stood with them on street corners and felt the same charged love I felt after first kisses, and shyly said goodbye. I have gone to their houses and eaten pasta salad standing up in their kitchens and talked about yelling. I have been buoyed from grimness by their comments on Instagram. I have taken their questions and listened to their advice. I sense this particularly with middle-aged women, the women who tell me, "You will get your self back, but it's different. It's richer."

I can feel now the way certain understandings pass through women's bodies. Natalie Angier writes in *Woman: An Intimate Geography*, "A woman's mother-lust, her need for the older female and for other women generally, is also ancient, and also worth heeding."

Sonia still has moments where she sits down on the floor and sobs and thinks she's a terrible mother. But, she says, some of that is normal. She only checks her baby monitor twice in the span of an hour now. That should be normal, right? The way she asks is only half-rhetorical. She knows that she'll never really know what is normal and what is not. "I realize I have to stop expecting to feel like I used to," she says, "because all the parameters have changed. I have a kid I'm going to worry about for the rest of my life." Worry and fear and loss are built into the system. They are part of the deal.

"I knew there'd be poopy diapers, I knew there'd be late nights," Sonia told me. "I was ready for all that. I was just not prepared for the emotional side of it."

She continued, "In my mind, postpartum depression was you want to drive into the lake with your kids. It never occurred to me that it was a spectrum. I certainly never thought I could be on it." Most of us fall somewhere in the middle of this spectrum, floundering in unspoken fears, sadness, isolation, loss, and wondering if all of this is normal.

I am not sure if the normative view of motherhood is more normal than the supposedly divergent one uncovered with the slightest nick of the surface. I'm not sure if it is helpful to insist *this is not normal*, because when persistent anxiety afflicts up to half of all mothers it might be considered the norm. This doesn't mean it shouldn't be treated. This doesn't mean it shouldn't be seen as problematic and troubling. This doesn't mean that there aren't extreme or serious cases that need immediate medical intervention, but rather that it may be possible that the norm is actually an extremely challenging and difficult one, debilitating and dangerous if ignored and taken for granted. The norm in childbirth used to include death. That norm was met with interventions, protocols, development, time, energy. We must establish norms of treatment and research and support and intervention to counter the current norm of fear.

Sonia worries now that she's probably scared several friends out of having children. "I think I was unfairly skewed to the dark side," she told me. "But then I also think most of the stories people told me were unfairly skewed to the other extreme." The dark stories are painful to tell. They are painful to examine within ourselves. I believe that no story, no matter how extreme, will influence other women's decisions about whether or not to have children. What stories can do is slowly shift collective awareness, illuminating realms of experience previously considered marginal or aberrant, deepening and complexifying our understanding of what it means to be human. "If we want to change our lives," Halifax wrote, "we have to change our stories, stories that contain the lessons for moving past the stuff of collective adaptation."

———————

I go running on a winter afternoon while my baby sleeps. Elena is snuggled beneath a comforter, a node of warmth in our chilly house. I leave her with Jorge, inhale December air in searing gusts and careen downhill toward the park, feeling heavy at first, then steadying into a smooth gait. What was a canopy of leaves is now a crunchy clutter at my feet. Running in this brisk air amid the bare trees, the sky a cold chamomile at early dusk, the geese at the distant pond's edge, I recall Elena's latest line of questioning: *Why geese not wear socks? Why geese not wear coats?* I feel a puncture in my composure and through it, deep sadness. I recall the scratch papers Elena played with at the Children's Museum, the waxy coat of black she scraped away, revealing the fluorescent colors beneath. I feel the black of my life suddenly scuffed and there is the electric pink of grief, a painful marvel.

It is a grief for my life already lived and gone, for my death: its possibility and its inevitability. It is a grief for what I have lost in becoming a parent and also for my limitations as a parent, the limitations of any one life. It is a grief much larger than me, a grief that feels borrowed from an ancient sorrow like a poem tacked to the wall above my desk, and a grief unmistakably mine, drawn from a swell of emotions whose origins and trajectories I can't begin to work out. It doesn't last long. By the fourth or fifth mile it is gone, by the time I get home and she's waking up and asking for "huevos boiled!" it is forgotten, although it leaves a drag like a receding wave.

Acknowledgments

At the start of this project, I remember trying to assess it from all angles, to get a scope of its scale and magnitude. I couldn't. It was too big. Maria Goldverg, my brilliant editor at Pantheon, walked me through this stage, helping me to envision the structure, form, and possibility of the book when I'd panic about its bigness. I cannot thank Maria enough for believing in me, for talking me through all kinds of uncertainty and stuckness, and for her guiding insight. She not only taught me how to conceive of and develop a work of this complexity, she also dug into an enormous and sprawling manuscript and edited it into crisp, startling coherency. Everyone who knows me knows I tend to write long: Maria knows just how long. Thank you for your patience and your brilliance and your dedication.

An enormous thank-you to the women who, while also living their very busy lives juggling family and work, spent hours upon hours sharing their stories with me. Thank you for trusting me and for being so willing to explore your experience, to believe that it matters. It does. It will change people's lives. A particular thank-you to April in Pittsburgh, who gave me the confidence to share my own story, and whose fearlessness and vulnerability have been such an inspiration.

Thank you to the many scientists I spoke with who very kindly and patiently walked me through subjects about which I know very little, and tolerated with warmth and equanimity my asking for the hundredth time, "What are receptors?" An enormous thank-you to Dr. Joseph S. Lonstein at Michigan State for not only answering my questions via phone and email, but also agreeing to read an early version of this manuscript. Thank you for believing in this project and for your patience in helping me grasp the science.

I am so grateful to my agent, Jane Dystel, for encouraging me to begin work on this project and for being so present every step of the way, always willing to answer a call or an email and to advocate for me. Thank you for making my work possible, and for being so reliable and solid in guiding me.

Thank you to the team at Pantheon: Holly Webber for scrupulous copyediting and fact-checking (and finding so many page numbers!), Josefine Kals and Rose Cronin-Jackman in publicity, Rachel Fershleiser in marketing, and Janet Hansen for her striking cover design.

Amanda Giracca, Simone Gorrindo, and Michelle Huh-Mounts all read early versions of this book and offered comments, feedback, and insights. Thank you so much for the encouragement and for helping to steer the work along; also, for beers, barbecues, commiseration about parenting woes, 5 a.m. sobbing phone calls, cross-country visits, road trips, and super-solid and lovely friendship in general.

Thank you to Dr. S, my therapist in Pittsburgh, whose insights are featured prominently here and who dramatically changed my thinking about anxiety.

In March 2019, with a month left before my final, final book deadline, my long-suffering dad and stepmom—parents not only of a writer, but a *musician*—allowed me to come crash in a tiny log cabin on their land and spend fourteen hours a day writing. They fed me when I straggled down at seven p.m. in a daze, and popped up occasionally to offer wood for the fire and make sure I was more or less coherent. This was my first-ever writing residency and it was a doozy. There is really no thanks large enough to put here on the page for Dad, Meg, and what they have given me: not just the space to write, but unwavering belief in my work and vision.

To Jack Menkedick: I can't imagine my artistic career without many an angsty, realization-strewn Skype conversation with you. Thank you for the commiseration and the willingness always to go deep, get curious, listen, and be present. Thank you to Mary Menkedick for taking Elena on many weekends and summer days so I could sit at your dining room table and Skype with neurobiologists, and for your optimism, support, and love. To my mom, Lois Carter: an infinite thanks for talking to me during so many long runs, helping me navigate the intricacies of the writing, and asking always in the same deadpan tone *How's the book,* thereby illuminating the absurdity of it all. Thank you for making me laugh and for being a goofball and for always being curious about new ideas.

Finally, to Jorge and Elena—you are my world. Thank you for all the dinner conversations, the rants in the car en route to the farm, the late-night beery musings, the back-and-forth on Frick Park hikes about this or that idea connected to this book. Thank you for climbing trees, for morning drawing on the front porch, for dancing to Lila Downs, for your sense of humor, your kindness, your gentleness, and your sweet and mellow foil to my neurotic self. Thank you for teaching me always to slow down and *chillax, Floyd.* You are the best—the very best—family I could have ever hoped for. You remind me every day of what really matters. You are everything.

Notes

Introduction

xiv "False notions of love": bell hooks, *All About Love: New Visions* (New York: HarperCollins, 1999), 159.

1 The Mother's Brain

9 "normal illness": D. W. Winnicott, "Primary Maternal Preoccupation," in *Collected Works of D. W. Winnicott* 5 (Oxford: Oxford University Press, 2016), 185.

9 "primary maternal preoccupation": Ibid.

9 "could be compared": Ibid.

9 "can feel herself": Ibid., 187.

9 "I do not believe": Ibid., 185.

14 Some scientists argue: Craig Howard Kinsley and Kelly G. Lambert, "The Maternal Brain," *Scientific American* (January 2006): 72–79.

15 "The hand—or paw—that rocks": Ibid., 72.

15 four hundred birth control pills a day: Jessica Grose, "Pregnancy and Prenatal Depression: Why Didn't Anyone Warn Me I Would Feel So Bad?" *Slate* (August 6, 2012). https://slate.com/human-interest/2012/08/pregnancy-and-prenatal-depression-why-didnt-anyone-warn-me-i-would-feel-so-bad.html.

16 "The infant creates": Craig Howard Kinsley and Elizabeth Amory Meyer, "Maternal Mentality," *Scientific American* (October 1, 2012). https://www.scientificamerican.com/article/maternal-mentality-2012-10-23/.

16 "Neurons that fire together wire together": Katherine Ellison, *The Mommy Brain: How Motherhood Makes Us Smarter* (New York: Basic Books, 2005), 17.

16 ground zero for maternal behavior: Kelly Lambert, interview by the author, June 22, 2017.

16 There are receptors in the MPOA: Jennifer Barrett and Alison Fleming, "Annual

Research Review: All Mothers Are Not Created Equal: Neural and Psychobiological Perspectives on Mothering and the Importance of Individual Differences," *The Journal of Child Psychology and Psychiatry* 52:4 (2010): 368–97.

16 Neurons that "ascend": Jodi L. Pawluski, Joseph S. Lonstein, and Alison S. Fleming, "Neurobiology of Postpartum Anxiety and Depression," *Trends in Neurosciences* 40 (February 2017): 106–20.

16 "rev up" MPOA: Kinsley and Lambert, "The Maternal Brain," 76.

17 "their release for the race": Ibid.

17 neuronal effect: Ibid.

17 Rats whose MPOA has been damaged: Michael Numan and Thomas Insel, *The Neurobiology of Parental Behavior* (New York: Springer, 2003), 134.

17 Hormones also ramp up: Kinsley and Lambert, "The Maternal Brain," 77.

17 "pregnancy brain": Katharina Maria Hillerer, Volker Rudolf Jacobs, Thorsten Fischer, and Ludwig Aigner, "The Maternal Brain: An Organ with Peripartal Plasticity," *Neural Plasticity* (2014). https://www.ncbi.nlm.nih.gov/pmc/articles/PMC4026981/.

17 Researchers have shown: Interview, Pilyoung Kim, July 27, 2017; and Pilyoung Kim, Lane Strathearn, and James Swain, "The Maternal Brain and Its Plasticity in Humans," *Hormones and Behavior* 77 (January 2016): 113–23.

18 (fMRI) studies have shown: Ellison, *The Mommy Brain*, 47.

19 Craig Kinsley has drawn a correlation: Kinsley and Meyer, "Maternal Mentality."

19 In virgin rats: Pilyoung Kim, interview by the author, July 27, 2017; and Kim, Strathearn, and Swain, "The Maternal Brain and Its Plasticity in Humans," 113–23.

19 The few fMRI studies: Ibid.

20 The amygdala is laden: Ibid.

20 Dr. James Swain: James E. Swain, "The Human Parental Brain: In Vivo Neuroimaging," *Progress in Neuro-Psychopharmacology and Biological Psychiatry* 35 (July 2011): 1242–54.

2 Postpartum Mood Disorders

25 Alison Fleming: Alison Fleming, interview by the author, July 6, 2017.

25 "implies that a certain level": Ibid.

26 A 2013 study by researcher Oliver Bosch: Oliver J. Bosch, "Maternal Aggression in Rodents: Brain Oxytocin and Vasopressin Mediate Pup Defence," *Philosophical Transactions of the Royal Society B* 368 (December 5, 2013).

26 Bosch worked in a lab: Oliver Bosch, interview by the author, June 14, 2017.

26 "When I compare": Ibid.

26 Dr. James Leckman: James Leckman, interview by the author, July 3, 2017.

27 "not an unfair hypothesis": Ibid.

27 Dr. Leckman's research: J. F. Leckman, R. Feldman, J. E. Swain, V. Eicher, N. Thompson, and L. C. Mayes, "Primary Parental Preoccupation: Circuits, Genes, and the Crucial Role of the Environment," *Journal of Neural Transmission* 111 (July 2004): 753–71.

27 Leckman revealed: Ibid., 756.

28 "just right": Diana Feygin, James E. Swain, James F. Leckman, "The Normalcy

of Neurosis: Evolutionary Origins of Obsessive-Compulsive Disorder and Related Behaviors," *Progress in Neuro-Psychopharmacology and Biological Psychiatry* 30 (July 2006): 854–64.

28 Leckman points out: James Leckman, interview by the author, July 3, 2017.

28 100 deaths per 1,000 births in 1900: CDC report, "Achievements in Public Health, 1900–1999: Healthier Mothers and Babies," October 1999, 849–58.

28 6 deaths per 1,000 births in 2014: CDC, "Morbidity and Mortality Weekly Report," November 18, 2016.

28 "Little wonder then": Leckman et al.,"Primary Parental Preoccupation," 757.

28 His interest in OCD: James Leckman, interview by the author, July 3, 2017.

29 1 in 4 girls will be sexually abused: National Sexual Violence Resource Center (NSVRC), https://www.nsvrc.org.

29 1 in 6 women: Rape, Abuse & Incest National Network, https://www.rainn.org.

29 1 in 4 women: Guttmacher Institute, https://www.guttmacher.org/united-states/abortion.

29 1 in 5 women: Mayo Clinic, https://www.mayoclinic.org/diseases-conditions/pregnancy-loss-miscarriage/symptoms-causes/syc-20354298.

29 1 in 3 women: Janice Goodman et al., "CALM Pregnancy: Results of a Pilot Study of Mindfulness-Based Cognitive Therapy for Perinatal Anxiety," *Archives of Women's Mental Health* 17 (October 2014): 373–87.

29 According to Samantha Meltzer-Brody: Samantha Meltzer-Brody, interview by the author, June 29, 2017.

29 "is a cultural organ": Bessel van der Kolk, *The Body Keeps the Score* (New York: Penguin, 2014), 86.

29 Dr. Pilyoung Kim: Pilyoung Kim, interview by the author, July 27, 2017.

29 Primatologist Sarah Hrdy: Sarah Hrdy, *Mother Nature: Maternal Instincts and How They Shape the Human Species* (New York: Ballantine, 1999).

29 "Today," Hrdy writes: Ibid., 3.

30 Hrdy warned: Ibid., 4.

30 "Research is me-search": Katherine Ellison, *The Mommy Brain: How Motherhood Makes Us Smarter* (New York: Basic Books, 2005), 35.

30 Dr. Joe Lonstein and Dr. Jodi Pawluski: Joe Lonstein and Jodi Pawluski, interview by the author, July 27, 2017.

30 There is more research: Ibid.

30 Dr. Lonstein's overview: Joseph S. Lonstein, "Regulation of Anxiety During the Postpartum Period," *Frontiers in Neuroendocrinology* 28 (August/September 2007): 115–41.

30 A 2014 study on mindfulness: Goodman et al., "CALM Pregnancy," 373–87.

31 Meanwhile, a 2006 literature review: Lori E. Ross and Linda M. McLean, "Anxiety Disorders During Pregnancy and the Postpartum Period: A Systematic Review," *Journal of Clinical Psychiatry* 67 (August 2006): 1285–98.

31 A 2016 literature review: Janice H. Goodman, Grace R. Watson, Brendon Stubbs, "Anxiety Disorders in Postpartum Women: A Systematic Review and Meta-analysis," *Journal of Affective Disorders* 203 (October 2016): 292–331.

31 As Dr. Kelly Lambert: Kelly Lambert, interview by the author, 6/22/17.

31 As Dr. Kim explained to me: Pilyoung Kim, interview by the author, July 27, 2017.

36 "Rather than feelings of sadness": MGH Center for Women's Mental Health, https://womensmentalhealth.org/specialty-clinics/postpartum-psychiatric-disorders/.

37 A 2014 study: Postpartum Depression: Action Towards Causes and Treatment (PACT) Consortium, "Clinical Phenotypes of Perinatal Depression and Time of Symptom Onset: Analysis of Data from an International Consortium," *The Lancet Psychiatry* 4 (June 2017): 477–85.

38 After lobbying on the part: Lisa S. Segre and Wendy N. Davis, "Postpartum Depression and Perinatal Mood Disorders in the DSM," Postpartum Support International, June 2013, https://www.postpartum.net/wp-content/uploads/2014/11/DSM-5-Summary-PSI.pdf.

39 "There's sort of suddenly thirty-five flavors": Samantha Meltzer-Brody, interview by the author, June 29, 2017.

45 It is impossible for anxiety or OCD alone: Amy Wenzel, interview by the author, June 28, 2017. Also Stephen Matthey, Bryanne Barnett, Pauline Howie, David J. Kavanagh, "Diagnosing Postpartum Depression in Mothers and Fathers: Whatever Happened to Anxiety?" *Journal of Affective Disorders* 74 (April 2003): 139–47.

46 Dr. Amy Wenzel: Amy Wenzel, interview by the author, June 28, 2017.

46 Dr. Ian Paul: Ian Paul, interview by the author, June 15, 2017.

46 "the principle of diagnostic parsimony": Matthey et al., "Diagnosing Postpartum Depression in Mothers and Fathers," 144.

46 In psychiatry, Goldberg says: Ibid.

46 According to psychology professor: Ibid.

47 Women with anxiety disorders: Ibid.

47 Matthey cites: Ibid.

47 In her 2003 study: Amy Wenzel, Erin N. Haugen, Lydia C. Jackson, and Kris Robinson, "Prevalence of Generalized Anxiety at Eight Weeks Postpartum," *Archives of Women's Mental Health* 6 (February 2003) 43–49.

47 A 2013 study: Ian M. Paul, Danielle S. Downs, Eric W. Schaefer, Jessica S. Beiler, Carol S. Weisman, "Postpartum Anxiety and Maternal-Infant Health Outcomes," *Pediatrics* 131 (April 2013): 1218–24.

47 When I asked Dr. Paul: Ian Paul, interview by the author, June 15, 2017.

48 "We have to find": Ibid.

49 Dr. Paul's office: Ibid.

50 major news story: "The Last Person You'd Expect to Die in Childbirth," Nina Martin and Renee Montagne, NPR/ProPublica, May 12, 2017, https://www.propublica.org/article/die-in-childbirth-maternal-death-rate-health-care-system.

50 The original Postpartum Worry Scale: Amy Wenzel et al., "Prevalence of Generalized Anxiety at Eight Weeks Postpartum," 43–49.

50 In 2014: Tracy E. Moran, Joshua R. Polanin, and Amy Wenzel, "The Postpartum Worry Scale—Revised: An Initial Validation of a Measure of Postpartum Worry," *Archives of Women's Mental Health* 17 (February 2014): 41–48.

3 The Risk Society

59 The concept of risk: Mary Douglas, *Mary Douglas: Collected Works: Risk and Blame: Essays in Cultural Theory* (New York: Routledge, 1992), 23.

59 "risk society": Ulrich Beck, *World at Risk* (Cambridge: Polity Press, 2009).

60 "Now I am become death": https://www.youtube.com/watch?v=lb13ynu3Iac.

60 Polish sociologist and philosopher Zygmunt Bauman: Alphia Possamai-Inesedy, "Confining Risk: Choice and Responsibility in Childbirth in a Risk Society," *Health Sociology Review* 15 (October 2006): 406.

61 This is reflective: Beck, *World at Risk*, 13.

61 "The risks which we believe": Ibid.

61 "In God's absence": Ibid., 4.

62 They must ask themselves: Ibid., 117.

62 The anthropologist Mary Douglas: Douglas, *Risk and Blame*, 23.

62 Douglas writes of risk: Ibid., 28.

67 In his book: Daniel Gardner, *The Science of Fear: How the Culture of Fear Manipulates Your Brain* (New York: Plume, 2009).

67 Gardner asks why: Ibid., 10.

68 Take, for example: Ibid., 185.

68 American parents wouldn't know this: Ibid., 183.

68 Multiple studies have shown: Ibid., 16.

68 on the rise: Ibid.

69 A study by psychologists: Ibid., 196.

69 Under the sway of emotion: Ibid., 82.

69 University of Oregon psychology professor: Ibid.

69 As neuroscientist Joseph LeDoux: Ibid.

69 Gardner quotes: Ibid., 230.

70 In her book *On Immunity*: Eula Biss, *On Immunity: An Inoculation* (Minneapolis: Graywolf, 2014).

70 As Gardner explains: Gardner, *The Science of Fear*, 64–65.

71 In an article: George F. Loewenstein, Elke U. Weber, Christopher K. Hsee, and Ned Welch, "Risks as Feelings," *Psychological Bulletin* 127 (2001): 267–86.

72 The irony is: Gardner, *The Science of Fear*, 105.

73 Gardner details: Ibid.

75 In the seventeenth century: Possamai-Inesedy, "Confining Risk," 406.

76 Mothers, writes sociologist Deborah Lupton: Deborah Lupton, "'Precious Cargo': Foetal Subjects, Risk and Reproductive Citizenship," *Critical Public Health* 22 (2012): 329–40.

76 The survey gave: Howard Minkoff and Mary Faith Marshall, "Fetal Risks, Relative Risks, and Relatives' Risks," *American Journal of Bioethics* 16 (February 2016): 3–11.

77 As an editorial on risk: Ellie Lee, Jan Macvarish, and Jennie Bristow, "Risk, Health and Parenting Culture," *Health, Risk & Society* 12 (August 2010): 293–300.

77 If at first: Ibid., 295.

77 Parents define themselves: Ibid., 299.

78 They open their piece: Minkoff and Marshall, "Fetal Risks, Relative Risks, and Relatives' Risks," 3.

78 Plus, they argue: Ibid.

79 magical thinking: Anne Drapkin Lyerly, Lisa M. Mitchell, Elizabeth Mitchell

Armstrong, Lisa H. Harris, Rebecca Kukla, Miriam Kuppermann, and Margaret Olivia Little, "Risk and the Pregnant Body," *The Hastings Center Report* 39
(November 2009): 34–42.

79 "Risk in the context": Mandie Scamell, "Childbirth Within the Risk Society,"
Sociology Compass 8 (July 2014): 917–28.

79 "reproductive asceticism": Deborah Lupton, "'Precious Cargo,'" 330.

80 Searching a modern academic library: Angela Ballantyne, Colin Gavaghan,
John McMillan, and Sue Pullon, "Pregnancy and the Culture of Extreme Risk
Aversion," *American Journal of Bioethics* 16 (February 2016): 21–23.

80 The responsibility for "making good choices": Rebecca Kukla, "The Ethics and
Cultural Politics of Reproductive Risk Warnings: A Case Study of California's
Proposition 65," *Health, Risk & Society* 12 (August 2010): 323–34.

80 Kukla points out: Ibid., 325.

80 The esteemed all-female authors: Lyerly et al., "Risk and the Pregnant Body,"
34–42.

81 However, as Kukla argues: Kukla, "The Ethics and Cultural Politics of Reproductive Risk Warnings," 323–34.

82 These omnipresent Prop 65 warnings: Ibid., 329.

82 In another article: Anne Drapkin Lyerly, Lisa M. Mitchell, Elizabeth M. Arm-
strong, Lisa H. Harris, Rebecca Kukla, Miriam Kuppermann, and Margaret
Olivia Little, "Risks, Values, and Decision Making Surrounding Pregnancy,"
Obstetrics and Gynecology 109 (April 2007): 979–84.

83 The women doctors: Ibid.

85 "Is Sleeping with Your Baby": Michaeleen Doucleff, "Is Sleeping with Your
Baby as Dangerous as Doctors Say?" NPR *Goats and Soda*, May 21, 2018. https://
www.npr.org/sections/goatsandsoda/2018/05/21/601289695/is-sleeping-with
-your-baby-as-dangerous-as-doctors-say.

4 The Risks Not Taken

89 *Conceiving Risk, Bearing Responsibility*: Elizabeth Armstrong, *Conceiving Risk,
Bearing Responsibility: Fetal Alcohol Syndrome and the Diagnosis of Moral Disorder*
(Baltimore: The Johns Hopkins University Press, 2003).

90 "wont to be fond of wine": Ibid., 24.

90 A passage in Plato's *Laws*: Ibid.

90 "wholesale poisoning of civilized": Ibid., 41.

91 "the enlightened nations": Ibid., 50.

91 "functions as a form": Ibid., 8.

91 "divinely appointed guardian[s]": Ibid., 60.

91 "In human beings it is difficult": Ibid., 70.

92 "social condiment": Ibid., 71.

92 "Probably the most serious effect": Ibid., 72.

92 "they smelled like a fruitcake": Ibid., 74.

93 "Back in the 50s and 60s": Ibid., 99.

95 false positives: Ibid.

95 One study looked: Nesrin Bingol, Carlotta Schuster, Magdalena Fuchs, Silvia
Iosub, Gudrun Turner, Richard K. Stone, Donald S. Gromisch, "The Influence

of Socioeconomic Factors on the Occurrence of Fetal Alcohol Syndrome," *Advances in Alcohol and Substance Abuse* (Summer 1987): 105–118.

96 developing FAS: Armstrong, *Conceiving Risk, Bearing Responsibility.*

96 "double damage by targeting": Ibid., 204.

96 "the greater the freedom": Ibid., 216.

97 Colin Gavaghan: Colin Gavaghan, "'You Can't *Handle* the Truth': Medical Paternalism and Prenatal Alcohol Use," *Journal of Medical Ethics* 35 (May 2009): 300–303.

97 "ensure that no one": Ibid., 300.

97 "For a relationship between": Ibid., 301.

97 "relatively low amounts": Ibid.

98 "a paternalistic exception": Ibid.

98 "formalis[ing] a connection": Pam K. Lowe and Ellie J. Lee, "Advocating Alcohol Abstinence to Pregnant Women: Some Observations About British Policy," *Health, Risk & Society* 12 (August 2010): 301–11.

98 "one less concern": Jacqueline Howard, "Is Light Drinking While Pregnant OK?," cnn.com, September 11, 2017, https://www.cnn.com/2017/09/11/health/drinking-alcohol-pregnant-study/index.html.

98 "when the risk is non-existent": Lowe and Lee, "Advocating Alcohol Abstinence," 302.

100 As psychologist Barry Schwartz: Scott Stossel, *My Age of Anxiety: Fear, Hope, Dread, and the Search for Peace of Mind* (New York: Knopf, 2014), 302.

100 "SuperBabies Don't Cry": Heather Kirn Lanier, "SuperBabies Don't Cry," *Vela,* April 2017. https://velamag.com/superbabies-dont-cry/.

101 "She believes her baby": Heather Kirn Lanier, "The Woman I Was Before I Knew," *Star in Her Eye,* January 12, 2015. https://starinhereye.wordpress.com/2015/01/12/the-woman-i-was-before-i-knew/.

101 "I got kicked out of the club": Heather Kirn Lanier, interview with the author, April 2018.

102 "controllable private nonsense": Judith Warner, *Perfect Madness: Motherhood in the Age of Anxiety* (New York: Riverhead, 2005), 56.

103 "It seems that Americans": Amy Fusselman, *Savage Park: A Meditation on Play, Space, and Risk for Americans Who Are Nervous, Distracted, and Afraid to Die* (New York: Mariner, 2015), 75.

103 "an administrator's heaven": Ibid., 73.

103 "American playgrounds that are designed": Ibid., 117.

103 "It seems that the first obligation" Janna Malamud Smith, *A Potent Spell: Mother Love and the Power of Fear* (Boston and New York: Houghton Mifflin, 2003), 25.

104 "As water given sugar": Jane Hirshfield, "Rebus," in *Given Sugar, Given Salt* (New York: Harper Perennial, 2002).

5 The White Advantage

113 black women are three to four times: Black Mamas Matter Alliance, "Setting the Standard for Holistic Care of and for Black Women," April 2018. http://blackmamasmatter.org/wp-content/uploads/2018/04/BMMA_BlackPaper_April-2018.pdf.

113 Black infants are twice: Ibid.

113 This is true for infants: Danyelle Soloman, "Racism: The Evergreen Toxin Killing Black Mothers and Infants," Center for American Progress, April 18, 2018. https://www.americanprogress.org/issues/race/reports/2018/04/18/449774/racism-evergreen-toxin-killing-black-mothers-infants/.

113 The white infant mortality rate drops: Imari Z. Smith, Keisha L. Bentley-Edwards, Salimah El-Amin, and William Darity, Jr., "Fighting at Birth: Eradicating the Black-White Infant Mortality Gap," Report from Duke University's Samuel DuBois Cook Center on Social Equity and Insight Center for Community Economic Development, March 2018.

114 For white women who grew up: Ibid.

114 White women smoke: Smith et al., "Fighting at Birth," 5.

114 After adjusting for gestational age: Margaret A. Harper, Mark A. Espeland, Elizabeth Dugan, Robert Meyer, Kathy Lane, and Sharon Williams, "Racial Disparity in Pregnancy-Related Mortality Following a Live Birth Outcome," *Annals of Epidemiology* 14 (April 2004): 274–79.

114 At all income and education levels: New York City, 2008–2012, Severe Maternal Morbidity: https://www1.nyc.gov/assets/doh/downloads/pdf/data/maternal-morbidity-report-08-12.pdf.

114 Black women with normal BMIs: Ibid.

114 The rate of preterm births: Smith et al., "Fighting at Birth," 1.

115 Genetic or biological differences: James W. Collins, Jr., Shou-Yien Wu, Richard J. David, "Differing Intergenerational Birth Weights Among the Descendants of US-born and Foreign-born Whites and African Americans in Illinois," *American Journal of Epidemiology* 155 (February 2002): 210–16.

115 After one generation: Ibid.

115 The weathering hypothesis: Arline T. Geronimus, Margaret Hicken, Danya Keene, and John Bound, "'Weathering' and Age Patterns of Allostatic Load Scores Among Blacks and Whites in the United States," *American Journal of Public Health* 96 (May 2006): 826–33.

115 "cumulative wear and tear": Ibid.

116 One 2017 study: Paula Braveman, Katherine Heck, Susan Egerter, Tyan Parker Dominguez, Christine Rinki, Kristen S. Marchi, and Michael Curtis, "Worry About Racial Discrimination: A Missing Piece of the Puzzle of Black-White Disparities in Preterm Birth?" *PLOS One* (October 11, 2017).

116 likely to have a preterm birth: Ibid.

117 Another retrospective study: Sarah Mustillo, Nancy Krieger, Erica P. Gunderson, Stephen Sidney, Heather McCreath, and Catarina I. Kiefe, "Self-Reported Experiences of Racial Discrimination and Black–White Differences in Preterm and Low-Birthweight Deliveries: The CARDIA Study," *American Journal of Public Health* 94 (December 2004): 2125–31.

117 In North Carolina: Nancy Dole, David A. Savitz, Anna Maria Siega-Riz, Irva Hertz-Picciotto, Michael J. McMahon, and Pierre Buekens, "Psychosocial Factors and Preterm Birth Among African American and White Women in Central North Carolina," *American Journal of Public Health* 94 (August 2004): 1358–65.

117 In Los Angeles: Tyan Parker Dominguez, Christine Dunkel-Schetter, Laura M. Glynn, Calvin Hobel, and Curt A. Sandman, "Racial Differences in Birth Out-

comes: The Role of General, Pregnancy, and Racism Stress," *Health Psychology* 27 (March 2008): 194–203.

117 Another set of studies by Northwestern pediatrics professor: James W. Collins, Jr., Richard J. David, Arden Handler, Stephen Wall, and Steven Andes, "Very Low Birthweight in African American Infants: The Role of Maternal Exposure to Interpersonal Racial Discrimination," *American Journal of Public Health* 94 (December 2004): 2132–38. Also James W. Collins, Jr., Richard J. David, Rebecca Symons, Arden Handler, Stephen N. Wall, and Lisa Dwyer, "Low-Income African American Mothers' Perception of Exposure to Racial Discrimination and Infant Birth Weight," *Epidemiology* 11 (May 2000): 337–39.

117 Finally, a study: Valerie A. Earnshaw, Lisa Rosenthal, Jessica B. Lewis, Emily C. Stasko, Jonathan N. Tobin, Tené T. Lewis, Allecia E. Reid, and Jeannette R. Ickovic, "Maternal Experiences with Everyday Discrimination and Infant Birth Weight: A Test of Mediators and Moderators Among Young, Urban Women of Color," *Annals of Behavioral Medicine* 45 (February 2013): 13–23.

118 One big study: Karen A. Ertel, Tamarra James-Todd, Kenneth Kleinman, Nancy Krieger, Matthew Gillman, Rosalind Wright, and Janet Rich-Edwards, "Racial Discrimination, Response to Unfair Treatment, and Depressive Symptoms Among Pregnant Black and African American Women in the United States," *Annals of Epidemiology* 22 (December 2012): 840–46.

119 one study of nearly two thousand mothers: Amelia R. Gavin, Jennifer L. Melville, Tessa Rue, Yuqing Guo, Karen Tabb Dina, and Wayne J. Katon, "Racial Differences in the Prevalence of Antenatal Depression," *General Hospital Psychiatry* 33 (March/April 2011): 87–93.

119 "PPD researchers have largely neglected": Robert H. Keefe, Carol Brownstein-Evans, and Rebecca S. Rouland Polmanteer, "The Challenges of Idealized Mothering: Marginalized Mothers Living with Postpartum," *Afflia* 33 (December 2017): 221–35.

119 *Ain't I a Woman*: bell hooks, *Ain't I a Woman: Black Women and Feminism* (New York: Routledge, 2014).

119 "passive nurturer": Ibid., 84–85.

120 "[These] women are faced": Rosenthal and Lobel, "Explaining Racial Disparities in Adverse Birth Outcomes," 980.

120 "Being expected to embody": Tope Fadiran Charlton, "The Impossibility of the Good Black Mother," *Time*, January 21, 2014. http://time.com/1311/the-impossibility-of-the-good-black-mother/.

120 black patients are less likely: Nina Martin and Renee Montagne, "Black Mothers Keep Dying After Giving Birth. Shalon Irving's Story Explains Why," NPR, December 7, 2017.

120 black health: Sandhya Somashekhar, "The Disturbing Reason Some African American Patients May Be Undertreated for Pain," *The Washington Post*, April 4, 2016. https://www.washingtonpost.com/news/to-your-health/wp/2016/04/04/do-blacks-feel-less-pain-than-whites-their-doctors-may-think-so/?noredirect=on.

121 Kristy Holloway: Kristy Holloway, interview by the author, February 25, 2019.

121 "face so many extra burdens": Ibid.

121 "badge of female glory": Ibid.

121 "I'm human": Ibid.
121 "The legacy of strength": Cheryl L. Woods-Giscombé, "Superwoman Schema: African American Women's Views on Stress, Strength, and Health," *Qualitative Health Research* 20 (February 2010): 668–83.
121 Katrina Pointer: Katrina Pointer, interview by the author, February, 27, 2019.
122 "Being a Good Mom": Sinikka Elliott, Rachel Powell, and Joslyn Brenton, "Being a Good Mom: Low-Income, Black Single Mothers Negotiate Intensive Mothering," *Journal of Family Issues* 36 (May 2013): 351–70.
122 "I could never be": Charlton, "The Impossibility of the Good Black Mother."
123 "It is not," she concludes: Ibid.
126 "a shadowy place": Kelena Reid Maxwell, "Birth Behind the Veil: African American Midwives and Mothers in the Rural South, 1921–1962," Dissertation, Rutgers University–New Brunswick.
127 "granny midwives": Keisha Goode and Barbara Katz Rothman, "African American Midwifery, a History and a Lament," *American Journal of Economics and Sociology* 76 (January 2017): 65–94.
127 "grand midwives": Ibid., 72.
127 A grand midwife: Maxwell, "Birth Behind the Veil."
127 "lights my pipe and waits": Ibid.
127 "a loose sisterhood": Ibid.
127 "syncretic, eclectic, and dynamic": Ibid.
128 for the rituals she carried out: Ibid.
128 "Prayers is the most important thing": Ibid.
128 "both," she writes, "were acts of healing": Goode and Rothman, "African American Midwifery, a History and a Lament," 67.
128 Finally, midwives washed and prepared: Keisha La'Nesha Goode, "Birthing, Blackness, and the Body: Black Midwives and Experiential Continuities of Institutional Racism," Dissertation, Graduate Faculty in Sociology, City University of New York.
128 "part of a long line of secret doctors": Maxwell, "Birth Behind the Veil."
128 the midwife would ritually escort: Ibid.
129 "a midwife-assisted home birth": Ibid.
129 Some scholars have argued: L. L. Wall, "The Medical Ethics of Dr. J. Marion Sims: A Fresh Look at the Historical Record," *Journal of Medical Ethics* 32 (June 2006): 346–50.
129 a statue next to Central Park: Meagan Flynn, "Statue of 'Father of Gynecology,' Who Experimented on Enslaved Women, Removed from Central Park," *The Washington Post*, April 18, 2018. https://www.washingtonpost.com /news/morning-mix/wp/2018/04/18/statue-of-father-of-gynecology-who -experimented-on-enslaved-women-removed-from-central-park/?noredirect =on&utm_term=.8a712b9e3d5e.
129 *The Warmth of Other Suns*: Isabel Wilkerson, *The Warmth of Other Suns* (New York: Vintage, 2010), 245.
130 "White women trusted midwives": Maxwell, "Birth Behind the Veil."
130 obstetrics was struggling: Goode, "Birthing, Blackness, and the Body."
130 The rise and positioning: Ibid.
131 "typical Italian midwife": Maxwell, "Birth Behind the Veil."
131 "except in some rare instances": Goode, "Birthing, Blackness, and the Body."

132 "Everyone was touched": Eileen Boris, "The Power of Motherhood: Black and White Activist Women Redefine the 'Political,'" in *Mothers of a New World: Maternalist Politics and the Origins of Welfare States*, Seth Koven and Sonya Michel, eds. (London: Routledge, 1993): 213–45.

132 the Children's Bureau: Jacqueline K. Parker and Edward M. Carpenter, "Julia Lathrop and the Children's Bureau: The Emergence of an Institution," *Social Service Review* 55 (March 1981): 60–77.

132 to fight an uphill battle: Boris, "The Power of Motherhood," in *Mothers of a New World*.

133 The act, written by Lathrop: Ibid.

6 Reproductive Rights

137 As part of the Children's Bureau's: Kelena Reid Maxwell, "Birth Behind the Veil: African American Midwives and Mothers in the Rural South, 1921–1962," Dissertation, Rutgers University–New Brunswick.

137 Maxwell cites: Ibid., 101.

137 Another significant 1922 study: Julius Levy, "Maternal Mortality and Mortality in the First Month of Life in Relation to an Attendant at Birth," paper read before the Child Hygiene Section at the American Public Health Association at the fifty-first annual meeting, Cleveland, October 18, 1922.

138 Statistics from major cities consistently supported: Keisha Goode and Barbara Katz Rothman, "African American Midwifery, a History and a Lament," *American Journal of Economics and Sociology* 76 (January 2017): 65–94.

138 "skilled care": Maxwell, "Birth Behind the Veil," 15.

138 "Twenty percent of white mothers": Ibid., 16.

138 "white folks' way": Keisha La'Nesha Goode, "Birthing, Blackness, and the Body: Black Midwives and Experiential Continuities of Institutional Racism," Dissertation, Graduate Faculty in Sociology, City University of New York, 58.

138 In 1921, Laurie Jean Reid: Kelena Reid Maxwell, "Birth Behind the Veil," 83.

139 "resplendent in garb": Ibid.

139 In order to maintain: Ibid.

139 The training focused: Ibid.

140 was repealed in 1929: Eileen Boris, "The Power of Motherhood: Black and White Activist Women Redefine the 'Political,'" in Seth Koven and Sonya Michel, eds., *Mothers of a New World: Maternalist Politics and the Origins of Welfare States* (London: Routledge, 1993).

140 Sheppard-Towner was radical: Ibid.

141 studies from 1930 to 1960: Goode and Rothman, "African American Midwifery, a History and a Lament," 85.

141 The largest study of home births: Keisha La'Nesha Goode, "Birthing, Blackness, and the Body," 21.

141 Still, by 2012: Ibid.

141 black women make up: Ibid.

142 "without talking about race": Ibid.

142 "We black women": Ibid.

143 "cellular knowledge:" Ibid.

143 In 2012, six members of the Midwives of Color: Ibid., 28–33.

144 In 2012, Certified Nurse Midwives: Goode, "Birthing, Blackness, and the Body," 15.

144 the Midwives Model of Care: National Association of Certified Professional Midwives (NACPM): http://nacpm.org/about-cpms/midwifery-model-of-care/

144 A narrative review: Hannah Yoder and Lynda R. Hardy, "Midwifery and Antenatal Care for Black Women: A Narrative Review," *SAGE Open* (January 23, 2018). https://journals.sagepub.com/doi/full/10.1177/2158244017752220.

145 A 2018 study: Saraswathi Vedam, "Mapping Integration of Midwives Across the United States: Impact on Access, Equity, and Outcomes," *PLOS One* (February 21, 2018).

145 "The difference": Jennie Joseph, interview by the author, February 21, 2019.

150 "American culture," writes Dorothy Roberts: Dorothy Roberts, *Killing the Black Body: Race, Reproduction, and the Meaning of Liberty* (New York: Vintage, 1997), 15.

150 "Regulating Black women's": Ibid., 6.

150 A pregnant slave: Ibid., 40.

150 "One of my sisters": Angela Davis, *Women, Race, and Class* (New York: Vintage, 1983), 9.

150 "the first example of maternal-fetal conflict": Roberts, *Killing the Black Body*, 40.

150 An early American law: Dorothy Roberts, "Racism and Patriarchy in the Meaning of Motherhood," Faculty Scholarship at Penn Law 595, 1993, 7.

150 Roberts quotes: Ibid., 24.

151 "I consider a woman": Ibid., 25.

151 "Damn you": Ibid., 26.

151 Fewer than two out of three: Ibid., 36.

151 "that trough was filled": Ibid., 37.

151 Slave children: Ibid., 52.

151 The son of activist: Crystal Lynn Webster, "In Pursuit of Autonomous Womanhood: Nineteenth-Century Black Motherhood in the U.S. North," *Slavery & Abolition* 38 (2017): 425–40.

152 "A fine fuss": Ibid.

152 "The notion that a white mother": Roberts, *Killing the Black Body*, 54.

152 "Rape was a weapon": Davis, *Women, Race, and Class*, 23–24.

153 Dorothy Roberts points out: Roberts, *Killing the Black Body*, 29.

153 In 1955, Till: Ruth Feldstein, *Motherhood in Black and White: Race and Sex in American Liberalism, 1930–1965* (Ithaca: Cornell University Press, 2000), 86.

153 The trial featured: Ibid., 91–92.

153 "to emerge as protective": Ibid., 92.

153 raised her son "correctly": Ibid.

154 Segregationist southern publications: Ibid., 100.

154 As black journalist and feminist: Roberts, *Killing the Black Body*, 30.

154 "white men first, white women": bell hooks, *Ain't I a Woman: Black Women and Feminism* (New York: Routledge, 2014), 52–53.

154 "Judged by the evolving": Angela Davis, *Women, Race, and Class*, 5.

154 "doubled discourse": Laura Briggs, "The Race of Hysteria: 'Overcivilization' and the 'Savage' Woman in Late Nineteenth-Century Obstetrics and Gynecology," *American Quarterly* 52 (June 2000): 246–73.

155 Scientists in the United States: Ibid.

156 labor "may be characterized": Ibid.

156 "the so-called blessings": Ibid.

159 *The Longest Shortest Time*: The Longest Shortest Time, "The Political Power of Black Motherhood," Episode 192, March 20, 2019. https://longestshortesttime .com/episode-192-the-political-power-of-black-motherhood.

163 Working as a public health nurse: Roberts, *Killing the Black Body*, 57–58.

163 "in the workhouse": Ibid., 58.

164 As Dorothy Roberts details: Ibid., 63.

164 "skull of a Negro murderer": Ibid., 82.

164 "social and racial crime": Ibid., 79.

164 "two of the most perverse": Ibid., 81.

164 "responsibility to the race": Ibid., 76.

165 "What was demanded": Davis, *Women, Race, and Class*, 210.

165 "More children from the fit": Roberts, *Killing the Black Body*, 80.

165 "epileptics, imbeciles, paupers": Ibid., 65.

165 Beginning in 1907: Ibid., 82.

165 "It is better for all the world": Ibid., 84.

166 "often bright and attractive": Ibid., 85.

166 "the normal aversions": Ibid., 84.

166 mass sterilization campaigns that began: Ibid.

166 As late as the 1960s: Ibid.

166 Roberts cites the example: Ibid., 94.

167 "The drawings are supposed": Davis, *Women, Race, and Class*, 218.

167 By 1976, at least a quarter: Roberts, *Killing the Black Body*, 95.

167 By 1970, two hundred thousand: Ibid., 90.

167 "Mississippi appendectomy": Ibid., 90.

167 Roberts writes that in 1972: Ibid., 91.

167 "In most major teaching hospitals": Ibid., 91.

168 "cavalierly subjecting women": Ibid., 91.

168 The district court declared: Southern Poverty Law Center, Relf vs. Weinberger, https://www.splcenter.org/seeking-justice/case-docket/relf-v-weinberger.

168 While one group of women activists: Ibid., 95.

169 "Black women's struggle": Ibid., 222.

169 "We have duped the American woman": Jennie Joseph, interview by the author, February 21, 2019.

170 "Then we've also undermined it": Ibid.

170 "Blindsided": Ibid.

170 "The levels of depression": Ibid.

170 "We've lost any sense": Ibid.

170 "Reproductive freedom": Roberts, *Killing the Black Body*, 6.

170 "This system": Jennie Joseph, interview by the author, February 21, 2019.

171 "more and more white mothers": Dorothy E. Roberts, "Racism and Patriarchy in the Meaning of Motherhood," *American University Journal of Gender, Social Policy & the Law* 1 (1992): 1–38.

7 A Woman's Role

178 Paleolithic cultures: Shari L. Thurer, *The Myths of Motherhood: How Culture Reinvents the Good Mother* (New York: Penguin, 1994).

178 voluptuous bellies and breasts: See Venus of Willendorf statue at Naturhistorisches Museum in Vienna, Austria, and other Venus figures uncovered in France and on display at European museums.

178 wombs or vaginas: Dana Cooper and Claire Phelan, eds., *Motherhood in Antiquity* (Basingstoke, England: Palgrave Macmillan, 2017), 230.

178 Paleolithic peoples carved: Carving found in Laussel, France, now at the Musée d'Aquitane in Bordeaux, France.

178 "Vagina symbols": Thurer, *The Myths of Motherhood*, 9.

179 "of the divine woman": Ibid., 10.

179 "Just as they were associated": Ibid., 34.

179 "a shift in magic": Ibid., 29.

179 Menstruation in particular: Ibid., 35–36.

179 A 2017 essay in *Aeon* magazine: Janie Hampton, "The Taboo of Menstruation," *Aeon*, May 2, 2017, https://aeon.co/essays/throughout-history-and-still-today -women-are-shamed-for-menstruating.

180 Aristotle wrote that: Thurer, *The Myths of Motherhood*, 65.

180 "the mother of the child": Ibid., 65.

180 In the early Enlightenment: Ibid., 149.

180 Darwinism largely pinned women in place: Patricia Fara, "Darwinian Differences: How the Theory of Evolution Viewed Women as Inferior," *The Big Think*, March 20, 2018. https://bigthink.com/big-think-books/patricia-fara -science-and-suffrage-in-the-first-world-war.

180 "equals of man": John Horgan, "Darwin Was Sexist, and So Are Many Modern Scientists," *Scientific American*, December 18, 2017. https://blogs.scientificamerican .com/cross-check/darwin-was-sexist-and-so-are-many-modern-scientists/.

181 Darwin's French translator: Sarah Hrdy, *Mother Nature: A History of Mothers, Infants, and Natural Selection* (New York: Pantheon, 1999), 20.

181 "Up until now science": Ibid., 21.

186 "minus appeal and magic": Thurer, *The Myths of Motherhood*, 154.

186 Instead of sleeping: Ibid., 143.

186 While mothers tended: Ibid., 154–57.

186 "soaked up all": Ibid., 155.

186 In their book: Barbara Ehrenreich and Deirdre English, *For Her Own Good: 150 Years of the Experts' Advice to Women* (New York: Anchor, 1979), 39–42.

187 the "expert" techniques: Ibid.

187 "A patient would have done better": Ibid., 48.

188 "A frequent treatment for leprosy": Ibid., 42.

188 "fell under the biological hegemony": Ibid., 108.

188 "a cozy dream": Ibid., 31.

188 White women deemed inappropriately feminine: Ibid.

189 "eating like a ploughman": Ibid., 136.

189 "one of the greatest causes": Ibid., 138.

189 "She has taken up": Ibid.

190 If the rest cure: Ibid., 135.

190 wet towels: Ibid., 34.
190 "Psychoanalysis," as historian Carroll Smith-Rosenberg writes: Ibid., 154.
191 "the primacy of the mother": Adrienne Rich, *Of Woman Born: Motherhood as Experience and Institution* (New York: W. W. Norton, 1995).
191 "Out of her body": Ibid.
192 "the terrain on which": Ibid.
192 "the fear of woman": Ibid.

8 Institutionalized

198 children were imbued: Ibid.
199 "The discovery of the child": Ibid.
199 the male solution: Ibid., 212.
199 "build up that tiny body": Jodi Vandenberg-Daves, *Modern Motherhood: An American History* (New Brunswick, NJ: Rutgers University Press, 2014), 84.
199 "walk—and speak": Ibid., 101.
199 a timeline of "milestones": Ibid.
200 "Anxiety was the lot": Ibid.
200 Permissive parenting was obsessively child-centered: Barbara Ehrenreich and Deirdre English, *For Her Own Good: 150 Years of the Experts' Advice to Women* (New York: Anchor, 1979).
200 "[was] now to train the parent": Sharon Hays, *The Cultural Contradictions of Motherhood* (New Haven: Yale University Press, 1996), 45.
200 "It is because I want": Vandenberg-Daves, *Modern Motherhood*, 188.
200 "the natural development of the child": Hays, *The Cultural Contradictions of Motherhood*, 45.
201 "ever-present, all-providing": Shari L. Thurer, *The Myths of Motherhood: How Culture Reinvents the Good Mother* (New York: Penguin, 1994), 258.
201 "Mother has become": Ibid., 258.
201 "encouraging certain behaviors": Ehrenreich and English, *For Her Own Good*, 238.
201 "the basic moral and spiritual value": Ibid., 256.
201 "From now on": Ibid., 233.
202 "intensive parenting": Hays, *The Cultural Contradictions of Motherhood*.
202 "applying sunscreen": Vandenberg-Daves, *Modern Motherhood*, 259–60.
202 "expert-guided, child-centered": Hays, *The Cultural Contradictions of Motherhood*, 46.
202 "instrumentally rational": Ibid., 16.
203 This admiration of the natural: Oliver Burkeman, "The Diabolical Genius of the Baby Advice Industry," *The Guardian*, January 16, 2018.
204 women made up: Women in the Labor Force, U.S. Department of Labor, https://www.dol.gov/wb/stats/NEWSTATS/facts/women_lf.htm###one.
204 "While often working more": Vandenberg-Daves, *Modern Motherhood*, 259.
204 "Childhood is filled with peril": Susan Douglas and Meredith Michaels, *The Mommy Myth: The Idealization of Motherhood and How It Has Undermined All Women* (New York: Free Press, 2004), 230.
204 "a degree of anxiety and guilt": Thurer, *The Myths of Motherhood*, 261.

205 "[Experts] have invented": Ibid., xviii.
214 "The words for mother and mud": Adrienne Rich, *Of Woman Born: Motherhood as Experience and Institution* (New York: W. W. Norton, 1995).
214 "In transfiguring and enslaving woman": Ibid.
215 "being initiated into high priestesshood": Louise Erdrich, *The Blue Jay's Dance: A Memoir of Early Motherhood* (New York: Harper Collins, 1995), 12.
216 In the earliest stages of pregnancy: Denise Grady, "The Mysterious Tree of a Newborn's Life," *The New York Times*, July 14, 2014. https://www.nytimes.com/2014/07/15/health/the-push-to-understand-the-placenta.html.
216 "[Trophoblasts] shove other": Ibid.
217 thirty-two miles of capillaries: Ibid.

9 Psychoanalysis

229 "as though they were a genus": Adam Phillips, *Missing Out: In Praise of the Unlived Life* (New York: Picador, 2012).
230 "to withstand the ever mounting tensions": Nellie L. Thompson and Helene Keable, "The Psychoanalytic Study of the Child: A Narrative of Postwar Psychoanalysis," *American Imago* 73 (Fall 2016): 343–65.
231 "a privileged entry": Margot Waddell, "Infant Observation in Britain: The Tavistock Approach," *International Journal of Psychoanalysis* 87 (August 2006): 1103–20.
231 In a 2006 article: Ibid.
232 Psychoanalyst Adam Phillips: Rozsika Parker, *Mother Love, Mother Hate: The Power of Maternal Ambivalence* (New York: Basic Books, 1995), 91.
232 "reify relationships": Nancy Chodorow, *The Reproduction of Mothering: Psychoanalysis and the Sociology of Gender* (Berkeley: University of California Press, 1978), 73.
232 Take, for example: Inge Bretherton, "The Origins of Attachment Theory: John Bowlby and Mary Ainsworth," *Developmental Psychology* 28 (1992): 759–75.
233 "lent the authority of science": Parker, *Mother Love, Mother Hate*, 196.
233 "This internalized something": Mary Main, "Mary D. Salter Ainsworth: Tribute and Portrait," *Psychoanalytic Inquiry* 19 (1999): 682–776.
234 "disease-provoking agent": Barbara Ehrenreich and Deirdre English, *For Her Own Good: 150 Years of the Experts' Advice to Women* (New York: Anchor, 1979), 227.
234 John Bowlby: Bretherton, "The Origins of Attachment Theory," 762.
234 In 1949, he was commissioned: Ibid., 761.
235 There were huge benefits: Ibid.
235 Yet there were also important consequences: Judith Warner, *Perfect Madness: Motherhood in the Age of Anxiety* (New York: Riverhead, 2005), 93.
235 "full-time employment of mother": Ehrenreich and English, *For Her Own Good*, 230.
236 Attachment derives: Parker, *Mother Love, Mother Hate*.
236 "Midcentury psychoanalytic thinking": Shari L. Thurer, *The Myths of Motherhood: How Culture Reinvents the Good Mother* (New York: Penguin, 1994), 270.
243 Parker explains that: Parker, *Mother Love, Mother Hate*, 196.

244 "You are offered": Rachel Cusk, *A Life's Work: On Becoming a Mother* (New York: Picador, 2001), 28.

244 "marooned in adulthood": Parker, *Mother Love, Mother Hate*.

244 "Mothers are expected": Ibid., 198.

245 As psychologist Alison Gopnik has put it: Alison Gopnik, *The Gardener and the Carpenter: What the New Science of Child Development Tells Us About the Relationship Between Parents and Children* (New York: Farrar, Straus, and Giroux, 2016), 9.

246 "who makes the stereotypical gestures": Parker, *Mother Love, Mother Hate*, 175.

246 "Our culture permits flexibility": Ibid., 1.

246 "the experience shared": Ibid., 1.

246 "as a source": Ibid., 48.

247 "Both mother and child": Ibid., 137.

247 "We owe the fairest flowering": Ibid., 15.

247 "My children cause me": Adrienne Rich, *Of Woman Born: Motherhood as Experience and Institution* (New York: W. W. Norton, 1995).

247 "In my experiences": Barbara Almond, *The Monster Within: The Hidden Side of Motherhood* (Berkeley: University of California Press, 2010), 11.

248 "Maternal ambivalence in its most extreme forms": Ibid., 226.

248 "The mother": D. W. Winnicott, "Hate in the Counter-Transference," *Journal of Psychotherapy Practice and Research* 3 (Fall 1994): 348–56.

248 "good-enough mother": D. W. Winnicott, "The Theory of the Parent-Infant Relationship," *International Journal of Psychoanalysis* 41 (1960): 585–95.

248 "A mother has to be able": Winnicott, "Hate in the Counter-Transference," 355.

10 Maternalism and Momism

253 In Puritan New England: Sharon Hays, *The Cultural Contradictions of Motherhood* (New Haven, Conn.: Yale University Press, 1996).

253 They were imagined: Ibid.

253 Fathers dressed children: Shari L. Thurer, *The Myths of Motherhood: How Culture Reinvents the Good Mother* (New York: Penguin, 1994), 167.

253 In the sixteenth and seventeenth centuries: Ibid., 168.

254 "not without regret": Ibid.

254 "trailing clouds of glory": Ibid., 195.

254 Culture became feminized: Rebecca Jo Plant, *Mom: The Transformation of Motherhood in Modern America* (Chicago: University of Chicago Press, 2010).

254 "agents of civilization": Ibid., 40.

255 "is forming the characters": Jodi Vandenberg-Daves, *Modern Motherhood: An American History* (New Brunswick, NJ: Rutgers University Press, 2014), 21.

255 "compromised maternal citizenship": Ibid., 17.

255 "[set] out to mother the world": Ibid., 44.

255 "would fulfill her traditional responsibility": Ibid., 104–5.

255 "Our girls": Ibid., 146.

256 Whereas in Europe: Ibid.

256 Some of these early women's activists: Angela Davis, *Women, Race, and Class* (New York: Vintage, 1983).

256 "If the vine": Ibid., 41.

257 "not even a passing reference": Ibid., 57.

257 "The whole history of feminism": bell hooks, *Ain't I A Woman: Black Women and Feminism* (New York: Routledge, 2014).

257 "I will cut off": Davis, *Women, Race, and Class*, 76.

257 Susan B. Anthony: Ibid., 116.

257 "Don't let her speak!": hooks, *Ain't I a Woman*, 159.

258 "black female immorality": Ibid., 131.

258 "Just as surely as the North": Davis, *Women, Race, and Class*, 126.

258 "The women's rights movement": hooks, *Ain't I a Woman*, 136.

258 Black suffragists demanded the vote: Eileen Boris, "The Power of Motherhood: Black and White Activist Women Redefine the 'Political,'" in Seth Koven and Sonya Michel, eds., *Mothers of a New World: Maternalist Politics and the Origins of Welfare States* (London: Routledge, 1993), 213–45.

259 "Black women were usually": Ibid.

259 "community of other mothers": Nancy A. Naples, "Activist Mothering: Cross-Generational Continuity in the Community Work of Women from Low-Income Urban Neighborhoods," *Gender & Society* 6 (September 1992): 441–63.

259 "The larger culture": Boris, "The Power of Motherhood," in *Mothers of a New World*.

260 "Momism" was essentially: Plant, *Mom*, 14.

260 "in no other nation": Ibid., 14.

260 Popular writer Philip Wylie's: Vandenberg-Daves, *Modern Motherhood*, 177.

261 "a veritable epidemic of mental illness": Plant, *Mom*, 98.

261 Psychiatrist Karl Menninger: Ibid., 49.

261 "emotional attitudes": Ibid., 130.

261 "Still largely barred from": Ibid., 116.

262 "[b]y reframing motherhood as a privilege": Karen Rinaldi, "Motherhood Isn't Sacrifice, It's Selfishness," *The New York Times*, August 4, 2017. https://www.nytimes.com/2017/08/04/opinion/sunday/motherhood-family-sexism-sacrifice.html.

262 "tending to our children": Ibid.

263 "reversed the trajectory of indebtedness": Plant, *Mom*, 87.

263 "[came] unhinged from": Barbara Ehrenreich and Deirdre English, *For Her Own Good: 150 Years of the Experts' Advice to Women* (New York: Anchor, 1979), 211.

263 Momism, with its pyrotechnic zeal: Plant, *Mom*, 26.

264 Thinkers like Simone de Beauvoir: Ibid., 30.

264 "If the homemaker does not regain": Ibid., 32.

11 Empowerment

270 The mainstream, ideal white mom: Rebecca Jo Plant, *Mom: The Transformation of Motherhood in Modern America* (New York: Penguin, 1994).

271 "Working for pay": bell hooks, *Ain't I A Woman: Black Women and Feminism* (New York: Routledge, 2014), 145.

272 "The Special Misogyny Reserved for Mothers": Hillary Frank, "The Spe-

cial Misogyny Reserved for Mothers," *The New York Times*, December 31, 2018. https://www.nytimes.com/2018/12/31/opinion/childbirth-injury-motherhood-misogyny.html.

273 "Since patriarchy wants women": E. Ann Kaplan, *Motherhood and Representation: The Mother in Popular Culture and Melodrama* (London: Routledge, 1992), 4.

273 "whatever remains unsatisfied": Daphne de Marneffe, *Maternal Desire: On Children, Love, and the Inner Life* (New York: Little, Brown, 2004), 105.

273 After my first book: Sarah Menkedick, "Why Don't People Take Writing About Motherhood Seriously? Because Women Do It," *Los Angeles Times*, April 16, 2017. https://www.latimes.com/opinion/op-ed/la-oe-menkedick-literary-value-of-motherhood-20170416-story.html.

274 "Though feminist activism": De Marneffe, *Maternal Desire*, xiii.

274 "We know more about the air we breathe": Adrienne Rich, *Of Woman Born: Motherhood as Experience and Institution* (New York: W. W. Norton, 1995).

275 De Marneffe writes: De Marneffe, *Maternal Desire*, xiii.

275 In 1957, the sociologist E. E. LeMasters: E. E. LeMasters, "Parenthood as Crisis": *Marriage and Family Living* 19 (November 1957): 352–55.

275 "psychiatric disability": LeMasters concluded this via interviewing the subjects' friends, which one could argue might not have been the most rigorous scientific method.

275 "The thirty-eight couples": Ibid., 12.

275 " 'We knew where babies' ": Ibid.

276 "To destroy the institution": Rich, *Of Woman Born*.

276 "Virtually all the messages": Shari L. Thurer, *The Myths of Motherhood: How Culture Reinvents the Good Mother* (New York: Penguin, 1994), 27.

277 "We are making a claim": Alexis Pauline Gumbs, China Martens, and Mai'a Williams, eds., *Revolutionary Mothering: Love on the Front Lines* (Oakland, Calif.: PM Press, 2016), 9.

278 "Mothering, radically defined": Ibid., xv.

12 Welfare

291 As historian Ruth Feldstein: Ruth Feldstein, *Motherhood in Black and White: Race and Sex in American Liberalism, 1930–1965* (Ithaca, NY: Cornell University Press, 2000), 92.

291 "When women misbehaved": Ibid., 14.

291 John Dollard, a social psychologist: Ibid., 22.

292 For Dollard, and for the great majority: Ibid.

292 "a weak, mother-centered family": Ibid.

292 "as accessible as animals": Ibid.

292 "the simple folkways": Ibid., 29.

293 "subordination of the woman": Ibid.

293 "[The] trouble": Ibid., 56.

294 "usually follow what might be": Ibid.

294 "Our constant control": Ibid., 55.

294 "In essence, the Negro Community": Dorothy Roberts, *Killing the Black Body: Race, Reproduction, and the Meaning of Liberty* (New York: Vintage, 1997), 16.

294 Moynihan was particularly concerned: Feldstein, *Motherhood in Black and White*, 143. This is evident in the quotes Moynihan cites from Whitney Young, a prominent civil rights leader: "Historically, in the matriarchal Negro society, mothers made sure that if one of their children had a chance for higher education the daughter was the one to pursue it." Daniel Patrick Moynihan, "The Moynihan Report," U.S. Department of Labor, 1965.

294 "The very essence": Ibid.

294 "what it takes for a working man": Ibid.

295 "Of all the negative stereotypes": bell hooks, *Ain't I a Woman: Black Women and Feminism* (New York: Routledge, 2014), 78.

295 "an 'orderly and normal' white family structure": Feldstein, *Motherhood in Black and White*, 149.

296 The income of black men: Emily Badger, Claire Cain Miller, Adam Pearce, and Kevin Quealy, "Extensive Data Shows Punishing Reach of Racism for Black Boys," *The New York Times*, March 19, 2018. https://www.nytimes.com/interactive/2018/03/19/upshot/race-class-white-and-black-men.html.

296 "Just as marital breakdown": Roberts, *Killing the Black Body*, 224.

297 "She is the agent of destruction": Ibid., 18.

302 "merely got back": Feldstein, *Motherhood in Black and White*, 34.

302 This distinction rendered: Roberts, *Killing the Black Body*, 236.

302 "worthy character": Jill Quadagno, *The Color of Welfare: How Racism Undermined the War on Poverty* (New York: Oxford University Press, 1994), 119.

302 Less than 3 percent: Roberts, *Killing the Black Body*, 220.

303 "insufficient to maintain normal family life": Feldstein, *Motherhood in Black and White*, 36.

303 "Americans now view welfare dependency": Roberts, *Killing the Black Body*, 218.

303 The category of "employable mother": Feldstein, *Motherhood in Black and White*, 36.

303 "man in the house": Quadagno, *The Color of Welfare*, 119–20.

304 "Should you be able": Ibid., 129.

304 945 billion: "Policy Basics: Where Do Our Federal Tax Dollars Go?" Center on Budget and Policy Priorities, January 29, 2019. https://www.cbpp.org/research/federal-budget/policy-basics-where-do-our-federal-tax-dollars-go.

304 16.7 billion: U.S. Department of Health and Human Services, Budget 2017 FY: https://www.hhs.gov/about/budget/fy2017/budget-in-brief/acf/mandatory/index.html.

304 "shiftless, lazy, immoral": Feldstein, *Motherhood in Black and White*, 67.

305 The Notification of Law Enforcement Officers: Ibid., 65.

305 Black civil rights activists began campaigning: Roberts, *Killing the Black Body*, 222.

305 "Black Brood Mares, Inc.": Ibid., 223.

305 As a result: Ibid., 222.

305 "in wretched hovels": Feldstein, *Motherhood in Black and White*, 70.

306 "Charges against ADC": Ibid., 70.

306 As Quadagno explains: Quadagno, *The Color of Welfare*.

306 Quadagno offers: Ibid.

307 "a racist unwillingness": Roberts, *Killing the Black Body,* 258.
313 "important and radical changes": Quoted in bell hooks, *All About Love: New Visions* (New York: HarperCollins, 1999), 85.
313 "In our society": Ibid., 98.

"Anxiety begins like . . ."

329 "real success stories": Mary Catherine Bateson, *Composing a Life* (New York: Grove Press, 1989), 6.
330 "We cannot find our enlightened minds": Mark Epstein, *Thoughts Without a Thinker: Psychotherapy from a Buddhist Perspective* (New York: Basic Books, 1985), 17.
330 "For those who suffer from alienation": Erich Fromm, *Psychoanalysis and Zen Buddhism* (New York: Open Road Media, 2013).
331 "The mind is always seeking": Pema Chödrön, *The Wisdom of No Escape and the Path of Loving-Kindness* (Boston and London: Shambhala, 2010), 147.
331 "Fear is a natural reaction": Pema Chödrön, *Comfortable with Uncertainty: 108 Teachings on Cultivating Fearlessness and Compassion* (Boston: Shambhala, 2002), 92.
333 "strange tangled imp": Dean Young, "Belief in Magic," *Poetry Magazine* (July/ August 2014). https://www.poetryfoundation.org/poetrymagazine/poems /57050/belief-in-magic.
333 "It is a meltdown": Joan Halifax, *A Buddhist Life in America,* The Wit Lectures, Harvard Divinity School, 1998. https://www.upaya.org/dox/BuddhistAmer3 .pdf.

14 The Fruitful Darkness

340 "I realized, as I was": Joan Halifax interviewed by Krista Tippett, "Buoyancy Rather Than Burnout in Our Lives," *On Being,* October 12, 2017. https:// onbeing.org/programs/joan-halifax-buoyancy-rather-than-burnout-in-our -lives-oct2017/.
340 "When a baby is born": Ibid.
340 In her book of that title: Joan Halifax, *The Fruitful Darkness: A Journey Through Buddhist Practice and Tribal Wisdom* (New York: Grove Press, 1993).
340 "illness is understood": Ibid., 193.
341 "the slow, difficult, and delightful": Daphne de Marneffe, *Maternal Desire: On Children, Love, and the Inner Life* (New York: Little, Brown, 2004), 112.
341 In his 1976 classic: Erich Fromm, *To Have or To Be?* (New York: Harper & Row, 1976).
341 "to grow, to flow out": Ibid., 76.
342 "Most people find giving up": Ibid., 77.
342 "the possibility of letting motherhood": De Marneffe, *Maternal Desire,* 124.
342 "Mommy Olympics": Ibid., 138.
342 "What were the consequences": Joan Halifax Roshi, "A Buddhist Life in America: Simplicity in the Complex," Wit Lectures, Harvard University, The Divinity School, 1998.

343 In a beautiful essay: Alyssa Knickerbocker, "X-Men," *Tin House*, January 30, 2018. https://tinhouse.com/x-men/.

343 "This is what I did": Ibid.

343 "Let it": Ibid.

343 "able to feel so deeply": Ibid.

343 "to label it postpartum depression": Ibid.

343 "Anxiety," Kierkegaard wrote: Rollo May, *The Meaning of Anxiety* (New York: W. W. Norton, 1950), 38.

348 "We think we know more": Adam Phillips, *Missing Out: In Praise of the Unlived Life* (New York: Picador, 2012).

348 "The ways we miss our lives": Phillips, *Missing Out*, xii.

348 "destroying the status quo": May, *The Meaning of Anxiety*, 40.

348 "In every experience of creativity": Ibid.

348 "meaningless frenzy": Ibid., 56.

349 "the Myth of Adam": Ibid., 35.

349 "the alarming possibility of being able": Ibid., 36.

349 "The self": Ibid., 153.

349 as Helene Deutsch has framed it: Helene Deutsch, *The Psychology of Women* (London: Grune & Stratton, 1944).

350 "elemental opposites": Rozsika Parker, *Mother Love, Mother Hate: The Power of Maternal Ambivalence* (New York: Basic Books, 1995), 203.

350 "Love and death are the great gifts": Halifax Roshi, "A Buddhist Life in America."

354 Paula Nicholson: "Loss, Happiness and Postpartum Depression: The Ultimate Paradox," *Canadian Psychology* 40 (May 1999): 162–78.

354 "So strong is the taboo": Ibid., 175.

354 "some degree of postpartum depression": Ibid., 176.

354 In the book: Jonathan Grayson, *Freedom from Obsessive-Compulsive Disorder: A Personalized Recovery Program for Living with Uncertainty* (New York: Berkeley Publishing Group, 2003).

356 "big squeeze": Pema Chödrön, *Comfortable with Uncertainty: 108 Teachings on Cultivating Fearlessness and Compassion* (Boston: Shambhala, 2002), 157.

357 "the gold of compassion": Halifax, *The Fruitful Darkness*, 5.

357 "A woman's mother-lust": De Marneffe, *Maternal Desire*, 259.

Index

ABOUT THE AUTHOR

Sarah Menkedick's debut essay collection *Homing Instincts* was long-listed for the PEN/Diamonstein-Spielvogel Award for the Art of the Essay. Sarah's writing has appeared in *Harper's Magazine, Pacific Standard, The New York Times, The Washington Post,* the *Los Angeles Times, The Guardian, Oxford American, The Paris Review Daily, Aeon, Guernica, The Kenyon Review, Buzzfeed,* and elsewhere. She holds a BA in history and the history of science from the University of Wisconsin–Madison and an MFA in nonfiction from the University of Pittsburgh, where she taught nonfiction writing. She lives in Pittsburgh with her family.

A NOTE ON THE TYPE

This book was set in Monotype Dante, a typeface designed by Giovanni Mardersteig (1892–1977). Conceived as a private type for the Officina Bodoni in Verona, Italy, Dante was originally cut only for hand composition by Charles Malin, the famous Parisian punch cutter, between 1946 and 1952. Its first use was in an edition of Boccaccio's *Trattatello in laude di Dante* that appeared in 1954. The Monotype Corporation's version of Dante followed in 1957. Although modeled on the Aldine type used for Pietro Cardinal Bembo's treatise *De Aetna* in 1495, Dante is a thoroughly modern interpretation of the venerable face.

Typeset by Scribe, Philadelphia, Pennsylvania
Printed and bound by Berryville Graphics, Berryville, Pennsylvania
Designed by Maggie Hinders